This *Cambridge Companion to Ezra Pound* contains fifteen chapters by lead-ing international scholars, who together reflect diverse but complementary approaches to the study of Ezra Pound's poetry and prose. They consider the poetics, foreign influences, economics, politics and publication history of Pound's entire corpus, and reveal his importance in developing some of the key movements in twentieth-century poetry. The book also situates Pound's work in the context of modernism, illustrating his influence on contemporaries such as T. S. Eliot and James Joyce. Taken together, the chapters offer a sustained examination of one of the most versatile, influential and certainly controversial poets of the modern period.

THE CAMBRIDGE
COMPANION TO
EZRA POUND

CAMBRIDGE COMPANIONS TO CULTURE

CAMBRIDGE COMPANIONS TO LITERATURE

THE CAMBRIDGE
COMPANION TO
EZRA POUND

EDITED BY
IRA B. NADEL

CAMBRIDGE
UNIVERSITY PRESS

PUBLISHED BY THE PRESS SYNDICATE OF THE UNIVERSITY OF CAMBRIDGE
The Pitt Building, Trumpington Street, Cambridge, United Kingdom

CAMBRIDGE UNIVERSITY PRESS
The Edinburgh Building, Cambridge, CB2 2RU, UK
40 West 20th Street, New York, NY 10011-4211, USA
10 Stamford Road, Oakleigh, VIC 3166, Australia
Ruiz de Alarcón 13, 28014 Madrid, Spain
Dock House, The Waterfront, Cape Town 8001, South Africa

http://www.cambridge.org

© Cambridge University Press 1999

First published 1999
Reprinted 2001

Printed in the United Kingdom at the University Press, Cambridge

Typeset in 10/13pt Sabon   [GC]

A catalogue record for this book is available from the British Library

ISBN 0 521 43117 4 hardback
ISBN 0 521 64920 X paperback

CONTENTS

CONTENTS

CONTRIBUTORS

DANIEL ALBRIGHT, Richard L. Turner Professor in the Humanities at the University of Rochester, has edited Yeats's poems and authored seven books, most recently *Quantum Poetics: Yeats, Pound, Eliot and The Science of Modernism* (1997).

MASSIMO BACIGALUPO, Professor of American Literature at the University of Genoa, is the author of *The Forméd Trace: The Later Poetry of Ezra Pound* (1980) as well as *L'ultimo Pound* (1981), and editor of *Ezra Pound: Un poeta a Rapallo* (1985). His numerous essays on Pound appear in English and Italian.

IAN F. BELL is Professor of American Literature at the University of Keele. Among his many books are *Ezra Pound: Critic and Scientist* (1981) and *Henry James and the Past* (1991). He has also edited *Ezra Pound: Tactics for Reading* (1982) and *Henry James: Fiction as History* (1985).

GEORGE BORNSTEIN, C. A. Patrides Professor of Literature at the University of Michigan, is the author of *Poetic Remaking: The Art of Browning, Yeats and Pound* (1988) and *The Postromantic Consciousness of Ezra Pound* (1977), as well as editor of *Ezra Pound Among the Poets* (1985) and *Representing Modernist Texts, Editing as Interpretation* (1991). He has also edited *The Wanderings of Oisin and Other Early Poems to 1895* by W. B. Yeats for the Cornell Yeats (1987).

RONALD BUSH is the author of *The Genesis of Ezra Pound's Cantos* (1976) and *T. S. Eliot: A Study in Character and Style* (1984). He is completing a study of *The Pisan Cantos* and is currently Drue Heinz Professor of American Literature at Oxford.

REED WAY DASENBROCK is Professor of English at New Mexico State University and the author of *The Literary Vorticism of Ezra Pound and Wyndham Lewis* (1985) and *Imitating the Italians, Wyatt, Spenser, Synge, Pound and Joyce* (1991).

HELEN M. DENNIS teaches in the Department of English and Comparative Literary Studies and at the Centre for the Study of Women and Gender at the University of Warwick. She has published on Pound and Medieval Provençal, gender in American literature and culture, and on Anglo-American modernism. Her book *A New Approach to the Poetry of Ezra Pound through Medieval Provençal* appeared in 1996.

WENDY STALLARD FLORY, Professor of English at Purdue University, has published *Ezra Pound and The Cantos, A Record of Struggle* (1980) and *The American Ezra Pound* (1989).

MICHAEL INGHAM, in addition to being Professor of Music and Chair of the Music Department of the University of California at Santa Barbara, is a professional singer. He has been featured as a recitalist or soloist with orchestras at a variety of European and North American festivals. He has also performed with such ensembles as the Los Angeles Chamber Orchestra and Vienna's Die Reihe and recorded for Orion, Pro Viva and Amcam Records.

IRA B. NADEL is Professor of English at the University of British Columbia, Vancouver. He has edited *The Letters of Ezra Pound to Alice Corbin Henderson* (1993) and written *Biography: Fiction, Fact & Form* (1984) and *Joyce and The Jews* (1989). He has also published a biography of the poet/singer Leonard Cohen entitled *Various Positions* (1996).

PETER NICHOLLS is Chair of the Department of English at the University of Sussex and the author of *Modernisms, A Literary Guide* (1995). He earlier published *Ezra Pound: Politics, Economics and Writing* (1984).

TIM REDMAN is Associate Professor of Literary Studies in the School of Arts and Humanities at the University of Texas at Dallas, where he teaches courses in American, British and Irish modernism, American Literature and Dante. He is the author of *Ezra Pound and Italian Fascism* (1991) and is currently completing a biography of Pound.

RICHARD TAYLOR, Professor of English and Comparative Literature at the Universitat of Bayreuth, has published *Variorum Edition of "Three Cantos," A Prototype* (1991) and co-edited *Ezra Pound in Europe* (1993). He is preparing a detailed chronology of the publication of *The Cantos* and a variorum edition of the poem.

HUGH WITEMEYER, Professor of English at the University of New Mexico, is the author of *The Poetry of Ezra Pound: Forms and Renewal, 1908–1920* (1969) and editor, most recently, of *Pound/Williams, Selected Letters* (1996). He is also co-editor of *Ezra Pound and Senator Bronson Cutting, A Political Correspondence 1930–1935* (1995).

MING XIE is a member of the Department of English at Beijing University. A graduate of the University of Nanjing, he received his PhD from Cambridge. His articles have appeared in *ELH* and *Paideuma*; his book on Pound and the translation of Chinese poetry is forthcoming.

ACKNOWLEDGMENTS

Numerous Poundians in various countries have assisted in the completion of this project and it is a pleasure to acknowledge their help. Mary de Rachewiltz in Italy willingly supported the Companion from its inception, as did the Ezra Pound Literary Trust through Peggy Fox of New Directions in New York. Kevin Taylor, and later Ray Ryan, both of Cambridge University Press, were continual enthusiasts who guided the work through its gestation and completion.

Individual contributors showed patience and determination in completing their essays and providing frequent guidance, George Bornstein, Ronald Bush, Tim Redman and Hugh Witemeyer among the most supportive of my numerous "Virgils." James Laughlin and Donald Gallup, premier Poundians, were important through their earlier efforts to publish Pound and record his publications. Professors Hugh Kenner and A. Walton Litz were in different ways instrumental in establishing and sustaining the critical study of Pound. Brenda Maddox and her London dining room, site of an important meeting in the summer of 1996 regarding the volume, are also to be thanked. Finally, I wish to acknowledge those many scholars who have directly and indirectly contributed to the elucidation of Pound's work, a task that is far from complete. Their support, as noted throughout these pages, remains ever valuable.

Letters by Dorothy Pound are Copyright © by Omar Pound. Previously unpublished material by Ezra Pound are Copyright © 1999 by the Trustees of the Ezra Pound Literary Property Trust. Grateful acknowledgement for permissions to publish material is offered to the Agents for the Trustees of the Ezra Pound Literary Property Trust: Mary de Rachewiltz, New Directions Publishing Corp. and Faber & Faber Ltd., as well as Hugh Kenner, James Laughlin, Gerald J. Pollinger, and Omar Pound. The following institutions are also acknowledged with very many thanks for permissions to include hitherto unpublished material from their various collections: Harry

Ransom Humanities Research Center, The University of Texas at Austin; Lilly Library, Manuscript Department, Indiana University, Bloomington; New York Public Library, Henry W. and Albert A. Berg Collection, Astor, Lenox and Tilden Foundations; Yale Collection of American Literature, Beinecke Rare Book and Manuscript Library, Yale University.

ABBREVIATIONS

AA	*Active Anthology*. London: Faber & Faber, 1933.
ABCE	*ABC of Economics*. London: Faber & Faber, 1933.
ABCR	*ABC of Reading*. 1934. New York: New Directions, 1960.
ALS	*A Lume Spento and Other Early Poems*. New York: New Directions, 1965.
ANT	*Antheil and The Treatise on Harmony*. Paris: Three Mountains Press, 1924.
AQY	*A Quinzaine for this Yule*. London: Pollock & Co., 1908.
C	*The Cantos*. 13th printing. New York: New Directions, 1995. This edition includes Pound's English translation of Canto LXXII. References are to Canto and page number.
CA	*Catholic Anthology*. London: Elkin Mathews, 1915.
CAC	*The Classic Anthology Defined by Confucius*. Cambridge, MA: Harvard University Press, 1954.
CAT	*Cathay*. London: Elkin Mathews, 1915.
CEP	*Collected Early Poems*. Ed. Michael John King. Intro. Louis L. Martz. New York: New Directions, 1976.
CFF	*Cantos*. London: Faber & Faber, 1986.
CL	*Cantos LII–LXXI*. London: Faber & Faber, 1940.
CN	*Canzoni*. London: Elkin Mathews, 1911.
CNJ	*Certain Noble Plays of Japan*. Intro. William B. Yeats. Churchtown, Dundrum: The Cuala Press, 1916.
CNTJ	*Classic Noh Theatre of Japan*. New York: New Directions, 1959.
CON	*Confucian Analects*. New York: Square $ Series, 1951.
CSP	*Collected Shorter Poems*. London: Faber & Faber, 1968.
CWC	*Chinese Written Character* in *Instigations*. New York: Boni and Liveright, 1920.
D17	*A Draft of The Cantos 17–27*. London: John Rodker, 1928.
DF	*Drafts & Fragments of Cantos CX–CXVII*. New York: New Directions, 1969.
DI	*Des Imagistes*. New York: Albert and Charles Boni, 1914.
DXVI	*A Draft of XVI Cantos*. Paris: Three Mountains Press, 1925.

DXXX   *A Draft of XXX Cantos.* Paris: Hours Press, 1930.

ENC   *Eleven New Cantos XXI–XLI.* New York: Farrar & Rinehart, 1934.

EP/DS   *Ezra Pound and Dorothy Shakespear: Their Letters.* Ed. Omar Pound and A. Walton Litz. New York: New Directions, 1984.

EP/JL   *Ezra Pound and James Laughlin, Selected Letters.* Ed. David M. Gordon. New York: W. W. Norton, 1994.

EPM   *Ezra Pound and Music.* Ed. R. Murray Schafer. New York: New Directions, 1977.

EP/MC   *Ezra Pound and Margaret Cravens.* Ed. Omar Pound and Robert Spoo. Durham: Duke University Press, 1988.

EPS   *"Ezra Pound Speaking," Radio Speeches of World War II.* Ed. Leonard W. Doob. Westport, CT: Greenwood, 1978.

EPVA   *Ezra Pound and The Visual Arts.* Ed. Harriet Zinnes. New York: New Directions, 1980.

EX   *Exultations.* London: Elkin Mathews, 1909.

FDC   *The Fifth Decad of Cantos.* London: Faber & Faber, 1937.

GB   *Gaudier-Brzeska.* 1916; New York: New Directions, 1974.

GCR   *Guido Cavalcanti Rime.* Genoa: Edizioni Marsano, 1932.

GK   *Guide to Kulchur.* London: Faber & Faber, 1938. New York: New Directions, 1968.

HR   *How to Read.* London: Harmsworth, 1931.

HSM   *Hugh Sewlyn Mauberley.* London: Ovid Press, 1920.

HSP   *Homage to Sextus Propertius.* London: Faber and Faber, 1934.

IC   *I Cantos,* a cura di Mary de Rachewiltz. Milano: Mondadori, 1985.

IMP   *Impact, Essays on Ignorance and the Decline of American Civilization.* Ed. Noel Stock. Chicago: Henry Regnery Company, 1960.

IND   *Indiscretions.* Paris: Three Mountains Press, 1923.

INS   *Instigations.* New York: Boni and Liveright, 1920.

J/M   *Jefferson and/or Mussolini.* London: Stanley Nott, 1935.

LE   *Literary Essays.* Ed. T. S. Eliot. Norfolk, CT: New Directions, 1954.

LUS   *Lustra.* London: Elkin Mathews, 1916.

MIN   *Make It New.* London: Faber & Faber, 1934.

NO   *"Noh" or Accomplishment.* London: Macmillan and Company, 1916.

P, 1909 *Persona.* London: Elkin Mathews, 1909.

P, 1926 *Persona, The Collected Poems of Ezra Pound.* New York: Boni and Liveright, 1926.

P, 1990 *Persona: The Shorter Poems.* Rev. edn, ed. Lea Baechler and A. Walton Litz. New York: New Directions, 1990.

PAI   *Paideuma: A Journal Devoted to Ezra Pound Scholarship.*

PC   *The Pisan Cantos.* New York: New Directions, 1948.

PD   *Pavannes and Divisions.* New York: Alfred A. Knopf, 1918.

PDD   *Pavannes and Divagations.* Norfolk, CT: New Directions, 1958.

PE   *Polite Essays.* London: Faber & Faber, 1937.

PM   *Patria Mia.* Chicago: Ralph Fletcher Seymour, 1950.

PS	*Poems 1918–1921.* New York: Boni and Liveright, 1921.
P/F	*Pound/Ford.* Ed. Brita Lindberg-Seyersted. New York: New Directions, 1982.
P/J	*Pound/Joyce.* Ed. Forrest Read. New York: New Directions, 1967.
P/I	*Letters to Ibbotson.* Ed. V. I. Mondolfo and M. Hurley. Orono, MA: National Poetry Foundation, 1979.
P/L	*Pound/Lewis.* Ed. Timothy Materer. New York: New Directions, 1985.
PV	*Provença.* Boston: Small, Maynard and Company, 1910.
Q	*Quia Pauper Amavi.* London: The Egoist, 1919.
R	*Ripostes.* London: Stephen Swift and Co., 1912.
SB	*Sonnets and Ballate of Guido Cavalcanti.* Boston: Small, Maynard and Company, 1912.
SC	*Selected Cantos.* London: Faber & Faber, 1967.
SCR	*Social Credit.* London: Stanley Nott, 1935.
SL	*Selected Letters of Ezra Pound.* Ed. D. D. Paige. New York: New Directions, 1971.
SP	*Selected Poems.* Ed. T. S. Eliot. London: Faber & Gwyer, 1928.
SPR	*Selected Prose, 1909–1965.* Ed. William Cookson. London: Faber & Faber, 1973.
SPS	*Selected Poems 1908–1959.* Ed. T. S. Eliot. London: Faber & Faber, 1975.
SR	*The Spirit of Romance.* 1910; New York: New Directions, 1968.
SRD	*Section: Rock-Drill.* 1955; New York: New Directions, 1956.
T	*Translations.* Intro. Hugh Kenner. London: Faber & Faber, 1953.
TC	"Three Cantos" (1917) in *Lustra.* New York: Alfred A. Knopf, 1917.
TAH	*Ta Hio.* Seattle: University of Washington, 1928.
TH	*Thrones 96–109 de los cantares.* New York: New Directions, 1959.
U	*Umbra.* London: Elkin Mathews, 1920.
UCH	Unpublished Materials. University of Chicago Library.
UP	*The Unwobbling Pivot & The Great Digest.* Norfolk, CT: New Directions, 1947.
WT	*Women of Trachis.* New York: New Directions, 1956.
WTSF	*Walking Tour of Southern France.* Ed. Richard Sieburth. New York: New Directions, 1992.
YC	Unpublished Material, Beinecke Rare Book and Manuscript Library, Yale University.

CHRONOLOGY

1885   Ezra Pound born in Hailey, Idaho, on October 30 to Homer
        and Isabel Weston Pound; his father in charge of the Federal
        Land Office supervising local mining.

1887   Winter. The Pounds abandon Idaho to live with Isabel's
        uncle Ezra Brown Weston and his wife, Aunt Frank, in their
        boarding house at 24 East 47th St., New York City.

1889   Family moves to Philadelphia where Homer Pound accepts
        job as an assistant assayer in the US Mint. Works there until
        his retirement in 1928.

1890   Pounds move to Jenkintown, Pennsylvania, a suburb just
        north of Philadelphia.

1892   Pounds settle into their long-term residence at 166 Fernbrook
        Avenue, Wyncote, Pennsylvania.

1894   Uncle Ezra Brown Weston, Pound's namesake, dies in New
        York.

1895   Pound enrolled in Wyncote Public School.

1897   Pound transfers to Cheltenham Military Academy.

1898   Aunt Frank Weston takes Pound and his mother to Europe,
        visiting Gibralter, Tunisia and Venice, later recalled in *The
        Cantos*.

1901   Enters University of Pennsylvania where in his second year
        he meets William Carlos Williams, a medical student. Also

meets Hilda Doolittle (H.D.) whose father teaches astronomy at the university and a tubercular artist named William Brooke Smith, one of his earliest friends.

1902   The Pounds and Aunt Frank take Pound on his second tour of Europe.

1903   Because of poor marks, Pound transfers to Hamilton College, Clinton, New York, where he studies Provençal and Anglo-Saxon.

1904   In Hamilton, meets Katherine (Kitty) Ruth Heyman, a travelling classical pianist, eleven years his senior. His poem, "Scriptor Ignotus" in *A Lume Spento* dedicated to her.

1905   Graduates Hamilton College with BA degree. In the fall, enrolls again at the University of Pennsylvania to study Romance languages. Begins to see H.D.

1906   Receives MA degree in the spring; Summer-Fall, travels to Madrid on a fellowship to study Spanish literature; returns to Penn to work with Professor Felix Schelling but does poorly.

1907   Falls in love with Mary Moore of Trenton in the summer. He will dedicate *Personae* (1909) to her; finds a teaching job in Crawsfordsville, Indiana, at Wabash College.

1908   February. Dismissal from Wabash College when he is accused by his landladies of harboring an actress overnight in his room.

        March-August. Jobless, he convinces his father to lend him some money to go off to Europe. Witter Bynner recommends this change. Pound settles in Venice for the summer; in July publishes his first book, *A Lume Spento*, at his own expense. 150 copies printed of the work dedicated to the deceased William Brooke Smith. Most of the ms. had been completed when Pound left the United States for Europe. In June, remeets Kitty Heyman who is in Venice on a concert tour and temporarily acts as her manager. By late August, heads to London where in December he publishes *A Quinzaine for this Yule* dedicated to Heyman.

1909   Meets Olivia Shakespear and her daughter Dorothy, his future wife; also meets Henry James, Ford Madox Ford, T. E. Hulme, Wyndham Lewis and W. B. Yeats; lives at 10 Church Walk, Kensington. Elkin Mathews issues *Personae* and *Exultations* in London.

1910   March 23. EP leaves London for Italy, stopping in Paris to visit Walter Morse Rummel, pianist. Goes on to Italy and remeets Olivia and Dorothy Shakespear.

            June. revisits New York and Pennsylvania; meets John Quinn through John B. Yeats, father of W. B. Yeats, then living in New York.

            The Spirit of Romance published in London by Dent; *Provença*, the first American edition of his poetry, published in Boston by Small, Maynard.

1911   February. Returns to Europe from America. Visits Rummel in Paris where he meets Margaret Cravens who would shortly offer him financial support. Goes to Giessen, Germany to meet Ford who ridicules his overwritten *Canzoni* published in July that year in London by Mathews. H.D. arrives in London. Meets A. R. Orage, editor of the *New Age* in which he will soon begin to appear, starting with the 12-part series on art and culture, "I Gather the Limbs of Osiris."

1912   With H.D., founds the new Imagist school. Becomes foreign correspondent of Harriet Monroe's *Poetry*.

            June. Margaret Cravens commits suicide in her Paris apartment.

            Ripostes published in London by Swift & Co.; *Sonnets and Ballate of Guido Cavalcanti* published in Boston by Small, Maynard.

1913   Becomes poetry editor of Dora Marsden and Harriet Shaw Weaver's *The New Freewoman*, soon to be called the *Egoist*. Meets French sculptor, Henri Gaudier-Brzeska and Mrs. Ernest Fenollosa. Works as Yeats's secretary for the first of three winters at Stone Cottage in Sussex. Writes to James

Joyce for a poem to include in his 1914 anthology, *Des Imagistes*. Publishes "A Few Don'ts by an Imagiste," in *Poetry*, I (March). Gaudier-Brzeska sculpts the Hieratic Head of Pound.

1914　April 20: marries Dorothy Shakespear and moves to 5 Holland Park Chambers, Kensington. With Wyndham Lewis develops the Vorticist movement through *Blast Magazine*. Publishes "Vorticism" essay in September issue of *Fortnightly Review*, same month he meets T. S. Eliot, arranged by Conrad Aiken. Pound sends "Prufrock" to *Poetry* in October; negotiates the publication of *A Portrait of the Artist* in the *Egoist*.

　　　　Des Imagistes anthology published in March in New York by Albert and Charles Boni; published in London by John Monro's The Poetry Book Shop a month later.

1915　June. Gaudier-Brzeska killed in battle. By September EP begins *Cantos* in disorganized manner. *Cathay*, his version of various Chinese texts, published in London by Elkin Mathews after working on the Fenollosa mss.; *Catholic Anthology*, with five poems by T. S. Eliot, two by William Carlos Williams and ten by Pound, appears from Elkin Mathews, London.

1916　*Gaudier-Brzeska: A Memoir*. London: John Lane, The Bodley Head; *Lustra*. London: Mathews; *Certain Noble Plays of Japan*. Churchtown, Dundrum: Cuala Press. Intro. Yeats. Reprinted as *"Noh" or Accomplishment* by Macmillan in London without the Yeats introduction. Actually appeared January 1917, although printed date on the volume is 1916.

1917　Works with Margaret Anderson and Jane Heap as foreign editor of the *Little Review* in which parts of Joyce's *Ulysses* would shortly appear. Publishes "Three Cantos" in *Poetry* 10 (June, July, August). Creates vortographs with American photographer Alvin Langdon Coburn.

1918　*Pavannes and Divisions* published in New York by Alfred Knopf. Writes music and art criticism for Orage's *New Age* under pseudonyms of William Atheling and B. H. Dias. Meets

Major C. H. Douglas who introduces EP to the Social Credit system which will strongly influence his economic ideas; Canto XXXVIII summarizes the Social Credit approach.

1919   *Quia Pauper Amavi* published in London by the Egoist Press in which "Three Cantos" and "Homage to Sextus Propertius" (dated 1917) appear. Tours Southern France with Dorothy and T. S. Eliot. C. H. Douglas's *Economic Democracy* serialized in the *New Age*.

1920   Begins work as foreign correspondent for *The Dial*. April trip to Venice via Paris. Meets Joyce in June at Sirmione on Lago di Garda where Pound and Dorothy have taken up temporary residence at the Hotel Eden. By July, the entire Joyce family moves to Paris, guided by Pound.

"Indiscretions," an autobiographical series, begins in *New Age* in May. *Instigations*, including Fenollosa's "The Chinese Written Character as a Medium for Poetry," published in April in New York by Boni and Liveright. *Hugh Selwyn Mauberley* appears in June from John Rodker's Ovid Press in 200 copies, the same month *Umbra, the Early Poems of Ezra Pound* was published by Mathews.

1921   In January Pound leaves London for France, eventually taking up residence in Paris in April; becomes acquainted with Cocteau, Picabia, Gertrude Stein, Brancusi, Hemingway, and George Antheil. Continues association with Joyce, begins friendship with e e cummings.

EP works on opera *Le Testament de Villon*. In November, Eliot, on his way to Switzerland, deposits ts. of *The Waste Land* for EP to edit. *Poems 1918–21* from Boni and Liveright in New York appears. Volume includes Cantos IV–VII.

1922   On New Year's Eve meets Picasso. In late January, returns *The Waste Land* to Eliot in London. Meets and boxes with Hemingway. Begins Bel Esprit philanthropic movement to help Eliot and other writers. Meets William Bird who will start the Three Mountains Press which will publish several of Pound's works. Quinn purchases *The Waste Land* which *The Dial* will publish in November.

Pound's translation of Remy de Gourmont's *Natural History of Love* published by Boni and Liveright.

1923   In Italy, he and Hemingway take a walking tour. In Paris, meets the violinist Olga Rudge from Youngstown, Ohio, in Natalie Barney's salon. Researches and writes the Malatesta Cantos, VIII–XI. Meets Harriet Monroe for the first time in Paris. Bride Scratton, whom Pound first met in 1910, divorces her husband, naming Pound as co-respondent. *Transatlantic Review*, edited by Ford and soon assisted by Basil Bunting, a disciple of Pound's, appears in Paris. Pound promotes and aids the journal. *Indiscretions* published by William Bird's Three Mountains Press.

1924   Meets William Carlos Williams in Paris in June; tours Italy again looking for permanent home. On October 10, Pound and Dorothy permanently leave Paris for Italy, first to Rapallo and then Sicily until January 1925 when they return to live in Rapallo. *Antheil and the Treatise on Harmony* published by William Bird in October.

1925   Deluxe edition of *A Draft of XVI Cantos* published in Paris in January by Bird's Three Mountains Press. Decorative initials by Henry Strater. Pound devotes himself to completing this "poem including history." Birth of daughter Mary in the Italian Tyrol July 9, child of Pound and Olga Rudge. Pound concentrates on composition of cantos, translation of Confucius and study of economics.

1926   Pound's opera *Le Testament de Villon* performed in Paris in June; September 10, birth of Omar Pound in Paris, son of Dorothy Pound. Hemingway drove her to the hospital. Son brought up in England.

        Personae, The Collected Poems of Ezra Pound published in December in New York by Boni & Liveright.

1927–28 Edits and publishes his journal, *Exile*, which lasts for only four issues. Begins friendship with Louis Zukofsky who would visit Pound in 1933. Pound and Olga begin to spend a great deal of time in Venice where she owned a small home at 252 Dorsoduro, just off the Calle Querini.

1928   Pound wins the 1927 *Dial* award for poetry. Pound's translation of the Confucian *Ta Hio or The Great Learning* published by the University of Washington Bookstore. In September, *A Draft of The Cantos 17–27* published by John Rodker in London with illuminated initials by Gladys Hynes. November saw the appearance of *Selected Poems* edited by T. S. Eliot and published by Faber & Gwyer. Visit by Homer and Isabel Pound to Rapallo.

1929   In January, Pound's parents relocate to Rapallo from Philadelphia. Olga Rudge closes her apartment in Paris and moves to her home in Venice where she and Pound would live, Pound referring to it as "the hidden nest" in Canto LXXVI.

1930   Meets Leo Frobenius, German anthropologist interested in the organic evolution of cultures which he likened to organisms; his ideas would influence Pound.

        200 copies of *A Draft of XXX Cantos* published in Paris in August by Nancy Cunard's Hours Press. October saw the appearance of *Imaginary Letters* printed by the Black Sun Press, Paris.

1931   *How to Read*. London: Harmsworth. Pound lectures at the Universita Bocconi, Milan on Jefferson and Van Buren. In admiration of fascism, begins to date his letters according to the Fascist calendar which begins with Anno I in March 1922 with the march on Rome.

1932   January. *Guido Calvalcanti: Rime*. Genoa: Edizioni Marsano. May. Edits *Profile: An Anthology*. Milan: Giovanni Scheiwiller. *Objectivist Anthology*, edited by Zukofsky, appears in August; dedicated to Pound who has two poems in it. Begins to publish in *Il Mare*, a Rapallo paper.

1933   January. Pound meets Mussolini in Rome, recounted in Canto XLI. Zukofsky visits Pound in Rapallo in early August, met first by Bunting in Genoa. In late August, first visit by the youthful James Laughlin, later to become Pound's publisher in America through New Directions press.

April. *ABC of Economics* London: Faber & Faber.

October. Edits *Active Anthology*. London: Faber & Faber.

1934   Correspondence with Laurence Binyon on his trans. of Dante's *Divine Comedy*; with W. H. Rouse on his trans. of the Odyssey; articles in Orage's new magazine, the *New English Weekly*, a Social Credit publication.

May. *ABC of Reading*. London: Routledge.

September. *Make it New*. London: Faber & Faber.

October. *Eleven New Cantos XXI–XLI*. New York: Farrar & Rinehart.

November. *Homage to Sextus Propertius*. London: Faber & Faber.

1935   In late summer, Ezra and Olga travel to Salzburg to meet James Laughlin and attend the music festival. On October 2, 1935 Mussolini declares war and invades Abyssinia. Throughout this period, Olga, Pound and Gerhart Munch constantly promote concerts in and around Rapallo. Olga also participates in the summer music school at Siena founded by Count Chigi Sarracini. Makes first radio broadcast from Italy to America.

May. *Social Credit: An Impact*. London: Stanley Nott.

July. *Jefferson and/or Mussolini*. London: Stanley Nott.

1936   Pound and Olga develop interest in Vivaldi via study groups, manuscript research and performances leading to the establishment of a Center for Vivaldi Studies at the Academy of Music in Siena.

Founding of New Directions by James Laughlin in Norfolk, Connecticut.

1937   January. *Polite Essays*. London: Faber & Faber.

June. *The Fifth Decad of Cantos*. London: Faber & Faber.

June. *Confucius, Digest of the Analects*. Milan: Giovanni Scheiwiller.

1938 July. *Guide to Kulchur*. London: Faber & Faber. Dedicated to Zukofsky and Bunting.

Initial contributions to *Il Meridiano di Roma*, a fascist publication, begin.

1939 April. Revisits America for the first time since 1910 in an attempt to avert war. Lobbies a series of US Congressmen, but to little avail. In May, gives a public reading of his poetry at Harvard, his first reading since the *BLAST* group in 1914. In June, receives honorary degree from Hamilton College; returns to Italy at the end of the month. June 26, death of Ford; Pound writes obituary. Publishes *What is Money For?*

1940 January. Dialogue with the philosopher George Santayana in Venice. Articles begin to appear in the *Japan Times* (Tokyo), often reprints of pieces from *Il Meridiano di Roma*. Work on *The Cantos* halts.

Cantos LII–LXXI. London: Faber & Faber. Contains the so-called Chinese Cantos. The American edition added a pamphlet with two essays: "Notes on the Cantos" by James Laughlin and "Notes on the Versification of the Cantos" by Delmore Schwartz.

1941 Begins regular radio broadcasts on shortwave from Rome to America and to American troops in support, he claims, of the US Constitution. They are highly critical of Roosevelt and the war effort, as well as antisemitic. To continue for three years, except for an interval beginning December 1941 when the US declared war on the Axis powers, ending in February 1943. In summer and autumn, unsuccessfully attempts to get passage on a plane from Rome for himself (and presumably Dorothy) to the States.

1942   February. Death of Homer Pound.

Mary Pound continues with an Italian translation of the Cantos. EP refused permission to join Americans being evacuated from Italy to Lisbon.

Carta da Visita. Rome: Edizione di Lettere d'Oggi. The first English edition, published as *A Visiting Card*, appeared in London in 1952 by Peter Russell.

1943   February. Resumes regular political broadcasts in Rome, criticizing American intervention in war.

July. Indicted *in absentia* on thirteen counts of treason by a Grand Jury in Washington, DC. The day before, July 25, Mussolini deposed from power.

September. EP leaves Rome on foot to begin 450-mile journey, partly by rail, to the Tyrol to see his daughter Mary. Italy occupied by the Germans.

1944   May. Dorothy and EP ordered by the Germans to leave Rapallo; they move in with Olga in Sant'Ambrogio, the hilltop town above the city. Writes the two "Italian Cantos," published in *Marina Repubblicana* in early 1945 but unprinted in a complete *Cantos* until 1985.

1945   April. The fleeing Mussolini apprehended and killed.

May. On the 2nd, Germany surrenders Italy to the Allies and the sixty-year-old Pound walks down the hill from Sant'Ambrogio to American troops in Rapallo to turn himself in. The soldiers do not know what to do with him and he returns home. The next day two Italian partisans arrest him at his home and take him to Zoagli just south of Rapallo. There being no reward, however, they let him go, but Pound, now with Olga, reports to the US Army authorities next door who take him to Genoa where he is formally arrested. He is sent to the US Army Disciplinary Training Center north of Pisa on May 24 where he is confined for nearly two and a half weeks in a solitary steel pen exposed to the elements.

Barbarous treatment creates a form of physical breakdown. Finally, moved to the medical tent and, by mid-July, to better accommodations, and given the use of a typewriter. Works on his translation of Confucius and the first draft of *The Pisan Cantos* (LXXIV–LXXXIV) before and after access to the typewriter. Dorothy visits in early October, followed by Mary and Olga Rudge.

November. On the 16th, Pound suddenly and secretly taken from the DTC to Rome where he begins flight to Washington, DC to be re-indicted for treason; new indictment issued on 26th increasing the number of treasonable offenses. Arraigned on November 27 in Washington but trial postponed until psychiatric examination completed. On December 21 Pound found medically unfit to stand trial; committed to St. Elizabeths Hospital for the Criminally Insane, Washington, DC where he would stay for the next twelve and a half years.

1946	February 13. A second jury hearing to determine the sanity of Pound held in Washington, DC. The decision "unsound mind" is upheld. Random House announces that it will exclude Pound's verse from their new edition of *Anthology of Famous English and American Poetry*. The first edition included twelve works by Pound.

T. S. Eliot visits Pound at St. Elizabeths in July. Mary Pound marries Prince Boris de Rachewiltz.

1947	Pound moved from criminal section of St. Elizabeths to the more amenable Chestnut Ward. In July, visited by Marianne Moore. Other visitors that year: Allen Tate, Randall Jarrell, Robert Duncan. Later guests included Thornton Wilder, Stephen Spender, Elizabeth Bishop, Katherine Anne Porter and Langston Hughes.

Confucius, *The Unwobbling Pivot & The Great Digest* (dated D.T.C., Pisa, Oct. 5–Nov. 5, 1945), a translation by Pound, published by New Directions, Norfolk, CT.

1948	February 9. Death of Pound's mother, Isabel Pound. Visit from Robert Lowell, at the time Poetry Consultant to the Library of Congress.

July. Visits from Marshall McLuhan and Hugh Kenner.

Mary de Rachewiltz and her husband Boris acquire Schloss Brunnenburg (Castel Fontana in Italian) built in the twelfth century, to become Pound's residence after his release from St. Elizabeths in 1958.

If This Be Treason... (Siena). Edited by and printed for Olga Rudge in January; six of Pound's radio broadcasts printed for the first time.

The Pisan Cantos published July 20 by New Directions in New York.

The Cantos. July 30. New York: New Directions. First publication of the complete cantos to date.

1949	February 20. Bollingen Prize for Poetry awarded to Pound for *The Pisan Cantos* amid controversy. *New York Times* headline reads: "Pound, in Mental Clinic, Wins Prize for Poetry Penned in Treason Cell."

Selected Poems published in October by New Directions in New York.

1950	Pound's *Money Pamphlets* translated into English and published in London.

Patria Mia published in May in Chicago by Ralph Fletcher Seymour. A reworking of articles on America originally in A. R. Orage's *New Age* from 1912 and 1913.

The Letters of Ezra Pound, 1907–1941, ed. D. D. Paige, published in New York by Harcourt, Brace and Company. Retitled *Selected Letters* in 1971.

1951	*Confucian Analects* (Square $ series).

1952	Olga Rudge finally visits Pound at St. Elizabeths. Sheri Martinelli, a painter and disciple, visits.

1953	Mary de Rachewiltz visits her father at St. Elizabeths.

The Translations. Intr. Hugh Kenner. London: Faber & Faber. Includes "Cavalcanti Poems," "Cathay," Noh plays and a selection of miscellaneous poems.

1954   Louis Zukofsky visits with his violinist son, Paul, who performs the music of Canto LXXV.

Literary Essays of Ezra Pound, ed. T. S. Eliot. London: Faber & Faber.

The Classic Anthology Defined by Confucius published by Harvard University Press.

1955   *Section: Rock-Drill.* Milano: All'Insegna del Pesce D'Oro.

1956   Sophokles, *Women of Trachis, A Version by Ezra Pound.* London: Neville Spearman, published in November.

1957   April. Marcella Spann visits Pound at St. Elizabeths. Will accompany him to Italy on his release and reside for a time at Brunnenburg with Dorothy Pound and Mary de Rachewiltz.

1958   April 18. Petition to release the seventy-two-year-old Pound from St. Elizabeths heard and granted in US District Court, Washington, DC, following the efforts of Archibald MacLeish, Robert Frost, Ernest Hemingway, T. S. Eliot and others. He is in the charge of his committee, Dorothy Shakespear Pound, responsible for his well-being, financial state and publications.

May 7. Pound officially discharged from St. Elizabeths. Before he leaves for Italy on June 30, he visits his childhood home in Wyncote, Pennsylvania, and then William Carlos Williams in New Jersey.

July 9. Arrives by boat in Naples with Dorothy and Marcella Spann and tells reporters "all America is an insane asylum." Poses onboard for cameras offering the Fascist salute.

1959   May. Pound, Dorothy and Marcella Spann leave Brunnenburg for an apartment in Rapallo. Marcella leaves by the end of the summer.

Thrones. Milano: All'Insegna del Pesce D'Oro.

1960   January. Pound goes alone to Rome to stay with Ugo Dadone. Interviewed in March by the poet Donald Hall. By May, returns to Dorothy in Rapallo. Enters a clinic to recover his health and by the fall returns to Brunnenburg. Silences and depression begin.

1961   Spring. Pound returns to Rome but by June is back at a clinic near Brunnenburg.

1962   Spring. Pound, improved, travels to Olga at Sant'Ambrogio above Rapallo and would not return to Brunnenburg. In June, he required an emergency operation to prevent uraemic poisoning of the blood. Released by the end of the summer, he returned to Olga at Sant'Ambrogio. They then went to Calle Querini in Venice.

1963   Pound receives Academy of American Poets Award. Operated on again for urinary problems.

        March 4. William Carlos Williams dies.

1964   *Confucius to Cummings* anthology prepared by Pound and Marcella Spann published by New Directions in New York.

1965   Attends the memorial service in London's Westminster Abbey for T. S. Eliot who died in January; visits Yeats's widow in Dublin. In summer visits the Spoleto Festival and publicly reads poems by Robert Lowell and Marianne Moore. Outside the theatre, he reads from *The Cantos* to a crowd. On October 30, Pound turns eighty. Visits Paris and Natalie Barney and attends performance of Beckett's *Endgame*. The next day Beckett visits Pound at his hotel.

1966   Pound becomes nearly silent; two years later he would declare, "I did not enter into silence; silence captured me." Depression cited as the principal cause.

        Archive of EP's papers, manuscripts, letters deposited at Yale University.

1967   Pound visits Joyce's grave in Zurich.

Cantos 110–116, New York: Fuck You Press; unauthorized publication.

In summer, Allen Ginsberg visits Pound first in Sant'Ambrogio and then in Venice in October, stimulating conversation.

Selected Cantos published in London by Faber & Faber. Pound made the selection in 1965.

1968   *Redondillas or Something of That Sort*. New York: New Directions. The poem and Pound's notes for it reprinted from a set of page proofs cut from *Canzoni* (1911).

1969   June 4. Pound unexpectedly arrives in New York with Olga Rudge to attend the opening of an exhibition of the ms. of *The Waste Land* and a meeting of the Academy of American Poets. Laughlin takes Pound to his country home. Pound and Olga then accompany Laughlin to Hamilton College where Laughlin receives an honorary degree. Pound sits on the stage and receives a standing ovation.

Drafts & Fragments of Cantos CX–CXVII. published in New York by New Directions.

1972   November 1: Pound dies in Venice at eighty-seven and is buried in the Protestant section of the island cemetery of San Michele on November 3.

Paideuma, the Pound journal, founded.

1973   December 8. Death of Dorothy Pound.

1996   March 15. Death of Olga Rudge.

I

IRA B. NADEL

Introduction   Understanding Pound

It is the artist's business to find his own *virtu*.

Pound, 1912

Understanding Ezra Pound has never been easy. His erudition and experimentation, not to say his orneriness, have constantly challenged readers. His life as an expatriate in Venice, London, Paris and Rapallo clouded his identity as an American; the war years obscured it when he delivered a series of anti-American and antisemitic radio broadcasts supporting Mussolini. That led to his subsequent arrest, trial and imprisonment in a Washington, DC mental hospital. It also led to *The Pisan Cantos*, which won the prestigious Bollingen Prize in 1949. His release in 1958 saw him return to Italy where he died in 1972. Yet as he wrote in 1920, "I *am* terribly, appallingly, but I am not sure about the 'deplorably' American."[1] That for Pound did not change.

Literature, not politics, was his calling. As poet, translator, editor, critic, librettist, and dramatist, drawing on medieval, Italian, American, English, Chinese, French, and contemporary traditions, Pound created works that were as complex as they were absorbing. From 1915 until 1969 he worked on an ambitious epic poem, *The Cantos*, which embraced the multiple traditions that informed his work. Its part-publication over the years marked its constant re-creation as new influences and sources appeared. Before and during that effort, he produced a series of innovative lyric and dramatic poems that were alternately identified as Imagist or Vorticist but were undeniably modern. Yet he knew what he was seeking which a 1946 letter to his American publisher, James Laughlin, makes clear:

> God Damn & buggar the punctuation
> The important thing is
> for the 1st time
> to
> emphasize
> the articulation
> of the thought.[2]

After a flirtation with pastiche and translation, rendered in *A Lume Spento* (1908), *Cavalcanti* (1912), and his magnificent effort at Chinese writing, *Cathay* (1915), Pound found an anchor in the work he labelled Imagist. But not before an engagement with romance which led to his belief that "art is vital" only when it interprets and manifests what the artist "perceives at greater intensity, and more intimately, than his public" (*SR*, 87). Imagism evolved as a reaction against abstraction in favor of precision, replacing Victorian generalities with the clarity found in Japanese haiku and ancient Greek lyrics. In "A Few Don'ts by an Imagist" (1913), Pound outlined the new aesthetic: an image was the presentation of "an intellectual and emotional complex in an instant of time" treated according to certain rules:

1. Direct treatment of the "thing," whether subjective or objective.
2. To use absolutely no word that does not contribute to the presentation.
3. As regarding rhythm: to compose in sequence of the musical phrase, not in sequence of a metronome. (*LE*, 3, 4)

The appearance of the slim, blue-bound anthology edited by Pound, *Des Imagistes* (1914), with work by Richard Aldington, H.D., F. S. Flint, Joyce, Williams and Pound, confirmed the importance of the new movement.

Throughout Pound's poetic career, he sought the objective presentation of material which he believed would stand on its own, without the need for symbolist, expressionistic or romantic attributes. In the *ABC of Reading* (1934), he outlined the essential properties of this method which relied on the direct examination of the object and the invention of a means to render it more concisely (*ABCR*, 20). To this end, the Chinese ideogram, to become integral for *The Cantos*, provided Pound with a direct example of the new objective method. The ideogram, he explained, "*means* the thing or the action or situation, or quality germane to the several things that it pictures" (*ABCR*, 21).

Supplementing Pound's thought at this juncture in his poetic development was his encounter with the Noh theatre of Japan which he examined with Yeats during the three winters they spent together at Stone Cottage (1913–1916) when Pound acted as Yeats's secretary. At the time, Pound was engaged with the work of Ernest Fenollosa, whose widow had given Pound her husband's papers: the first product was *Cathay*; the second was *Certain Noble Plays of Japan* (1916) with an introduction by Yeats; the third was "The Chinese Written Character as a Medium for Poetry" (1919). Collectively, the result was to intensify Pound's determination to make poetry "as much like granite as it can be . . . . austere, direct, free from emotional slither" (*LE*, 12).

To incorporate the emergence of Vorticism, appearing as a system of energies in response to modern dynamism and technology, and rendered in Wyndham Lewis' typographically explosive magazine *BLAST* (1914–15), Pound redefined the image. It now became not an idea but "a radiant node or cluster . . . a VORTEX from which, and through which, and into which, ideas are constantly rushing" (*GB*, 92). But Noh theatre rather than the dynamism of the Vortex provided Pound with new direction for his work, for in Noh "Unity of Image" replaced plot: "the better plays . . . all are built into the intensification of a single Image" (*NO*, 27). But soon, as he embarked on *The Cantos*, even this approach would appear limited to Pound who had to find a way for the image to arrest the tension of competing materials while functioning as an element of reference and allusion. The image had to link different times together, one supplementing not cancelling the other.

Pound's progress can be noted in the quasi-autobiographical and satirical *Hugh Selwyn Mauberley* (1920), a poem that undermines the authenticity of one aesthetic while suggesting another. A lyric tradition founders in a new climate that demands a mimetic image of decay, he argues. Representational art is hollow. The second part of the poem shows Mauberley's failure as an artist, one who can reveal no more than a profile, "Not the full smile." He becomes a drifting figure inclined to postpone rather than encounter, although such idleness is soon shattered:

> The coral isle, the lion-coloured sand
> Burst in upon the porcelain reverie:
> Impetuous troubling
> Of his imagery   (*SP*, 167, 169)

"Medallion," the final poem of the sequence and a companion piece to the opening "Envoi," is a further critique of aestheticism. A hard, ornamental imagism replaces the mimetic.

Mauberley marks a plateau, for with it Pound recognized what he hoped he would find in the poetry of his time which he outlined in "A Retrospect" (1918):

> the poetry which I expect to see written during the next decade or so, it will, I think, move against poppy-cock, it will be harder and saner, it will be what Mr. Hewlett calls "nearer the bone . . ." it will not try to seem forcible by rhetorical din, and luxurious riot. We will have fewer painted adjectives impeding the shock and stroke of it.   (*LE*, 12)

Ahead of him lay the work of five decades, *The Cantos*.

II

> Afraid the whole damn poem is rather obscure, especially in fragments. Have
> I ever given you outline of main scheme : : : or whatever it is?
>   I. Rather like, or unlike subject and response and counter subject in fugue.
>   A. A. Live man goes down into world of Dead
>   C. B. The "repeat in history"
>   B. C. The "magic moment" or moment of metamorphosis, bust
>   thru from quotidien into "divine or permanent world."
>   Gods, etc.   (*SL*, 210)

Pound's 1927 outline of his epic poem to his father describes a scheme he
desired but could not achieve. The completed poem, stretching over fifty-
four years of effort, is more varied, digressive, repetitive and exciting than
he suggests. "Various things keep cropping up in the poem" he added in
the original letter and he was right (*SL*, 210). From the classical world of
Greece to Renaissance Italy, from China in the T'sung dynasty to America
during and after the War of Independence, the poem contains an encyclo-
pedic range of allusion and reference. Languages are equally divergent
with Greek, Latin, French, Chinese, German, Provençal, and English, among
other languages, present. Canto XX, dealing with Nicolo d'Este's reaction
to the execution of Parisina and Ugo, is a jumbled reminiscence. But one
should "take that as a sort of bounding surface from which one gives the
main subject of the Canto, the lotophagoi: lotus eaters, or respectable dope
smokers; and general paradiso. You have had a hell in Canti XIV, XV;
purgatorio in XVI etc." he explains (*SL*, 210).

The outlines Pound refers to are not exact and critics (including Yeats
in *A Packet for Ezra Pound* [1928]) have often been misled by the determination to see the poem as ordered with a structured plot and series of
developing characters. But as Pound reminds us, "there is a corking plot to
the *Iliad*, but it is not told us in the poem" (*LE*, 394). *The Cantos* incorporates the concepts Pound summarized in an essay on medievalism when
he wrote that

> We appear to have lost the radiant world where one thought cuts through
> another with clean edge, a world of moving energies "*mezzo oscuro rade*,"
> "*risplende in sè perpetuale effecto*", magnetisms that take form, that are
> seen, or that border the visible, the matter of Dante's *paradiso*, the glass
> under water, the form that seems a form seen in a mirror . . .   (*LE*, 154)

Intersections of radiant forms is one concept of *The Cantos*; the lessons
of history from the Italian Renaissance, Chinese dynasties and American
Revolution is another.

The Cantos was published in nine separate volumes beginning in 1925 and ending in 1969; its first periodical publication was in 1917. The titles were tentative, allowing Pound the freedom to revise, or restructure. Four of the nine volume titles use the word "Draft" to suggest the temporal nature of their form. Indeed, "Three Cantos," the first publication of the long work which appeared in *Poetry Magazine* in 1917, was entirely re-cast with the material from Canto III becoming that of a new Canto I in 1925. But early readers were hardly enthusiastic. On first scanning "Three Cantos," Harriet Monroe, editor of *Poetry*, became ill: "I read two or three pages of Ezra's Cantos and then took sick – no doubt that was the cause. Since then, I haven't had brains enough to tackle it." When she recovered a month later, she wrote: "I can't pretend to be much pleased at the course his verse is taking. A hint from Browning at his most recondite, and erudition in seventeen languages" (*EP/ACH*, 194). Yet as Basil Bunting would later remark of this monumental text, "you will have to go a long way round / if you want to avoid them."[3]

"An epic is a poem including history," Pound wrote in "Make It New" (*LE,* 86) and in this *The Cantos* excel. His range was wide and incorporated documents of various times and cultures to enhance the objectivity and authenticity of his work. Whether it was the correspondence of John Adams, the letters of Malatesta or the documents and literal signs he saw at various stops in his life, Pound integrated them into his text to create a visual history. Canto XXXIV, for example, contains a pyramid filled with words in English and Hebrew, while Canto XCIII contains hieroglyphics. Visual musical notation appears in Canto LXXV, and as late as Canto XCVII a symbol representing a temple augments the line of poetry (XCVII/696). Throughout the poem, Chinese ideograms, the very embodiment of picture and thing populate the text, while actual signs are reproduced as in Canto LXV/371. The presence of historical figures lends referentiality to the text, whether it is Adams, Napoleon or Mussolini.

The lyrical engages the dramatic. Often, in the midst of the sweep of history, there is a pause and a single voice speaks. Canto XXXIX ends with

> Dark shoulders have stirred the lightning
> A girl's arms have nested the fire,
> Not I but the handmaid kindled
>   Cantat sic nupta
> I have eaten the flame.　　　　　　　　　(XXXIX/196)

Throughout *The Pisan Cantos*, the most personal section of the entire work, narrative, personal history and lyrical retrospection mingle:

> Serenely in the crystal jet
>> as the bright ball that the fountain tosses
> (Verlaine) as diamond clearness
>> How soft the wind under Taishan
>>> where the sea is remembered
>> out of hell, the pit
>> out of the dust and glare evil   (LXXIV/469)

Pound unknowingly comments on this process when John Adams reflects that

>> whenever
> we leave principles and clear propositions
> and wander into construction we wander into a wilderness
> a darkness   (LXIV/359)

The Cantos seeks to undo the hard categories of drama, satire, documentary, diaries, hymns, elegies, epigrams, essay, catalogues and sermons, to cite only a few of its other genres. The overlaying of so many genres has the effect of eliding their differences, fulfilling Pound's dictum that literary forms often subvert the distinction between them. The poem, an intellectual autobiography simultaneously manifesting a history of literature and culture, also incorporates myth which mediates the personal into something unusual. Consequently, *The Cantos* is polyphonic in theme and serial in form, with recurrence rather than linearity its thrust. In his quest for *vers libre* ("To break the pentameter, that was the first heave"[4]), Pound rejected formal completeness and proportion, substituting flux and openness, supplemented by a poetics of quotation. This is Pound's use of statements by others to elucidate his own argument. "Beauty is difficult," he writes, a multi-layered declaration first used by Beardsley, referenced by Yeats and repeated by Pound in Canto LXXIV/464.

An outline of *The Cantos*, corresponding to their publication in book form, begins with

Cantos I–XVI (*A Draft of XVI. Cantos*, 1925). The opening seven deal with mythical, visionary and legendary materials, including Odysseus' descent to Hell, the metamorphoses of Dionysus, and troubadour and Italian parallels to Ovid. Modern life, by contrast, is shown to be lifeless. Cantos VII–XI focus on Sigismundo Malatesta, master of fifteenth-century Rimini, and his struggle to enhance the art of his city. Cantos XII to XVI criticize modern monopolists, idealize Confucian order, and conclude with an escape to Elysian fields.

Cantos XVII–XXVII (*A Draft of the Cantos 17–27*, 1928). Modern profiteers versus Renaissance life and pleasure, following a return to Venice in Canto XVII. The goals of the Quattrocento in contrast to the lack of direction and destructiveness of the modern age.

Cantos XXVIII–XLI (*A Draft of XXX Cantos*, 1930; *Eleven New Cantos*, 1934). The so-called Jefferson Cantos which celebrate the New World and the rationality of the American Founding Fathers contrasted with the darkness of Europe (Cantos XXXI–XXXIV). Canto XXXVI successfully translates Cavalcanti's "Donna mi prega." The section ends with the battle between institutionalized swindling and the voyage of Hanno; it concludes with a comparison between Mussolini's *virtu* against monopolists and that of Jefferson.

Cantos XLII–LI (*The Fifth Decad of Cantos*, 1937) Reforms in Leopoldine Italy and an examination of Siena in the eighteenth century where money was not hoarded but shared. The anathema of usury in Canto XLV, while corrupt England is castigated in XLVI. The peace experienced in Chinese landscape, the destructive victory of Waterloo where usury triumphed and the battle of usury against light and nature (LI).

Cantos LII–LXXI (*Cantos LII–LXXI*, 1940) The Chinese Cantos stress a Confucian presentation of Chinese imperial history from the Book of Rites through the Manchu period. Pound shows that only when Confucian ethics rule does the empire flourish; Taoists and Buddhists stunt the growth of the kingdom. The ideal emperor is Yong Tching who died in 1735.

The Adams Cantos (LXII–LXXI) present in detail John Adams and his fundamental contribution of integrity and energy to America; from documents and other sources, Pound presents Adams's impressions of France and England, and his role in creating the Constitution. Focus in this section on the art of government. Cantos LXXII and LXXIII form the "Italian Cantos," unavailable in a complete *Cantos* until 1985.

Cantos LXXIV–LXXXIV (*The Pisan Cantos*, 1948). Pound, in the Disciplinary Training Center near Pisa after his arrest, meditates on the fall of Italy and the end of his dreams of an improved society; the test becomes an elegy for a Europe that has disappeared with details of his early experiences with Joyce, Ford and others. Mythic visions and Confucian ideals sustain him as he discovers that "What thou lovest well remains." Conflict between the paradisal possibilities of nature and the dark night of the soul as he faces imprisonment and even death. Pound's presence in the poem increases from this section on.

Cantos LXXXV–XCV (*Section: Rock-Drill*, 1955). First part refers back to the American and Chinese Cantos; second looks forward to a possible *paradiso*. Celebration of civic virtue and courage, as well as pagan mysteries and the neo-Platonic strain in medieval thought. Presents the natural universe through an animistic vision. Canto XCV ends with the shipwreck of Odysseus and his rescue by the nymph Ino.

Cantos XCVI–CIX (*Thrones*, 1959). With a title from Dante's *Paradiso*, the poem now blends two themes from *Rock-Drill*: the examination of history and the celebration of virtue and intelligence. Explores early Christian Europe as well as nineteenth-century European and American governments. Details on the regulation of civic and guild life in Constantinople and the philosophers of Light in the so-called Dark Ages. Early English history plus the Parliamentary crisis of the seventeenth century is interrupted by flashes of Eleusinian mystery and pagan theophanies. Nature and light celebrated.

Cantos CX–CXVII (*Drafts & Fragments*, 1969). A return to Venice and the poet's private situation; reflections on the failure of the long poem but a celebration of life despite its fragmentation.

History, myth and anecdote embody the inclusiveness of *The Cantos* whose verse forms transcends periods and genres. The work embraces patterns that are Homeric, Dantescan and even Quattrocento, which Pound summarized as the mysteries, whether of Eleusis, Dionysus, or Pythagoras. The structure or method of arrangement Pound follows is fragmentation and contrast so that Confucius is set against the modern Inferno of Cantos XII–XV or Vienna set against Cavalcanti (XXXV–XXXVI). This establishes a radical break from the organic structures found in many of his predecessors. Pound prefers collage to the sequential, organic, lyric poem. For Pound, his discrete structures are the meaning; the form of the poem is its reality. A line from Canto CXIII presenting "the mind as Ixion, unstill, ever turning" (810), summarizes the tension between order and chaos in this form of poetics.

III

It has been complained, with some justice, that I dump my notebooks on the public.
                                                                                    Pound, 1918

Reception of Pound's poetry in general, and *The Cantos* in particular, has been mixed. Readers were generally confused and anxious by the seemingly twisted forms of his work. Early critics such as T. S. Eliot and Louis Zukofsky recognised the difficulties in Pound's violation of lyric norms and offered guides. Eliot anonymously wrote *Ezra Pound His Metric and Poetry* in 1917, Pound editing the work before sending it on to John Quinn for publication in New York by Knopf to coincide with the appearance of *Lustra* (1917). Zukofsky published an essay in 1929 on *The Cantos*, acknowledging Pound as "both the isolated creator and the worldly pamphleteer."[5] In 1940 James Laughlin, Pound's publisher, was so concerned about the reception of *Cantos LII–LXXI* that he convinced Pound of the usefulness of pasting a small explanatory pamphlet into the first 500 copies of the volume. *Notes on Ezra Pound's Cantos* contained two essays, one unsigned by Laughlin, the other by the poet Delmore Schwartz.

Critics have wrestled with Pound's texts since their first publication and various reference books, guides and annotations have seemed necessary, despite Pound's repeated admonition that the best way to read *The Cantos* is simply to engage the text, without cribs, dictionaries or phrase books. In 1934 he wrote to one reader that she should

> skip anything you don't understand and go on till you pick it up again. All tosh about *foreign languages* making it difficult. The quotes are all either explained at once by repeat or they are definitely *of* the things indicated.
>
> (*SL*, 250–251)

The discontinuity of the poem, however, put readers off, while Pound's own comments in the work ("I cannot make it cohere," CXVI/816), plus various errors of fact and misuse of sources, gave many scholars cause to reject his effort. Some critics ungenerously refered to *The Cantos* as "a shifting heap of splinters" or a "nostalgic montage without unity, a picaresque of styles." Others countered by arguing that the first fifty years of this century are "the Pound Era" and understood the poem as generating a new aesthetic with "syntax yielding to parataxis" as Pound juxtaposes "concrete particulars that he considers meaningful in the conviction that they will speak for themselves."[6] Supporters declared that collage was the designated form of the work, linked to elements of Cubism and modern art, with metonymic preference replacing metaphoric expansion in the text. Detractors condemned the work as a textual mess. Pound himself unknowingly provided a guide to *The Cantos* when he wrote in 1916 that "the work of art which is most 'worth-while' is the work which would need a hundred works of any other kind of art to explain it. A fine statue is the core of a hundred poems" (*GB*, 84).

Casting a shadow over these formal assessments, however, are Pound's politics and antisemitism which Charles Olson, among others, evaluated:

> Shall we talk a 100 Cantos and not answer the antisemite who wrote them? Shall we learn from his line and not answer his lie? . . . For Pound is no dried whore of fascism. He is as brilliant a maker of language as we have had in our time. The point is not that this mitigates, or in any way relates to the punishment the U.S. shall deal to him . . . what is called for is a consideration, based on his career, of how such a man came to the position he reached.[7]

Pound was an activist who insisted on "ideas which are intended to 'go into action,'" or "to guide action and serve as rules (and/or measures) of conduct," an aesthetic for his writing as much as a guide to his thought (GK, 34). But from 1941 to 1943, they took on a particular coloration in his radio broadcasts which altered his ideas from the thirties when he espoused the Social Credit views developed by C. H. Douglas who sought to correct the inequitable distribution of wealth, purchasing power and credit. The control and exploitation of credit by private banks was for Douglas – and soon for Pound – the main culprit. Because the banks charge excessive interest (Pound labelled it usury) for the use of money and credit, prices would always be higher than purchasing power. Government control of credit and interest rates and the issuance of "national dividends" directly to the consumers was the Social Credit answer.

By the time of the Depression, Pound was convinced that the forces which caused the First World War were accelerating to a second. Simple economic reforms would be the only answer. In Italy, however, he began to admire Mussolini's form of National Socialism and continuously sent a barrage of articles and "letters to the editor" to a wide range of American periodicals; they mostly dealt with political and economic issues. These instigations found their way into such venues as the *Boston Herald*, the *New York World Telegram*, the *New Republic*, *Time*, and *Esquire*, as well as college publications, little magazines and local newspapers in far-flung communities. In 1935 alone, he sent approximately 150 items to such journals. He also spent time writing to US Congressmen including Senator Bronson Cutting, Representative George Holden Tinham and Senator William E. Borah, visiting the last in Washington in 1939.

During the thirties Pound also published a good deal of writing instructional in tone, from the *ABC of Economics* and the *ABC of Reading* to *Jefferson and/or Mussolini* and *Guide to Kulchur*. With a determined voice, he taught his readers how to understand the centrality of economics, the value of literature and the necessity of reaffirming what he believed to be fundamental political ideals. What he sought was to aestheticize the political. Various pamphlets, mostly dealing with money and economic matters, supplemented his prose works – all while he added forty new sections to *The Cantos*, sections that reflected his focused engagement with American politics and history. Van Buren, Jefferson and John Adams became the poem's new heroes.

While concentrating on American politics and politicians, Pound was also pursuing Mussolini. He wrote first to Il Duce's private secretary in April 1932. He finally met Mussolini himself in January 1933, the memorable event recorded at the opening of Canto XLI. In *Guide to Kulchur*,

Pound expressed tentative faith in Mussolini because he "told his people that poetry is a necessity *to the state*" (*GK*, 249). Pound admired Mussolini's determination to rid Italy of its historical clutter (see *J/M* 66) and initiate his vision of a new, productive Italy: "Producers represent the new Italy, as opposed to the old Italy of balladeers and tour-guides," Mussolini proclaimed.[8]

By the forties, Pound took an active role in supporting fascism, making more than 100 short-wave broadcasts over Rome Radio between 1941 and 1943. Criticizing the American government, he defended the policies of Mussolini and Hitler and developed a litany of antisemitic attitudes and remarks. In July 1943, after several of his broadcasts were monitored in Washington, he was indicted for treason by a US Grand Jury. Apprehended in Rapallo in May 1945, he spent six months in the Army's Disciplinary Training Center near Pisa; suddenly flown to Washington, he underwent a psychiatric examination, a federal court then declaring him mentally unfit to stand trial. From December 1945 until May 1958, he was imprisoned in St. Elizabeths Hospital, Washington, D.C., a federal institution for the criminally insane. The controversy surrounding him intensified when he won the Bollingen Prize for Poetry in 1949 for *The Pisan Cantos*. But his goal remained clear: "I must find a verbal formula to combat the rise of brutality – the principle of order versus the split atom."[9]

Pound busied himself with many other activities while he was writing his epic, none more important than that of anthologist, a task he understood as shaping literary history as well as taste. He began with *Des Imagistes* (1914) and continued with the *Catholic Anthology* (1915) *Profile* (1932), the *Active Anthology* (1933), and *Confucius to Cummings* (1964). His efforts not only established connections with such notable writers as Joyce, whom he approached for *Des Imagistes*, but he managed to organize volumes that reflected critical developments in the movement of literature at the same time he expanded his own readership. What the anthologies collectively illustrate is Pound's belief that "a man can learn more about poetry by really knowing and examining a few of the best poems than by meandering about among a great many" (*ABCR*, 43). An anthology for Pound was a laboratory for readers because for him the "proper METHOD for studying poetry and good letters is the method of contemporary biologists, that is careful first-hand examination of the matter, and continual COMPARISON of one 'slide' or specimen with another" (*ABCR*, 17). And readers of Pound's letters know that he was forever making lists of texts for his recipients to read, lists that were eclectic, inclusive and confident. "Rub it in that EP has spent 30 years introducing the BEST of one nation to another & not the worst . . . ," Dorothy Pound told James Laughlin in 1947, after spending a morning discussing anthologies and selections with "the boss" (*EP/JL*, 167).

Pound was similarly energetic as an editor and literary promoter. Best known perhaps for his editing of *The Waste Land* in 1921 from nearly 1,000 lines of poetry to 434, he not only refashioned the text, but trumpeted its virtues. To John Quinn in New York he declared "about enough, Eliot's poem, to make the rest of us shut up shop," characteristically adding, "I haven't done so; have in fact knocked out another Canto (not in the least *à la Eliot*, or connected with 'modern life')" (*EP/JQ*, 206). Yeats earlier benefited from Pound's sense of precision and exactness in poetic expression during the three winters they spent together at Stone Cottage, just as Williams and Zukofsky would profit from his direction.

Joyce, although not directly subject to Pound's editorial knife, also gained from his efforts: in late 1913, and at the suggestion of Yeats, Pound first made contact with Joyce. The letter was a pure solicitation: Pound was looking for new material for a host of periodicals and ended his note with this declaration: "I am *bonae voluntatis*, – don't in the least know that I can be of any use to you – or you to me. From what W. B. Y. says I imagine we have a hate or two in common – but thats a very problematical bond on introduction" (*P/J*, 18). Pound then decided he wanted to print Joyce's poem "I Hear an Army" in *Des Imagistes* and would pay for it. Joyce, impressed with this aggressiveness, sent Pound the first chapter of *A Portrait of the Artist*. Pound sent it at once to the *Egoist*, the first to print any portion of the work; a few years later, Pound convinced Margaret Anderson and Jane Heap, editors of the *Little Review* to publish episodes of *Ulysses* beginning in 1918. Pound also convinced Joyce of the value of moving to Paris, thereby making it possible for him to be in contact with such figures as Sylvia Beach who, of course, published *Ulysses*.

As a foreign correspondent, Pound maintained his American identity and link with North America. Whether it was *Poetry*, the *Smart Set*, the *Little Review* or *The Dial*, Pound found an identity as America's agent in Europe, transmitting back home the newest voices and works that he discovered in Europe. He relished the role and when he found out in March 1923, for example, that he would no longer be a contributor to *The Dial*, he confided to Kate Buss that "I don't know where to go next. As far as I can see, my communication with America is over. I.e., public communication. The last link severed" (*SL*, 186). But he enjoyed being a promoter/agent for foreign journals as well. He acted as liaison between a series of writers and Ford Madox Ford's *English Review*, Dora Marsden's *Egoist* and Henry Davray's *Mercure de France*. A great deal of his early time in London was spent in finding new talent, a habit he continued throughout the later part of his career.

Yeats, in commenting on Pound's preference for style rather than form – the style always "interrupted, broken, twisted into nothing by its direct opposite, nervous obsession, nightmare, stammering confusion" – also recognized that "he has great influence, more perhaps than any contemporary except Eliot."[10] This admission acknowledged the inescapability of Pound among the moderns and his centrality in the moral and literary geography of European literary culture, something Pound himself observed. To an interviewer in 1960, he asserted that "I am the last American living the tragedy of Europe."[11]

IV

We advance by discriminations.

Pound, 1912

Eliot, one might argue, initiated the recuperation of Ezra Pound with his edition of Pound's *Literary Essays* in 1954. Pound was still in St. Elizabeths, writing, translating and officiating over the development of American poetry from his post in what he called the nut house. Many came to bear witness: Charles Olson, Robert Lowell, Allen Ginsberg, Louis Zukofsky, Archibald MacLeish, William Carlos Williams and Eliot. Marshall McLuhan also came in the company of Hugh Kenner, the critic who advanced an understanding of Pound's work with *The Poetry of Ezra Pound* which preceded Eliot's work by three years. It began with the assertion that "there is no great contemporary writer who is less read than Ezra Pound."[12] Buttressed by the appearance of Pound's literary essays, canonizing his ideas on the art of poetry, tradition and contemporaries, Pound's work was open for review. A cascade of critical titles followed.

Studies of individual poems soon appeared, showing the new confidence of critics, supplemented by a series of textual examinations beginning with Donald Gallup's essential bibliography published in 1963, revised in 1983. Guides to Pound's poetry soon appeared, culminating in 1971 with the appearance of Hugh Kenner's magisterial *The Pound Era*, a work that re-established the centrality of Pound for a post New Criticism generation, one that was taught to see Pound as not only a progenitor but pillar of modernism.

By 1970, a retrospect was already underway: Eric Homberger edited *Ezra Pound: The Critical Heritage*, while J. P. Sullivan edited *Ezra Pound: A Critical Anthology*. In 1972, *Paideuma*, a journal devoted to Pound scholarship, began. In 1976, Ronald Bush's *The Genesis of Ezra Pound's Cantos* provided the first detailed study of the origin and structure of the poem, extended by the more recent textual studies of Richard Taylor and his efforts to construct a variorum edition. Carroll F. Terrell's fundamental research tool, the two-volume, *A Companion to the Cantos of Ezra Pound*, appeared in 1980. Barbara Eastman's *Ezra Pound's Cantos: The Story of the Text* (1979) and Christine Froula's *To Write Paradise: Style and Error in Pound's Cantos* (1984) furthered textual interest, extended by Peter Stoicheff's study of *Drafts & Fragments* entitled *Hall of Mirrors* (1995).

Keeping pace with the critical and textual discussion of Pound has been several editorial projects. In 1985 Mary de Rachewiltz published *I Cantos*, a dual language version of the poem and the first complete edition containing the formerly excluded Cantos LXXII and LXXIII, the "Italian Cantos." It also incoporated several final revisions by Pound to the text, resulting in what Massimo Bacigalupo has called "a new Cantos for Pound's second century" (*PAI*, 15 [1986], 298). A revised edition of *Personae* with corrected texts appeared in 1990. On a larger scale is the notable eleven-volume 1991 Garland facsimile edition of all of Pound's periodical contributions in poetry and prose. This is a fundamental research tool making accessible a major corpus of Pound's writing. A volume of formerly inaccessible or unpublished prose, entitled *Machine Art and Other Writings*, appeared in 1996. A continuous set of letters has also emerged, supplementing the 1950 publication of Pound's correspondence edited by D. D. Paige and retitled *Selected Letters* in 1971. The bibliography to this *Companion* lists the principal editions of these and other texts.

In this current collection, a variety of critical approaches seek to present the work of Pound from complementary perspectives: descriptive, analytical, historical, cultural, and textual. The opening essay establishes Pound's prominence and importance in shaping the modernist enterprise. George Bornstein documents Pound's efforts in literary politics as he helped "to produce, distribute and institutionalize modernist works." Advice that was practical, technical, and even personal was freely offered to Yeats, Eliot, Lewis, H.D., Joyce and others. Pound, Bornstein argues, acted as a "permanent principle of innovation," a point borne out by Yeats: "to talk over a poem with him is like getting you to put a sentence into dialect. All becomes clear and natural."[13] The modernist insistence on poetic accuracy and the effort to fuse elite and popular culture were further goals Pound promoted.

Hugh Witemeyer looks closely at Pound's early poetic development, detailing the tension between the worship of beauty and the reform of culture. From early lyrics and translations to the satire and experiment of *Mauberley* (1920), Pound's texts embody the neo-classical ideal of the epic poet as a man of learning as well as imagination, argues Witemeyer. The three following essays study Pound's epic text, *The Cantos*, in detail, beginning with Daniel Albright's analysis of the dual, self-scrutinizing structure of the early Cantos which both erase and reinscribe their content. Beginning with a discussion of the term "canto" and its application to the poem, Albright shows Pound's reluctance to model his work on classical or medieval European examples *or* modernist experiments. Browning was his example, although after "Three Cantos" (1917), Albright discloses how Pound reconceived the poem, replacing a centralizing consciousness with a fragmented perception affirming dislocation through juxtaposition. Japanese Noh theatre provided the clue for Pound with its anti-discursive, incisive style of "ragged surfaces imprinted with voices"; the shape of *The Cantos* started to take form. Succeeding the Noh theatre as a modeling influence were satire, fugal patterns, and the ideogram, all contributing but also challenging the structure of the work – challenges that Pound would spend more than fifty years struggling to resolve.

In Pound's "Middle Cantos," Ian F. Bell charts some of the solutions. Reading these works as a cultural map, Bell shows how Pound constructs a means of settlement through the founding of a sixteenth-century Italian bank in Siena, eighteenth-century reforms in Tuscany, the history of China and the career of John Adams. In his diagnosis of the corruption of culture brought about by usury, Pound returns to the values of Confucian thought and the ideal of the American Republic. Recapitulation and anticipation are the historical moves Pound undertakes between Cantos LXII–LXXI where accuracy and precision become the keynotes, Pound appropriately concluding *The Fifth Decad* with the ideogram for the "right name" (LI/252). Bell underscores the dynastic impulse of the poem designed to maintain Confucian reverence for the work of documents and the preservation of the law.

The law takes on a different meaning, however, in Ronald Bush's essay "Late Cantos." Allied with fascist doctrine and antisemitic harangues, the poetry nonetheless possesses moments of "tragic enlightenment." Pound's arrest, detention, trial and imprisonment, the law now understood as punishment, contributed heavily to a new urgency and retrospective tone in his long poem. Written between 1945 and 1958 exclusively in captivity (first in Pisa and then St. Elizabeths), the late Cantos contain both the most accessible and troubling passages of the entire work. After affirming natural order and hierarchy in his poems of the thirties, Pound, especially in *The Pisan Cantos* and the final volume *Drafts & Fragments*, rediscovered earlier sympathies for the bohemian and the outcast.

During the war, Pound wrote only fragments, although in 1944 he wrote the two formerly unpublished Italian Cantos, Cantos LXXII and LXXIII. Yet in Pisa, he sought to redeem the energies of light and reason through his writing. Diary and reminiscence impose themselves on visionary poetry. *Section: Rock-Drill* and *Drafts & Fragments* incorporate Confucian wisdom into a response to the atmosphere of decayed post-war culture which *Thrones* shifts to the mythic world of Odysseus and harmony, at times so abbreviated as to be unreadable and hermetic. *Drafts &* *Fragments* mixes a melancholy lyricism with an elegiac tone, with nature offering a lament: "A wind of darkness hurls against forest" (CX/801). But as he strove to celebrate light, Pound also understood that "my errors and wrecks lie about me" (CXVI/816).

Tentativeness replaces dogmatism as *The Cantos* comes to its open-ended close, surrounded by textual confusion which Bush unravels, including the addition of Canto CXX, a revision of lines from Canto CXV with its paradisal closure:

> I have tried to write Paradise
> * * * * * * * * *
> Let the Gods forgive what I
>   have made
> Let those I love try to forgive
>   what I have made.
>   (Notes for CXVII et seq./822)

James Laughlin added these words as the conclusion to the 1972 edition of the poem, but Faber & Faber rejected them, complicating matters. In the past twenty-five years, there have been no less than six significant versions of the ending of *The Cantos*.

Richard Taylor addresses many of these matters in his essay on the textual history of the poem. Against the dramatic changes in textual criticism over the last twenty years, Taylor examines the difficulties in sorting out the compositional history of *The Cantos*. Interferences in the production of text – from accidental errors to substantial editorial interventions – have affected the publication of the poem, and reprinted editions have only exacerbated the level of inaccuracy, introducing new errors. The instability of the text of *The Cantos* originates in its disparate composition and publication over a lengthy period and its peculiar history of attempts to revise and correct the poem, often marked by non-authorial changes.

The numerous quotations and more than twenty languages in the work present immense challenges to publishers, editors and printers. Taylor tries to sort them out by outlining the value of a variorum edition and a proper publishing history of the poem. For example, the 1970 New Directions printing of the poem incorporated no less than 138 changes to the text but no public record of them exists. Differences between British and American editions did not help the textual confusions. Errors and corrections to the text of *The Cantos* plus inconsistent methods and contradictory intentions prevented the establishment of a definitive edition of the work during

Pound's lifetime. But such errors, must not continue, Taylor concludes, although two troubling questions persist: just what *is* the text of *The Cantos* and how can it be established? These questions are of central importance to any understanding of the poem.

Peter Nicholls considers the impact of *The Cantos* on a generation of younger writers, arguing that the poem functions as a kind of matrix, a textual world inhabited in different ways by different writers. "Emulation and resistance" describe the poetic response to Pound's work by a younger generation. Creeley, Duncan and Olson, not to say Ginsberg, Ashbery and Howe, realized that "the fact of Ezra Pound and his work is inescapable" as Creeley declared, adding, perhaps more importantly, that "Pound has given us . . . possibilities." Pound, Nicholls demonstrates, presented a tradition counter to that of Eliot and the New Critics. He showed what is possible in a new poetics if the poet dared to violate the traditional academic constraints and protocols. Pound's influence was both enabling and prescriptive: he opened poetry up to a range of different knowledges, while embedding the poetic act within a complex historicity – yet monumentally imposing himself on the poetic landscape.

"Pound as Critic" is the focus of Massimo Bacigalupo's essay, an exploration of the ways Pound's poetic aesthetic mirrors his prose criticism. The numerous volumes he published beginning with *The Spirit of Romance* (1910) and ending with the anthology *Confucius to Cummings* (1964), display a surprisingly unified approach and focus for his persistent topics: the virtue of close reading, the essential union of poetry and history, the necessity of representing the objective in art, literature as source data for the study of man, and a belief that a few dozen facts could give us the intelligence of a period (*LE*, 46; *SPR*, 22–23). Or as Pound preferred to say, hard bits of mosaic can contain the world.

Catch phrases and quotations Bacigalupo shows to be the première stylistic feature of Pound's prose. His model? The spoken word with its shifting tones and emphases. The search for "passionate simplicity" (*LE*, 53) in his prose reflects the intensity of his quest for exactness in his poetry. Literature and the artist, the subject of his pre-World War I writing; individual writers such as Gourmont and James, the focus of his prose in the 1920s; textbooks on literature and economics, the center of his work in the 1930s; politics and economics, his obsession in the 1940s; translation, his concern in the 1950s – these form the nexus of Pound's prose whose goal was simple: to teach us through language to "Wake up and live!" (*EP/JL*, 180).

Ming Xie investigates Pound's abilities as a translator and his treatment of language in the establishment of a set of new texts based on primary forms, admitting that Pound's new English versions often substitute for the originals. But translation strengthened his own poetic innovations which, in turn, guided his translations. Hardly a scholar of foreign languages, although he studied Romance Languages at university, Pound pays more attention to meaning and its equivalences than to grammar. Pound conceived of translation as an invented turning of previous material, originating in his understanding of "troubadour," which in Provençal derives from *trobar*, to invent, from the Latin, *tropus*. Translation for Pound is to approximate the sound and alliterative stress of the original language. His aim was always fidelity to the original in both meaning and atmosphere. Or as he told W. H. D. Rouse in 1935, "no need of keeping verbal literality for phrases which sing and run naturally in the original" (*SL*, 273). What he sought in his rendering of originals was the "raw cut of concrete reality combined with the tremendous energy, the contact with the natural force" (*SL*, 273). And as Xie explains, *The Cantos* is itself an "epic of translation" with a multilingual, intertextual web of cultures simultaneously existing in various modes of translation from allusion to quotation and even parody.

Reed Way Dasenbrock initiates the final section of the collection, a series of essays on Pound and extra-literary topics. He begins with a new look at the Pound/Visual Arts nexus, arguing that Pound was attracted to the social and public nature of art, not the art itself. The public nature of art meant that it demanded patronage, a topic which fascinated Pound who sought a similar state for poetry – and partially found it for his own work in his relationship with the New York lawyer John Quinn. Drawing an analogy between the patronage of the Italian Renaissance and the conditions of his own time, Pound sought to get poetry into the public spotlight through its link with the visual arts. Hence, Vorticism and Pound's efforts, along with Wyndham Lewis, to promote it. And later, in the important Malatesta and Venetian Cantos (VIII–XII, XXIV–XXVI), he explored the impact of patronage on the arts. Dasenbrock completes his analysis with an original reading of the role of the visual arts in Pound's political thinking and, in particular, his attraction to Mussolini.

Michael Ingham examines the link between Pound and music, noting the compelling connections between poetry and musical sound. He demonstrates the depth of Pound's 1920 remark to Agnes Bedford, "meaning is all tied up with sound" (*SL*, 161), through a survey of Pound's efforts at musical composition – principally his two operas, *Le Testament de Villon* and *Cavalcanti* – and his various musical criticism. Ingham details the roots of Pound's absorption with music through his friendship with Walter Morse Rummel, Arnold Dolmetsch, George Antheil and, of course, Olga Rudge. He also provides an intriguing comparison between Pound and

Charles Ives, and argues that the order of *The Cantos* is the order of the voice – found in song, conversation, politics and love.

Tim Redman tackles the knotty issue of Pound's politics and economics – not only their origins but influence on Pound's writing. Redman argues that Pound's political philosophy "largely conforms to a set of populist beliefs deeply rooted in American history." He begins by explaining the importance of Thaddeus Pound, the poet's paternal grandfather, in state and national politics, and his influence on the political consciousness of his grandson. His mother's side was equally prominent, since his maternal grandmother was the daughter of Mary Wadsworth whose family arrived in America in 1632. And while aesthetics, rather than populist politics, shaped Pound's early years in Europe, politics was always at hand. Redman traces the importance of A. R. Orage and the *New Age* circle, the influence of C. H. Douglas and Social Credit, and the politics of art on Pound, notably how copyright laws, passports and publication restrictions exercised him into action.

Moving to Italy in 1924 brought for Pound a new interest in Mussolini's fascism and, by the early thirties, a renewed study of economics. Redman analyzes Pound's political philosophy (stimulated by his re-reading Jefferson and Adams) as a development of his economic concerns and shows how it influenced his conception of *The Cantos*. Other economists such as Silvio Gesell and Odon Por – later supplemented by Brooks Adams and Alexander del Mar – supplied ideas which Pound drew on and combined with his notions of Social Credit and Confucius to formulate his political and economic principles which *Guide to Kulchur* (1938) summarizes.

One origin for Pound's sympathy with the Social Credit/fascist ideal, Redman concludes, is in a so-called American fascism which has its roots in American populism. Reacting to rule by a predatory economic plutocracy, this group supports a strong executive which will control civil liberties and eliminate the opposition between financier and producer in an effort to restore to the population their sovereign right to control money. From Pound's understanding of Chinese history, Social Credit philosophy, the achievements of Mussolini and the ideal of Jefferson and Adams emerges the foundation of his political and economic theories.

Helen M. Dennis shows that although Pound's poetry encodes conservative configurations of the feminine, this did not prevent Pound from collaborating with a range of unusual, independent women – H.D., Mrs. Mary Fenollosa, Harriet Monroe, Marianne Moore, and Olga Rudge to name but a few. The enigma exists in his personal life as well as poetry, since he outwardly maintained a marriage but inwardly sustained a personal romance with Olga Rudge for forty-nine years. Beginning with a survey of

Pound's association with various women who encouraged or supported his work, especially Dorothy Shakespear and Margaret Cravens, Dennis analyzes the tension that often surrounded Pound's relation with women, whether it was Bride Scratton or Sheri Martinelli. Dennis also carefully documents the way Pound transformed so many to these women into mythological figures in his poetry, acknowledging that in the cultural exchange of marriage (and sometimes love) the female body absorbs spiritual and aesthetic value. For Pound, the female is always a presence, immanent and transcendent in his work.

Concluding the volume is Wendy Flory's review of Pound and antisemitism, this issue, rather than treason – the original charge against him in July 1943 – taking precedence as the source of outrage against him. The context of the Holocaust has intensified the denunciations of Pound's antisemitism, she notes, but also delayed a careful analysis of his position. Reluctance to confront the extent of American antisemitism at the time of the Holocaust, Flory explains, determined the attitudes toward Pound. His antisemitism served as "a convenient place-holder for all those whose antisemitism was not being confronted." Denouncing Pound as "the real antisemite" became an effortless alternative to any serious analysis of the problem of antisemitism in America and in oneself.

Flory explains the antisemitism of Pound, dominant from 1935 on, as his suffering from paranoid psychosis. She focuses on Pound's state of mind and notes the absence of any but passing and immaterial antisemitic allusions in *The Cantos*. His radio broadcasts she reads as disorganized rantings reflecting his confused and delusional attitude. Pound's fixation on an economic-conspiracy theory, linked to his manic component, determined the erratic tone of his radio broadcasts and his frequently psychotic response to the political and economic topics he discussed at St. Elizabeths. Such distortions help to explain his antisemitism and clear the way for a sharper understanding of his poetry.

Has literature a function in the state? This is the provocative question Pound asks at the opening of "How to Read" and answers through his work and its aesthetic. He disputes the Senecan tag, *litterae nihil sanates* (literature heals nothing), quoted twice in *The Cantos*, by arguing for writing that galvanizes its readers. Literature, he argues, renews the past through the language of the present, while giving it fresh meaning. "The news in the Odyssey is still news" he wants us to understand, just as he tries to convince us that literature is the first step to moral action (*ABC*, 44). Books feed us with energy; the "Arts work on life as history works on the development of civilization and literature. The artist seeks out the luminous detail and presents it" (*SPR*, 23). Our job is to spot it.

NOTES

1 Pound in Walter Sutton (ed.) *Pound, Thayer, Watson and The Dial, A Story in Letters* (Gainesville: University Press of Florida, 1994), p. 169.

2 Pound in David M. Gordon (ed.), *Ezra Pound and James Laughlin, Selected Letters* (New York: Norton, 1994), p. 145.

3 Basil Bunting, "On the Fly-Leaf of Pound's Cantos," in *Collected Poems, New Edition* (Oxford: Oxford University Press, 1978), p. 110.

4 Pound in Marjorie Perloff, "Pound/Stevens: Whose Era?" in Perloff, *The Dance of the Intellect* (Cambridge: Cambridge University Press, 1985), p. 17.

5 Louis Zukofsky, "Ezra Pound," in *Prepositions, The Collected Critical Essays of Louis Zukofsky*, expanded edn (Berkeley: University of California Press, 1981), p. 69. Zukofsky also reminds his readers that "the poet and his personae in the *Cantos* are not present in sharp, medieval outline. Dante wore robes and had a theology to accompany him on his journey" (p. 75).

6 Lucy Beckett, *Wallace Stevens* (Cambridge: Cambridge University Press, 1974), p. 64; Geoffrey Hartman, "Toward Literary History," in *Beyond Formalism* (New Haven: Yale University Press, 1970), p. 358; Hugh Kenner, *The Pound Era* (Berkeley: University of California Press, 1971); Eva Hesse, "Introduction," in Hesse (ed.), *New Approaches to Ezra Pound* (Berkeley: University of California Press, 1969), p. 48.

7 Charles Olson in Catherine Seelye (ed.), *Charles Olson and Ezra Pound* (New York: Grossman/Viking, 1975), pp. 17, 19.

8 Benito Mussolini, "Orientamenti e problemi," in Edoardo and Duilio Susmel (eds.), *Opera Omnia di Benito Mussolini*, 36 vols. (Florence: La Fenice, 1951–63), XI, p. 283.

9 Pound, interviewed in Rome in late February 1960 by Donald Hall, printed in "Ezra Pound: An Interview," *Paris Review*, 28 (1962), 47.

10 W. B. Yeats in J. P. Sullivan (ed.), *Ezra Pound, A Critical Anthology* (Harmondsworth: Penguin, 1970), p. 184.

11 Pound, in Hall, "Ezra Pound: An Interview," 51.

12 Hugh Kenner, *The Poetry of Ezra Pound* (1951; Lincoln: University of Nebraska Press, 1985), p. 16.

13 Yeats to Lady Gregory, January 3, 1913, in Richard Ellmann, "Ez and Old Billyum," in Ellmann, *Eminent Domain: Yeats among Wilde, Joyce, Pound, Eliot and Auden* (New York: Oxford University Press, 1967), p. 66. In the same letter, Yeats added that Pound "spoils himself by too many experiments and has more sound principles than taste."

2

GEORGE BORNSTEIN

Ezra Pound and the making of modernism

"It is after all a grrrreat litttttterary period," wrote Ezra Pound to
T. S. Eliot with typical exuberance at the end of a famous 1921 letter accompanying major suggestions for revising Eliot's masterpiece *The Waste
Land* (*SL*, 170). That mixture of showmanship, judgement, and genuine
enthusiasm typifies Pound's contribution to the making of the great period
of modernism, particularly when we remember its context of the brilliant
reshaping of Eliot's original chaotic manuscript into the poem we now think
of as one of the modernist monuments. Pound's remark also displays a canny
awareness of literary politics, not least the potential of periodicity itself.

Besides the example of his own work, Pound helped to make modernism
by supporting and encouraging other modernists and by helping to produce, distribute, and institutionalize modernist works. He presented the
spectacle of "Pound the major poet devoting, say, one fifth of his time to
poetry," wrote Ernest Hemingway appreciatively in 1925. "With the rest
of his time he tries to advance the fortunes, both material and artistic, of
his friends . . . he defends them when they are attacked, he gets them into
magazines and out of jail . . . sells their pictures . . . arranges concerts for
them . . . writes articles about them . . . introduces them to wealthy women
[patrons] . . . gets publishers to take their books."[1] Those friends were the
people whose work Pound admired. As Hemingway suggests, Pound's artistic service to the writers among them ran a gamut from aesthetic advice
and technical expertise to practical support through creating a network of
editors, publishers, and patrons. This essay stresses Pound's interaction
with other poets – especially W. B. Yeats, Hilda Doolittle (H.D.), and
T. S. Eliot – and with James Joyce during the London years (1908–1920)
and their Parisian coda (1921–1925), when Pound was most actively
and collaboratively involved in the modernist project. The collaboration
involved personal interaction and intertextuality, a common set of themes
and discursive practices, and an astute awareness of the material grounding
of texts in institutions of production and dissemination.

During this period Pound functioned as a permanent principle of innovation in modernist literature, establishing one interaction, technique, or institution only to hurry on to the next. "The artist is always beginning," he wrote in "How I Began" (1913). "Any work of art which is not a beginning, an invention, a discovery, is of little worth." Indeed, the slogan "make it new" which he later adopted from the Shang dynasty founder Tching Tang (see Canto LIII) demanded continual renewal rather than ossification yet gestured also toward an "it" to be remade. Such thinking entailed a dialectic of continuity and disruption, totality and openness, hierarchy and subversion, with Pound usually favoring the more radical terms. His vent for transgression, openness, and baring the device epitomizes those very modernist qualities most often appropriated for postmodernism. Pound displayed them both in his work and in his career, most notably in the first two decades of his European sojourn.

First in London and then in Paris, Pound rushed through an astonishing series of interactions with other writers, some of which would last for a lifetime and others of which quickly end. Among the most significant would be William Carlos Williams and H.D. (both friends from his American university days), Yeats, Eliot, T. E. Hulme, Richard Aldington, Robert Frost, D. H. Lawrence, e e cummings, Marianne Moore, Joyce, Ford Madox Ford, Wyndham Lewis, and Hemingway. These interactions seem characterized by a more cooperative model than the (male) "anxiety of influence" popularized by Harold Bloom. Pound's emphasis on conscious craft, on ideogrammic organizations of literary history, and on comparative traditions involving multiple languages led, instead, to more generous interactions with others and more genuine efforts on their behalf.[2] An impressive range of talents and personalities have testified to Pound's ongoing generosity. "The strange thing is that Ezra was so inexpressibly kind to anyone who he felt had the faintest spark of submerged talent," recalled H.D., who knew Pound most of his adult life. In his autobiography *Troubadour*, Alfred Kreymborg observed at an earlier date that "In a world where most people slavishly coddled their own egos, here was a fellow with a heart and intelligence at the service of other contemporaries." And Wyndham Lewis, whose relationship to Pound passed through several phases, could remark that

in his attitude towards other people's work Pound has been superlatively generous . . . [his critical sympathy] extends far and wide. He does not in the least mind being in service to somebody (as do other people it is usually found) if they have great talent . . . I have never known a person less troubled with personal feelings. This probably it is that has helped to make Pound that odd figure – the great poet and the great impresario at one and the same time. Also, he is the born teacher; and by his influence, direct and indirect, he has brought about profound changes in our literary techniques and criticism.[3]

Such magnanimity did not insulate Pound from the normal course of literary feuding or backbiting, of course. He could challenge Lascelles Abercrombie to a duel because of Abercrombie's Georgian devotion to Wordsworth. And Pound could be on the receiving end as well, for instance when one of his and Hemingway's arch-nemeses, Gertrude Stein, remarked tartly in *The Autobiography of Alice B. Toklas* that "Ezra Pound . . . was a village explainer, excellent if you were a village, but if you were not, not."[4]

Pound's first major encounter with an older poet after arriving in London was with W. B. Yeats, the one he most admired. In general Pound viewed the verse of turn-of-the-century London scathingly, seeing in it vague diction, twisted syntax, conventional imagery, and clumsy rhythm. It appeared derivative, "a horrible agglomerate compost, not minted, most of it not even baked, all legato, a doughy mess of third-hand Keats, Wordsworth, heaven knows what, fourth-hand Elizabethan sonority blunted, half melted, lumpy" (*LE*, 205). Those metaphors of composting, minting, and baking all suggest transformation, and Pound would hurl himself into transforming British verse. He sought to do so with the aid and example of Yeats, himself in midst of one of his great periods of remaking himself. Indeed, Pound said that he "went to London because I thought Yeats knew more about poetry than anybody else" and that he organized his life there by visiting "Ford in the afternoons and Yeats in the evenings."[5] His goal was to find out "how Yeats did it" (*L*, 296). By that Pound meant that Yeats had already thrown off his nineties manner and was writing direct lyrics incorporating images, natural syntax, and more conversational language. Pound himself had not done so yet, and in that respect Yeats was in advance of his younger admirer. Poems like "The Folly of Being Comforted" or "Adam's Curse" from Yeats's *In the Seven Woods* (1903) seemed far more modern than "Cino" or "Villonaud for this Yule" from Pound's volume *A Lume Spento* (1908) five years later.

Having known Yeats's works well for at least a decade, Pound finally met the older poet in May of 1908 through the auspices of Yeats's intimate friend Olivia Shakespear. She brought the young admirer to one of Yeats's Monday evening salons in Woburn Buildings and arranged a more extensive visit when Yeats returned to London in October. Part of the intricate web connecting major modernist writers, Olivia Shakespear was herself a novelist as well as the cousin of Yeats's friend Lionel Johnson and the mother of Dorothy Shakespear, whom Ezra would marry in 1914 after more than five years of complicated courtship. Through the Shakespear women, Yeats in turn would meet Dorothy's best school-friend, George Hyde-Lees, whom he married in 1917.

The poets' initial reactions to each other varied. Pound was elated, and by May of 1909 could write exuberantly to his friend William Carlos Williams that "I have been praised by the greatest living poet" (SL, 7). In Pound's slangy patois, Williams would henceforth be Little Bill and Yeats would be Big Bill. For his part, the older poet's response was at first more reserved. In 1909 he wrote to Lady Gregory about "this queer creature Ezra Pound, who . . . has I think got closer to the right sort of music for poetry than Mrs. Emery . . . however he can't sing as he has no voice."[6] Yet soon Pound was presiding over Yeats's Monday evenings, distributing the cigarettes and wine along with his own copious opinions about literary art. Within a few years, Yeats would confide again to Lady Gregory that Pound's criticism was a great help to him in midst of the self-remaking leading to *Responsibilities* (1914). "He is full of the middle ages and helps me to get back to the definite and the concrete away from modern abstractions," wrote Yeats. "To talk over a poem with him is like getting you to put a sentence into dialect. All becomes clear and natural."[7] The definite, the concrete, the clear, the syntactically natural were all modernist virtues, though Pound's generation would take them farther than Yeats did, with his lingering attraction to suggestion, symbolism, and mood. Even at this stage Yeats still thought Pound too experimental in his own work, with more sound principles than taste.

Pound's role as foreign editor of *Poetry* magazine beginning in 1912 provides one index of his growing relation with Yeats. After assuming his post, Pound urged that the magazine establish its own credentials by printing some of Yeats's work at once. Upon soliciting the poems from Yeats in October 1912, he could not resist changing Yeats's wording in three cases. Pound deleted "as it were" from "Once walked a thing that seemed as it were a burning cloud" from "Fallen Majesty," changed "or the" to "nor with" in "Nor mouth with kissing or the wine unwet" in "The Mountain Tomb," and "he" to "him" in "Nor he, the best labourer, dead" in "To a Child Dancing upon the Shore." Yeats predictably hit the ceiling, though he eventually accepted Pound's changes in whole or in part. In his "Status Rerum" essay in *Poetry* for January, Pound pronounced Yeats the only contemporary poet worth studying. The next summer Pound badgered Harriet Monroe to award the Guarantors' Prize to Yeats for "The Grey Rock," but Yeats himself declined all but ten pounds ($50) of the fifty pound prize in favor of Pound, whose experiments he still distrusted but who possessed a "vigorous creative mind." And it was in *Poetry* that Pound a year later would review *Responsibilities*, calling Yeats the best poet in England even while labelling him a symbolist rather than an imagist.[8]

The mutual support and interaction of Yeats and Pound reached its highpoint during the three winters commencing in 1913–1914, when they shared lodgings in Sussex, with Pound serving as Yeats's secretary. The place they selected was Stone Cottage, near both the village of Coleman's Hatch and the Hundred-Acre Wood which A. A. Milne would make famous in his Winnie-the-Pooh books. With the aid of his new Civil List pension, Yeats intended for Pound to handle his correspondence and read to him at night. Pound told his mother that he had taken the post as a duty to posterity, but he also keenly appreciated its benefits to both his poetic craft and public reputation. With Pound finishing *Lustra* and Yeats *Responsibilities*, the two poets reinforced each other's drive toward modernization. Pound's retrospective portrait in Canto LXXXIII of those winters begins with an account of Yeats composing "The Peacock":

> so that I recalled the noise in the chimney
> as it were the wind in the chimney
>   but was in reality Uncle William
> downstairs composing
> that had made a great Peeeeacock
>   in the proide ov his oiye.   (LXXXIII/553–4)

The rhythm of the lines renders with comic affection Yeats's characteristic humming and chanting during poetic composition, though Pound immediately signals respect with the assertion "as indeed he had, and perdurable." The poets pressed on to folklore and to the occult for their own art, with Pound closing the passage by remembering Yeats "hearing nearly all Wordsworth / for the sake of his conscience but / preferring Ennemosor on Witches."

Folklore led to a multicultural perspective, with Lady Gregory's *Visions and Beliefs in the West of Ireland* and Joseph Ennemoser's *History of Magic* leading on to reworking of folk themes in the high art of Noh drama. Yeats had already stimulated Pound's interest in the Bengali poet Rabindranath Tagore, whom they had both boomed the year before. Now Pound was busily finishing his translations of Ernest Fenollosa's notes on Noh drama, an enterprise that would affect both his own adaptations and Yeats's *Four Plays for Dancers*, particularly *At the Hawk's Well*. Sometimes the conjunction could have unintentionally humorous results, as when a ghost in the Pound–Fenollosa version of *Nishikigi* speaks with an accent not far from Lady Gregory's Kiltartan: "Times out of mind am I here setting up this bright branch, this silky wood with the charms painted in it as fine as the web you'd get in the grass-cloth of Shinobu, that they'd be still selling you in this mountain" (*T*, 286). More often, though, the impact of the Noh resulted in a gain of real power, exemplifying the openness to non-Western cultures characteristic of modernist authors. The Noh was also an aristocratic form, of course, and its elitism constituted part of its appeal to both poets at this period, though usually in conjunction with more populist elements such as its reworking of folk motifs. Indeed, the effort to fuse elite and popular culture would remain a central tenet of modernist constructions such as Eliot's *Waste Land* or Joyce's *Ulysses*.

Two other tendencies of these years deserve mention as reinforcing already existing habits of both writers. Both pertain to form. First was a tendency to think of the volume rather than the individual lyric as unit, a habit missed by the New Critical construction of modernism and virtually every subsequent reconstruction. Yet Yeats had from *The Wanderings of Oisin and Other Poems* (1889) onward spent considerable care in arranging and then subsequently rearranging his collections of verse, and so too had Pound from at least *Canzoni* onwards. Both freely urged such considerations on other writers. "My ten or more years of practice, failure, success, etc. in arranging tables of contents, is à votre service," wrote Pound to Marianne Moore in 1918. "I would warn you of the very great importance of the actual order of poems in a booklet" (*SL*, 143). Pound was possibly the most public partisan of that principle for his generation, arranging the contents of several landmark volumes of modernist verse. The second principle would become a more widely recognized modernist trademark, the creation of structure by the continuous paralleling of past and present. Pound, Eliot, and Joyce would all take this technique farther than Yeats, but as Eliot pointed out in his famous review "*Ulysses*, Order, and Myth," Yeats had been the first to "adumbrate" it. For example, Yeats had paralleled the modern and Homeric worlds in poems from *The Green Helmet* like "No Second Troy," which Pound singled out for praise in his 1914 review of *Responsibilities*. Clearly, the poets had much to discuss during those three winters at Stone Cottage.

After the three winters Pound and Yeats went their separate ways, Yeats ever more toward Ireland and Pound eventually toward the Continent. Yet besides continued personal contact and correspondence, they kept up through their published works that episodic intertextuality already begun by poems of Pound's like "Au Jardin" or "The Lake Isle." Yeats, for example, slyly opened the revised version of the occult *A Vision*, his work most concerned with that afterlife which Pound like Confucius thought a distraction from practical ethics, with "A Packet for Ezra Pound." Though he began by praising Pound's conversation as an inducement to winter in Rapallo and ended by quoting "The Return," Yeats took care both to tease Pound for indiscriminate pity of the local cats and to remind him of Yeats's greater political experience by admonishing, "Do not be elected to the Senate of your country," an event of which there was little likelihood anyway. Pound, in turn, could give as good as he got, as in referring to Yeats's tower at Ballylee as "Ballyphallus." He continued to suggest emendations in Yeats's verse, as by improving the chorus "From the 'Antigone'" that now closes *The Winding Stair and Other Poems*. And as Yeats flickers in and out of *The Cantos*, Pound identified perhaps their most central difference in a passage near the beginning of Canto LXXXIII:

> Le Paradis n'est pas artificiel
> and Uncle William dawdling around Notre Dame
> in search of whatever
> > paused to admire the symbol
> with Notre Dame standing inside it.   (LXXXIII/548)

Pound saw Yeats for all his modernism as remaining at heart a symbolist, always gesturing beyond surface, language, or concreteness, whereas for Pound the route his own generation took toward modernism ran through Imagism as a way station.

As T. S. Eliot remarked in "American Literature and the American Language," "The *point de repère* usually and conveniently taken, as the starting-point of modern poetry, is the group denominated 'imagists' in London about 1910."[9] The tangled and contested history of Imagism runs through three main stages. Dominated by the assertive T. E. Hulme fresh from his Cambridge expulsion, the first phase involved a group of young writers in 1908–09 who first formed a Poets' Club and then reconstituted themselves as members of a School of Images dedicated to accurate expression without verbiage. The second phase, orchestrated by Pound himself, may be dated from November 1912, when he humorously included in his *Ripostes* volume five brief lyrics labelled "The Complete Poetical Works of T. E. Hulme" and declared in a prefatory note that "As for the future, *Les Imagistes*, the descendants of the forgotten school of 1909, have that in their keeping" (*P* 1990, 266). The identities of the mysterious Imagists of the second stage would become clear over the next few months as principally H.D., Richard Aldington, and Pound himself. As represented in Pound's *Des Imagistes* anthology of 1914, the full group also came to include to varying degrees F. S. Flint, Skipwith Cannell, Amy Lowell, William Carlos Williams, James Joyce, Ford Madox Hueffer (later Ford), Allen Upward, and John Cournos. But by then Pound was already losing control of the movement to the talented, rich, and equally well-organized Amy Lowell of Boston, who for three years beginning in 1915 assembled an expanded group in her own annual *Some Imagist Poets*. Pound derided this third phase of the movement as "Amygism" and countered by assembling a still wider circle for his own *Catholic Anthology* (1915), but by then he had already gone on himself to Vorticism instead.

For launching his own stage of Imagism, Pound skillfully exploited his position at *Poetry*. Previously, he had utilized Ford's year-and-a-half at the *English Review* to get his first poem published in a British magazine ("Sestina: Altaforte"), and in late 1911 through Hulme he had met A. R. Orage, the socialist-minded editor in whose *New Age* Pound would publish nearly 300 contributions over the coming decade. But in *Poetry* Pound saw an opportunity to select and disseminate poetry that he admired, and hence to construct a sense of modernist verse for a small but influential public; he would later coopt *The Egoist, The Little Review*, and *The Dial* in the same way.

Pound's first step was to establish a semi-independent editorial position. When Harriet Monroe, twenty-five years Pound's senior, wrote to solicit his participation in the literary magazine that she was planning, Pound saw the chance it offered for an outlet against the derivative and conventional poetry of the day. He responded both by authorizing her to "announce, if it's any good to you, that for the present such of my work as appears in America (barring my own books) will appear exclusively in your magazine" and offering to act as British and French talent scout (*SL*, 9). By the time the first issue of *Poetry* appeared in October 1912, it both carried his announcement and listed him as "Foreign Correspondent."

Pound would hold that position through seven sometimes stormy years of connection with the magazine and would alternately cajole, bully, flatter, rant, and instruct, trying all the time to push *Poetry* toward a more cosmopolitan stance and more Poundian view of which modernist writers mattered. In turn, Monroe and her assistant Alice Corbin Henderson followed their own, more populist lights but valued Pound's contributions even while striving to remind him that they were running the magazine. Perceptively recruiting him when he was almost unknown in America, Monroe recorded in her autobiography that Pound's letters "were a tonic and an inspiration, for at that time, as I firmly believe, he was the best critic living, at least in our specialty, and his acid touch on weak spots was as fearsomely enlightening as a clinic."[10]

One of Pound's first campaigns in *Poetry* was to establish Imagism in general and H.D. in particular. After forwarding work of Yeats to establish the "tone" of the magazine and of Tagore to further the ideal of world literature, Pound sent to Monroe poems by H.D. and by Richard Aldington. "I've had luck again, and am sending you some *modern* stuff by an American, I say modern, for it is in the laconic speech of the Imagistes," he wrote of H.D. "Objective – no slither; direct – no excessive use of adjectives, no metaphors that won't permit examination" (*SL*, 11). Those qualities helped to enable modernism's technical break with the nineteenth century, to facilitate what Yeats called everyone getting down off their stilts. Forty-five years later H.D. remembered Pound's reaction to her poems in the British Museum tea room this way:

> "But dryad," (in the Museum tea room), "this is poetry." He slashed with a pencil. "Cut this out, shorten this line. 'Hermes of the Ways' is a good title. I'll send this to Harriet Monroe of *Poetry*. Have you a copy? Yes? Then we can send this, or I'll type it when I get back. Will this do?" And he scrawled "H.D. Imagiste" at the bottom of the page. (*End to Torment*, 18)

Pound himself later recalled that the name Imagism was invented to launch H.D. and Aldington before they had enough material for their own books (*SL*, 213), just as the initials H.D. created a sort of mystery about the new author, who then chose to continue them for the rest of her publishing career. Pound generously admonished Monroe to print his friend's work before printing his own in the magazine. The prose manifestos at which Pound excelled soon followed. Two early ones were "Imagisme" signed by F. S. Flint but ghost-written by Pound and "A Few Don'ts by an Imagiste." The first announced direct treatment, concise wording, and flexible rather than mechanical rhythm as key principles of the new movement, while the second defined an "Image" as "that which presents an intellectual and emotional complex in an instant of time" (*LE*, 4). While "intellectual and emotional" identifies the Image as focus for a range of thoughts and feelings, the phrase "instant of time" in that definition anticipates the static quality that Pound came to see in Imagism and that propelled him toward the more dynamic Vorticism of Wyndham Lewis and the short-lived periodical *Blast* instead.

H.D. and Pound always held special places in each other's development. They had met at a Halloween party in Pound's first year at the University of Pennsylvania, become part of the "gang" that included William Carlos Williams, and eventually courted before Pound's departure first for Wabash College and then for Europe. He called her "Dryad," a term she would use for signing her letters to him throughout her life, and assembled the vellum manuscript *Hilda's Book* out of his early poems for her. He was a large part of the attraction for her in moving to London, and the Imagist phase marked Pound's period of greatest enthusiasm for her work and greatest service to her reputation. Later they would both write long modernist poems structured partly by classical myth, with Pound relying more on male figures such as Odysseus and H.D. on female ones such as Helen. Both would gradually fade from public view during the 1930s and Second World War, Pound isolated geographically in Italy and intellectually by his increasingly pro-fascist views of Mussolini, H.D. by the luxury made possible by her lover Bryher, who published H.D.'s work in limited editions for a coterie audience. In 1958, the year Pound was finally released from St. Elizabeths and three years before her own death, H.D. constructed the memoir *End to Torment* as a prolonged meditation on their lifelong interaction. After an earlier period in which scholars looked at their relationship sympathetically from Pound's point of view and then more hostilely from a position imputed to H.D. (though different from that recorded by both her and her daughter Perdita), the pendulum now seems to have swung back toward a more balanced understanding. Perhaps the best verdict remains that of H.D. herself toward the end of the memoir: "He gave, he took," she wrote. "He gave extravagantly" (*End to Torment*, 49).

Part of Pound's giving meant offering a forum in *Poetry* for emerging poets. Besides the established Yeats and newly fashionable Tagore, we have seen that he sent Harriet Monroe work by Aldington and H.D. with the insistence that their poetry appear before any of his own in the magazine. Other recruits included Robert Frost, whom Pound described in Ezraic dialect as "VURRY Amur'k'n" (*SL*, 14) and whom he had to persuade Monroe to print despite her own distaste. As he had with Yeats, H.D., and others, Pound tried to rewrite some of Frost's work for *Poetry* but this time received the reproof that omitting two words had "spoiled my metre, my idiom, and idea."[11] Old friend William Carlos Williams and new acquaintance D. H. Lawrence soon joined those whose work Pound both sent to the magazine and reviewed there.

And Pound soon began sending his own verse, most importantly at first the sequence "Contemporania". Occupying the first dozen pages of the April 1913 number, those dozen poems included Pound's most famous Imagist work, the two-line "In a Station of the Metro." Its Haiku-like terseness, meter, and subject exemplified the Imagist principles he was promulgating. Four years later, Pound chose *Poetry* to publish "Three Cantos," the so-called Ur-cantos from which the epic that occupied the rest of his poetic career would derive. The *Poetry* version differs dramatically from the final one, beginning as it does with a canto featuring not Homer but rather the Browning of *Sordello*, and not arriving at the *Odyssey* until Canto III. Such discrepancies belong to the openness, fluidity, and resistance to closure of many modernist texts which most readers know only from their copyright book versions, and which contemporary textual theory is beginning to learn how to excavate.[12]

Perhaps Pound's biggest discovery for *Poetry* was T. S. Eliot, whom he met in September of 1914 through the American poet Conrad Aiken. Their careers would intertwine tightly over the next decade both with each other and with magazines such as *Poetry* or *The Dial*, publishers such as The Egoist Ltd. or Alfred A. Knopf, and patrons such as John Quinn. "He has sent in the best poem I have yet had or seen from an American," exulted Pound to Monroe over "The Love Song of J. Alfred Prufrock." "PRAY GOD IT BE NOT A SINGLE AND UNIQUE SUCCESS" (*SL*, 40). Pound considered Eliot the only American he knew who had both trained and modernized himself in the art of poetry, and delighted in maneuvering Eliot into print past the objections and sometimes the rejections of more conventional editors. He deliberately chose "Prufrock" rather than "Portrait of a Lady" for Eliot's debut, viewing "Prufrock" as more experimental and distinctive, and hence more helpful for differentiating Eliot at once from other poets. Indeed, the leaps, allusions, and rhythms of "Prufrock" seemed so experimental that Pound had to coax Monroe into printing it at all, assuring her that winter from the Sussex cottage he again shared with Yeats, that the poem did not "go off at the end." To her credit, Monroe finally did publish it in the June 1915 issue, Eliot's first verse to appear in print since his undergraduate publications in the *Harvard Advocate* of 1908–10. Pound also arranged Eliot's other three appearances in magazines that year – "Preludes" and "Rhapsody of a Windy Night" in Pound and Lewis's *Blast*, "Portrait of a Lady" in Alfred Kreymborg's *Others*, and a group of three Boston poems in *Poetry* for October. 1915 closed with a gathering of those poems and a new one ("Hysteria") in Pound's *Catholic Anthology*, the first presentation of any of Eliot's poetry in book form. All of Eliot's verse to appear in his first year of new publication thus resulted from Pound's interventions.

What *Poetry* was to "Prufrock," Eliot's first mature lyric, *The Egoist* was to *Prufrock and Other Observations*, his first volume of verse. Originally a women's suffrage magazine, *The New Freewoman*, under the control of the Philadelphia Quaker Harriet Shaw Weaver and ardent feminist editor Dora Marsden, had approached Pound for literary help. In return both for his contributions and for arranging a cash subsidy (from John Gould Fletcher), Pound emerged as literary editor with control over a specific section of the magazine. Changing its name to *The Egoist* at the end of the year, that little magazine became another of the literarily distinguished but economically marginal outlets for modernist work, both in its own pages and in its associated small press. Through it Pound arranged for Joyce's

Portrait of the Artist as a Young Man, Lewis's *Tarr,* and his own "Dialogues of Fontenelle" to appear in print. He persuaded Marsden and Weaver to install Richard Aldington as literary subeditor of the *Egoist,* and when over Christmas 1916 Aldington left for the war, Pound nominated Eliot as his successor.

Pound also arranged the contents of *Prufrock and Other Observations* and got it published by the magazine's press by clandestinely advancing the cost of the printing bill himself. Pound promptly reviewed the volume for *Poetry,* emphasizing Eliot's portrait of the contemporary condition, use of metaphor and concreteness, fusion of intelligence and emotion, and mastery of rhythm. He also forwarded the book to his New York patron John Quinn, whose enthusiasm it ignited. Though his efforts to get the American firm of Alfred Knopf to publish Eliot's poetry had to wait until the expanded *Poems* volume of 1920, Quinn successfully arranged for Knopf to publish both Pound's *Lustra* and Eliot's anonymous appreciation of Pound in the pamphlet *Ezra Pound His Metric and Poetry.* There Eliot surveyed Pound's career to date, accurately identified Browning and Yeats as chief influences, and called particular attention to Pound's rhythmic and formal innovations. It seemed as though the relation between the two poets could hardly be more cooperative, yet shortly they would work together even more closely, first in short poems and then in shaping Eliot's epic, *The Waste Land.*

Despite its breaking of traditional forms, modernism sought a balance between form and dispersal. By the end of the second decade of the new century, both Pound and Eliot saw that the effect of their own formal experiments could lead to anarchy rather than liberation. As Pound later described it, they "decided that the dilutation of vers libre, Amygism, Lee Masterism, general floppiness had gone too far and that some counter-current must be set going."[13] Dilution and floppiness contradicted the goals of concentration and concreteness that had inspired the original break-throughs. As a corrective, Pound and Eliot temporarily returned to rhyme and regular strophes, producing the quatrain poems of Eliot's second volume (for example, the Sweeney lyrics) and Pound's great sequence *Hugh Selwyn Mauberley.* Their modernist meters and juxtapositions drew strength from their tension with tight formal constraints. Pound in particular played deliberately against the quatrain form, abandoning it altogether under pressure of emotion in the great anti-war chant of the fourth lyric of the *Mauberley* sequence ("These fought in any case . . .").

Pound's interaction with Eliot crested in their collaboration on *The Waste Land* manuscripts during the winter of 1921–22. In December Eliot sent Pound a welter of manuscripts, more than twice as long as the published poem would be, to ask his advice. Believing in the serendipitous entry he found in a German–Latin dictionary that "dichten=condensare," Pound characteristically advocated cuts, as he had earlier with H.D., Frost, and others. He particularly urged dropping three long sections – an introductory account of a night on the town, a passage of satiric Popean couplets, and the narrative account of sailing off the coast of Massachusetts that prefaced the Phlebus the Phoenician passage. Pound also recommended the elimination of several related lyrics at the end. "The thing now runs from 'April . . .' to 'shantih' without a break. That is 19 pages, and let us say the longest poem in the English langwidge," he advised Eliot. "Don't try to bust all records by prolonging it three pages further" (SL, 169). Besides major structural suggestions, Pound worked over the minutiae of particular passages. The results can be viewed in Valerie Eliot's edition of The Waste Land: A Facsimile and Transcript of the Original Drafts. Sprinkled among favorite encouragements like "O.K." and "echt" appear pungent Poundiana like "Too tum-pum" and "Too easy." Perhaps most memorably, Pound objected to the "may" in "may pass" at the end of the encounter between the young man carbuncular and the typist: "make up yr. mind[.] You Tiresias if you know know damn well or else you dont." Such comments reveal Pound's penchant for meters of the musical phrase rather than the metronome and his confident firmness of presentation, even while their tone reflects the jaunty combination of mutual respect, high spirits, and devotion to craft.

When Eliot reprinted The Waste Land in the 1925 edition of his poems, and in all subsequent versions, he included the dedication "For Ezra Pound / il miglior fabbro." That Italian phrase for "the better craftsman" came from Purgatorio 26, where Dante uses it to pay tribute to the superior technical skill of Arnaut Daniel over all other Provençal poets. In using it, Eliot later said that he meant particularly to honor Pound's craftsmanship and critical ability, which had turned The Waste Land "from a jumble of good and bad passages into a poem." Pound himself identified Eliot and Yeats as the only two poets who had been able to stand up to his criticism for a protracted period of time. The result was impressive. It also challenges the paradigms of the artist as isolated genius or as autonomous author of a work. The intensely collaborative Waste Land belongs almost as much to Pound as to Eliot. Without going as far as those critics who puckishly refer to it as Pound's greatest poem, we can still readily admit that like parts of Wordsworth and Coleridge, or John Stuart Mill's Autobiography, or the turn-of-the-century plays of Lady Gregory and W. B. Yeats, The Waste Land belongs to the surprisingly large class of works ostensibly by a single writer but more properly understood as products of multiple authorship.

Typically, Pound's service to the poem did not stop with editorial service but continued on to publication as well. His own situation in England had deteriorated to the point where moving to Paris seemed expedient. Toward the end of the London years, a concerned Eliot had written to John Quinn that "there is now no organ of any importance in which [Pound] can express himself, and he is becoming forgotten . . . Pound's lack of tact has done him great harm." The resourceful Quinn them intervened with Scofield Thayer and Gilbert Seldes to secure Pound a post as foreign correspondent of their *Dial* magazine. Pound in turn played a leading role in the complicated negotiations that resulted in *The Waste Land* appearing simultaneously in the first issue of Eliot's own journal *The Criterion* in London and in *The Dial* in New York, followed closely by book publication with Boni and Liveright. As a result, Eliot received not only the original offer of $150 from *The Dial* for the poem, but also the $2,000 *Dial* award plus over $500 royalties from Boni and Liveright – the first time in years he had an income about equal in today's prices to that of a junior faculty member. Further, publication in *The Dial* marked a stage in the dissemination of modernism to a wider audience. While not a mass market magazine nor even a major literary outlet like the *New York Review of Books* or the *Times Literary Supplement*, *The Dial* – with its 1922 circulation of 9,000 copies per month – marked a step up from the few hundred circulation of *The Egoist* or even few thousand of *The Little Review*. Pound did not doubt the poem's significance for modernism generally. "Eliot's *Waste Land* is I think the justification of the 'movement,' of our modern experiment, since 1900," he told his old professor Felix Schelling (*SL*, 180).

Although Eliot praised Pound as critic for seeing what other poets were trying to do and then helping them to do it, in some ways Pound's changes in *The Waste Land* both made the poem more Poundian and prefigured the differences that caused him and Eliot to move apart. The poem as we know it, for example, follows the abrupt jumps characteristic of Pound's *Cantos* but which Eliot would forsake for the fuller syntax of *Four Quartets*. It diminishes the religious, specifically Christian content foregrounded in excised portions such as "The Death of Saint Narcissus." And its condensed technique can lead to a bewildering concentration of allusions.

Pound and Eliot would diverge increasingly over social issues, with "Possum" or "Reverend Eliot" (as Pound took to calling him) increasingly championing the idea of a Christian society, and "Brer Rabbit" (Pound's name for himself in their correspondence) increasingly favoring Confucian and Italian fascist ones. But Eliot seems to have felt that he could never repay what he owed Pound: he stoutly included his contributions in *The Criterion* even though they threatened to sink the review, got Faber to publish his work, and was one of the ten fellows who voted for awarding Pound the controversial Bollingen Prize after World War II. Yet he seemed increasingly to honor Pound less for what he said than for the way he said it, and in *After Strange Gods* pointedly denounced Pound's hell as a hell for other people. Correspondingly, Pound's *Pisan Cantos* would open with an allusion to "The Hollow Men," though in Canto XCVIII he would maintain that "Yeats, Possum and Wyndham / had no ground beneath 'em" because of inattention to the proper economics (705). Yet when Eliot died, an ailing Pound rallied his forces to produce a late tribute to a memorial volume. "Who is there now for me to share a joke with?" asked Pound. "His was the true Dantescan voice – not honored enough, and deserving more than I ever gave him."[14]

At the opposite extreme from Pound's close personal friendship with Eliot was his equally long but largely epistolary relationship with Marianne Moore, with whom he exchanged hundreds of letters over half a century but met in person only a few times. Again their relation intertwined with that of journalistic institutions, with Pound becoming aware of Moore through *Poetry* and the *Egoist*, which printed both her poems and an appreciation of her by H.D. When their correspondence began in 1918, Pound welcomed her contributions to *The Little Review* and offered to help her get a book published. By the early 1920s he ranked her with William Carlos Williams and Mina Loy as the three most interesting poets in America and came to regard her increasingly as one of international modernism's chief advocates in the United States. Partly through Pound's influence, she came to the attention of *The Dial*, where she used her post as editor from 1925 until the magazine's demise in 1929 to help Pound and other modernists stay regularly in print. Throughout the thirties Pound continually hoped that she would again edit a journal promoting modernist literature, at one point envisioning her as Harriet Monroe's successor at *Poetry*. He took care to include her prominently both in his *Profile* anthology of 1932 and his *Active Anthology* the next year.

Pound met Moore for the first time only in 1939, just before the war years interrupted their relationship. After that gap, Moore visited Pound at St. Elizabeths and supplied one of the testimonials for his eventual release. Despite the huge gulf in Pound's extroverted bohemian manner and Moore's more proper gentility, their shared standards and craftsmanship drew them together. Pound particularly admired Moore's intricate metrics, deft use of quotation, and passion for the *mot juste*. Moore, in turn, published two perceptive reviews of *A Draft of XXX Cantos*, praising Pound's ability to concentrate the past on the present and his unerring ear, but politely demurring at his lapses into rhetorical denunciation or feminolatry. In the

1950s she generously acknowledged how Pound's technical advice had improved her translation of *The Fables of La Fontaine*, a project he always stoutly supported. At their last meeting, in the lobby of the New York Public Library during an American Academy of Arts and Letters evening in 1969, the two poets clasped hands after fifty years of friendship and alliance to exclaim movingly "Oh, Ezra" and "Oh, Marianne."

The *annus mirabilis* 1922 saw the publication of another modernist masterpiece besides *The Waste Land* whose appearance owed much to Pound, James Joyce's *Ulysses*. Indeed, Pound's complex relation with Joyce recapitulates his myriad contributions to modernism during the London and Paris years – personal interaction and support, shared themes and techniques, and discovery or creation of institutions for producing and disseminating the new work. Contact began when Yeats mentioned Joyce to Pound at the Coleman's Hatch cottage in December 1913 as a potential contributor to the *Des Imagistes* anthology. Pound wrote at once to Joyce, and then a second time when Yeats discovered a manuscript of Joyce's lyric "I Hear an Army," which Pound asked to include in the forthcoming book. Joyce accepted, and also in January sent *Dubliners* and the first chapter of *A Portrait of the Artist as a Young Man*. "Dear Joyce," replied Pound immediately, "I'm not supposed to know much about prose but I think your novel is damn fine stuff" (P/J, 24). For the next decade Pound boosted Joyce both enthusiastically and effectively.

The first step was to get *Portrait* into print, initially as a serial and then as a volume. Pound quickly arranged for its publication in the *Egoist*, initiating Harriet Shaw Weaver's extensive future support of Joyce. The author forwarded *Portrait* to Pound chapter by chapter for appearance in the magazine, with the pressure of deadlines often driving him to complete sections of the novel. That publication helped persuade Grant Richards to publish the book *Dubliners* at long last. Subsequent efforts to put *Portrait* into book form proved especially difficult because the recent prosecution of Lawrence's *The Rainbow* had made printers, publishers, and booksellers leery of censorship and obscenity laws. Pound himself ran into similar problems trying to get his own *Lustra* volume into print, with printers and publishers objecting to such poems as "To a Friend Writing Upon Cabaret Dancers," "Salutation the Second," or "Coitus." As Pound later wrote to William Carlos Williams, he had "the whole stinking sweat of providing the mechanical means for letting through the new movement, i.e., scrap for the mot juste, for clear honest statement" (P/J, 63).

After complicated maneuvers by Pound and Weaver, *Portrait* appeared first from B. W. Huebsch in New York, with Weaver agreeing to take 750 copies for distribution in England through Egoist Press. Pound's early campaigns for funds for Joyce also paid off, and with Yeats's help he wangled seventy-five pounds for Joyce from the Royal Literary Fund and then in August 1916 one hundred pounds from the Civil List. No wonder that Joyce wrote exuberantly to Yeats, "I have every reason to be grateful to the many friends who have helped me since I came here and I can never thank you enough for having brought me into relations with your friend Ezra Pound who is indeed a wonder worker" (*P/J*, 80).

While Pound could never muster the admiration that Joyce wanted for his play *Exiles*, he did respond ebulliently to *Ulysses*. "I went out with the big bass drum, cause a masterwork is a masterwork," Pound later recalled of his campaign for that novel (*P/J*, 267). Once again, he found a serial home for a work in process of composition, this time in *The Little Review*, which Margaret Anderson operated with the help of her friend Jane Heap. The mildly anarchist Anderson had started the magazine in Chicago in 1914, moved it to New York with Heap at the end of 1916, and eventually would relocate it and herself in Paris. She began to publish Pound in 1916, who at that time thought of *The Little Review* as second fiddle to Monroe's *Poetry*. But in early 1917 Anderson gladly accepted Pound's terms for joining the magazine, "a glorious surprise" she promised to her readers.

Pound in effect would run his own magazine within hers, with a guaranteed number of pages for the regular appearance of Eliot, Lewis, Joyce, and himself. With a gap in the middle, Pound would remain with the magazine until 1923, securing contributions from Ford, Lady Gregory, Lewis, Yeats, Eliot, and Iris Barry among others. But his greatest coup as editor was to publish Joyce's *Ulysses* serially from March 1918 until the fall of 1920, when suppression by the Post Office authorities for the fourth and final time caused publication to halt after episode fourteen ("Oxen of the Sun") and the last few chapters to appear first in book form. As with *Portrait*, Joyce would forward chapters of his work-in-progress to Pound for serial publication as he finished them. And as with other writers, Pound could not forbear tinkering and making suggestions, though Joyce politely held firm once he had made up his mind. Pound's enthusiasm for the novel had wavered with the "Sirens" episode (where he worried about potential censorship) but bounced back strongly with "Cyclops" and its parodies of style. "Our James is a grrreat man," he crowed to John Quinn. In the spring of 1922, Pound even published the celebratory "Little Review Calendar," an elaborate pagan construction for "Year 1 p.s.U." (*post scriptum Ulixes*).

Pound's practical help to Joyce continued during this period. He was able to pay *Little Review* contributors through the generosity of Quinn, who organized financial backing for the magazine for a two-year period. Quinn in New York was perhaps the most valuable of the patrons of modernist work, excelling even Margaret Cravens, Lady Cunard, or Winifred Ellerman in effectiveness of support. At Pound's instigation, Quinn would later purchase manuscripts from Joyce, too, though Joyce characteristically became ambivalent about the proceeds. Pound and Joyce themselves had not met until 1920, when Joyce came to visit at Pound's beloved Sirmione on the Lago di Garda in northern Italy. Joyce thought Pound "a miracle of ebulliency, gusto, and help," but accurately suspected that Pound considered him "a hopeless bourgeois" though great artist (P/J, 178). In perhaps the most comic effort to lend Joyce support, Pound remembered Joyce's complaints about lacking adequate clothing, and later dispatched T. S. Eliot and Wyndham Lewis to deliver a large and mysterious brown paper parcel to Joyce in Paris. When unwrapped, the parcel turned out to contain used shoes and other items of second-hand clothing. An embarrassed Joyce insisted on treating Lewis and Eliot whenever they were together for the rest of their visit.

More enduringly, Pound introduced Joyce to his circle in Paris, and engineered his meeting with Sylvia Beach of Shakespeare and Company, who would do so much toward arranging the book publication of *Ulysses*. That volume appeared first in Paris on Joyce's fortieth birthday, February 2, 1922, under the imprint of Shakespeare and Company, from type set by hand in the shop of Maurice Darantière, master printer of Dijon, by typesetters largely ignorant of English. The volume thus belongs to the surprisingly large number of modernist works that first appeared as books from such small presses as the Dun Emer (later Cuala) Press of Yeats and his sisters, Elkin Mathews's shop in Vigo Street, Marsden and Shaw's Egoist Press, Bryher's Brendin Press, John Rodker's Ovid Press, William Bird's Three Mountains Press, or Nancy Cunard's Hours Press. Even today, important works by Pound, Williams, and H.D. among others find their American audience through New Directions, which started as a pioneering publishing company founded by Pound's sometime disciple James Laughlin in 1936 to circulate modernist literature.

Not content with getting Joyce both published and subsidized, Pound undertook a publicity campaign for him, too, producing a dozen major statements on the novelist (three of which are reprinted in *Literary Essays*). These included reviews of *Dubliners*, *Portrait*, and *Ulysses*, works that Pound regarded as permanent contributions to literature. In his *Egoist* notice of 1914, for example, Pound praised *Dubliners* for its clear prose, condensation, and extension of the tradition of Flaubert. He similarly detected Flaubertian virtues in the later *Portrait* for *Egoist* readers three years later, again praising particularly Joyce's style. He saved perhaps his finest review for *Ulysses* in *The Dial* during 1922. Urging readers to "unite to give praise to Ulysses," Pound yet again invoked Flaubert along with Rabelais, noted that the varied dialects enabled Joyce to present subject matter and tones of mind succinctly, saw the novel as poaching on the epic, identified the Homeric parallels as a scaffold or means of construction leading to a triumph in form, admired both Bloom and Molly, and pronounced the whole work "an epoch-making report on the state of the human mind in the twentieth century" (*P/J*, 199). Many of those terms seem to fit Pound's own ambitions for *The Cantos*, which in the early 1920s he revised into something like its current opening form. He replaced the original beginning that meditated on Browning with the current opening translation of Homer, shifted abruptly between varied dialects, foregrounded the Pound-Odysseus figure whose encounter with the *periplum* creates one of the poem's structural devices, and clearly aimed himself at a report on the "state of the human mind in the twentieth century."

Yet Pound's conception of epic as a poem including history and economics points toward his increasing divergence from Joyce over contemporary politics. Whereas Joyce resisted overt politicization of art, continued his formal experiments, and acquired an early distaste for both authoritarian politics and antisemitism, Pound turned instead toward increasingly doctrinaire presentations tainted with fascism and bigotry. The psychological and linguistic explorations of Joyce and Stein in the 1930s ceased to interest him. By 1936 he could tell his fellow authoritarian Wyndham Lewis that "this flow of conSquishousness Girtie/Jimmee stuff has about FLOWED long enuff" (*P/J*, 256).

Neither Pound nor Joyce admired the other's new work in the thirties, Pound disdaining *Finnegans Wake* and Joyce perhaps not even reading the newer *Cantos*. Yet Pound stoutly defended Joyce's right to experiment as the due of a writer who had produced three masterpieces already. Joyce in turn responded warmly to appeals for endorsement of Pound, though taking care to praise the man rather than the work, as in his testimonial for Ford's promotion of *A Draft of XXX Cantos* where he emphasized that but for Pound "I should probably be the unknown drudge that he discovered – if it was a discovery" (*P/J*, 245). And Pound appears fleetingly several times in *Finnegans Wake* itself, including phrases that memorialize his famous bluntness (like "unbluffingly blurtubruskblunt as an Esra, the Cat") or his Chinese translations (A maundarin tongue in a pounderin jowl") (*P/J*, 263).

Fittingly, Pound's reconciliation with Joyce, as with so much of his earlier career, comes in the partial purgatory of the *Pisan Cantos*. With

Europe and his own mind and career in ruins, the speaker looks back over a lifetime's *periplum*, and particularly to the years so central to the formation of modernism. In a moving roll call from Canto LXXIV Pound begins by recalling three of his foremost companions in making modernism – Ford, Yeats, and Joyce:

> Lordly men are to earth o'ergiven
>   these the companions:
> Fordie that wrote of giants
> And William who dreamed of nobility
> And Jim the comedian singing:
>   "Blarrney castle me darlin'
>   you're nothing now but a Stowne."
>
> (LXXIV/452–3)

Ford and Yeats had both died in 1939, and Joyce in 1941. Elsewhere in the *Pisan Cantos* Pound wondered what was left of the London and Paris that he knew in the great modernist years. It seems clear that one thing left is modernism itself, an achievement and a legacy that Pound himself did so much to construct as well as to memorialize. In that process, as much as in his own work or in his contributions to that of others, he most truly proved himself *il miglior fabbro*.

NOTES

1 As quoted in Charles Norman, *Ezra Pound* (New York: Macmillan, 1960), p. 275.
2 I have discussed this aspect at greater length in "Pound's Parleyings with Robert Browning," originally published in the collection *Ezra Pound Among the Poets* (Chicago and London: University of Chicago Press, 1985), pp. 106–127, and reprinted in my critical study *Poetic Remaking: The Art of Browning, Yeats, and Pound* (University Park and London: Pennsylvania State University Press, 1988). See also the "Introduction" to Reed Way Dasenbrock, *Imitating the Italians: Wyatt, Spenser, Synge, Pound, Joyce* (Baltimore and London: Johns Hopkins University Press, 1991).
3 H.D., *End to Torment: A Memoir of Ezra Pound* (New York: New Directions, 1979), p. 10; Alfred Kreymborg, *Troubadour: An Autobiography* (New York: Boni and Liveright, 1925), p. 204; Wyndham Lewis, *Blasting and Bombardiering* (Berkeley and Los Angeles: University of California Press, 1967), p. 280.
4 Gertrude Stein, *The Autobiography of Alice B. Toklas* (New York: Harcourt, Brace, 1933), p. 246.
5 Interview "Ezra Pound," in *Writers at Work: The Paris Review Interviews*, Second Series, ed. George Plimpton (New York: Viking Press, 1965), p. 47.
6 Allaw Wade (ed.), *The Letters of W. B. Yeats* (London: Rupert Hart-Davis, 1954), p. 543.

7 As quoted in Richard Ellmann's helpful essay "Ez and Old Billyum," in Ellmann, *Eminent Domain: Yeats Among Wilde, Joyce, Pound, Eliot and Auden* (New York: Oxford University Press, 1967), p. 66.

8 Ezra Pound, "The Later Yeats," *Poetry*, 4 (May 1914), 64–69.

9 T. S. Eliot, *To Criticize the Critic* (New York: Farrar, Straus & Giroux, 1965), p. 58.

10 Harriet Monroe, *A Poet's Life* (New York: Macmillan, 1938), p. 266. Cf. p. 268:

> Thus began the rather violent, but on the whole salutary, discipline of the lash of which the editor of the new magazine felt herself being rapidly educated, while all incrustations of habit and prejudice were ruthlessly swept away. Ezra Pound was born to be a great teacher ... At any rate, *Poetry* was the first of the numerous "little magazines" which he has fostered or founded and then tired of. Its editor has always acknowledged gratefully what she owed to his help during those first diverting and experimental years.

11 Robert Fost to Pound in Ellen Williams, *Harriet Monroe and the Poetry Renaissance: The First Ten Years of Poetry, 1912–1922* (Urbana: University of Illinois Press, 1977), p. 64.

12 For an example involving *The Cantos*, see Ron Bush's careful archeological work in "Excavating the Ideological Faultlines of Modernism: Editing Ezra Pound's *Cantos*," in George Bornstein (ed.), *Representing Modernist Texts: Editing as Interpretation* (Ann Arbor: University of Michigan Press, 1991).

13 *Criterion*, July 1932, 590.

14 "For T.S.E.," *Sewanee Review*, Special Issue for T. S. Eliot, January–March 1966, p. 109.

3

HUGH WITEMEYER

Early poetry 1908–1920

Writing of W. B. Yeats at the end of the 1930s, T. S. Eliot described him as "born into a world in which the doctrine of 'Art for Art's sake' was generally accepted, and living on into one in which art has been asked to be instrumental to social purposes."[1] Eliot and his contemporaries experienced this transition as well. Like Yeats and Ruskin before him, they had somehow to reconcile the competing claims of aestheticism and social commitment. The early poetry of Ezra Pound registers this tension vividly, as it oscillates between the worship of beauty and the reform of culture. Through many changes of style, from the *fin-de-siècle* romanticism of *A Lume Spento* (1908) to the hard-edged satire of *Hugh Selwyn Mauberley* (1920), Pound's writing served this double imperative.

From the age of fifteen, Pound says in a memoir entitled "How I Began" (1913), he knew that he was to be a poet. Moreover, he was to be a national epic poet, on the model of Homer, Dante and Whitman. His mother encouraged him to write an epic of the American West, and the early poem entitled "Scriptor Ignotus" speaks prophetically of "that great forty-year epic / That you know of, yet unwrit" (*CEP*, 24–5). The young man from Hailey, Idaho, and Wyncote, Pennsylvania, embraced as his destiny a high romantic ideal of the poet as bard, prophet, sage, and visionary seer. In this paradigm, the service of art and the service of society are one.

Since it was traditional for epic poets to commence modestly, learning their craft through an apprenticeship to lesser genres first, Pound began as a writer and translator of lyrics and dramatic lyrics. For a time he wrote a sonnet a day for practice, though few of these were ever published. Technique, the young poet believed, can be learned by conscious effort and discipline. Inspiration – or "delightful psychic experience," as he sometimes called it (*SR*, 92) – can not; like lightning, it comes unbidden from the gods. Thus, Pound prepared himself for his great vocation by creating in his early work a programmatically wide variety of lyric forms and modes. Between 1908 and 1912, he published no fewer than six volumes of verse; they are now gathered in *Collected Early Poems* and *Personae*. These imaginative exercises included several forward-looking experiments in the combining of discrete lyrics into longer sequences, such as "Und Drang" in *Canzoni* (*CEP*, 167–74).[2]

Training himself in this manner, Pound followed the neo-classical ideal of the epic poet as a man of no less learning than imagination. As refurbished by Matthew Arnold in the later nineteenth century, the neo-classical ideal emphasized a cosmopolitan internationalism of intellect and culture, a transcendence of provincial, monolingual perspectives, and an awareness of the best that has been thought and said (at any rate by Europeans). Pound, like Eliot, belonged to the first generation of American literary aspirants to take Arnold's prescriptions to heart as educational imperatives.

Thus, Pound visited Europe in 1898, 1902 and 1906; and he became a student of comparative literature at Hamilton College and the University of Pennsylvania, where he learned Classical, Romance, and Germanic languages to varying degrees of proficiency. His special field of interest was late-medieval literature in the Romance languages, including Provençal. The lectures he gave on this subject shortly after he came to London were published as *The Spirit of Romance: An Attempt to Define Somewhat the Charm of the Pre-Renaissance Literature of Latin Europe* (1910). He later acquired some Chinese and ancient Egyptian, as the horizons of his multiculturalism expanded beyond a Eurocentric outlook.

Pound's early creative work moved in tandem with his scholarly pursuits. He translated and wrote in imitation of his favorite medieval poems, from "The Seafarer" to Villon's *Testament*. His chameleonic style ranges from the rough-and-ready to the dreamy and archaic. He employs allusion and other techniques of "criticism in new composition" to direct his readers' attention to neglected periods, unknown authors, and obscure works – especially those which, in Pound's opinion, have made "donative" contributions to the development of poetry.[3] Like the lectures comprising *The Spirit of Romance*, many of his early poems seek to recreate the unique *virtù* of an individual writer or body of literature now largely forgotten. By the same token, Pound's dramatic monologues or *personae* have a didactic as well as an expressive function. They attempt to whet the reader's interest in the sensibility and accomplishments of vital but little-known historical figures such as the Provençal troubadours.

In showcasing relatively obscure authors, Pound extends the late-Victorian cult of the minor artist; but he also signals his ambition to revise the traditional canon by leaving his favorites in a considerably more prominent position than they held before Pound took them up. Like Eliot, who in his early poems and essays sought to change the canon of early seventeenth-century English literature, Pound attempted to alter and expand the limited cultural curriculum of his English-speaking readers. His constructive attitude toward the literary predecessors in his personal pantheon illustrates what George Bornstein calls a "beneficent conception of literary influence," as opposed to "the anxiety model" propounded by Harold Bloom and others.[4]

Yet even as Pound was drawn to a learned, neo-classical conception of poetry, he was no less powerfully attracted to a visionary, neo-romantic ideal. Thus, many of his early lyrics evoke a mystical and ethereal imaginative world, whose recurrent elements include disembodied spirits, magical metamorphoses, refracted light, inspiring winds, and emblematic minerals. In this realm, the religious-aesthetic worship of an idealized female figure signals a renewal of the medieval cult of courtly love, as nineteenth-century romanticism conceived it. The central male figure is often an itinerant, bohemian troubadour, a rebellious artist and lover in exile. The underlying metaphysic is a vitalistic neo-Platonism, according to which *personae* are not so much impersonations as momentary reincarnations of the great souls of the past. "Thus *am I* Dante for a space and *am* / One François Villon, ballad-lord and thief," Pound says in "Histrion" (*CEP*, 71; emphasis added).

These romantic proclivities shaped Pound's early life as well as his work. His bohemian appearance and behavior resulted in his being dismissed in 1908 from his first teaching job at Wabash College in Crawfordsville, Indiana. Convinced by this and other experiences that no serious artist could thrive in the Puritanic and materialistic environment of the United States, Pound left his homeland later in the same year. He migrated first to Venice and then to London, where his personal and poetic styles found a more receptive audience. He persuaded a London publisher, Elkin Mathews, to take him on as a regular author.

In his new milieu, Pound gravitated naturally to W. B. Yeats, whom he regarded as the premier poet writing in English. The two men became life-long friends. Pound shared many of Yeats's esoteric and occult interests, adopted his Irish intonation for public readings, served as Yeats's personal companion and secretary at Stone Cottage in Sussex during the winters of 1913–16, and married the daughter of Yeats's close friend, Olivia Shakespear.

Furthermore, the early poetry of Yeats became one of two poles between which Pound's own early poems tend to gravitate. The opposite pole is the work of Robert Browning, the most important Victorian influence upon the young American. Yeats and Browning appealed to two tendencies which Pound held in creative tension.[5] If Yeats was mystical and visionary, Browning was empirical and historical. Whereas Yeats strove for a poetry of timeless moods, pure emotion, and lyric ecstasy, Browning sought to revitalize history and to contextualize the utterances of a wide range of dramatic speakers.

Thus Pound's *personae* can be ranged along a Yeats–Browning spectrum. At the Yeatsian end there is "La Fraisne," a demented, metamorphic monologue which echoes Yeats's "The Madness of King Goll." At the Browningesque end we find "Marvoil," a careful reconstruction of an artist's life which echoes Browning's "Fra Lippo Lippi." If we seek a generalization that encompasses both poles of Pound's early art, we might say that his dramatic speakers are vital historic or pseudohistoric figures, caught in mid-career at some rare moment of intense passion, ecstasy, or contemplative lucidity.

These different aspects of Pound's talent work together in one of the troubadour monologues, "Piere Vidal Old" (1909). The poem recreates the circumstances of a medieval poet's legendary life at the same time that it evokes the ecstatic frenzy of eros. In good Edwardian fashion, it appeals to a sense of traditional decorum even as it challenges conventional proprieties.

Pound's scholarly source is the *vida* of the Provençal troubadour, Piere Vidal (1175–1215). From it, we learn that Vidal was enamored of the Countess of Penautier, who did not return his regard. Because the Countess was nicknamed *Loba*, Vidal dressed himself in a wolf's pelt to dramatize his desire to be her mate. The "wolf" was hunted down by the Countess's shepherds, mauled by their dogs, and

> brought as one dead to the dwelling of the She-Wolf of Penautier. And when she saw that it was even Peire Vidal, she made right merry over his folly, and laughed greatly, and also her husband . . .[6]

As presented in the Provençal *vida*, the tale is a medieval *exemplum* of the follies of love, hard-eyed and unromantic. Pound echoes this tone when, in *The Spirit of Romance*, he calls Vidal a "mad poseur" (*SR*, 178).

Yet in his poem Pound offers more than a lesson in Provençal literary lore. He brings history to life by evoking Vidal's passion. To this end, he thoroughly romanticizes the tale. He suggests that Vidal, touched by divine inspiration, truly went mad, thought himself a wolf, hunted deer, and attacked the hounds:

> Even the grey pack knew me and knew fear.
> God! how the swiftest hind's blood spurted hot
> Over the sharpened teeth and purpling lips.
>
> (*P, 1990*, 28–9)

Responding to Vidal's "splendid madness," the Countess gives herself to him for one consummate night of love. The memory of that night returns to Vidal midway through the monologue, disrupting its fluent syntax and regular stanzas. The speaker begins to stammer, and the *abcbdb* rhyme-scheme gives way, in the sixth stanza, to something irregular and unpredictable.

Though old, Piere Vidal lays claim to a vitality superior to that of his auditors. The "Age gone lax" which he upbraids is not only that of his implied thirteenth-century listeners but also Pound's own and ours, capable of a life like Vidal's only vicariously, through the masks of poetry. We are the "stunted followers / That mask at passions and desire desires" – the hollow men of the modern world, too inhibited to acknowledge real feeling. Here the created mask turns an unflattering mirror upon both its creator and its audience.

Pound's ambivalence toward the Edwardian–Georgian reading public was increasing. On the one hand, London had received him generously and reviewed his work appreciatively.[7] He relished his growing readership and catered to its Keatsian taste for purpling lips. On the other hand, he chafed against the residual Victorian decorum that required him to speak of half-sheathed and naked daggers instead of the real phallic thing. He yearned to challenge prevailing bourgeois proprieties, even at the risk of alienating admirers. Pound's sense of his audience was to become more troubled and problematic as the century unfolded.

Ripostes (1912) marks the transition between Pound's early romantic style and a self-consciously modern style. The diction of the poems in this volume oscillates between the archaic and the slangy, the medieval and the contemporary, "The Seafarer" and "The Plunge." A deliberate process of self-modernization is under way.

Influenced by developments on the continent, Pound and other London artists adopted the *avant-garde* mode of cultural politics, aggressively manipulating the media to promote their activities and to shock bourgeois taste by means of outrageous manifestoes, proclamations, interviews, exhibitions, and readings. In the latter part of 1912, Pound banded together with several other poets, including Hilda Doolittle (H.D.), Richard Aldington, and F. S. Flint, to start a movement called *Imagisme*. Its principal outlets were *Poetry* magazine, founded in Chicago in 1912 by Harriet Monroe with Pound as Foreign Editor; *The New Age*, a dissident socialist journal edited in London by A. R. Orage; and *The Egoist*, which had begun in London as a feminist-transcendentalist periodical entitled *The New Freewoman*. In these and other little magazines, Pound tirelessly promoted not only his own ideas and works but also those of his friends:

James Joyce, T. S. Eliot, Wyndham Lewis, W. B. Yeats, Ford Madox Ford, H.D., Robert Frost, William Carlos Williams, Henri Gaudier-Brzeska and others.

Imagism is probably the most important single movement in English-language poetry of the twentieth century. Hardly any prominent poet, in Pound's generation and the next two after it, went untouched by Imagist theory and practice. The aesthetic of Imagism might nowadays be called minimalist. It emphasized a romantic return to origins, a simplification of needless complexities, a zealous Puritanical stripping-away of the excrescences which had attached themselves to the art of poetry like barnacles to a clean hull. Among the luxuries to be relinquished were traditional meter and rhyme, artificial poetic diction, superfluous verbiage, rhetoric, explicit philosophizing and editorializing, and transitional filler. The poem was to be made as economical and functional as possible, and its chief *raison d'être* was to present images unmediated by authorial commentary. This stress upon precision and economy was indebted both to Ford Madox Ford's campaign to import Flaubertian stylistic values into English prose fiction, and to T. E. Hulme's doctrine of the image, propounded in meetings of a poets' club which Pound attended in London around 1909.[8]

The image of Imagism was not just a verbal evocation of sensory experience. Often spelled by Pound with a capital I, it had a quasi-mystical significance as well. The Image conveys meaningful experience virtually without the mediation of language. It "presents an intellectual and emotional complex in an instant of time," Pound said; it "gives that sense of sudden liberation; that sense of freedom from time limits and space limits; that sense of sudden growth, which we experience in the presence of the greatest works of art" (*LE*, 4). Although Pound denied it, his emphasis upon the numinous significance of the Image is indebted to Yeatsian symbology – in other words, to a neo-Platonic belief in the transcendental origin and visionary resonance of some of the eidolons which present themselves to the poet's waking or dreaming mind. The Image likewise has affinities with James Joyce's concept of the secular epiphany; both are pattern-disclosing revelations which manifest themselves in the course of everyday life, hallowing the quotidian and bestowing an aura of sacredness upon the profane.

When Imagism began to attract a school of imitators in 1914, Pound abandoned it and declared himself a "Vorticist" instead. Actually, his poetics changed very little, but Vorticism was a more interdisciplinary movement than Imagism. The Vorticists included non-representational painters (Wyndham Lewis, David Bomberg, Edward Wadsworth) and sculptors (Henri Gaudier-Brzeska, Jacob Epstein) as well as writers. Influenced by continental Cubism, Futurism and Expressionism, the Vorticists championed the principles of abstract formalism and celebrated the dynamic nature of creative processes and products.

A "Vortex" is a swirl of creative energy within an artist's psyche, within his work, or within his milieu. The Italian Renaissance was a Vortex, and Pound hoped for another, modernist renaissance, which, radiating from London, would transform the world. But the transformation would not be welcome in all quarters. As an *avant-garde* movement, Vorticism adopted an antagonistic and elitist stance toward the bourgeois public, which it saw as invincibly ignorant in matters of aesthetic importance. From a Vorticist viewpoint, art best serves society by subverting its most cherished beliefs.

Radical though it was, the Vorticist revolution was conservative as well. It would not break with the past entirely, but sought to preserve its most vital elements. Thus, in the poetry of his Imagist and Vorticist period (1912–16), Pound emulates a variety of precedents which embody the dynamic concision he values so highly. The lyrics of the *Greek Anthology*, the epigrams of the Roman satirists, and the *haiku* of the classical Japanese poets all provide distilled models for the poems in *Lustra* (1916).

The shorter poems of these years fall into two general groups: lyrics and satires. The lyrics celebrate beauty, vitality, fertility and desire; whereas the brash, insouciant satires scathingly register the absence of these life-forces in contemporary society and art. The principles of Imagism are primarily embodied in the lyrics, as Pound explained in 1914:

> no artist can possibly get a vortex into every poem or picture he does. One would like to do so, but it is beyond one . . . [Yet certain subjects], though they do not contain a vortex, may have some interest, an interest as a "criticism of life" or of art. It is natural to express these things, and a vorticist or imagiste writer may be justified in presenting a certain amount of work which is not vorticism or imagisme. (GB, 109)

Much of the non-Imagist work in *Lustra* is criticism or satire of this type, ranging from punchy Latinate epigrams to rambling Whitmanian harangues.

The classic Imagist poem is the haiku-like "In a Station of the Metro," with its epiphany of beauty in a crowded Paris underground-railway station. Pound's metaphoric leap from luminescent faces to "petals on a wet, black bough" generates "that sense of sudden liberation; that sense of freedom from time limits and space limits" to which Imagist revelation aspires (*LE*, 4). An even more compact example is "Papyrus," which, as its title suggests, pretends to translate a Greek lyric accidentally and only partially preserved on a recycled manuscript. In how few words can the essence of a Sappho love-poem be conveyed?

> Spring . . . . . .
> Too long . . . . . .
> Gongula . . . . . .   (*P, 1990*, 115)

In theme and form, the poem enacts a drama of presence and absence. The presence of spring whets Sappho's appetite for the absent Gongula. The presence of three line-beginnings whets our appetite for an absent text. By honing language's presence to an absolute minimum, the Imagist poem sharpens our intuition of its expressive gaps and omissions.

In the satires of *Lustra*, such absences connote not beauty and desire but ugliness and sterility. The lady in "The Garden," for example, has no vital centre:

> Like a skein of loose silk blown against a wall
> She walks by the railing of a path in Kensington Gardens,
> And she is dying piece-meal
>   of a sort of emotional anaemia.

Coleridge called this condition "Death-in-Life," and Pound's pun shows it to be both psychological and biological: "In her is the end of breeding" (*P, 1990*, 85).

Confirmation of the Imagist aesthetic came out of the blue in late 1913, when Pound unexpectedly received a packet of manuscripts from the widow of Ernest Fenollosa (1853–1908), a distinguished American historian of Oriental art. At the time of his death, Fenollosa had been translating a number of classic Chinese poems and Japanese Noh plays, and working on an essay about the Chinese written character as a medium for poetry. In the essay, Fenollosa praised Chinese words for their pictographic concreteness and Chinese syntax for its dynamic word order. Because the Chinese language mimes natural objects and processes so closely, Fenollosa argued, it is an ideal medium for poetry.

These conclusions seemed to rhyme with the Imagist emphasis upon concrete presentation and natural speech; and so Pound, undeterred by the fact that his own knowledge of Chinese was rudimentary, hastened to complete Fenollosa's translations as illustrations of the Imagist program. *Cathay* appeared in 1915 and was incorporated into Pound's *Lustra* in 1916. The Noh translations were also published in 1916; they strongly influenced the later plays of W. B. Yeats.

The imagistic qualities of the *Cathay* translations are immediately apparent and immensely appealing. Unlike some modern Imagist lyrics, moreover, the *Cathay* poems maintain traditional unities of viewpoint and emotional tone. Acknowledging this, Pound compared them to Ovid's heroic epistles and Browning's dramatic monologues, the genre he himself had imitated so often.[9] Abrupt juxtapositions of images and lines are grounded in the familiar convention of a stable lyric voice with which the reader may identify. "Emotion is born out of habit," says the speaker of "South-Folk in Cold Country":

> Yesterday we went out of the Wild-Goose gate,
> To-day from the Dragon-Pen.
> Surprised. Desert turmoil. Sea sun.
> Flying snow bewilders the barbarian heaven.
> Lice swarm like ants over our accoutrements.
> Mind and spirit drive on the feathery banners.   (*P, 1990*, 143)

The voice is clearly that of a disillusioned soldier who conveys his exhaustion and disorientation through a jumble of images drawn from the hostile environments he has experienced.

In contrast, the stroboscopic images of "The Game of Chess" are not grounded in a particular personality. Their function is to evoke the visual patterns on a chessboard as a projected subject for a set of dynamic, abstractionist paintings or prints.

> Whirl! Centripetal! Mate! King down in the vortex,
> Clash, leaping of bands, straight strips of hard colour,
> Blocked lights working in. Escapes. Renewal of contest.
>
> (*P, 1990*, 124)

The voice is excited but objective and impersonal. As a manifesto for Vorticism, the poem programmatically eschews sentimental humanism, denying its readers the pleasures of empathy. With the coming of the Great War, Pound's poetry adopts an increasingly impersonal mode, in which *personae* play subordinate and intermittent roles.

Homage to Sextus Propertius (1919) is the key poem in this transition. It is the last major single *persona* in Pound's work. Like *Cathay*, it is a free translation of ancient lyrics which employ the convention of a unitary dramatic speaker – in this case, the Latin elegies of the Roman poet Sextus Propertius. Pound selects and arranges the elegies to build up a complex and unorthodox portrait of Propertius, one that both interprets the historical original and expresses the preoccupations of the modern translator.[10]

The recurrent themes of the sequence are those of much World War I verse: love, war, death, and poetry itself. As in "South-Folk in Cold Country" and several other *Cathay* poems, the speaker registers his disillusion with imperial wars, thereby obliquely conveying the translator's protest against the analogous conflict of his own era. The *Homage*, Pound said, "presents certain emotions as vital to me in 1917, faced with the infinite and ineffable imbecility of the British Empire, as they were to Propertius some centuries earlier, when faced with the infinite and ineffable imbecility of the Roman Empire" (*L*, 231). Pound's Propertius rejects the demand that his art aggrandize the war effort through an over-inflated and derivative patriotic rhetoric. Instead, he will celebrate love and precious private life, a sphere which contains its own brushes with death and conflict enough.

On one level, *Homage to Sextus Propertius* is Pound's elegy to the literate, Edwardian–Georgian reading public which he was able to take for granted in most of his pre-war work. Even the *Lustra* satires presuppose the existence of an audience interested enough in poetry to resent or enjoy being abused. But the *Homage* declares that readership a casualty of the war – or, more precisely, of the same systemic corruption of language and cultural values that prolonged the war. The greater that corruption, the greater the poet's urge to expose and denounce it, but the smaller the audience capable of understanding and crediting his message. He ends up writing for a tiny coterie and an imagined posterity:

> I shall triumph among young ladies of indeterminate character,
> My talent acclaimed in their banquets,
> > I shall be honoured with yesterday's wreaths.
> And the god strikes to the marrow.
>
> > > . . .
>
> For the nobleness of the populace brooks nothing below its own altitude.
> One must have resonance, resonance and sonority . . . like a goose.
>
> > > > > > > (*P, 1990*, 224)

The incomprehension with which the *Homage* was received by reviewers and readers seemed to confirm Pound's point. Seldom again would he bother to publish a poem that attempts to meet its audience halfway. After the war, readers had to take Pound on his own terms or not at all. As his sense of social mission deepened, his circle of readers paradoxically contracted.

The difficulty of finding an alternative to *personae* as an organizing principle for a long poem is the main topic of Pound's *Three Cantos* (1917). Begun in the year he turned thirty, these poems were the first installment of the epic he had long projected. Instead of a traditional declaration of theme and invocation of a muse, however, *Three Cantos* begins with an appeal to Robert Browning, whose *Sordello* Pound sees as the most recent long poem that offers a viable model for his own ambitious endeavor. We detect an uncharacteristic note of the anxiety of influence, when Pound complains that Browning has pre-empted him.

> So you worked out new form, the meditative,
> Semi-dramatic, semi-epic story,
> And we will say: What's left for me to do?
> Whom shall I conjure up: who's my Sordello,
>
> (P, 1990, 231)

Pound's dilemma is exacerbated by the demise of the Victorian audience.

> Ah, had you quite my age, quite such a beastly
>   and cantankerous age?
> You had some basis, had some set belief.
> Am I let preach? Has it a place in music?   (P, 1990, 230)

The interrogation ends inconclusively, and Pound was unable to go on with the poem for five years.[11] To whom was he preaching?

In the meantime, others were preaching to Pound, and he was being converted. In the offices of *The New Age*, Pound was exposed in 1919 to the doctrine of Social Credit, as expounded by its founder, Major C. H. Douglas. An engineer-turned-economist, Douglas believed that he had identified the economic causes of poverty and war in modern industrial society. His analysis made sense to Pound as a rational explanation of the incomprehensible carnage which had shattered the Vortex and its attendant hopes for a cultural renaissance.

Douglas argued that both poverty and war result from the inequitable distribution of consumer purchasing-power in the capitalist economies of modern nation-states. What skews the distribution of purchasing-power is the control of credit by private bankers and the charging of excessive interest or usury for the use of credit. These interest charges are reckoned into prices, but do not reach consumers, according to Douglas; therefore, the price of goods is always higher than available purchasing-power. Until credit is nationalized in the public interest, poverty and war are inevitable, as nations compete for foreign markets to absorb their surplus of domestic products. Social Credit was thus a sophisticated version of the conspiracy theories which traced the causes of the Great War to the greed of those who most profited from it: bankers, munitions-makers, generals, and top politicians.

These new convictions altered Pound's sense of the relationship between art and society. Like Ruskin around 1860, Pound came to see the faulty economic organization of society as the root of many evils which impair the quality of modern life. If art is to flourish, the society which produces it must be healthy; but bourgeois capitalist democracy is corrupted by rampant greed and mediocrity. In Pound's view, the onset of the Great Depression ten years later only served to confirm the accuracy of the Social Credit diagnosis.

The first major work in which Pound expresses this embittered social vision is *Hugh Selwyn Mauberley* (1920). Pound wrote the sequence as a poetic farewell to London on the eve of his departure for Paris. In it, he adumbrates the reasons why, after a residence of twelve years, he no longer finds England congenial to art and artists.

His analysis is complex and uncompromising. To begin with, his formidable style makes few concessions to the common reader. Those tackling the poem for the first time may well come away with little more than a general impression of angry urgency and bitter irony. A major source of difficulty is the extreme condensation of the images and allusions, which often imply discursive arguments made elsewhere in Pound's writings but not repeated here. In the absence of an easily identifiable central speaker or *persona,* another problem lies in gauging the point of view and tone of voice of the various sections of the sequence. The reader is forced to construe unfamiliar, heterogeneous materials juxtaposed according to a logic that is not immediately apparent. It is as though the imagistic technique of "In a Station of the Metro" had fissioned.

To bring the *Mauberley* sequence under control, each reader must make a set of personal hermeneutic decisions about the meaning and connection of its various elements. Here is one set of choices that may prove helpful. In its first twelve sections, the sequence analyzes the false values of modern civilization by showing their effects upon the market for art and upon the careers of a series of minor artists. As in many of his earlier poems, Pound takes the *vida* of the secondary artist to be a valid index of the general culture of his society. The poem is by no means a neo-romantic "*Kunstlerroman*" (novel of the education of the artist) in verse, however. Ironically, the title character, a fictive poet named Hugh Selwyn Mauberley, does not even appear until the second part of the sequence, beginning with "Mauberley 1920." Instead of spotlighting a protagonist, the first part of the poem presents a critique of "the age" and shows its effects upon the lives and works of other English artists, from the mid-Victorian period on.

These portraits provide an aesthetic heritage for Mauberley and a glance at some contemporary careers with which his may be compared. The voice that knits the sequence is the flexible voice of Pound himself, speaking in various tones of irony, rage, detachment and impersonal sympathy; but the voice does not build up a *persona* or generate an illusion of dramatic character. There are moments of lyric affirmation, especially in the "Envoi" and "Medallion," but the predominant tone is diagnostic, ironic, and satiric.[12]

Pound's criticism is two-edged. First, he condemns the philistine priorities of a society which values money more than life, profit more than beauty. Secondly, he criticizes modern artists themselves for their escapist responses to the pressures of the age, for either giving up or taking refuge in a hedonistic aestheticism. In other words, *Mauberley* is an extended case study of what happens when, as Eliot put it, the doctrine of "Art for Art's sake" is challenged by the demand that art "be instrumental to social purposes."

After the opening "Ode," sections II–V present Pound's critique of British values in an era of "tawdry cheapness." In art, the age demands a prettified image of itself, a "mould in plaster" or a photographically realistic drama and fiction which are endlessly replicable for a mass market. When beauty (TO KALON) is "decreed in the market place," art becomes mechanical; the pianola which "replaces" Sappho's barbitos or lyre symbolizes this decline (*P, 1990,* 186–187). In politics, a mechanical democracy of electoral franchise and mass-circulation newspapers displaces a traditional religious sense of community and chooses corrupt or ineffectual leaders. Aesthetic and political ideals "defect" and turn into hollow mockeries.

The Great War of 1914–18 was the logical outcome of this displacement of life values by money values. Those who went to battle out of patriotic idealism returned with no illusions:

> believing in old men's lies, then unbelieving
> came home, home to a lie,
> home to many deceits,
> home to old lies and new infamy;
> usury age-old and age-thick
> and liars in public places.   (*P, 1990,* 188)

The Social-Credit conspiracy-theory of the economic and political causes of the war underpins these bitter lines, which mark the first appearance of the term *usury* in Pound's poetry.

Pound traces the philistine phase of modern British society back some seventy-five years, to the Pre-Raphaelite controversies of the mid-Victorian period. Much of *Mauberley* is devoted to showing how different artists have responded to economic and social pressures during this period. Pound does not let his sympathy for the artists' cause prevent him from making an unsentimental diagnosis of the flaws in their will and their aesthetic views. After all, "the age" is not wholly to blame if its minor talents do not succeed.

Mauberley's gallery of impaired, failed, and compromised artists begins with the "E.P." of the opening ode, a version of Pound himself in the years just after his arrival in London. Well-meaning but immobilized by the dated cultural baggage of his provincial American upbringing, "E.P." fails to modernize his style and falls behind, trapped in the contemplation of an old-fashioned ideal of beauty.

The gallery resumes in "Yeux Glauques" and proceeds in roughly chronological order, from Ruskin, Rossetti, Swinburne and Burne-Jones, to the Rhymers of the Nineties (Lionel Johnson, Ernest Dowson), to Max Beerbohm ("Brennbaum"), Arnold Bennett ("Mr. Nixon") and Ford Madox Ford ("the stylist").[13] In Sections XI and XII, the focus shifts from the artists to their audience, as Pound satirizes bourgeois, aristocratic and popular representatives of modern public taste. If the economic and social demands of the age induce escapism or compromise among artists, among consumers of the arts they erase all notions of patronage based upon aesthetic merit.

The second part of the sequence, beginning with "Mauberley 1920", traces the effect of these forces upon the career of a fictive English poet. Hugh Selwyn Mauberley is not modelled upon any identifiable, historical individual. Rather, he is a type of the aesthete. Mauberley begins as an Imagist poet but declines, under the pressures of the age, into hedonistic impressionism.

Mauberley starts out as an admirer of the Parnassian poetry of Théophile Gautier in *Emaux et Camées*. (The "eau-forte / Par Jacquemart" is the engraved portrait bust of Gautier on the frontispiece of the 1881 edition. With this allusion, the poem is also declaring its own aesthetic allegiances, for Gautier's quatrains are one model for those of *Mauberley* itself.) The connoisseur admires engravings, coins, medallions, relief sculpture and the linear style of Italian Renaissance portraiture. With Flaubertian precision, he models his own imagistic poetry upon this lapidary visual art. Indeed, the "Medallion" which closes the entire poem should probably be read as a work by Mauberley himself, a typical profile portrait in "sculpted" rhyme of a beautiful woman singing. (The "Envoi" offers a more melodic treatment of the same subject).

After three productive years, however, Mauberley's talent recedes into silence. He misses an opportunity for love because he simply lacks erotic desire. (For Pound, as the French epigraph from "Caid Ali" suggests, eros and creativity are different manifestations of the same energy.) Mauberley's response to the age is not to yield to its demands but to withdraw into a private, subjective world of "selected impressions," rare and exquisite apperceptions of beauty passively received but not returned to the world as art.

A pale gold, in the aforesaid pattern,
The unexpected palms
Destroying, certainly, the artist's urge,
Left him delighted with the imaginary
Audition of the phantasmal sea-surge.   (*P, 1990*, 200)

Mauberley drifts into psychic isolation or solipsism, depicted as a tropical lotos-land where he need do nothing but enjoy the "overblotted / Series / Of intermittences" which now constitutes his consciousness. His poetic quest is over. Like one of the failed crewmen of Odysseus, he leaves an engraved oar (his "Medallion") to commemorate his passing.

With this bleak critique of the modern poet's dilemma, Pound himself ceased to write minor poetry. He did not lapse out like Mauberley, but turned his considerable energies to his epic. After 1921, all of Pound's serious, original poetry went into *The Cantos*. But his conception of that project had changed since the palmy days of his novitiate. After writing *Propertius* and *Mauberley*, he was convinced that only a huge, indigestible poem would stick in the craw of a monstrous, all-consuming age. Into that poem he would put what needed saving. Few might read it, yet only thus could he continue to serve both art and society.

NOTES

1 Frank Kermode (ed.), *Selected Prose of T. S. Eliot* (London: Faber and Faber, 1975), p. 257.
2 See Bruce Fogelman, *Shapes of Power: The Development of Ezra Pound's Poetic Sequences* (Ann Arbor, MI: UMI Research Press, 1988), chapter 2.
3 See Hugh Witemeyer, *The Poetry of Ezra Pound: Forms and Renewal, 1908–1920* (Berkeley: University of California Press, 1969), chapter 1.
4 George Bornstein, *Poetic Remaking: The Art of Browning, Yeats, and Pound* (University Park: The Pennsylvania State University Press, 1988), p. 140.
5 See N. Christoph de Nagy, *The Poetry of Ezra Pound: The Pre-Imagist Stage*, 2nd edn (Berne, Switzerland: Francke Verlag, 1960), chapter 5; and Witemeyer, *Poetry of Ezra Pound*, chapter 4.
6 Ida Farnell (trans.), *The Lives of the Troubadours* (London: David Nutt, 1896), p. 86. For evidence that Pound knew this translation, see *SR*, 62.
7 For reviews of Pound's early books, see Eric Homberger (ed.), *Ezra Pound: The Critical Heritage* (London and Boston: Routledge & Kegan Paul, 1972), pp. 43–98.
8 See Stanley Coffman, *Imagism: A Chapter in the History of Modern Poetry* (Norman: University of Oklahoma Press, 1951). More recent studies of Imagism include Herbert Schneidau, *Ezra Pound: The Image and the Real* (Baton Rouge: Louisiana State University Press, 1969); J. B. Harmer, *Victory in Limbo: Imagism 1908–1917* (New York: St. Martin's Press, 1975); and John T. Gage, *In the Arresting Eye: The Rhetoric of Imagism* (Baton Rouge: Louisiana State

University Press, 1981). For poststructuralist treatments of the subject, see Joseph N. Riddell, "'Neo-Nietzschean Clatter' – Speculation and/on Pound's Poetic Image," in Ian F. A. Bell (ed.), *Ezra Pound: Tactics for Reading* (London: Vision Press, 1982), pp. 187–220, and Daniel Tiffany, *Radio Corpse: Imagism and the Cryptaesthetic of Ezra Pound* (Cambridge, MA: Harvard University Press, 1995).

9 Ezra Pound, "Chinese Poetry," *To-Day*, 3 (1918), 54–57, 93–95. For discussions of *Cathay* by native speakers of Chinese, see Wai-lim Yip, *Ezra Pound's Cathay* (Princeton: Princeton University Press, 1969), and Zhaoming Qian, *Orientalism and Modernism: The Legacy of China in Pound and Williams* (Durham and London: Duke University Press, 1995), pp. 65–87.

10 See J. P. Sullivan, *Ezra Pound and Sextus Propertius: A Study in Creative Translation* (Austin: University of Texas Press, 1964).

11 For the evolution of the early Cantos, see Ronald Bush, *The Genesis of Ezra Pound's Cantos* (Princeton: Princeton University Press, 1976), and Christine Froula, *To Write Paradise: Style and Error in Pound's Cantos* (New Haven and London: Yale University Press, 1984), chapters 1 and 2.

12 My reading of *Mauberley* is indebted to John J. Espey, *Ezra Pound's Mauberley: A Study in Composition* (Berkeley: University of California Press, 1955). For an opposing view, see Jo Brantley Berryman, *Circe's Craft: Ezra Pound's Hugh Selwyn Mauberley* (Ann Arbor, MI: UMI Research Press, 1983). For the critical history of the poem, see Stephen J. Adams, "Irony and Common Sense: The Genre of *Mauberley*", *Paideuma*, 18 (1989), 147–160, and Ronald Bush, "'It Draws One to Consider Time Wasted': *Hugh Selwyn Mauberley*", *American Literary History*, 21 (1990), 56–78. For a Bakhtinian reading, see Brian G. Caraher, "Reading Pound with Bakhtin: Sculpting the Social Languages of *Hugh Selwyn Mauberley*'s 'Mere Surface,'" *Modern Language Quarterly*, 49 (1988), 38–64.

13 See K. K. Ruthven, *A Guide to Ezra Pound's Personae (1926)* (Berkeley: University of California Press, 1969), pp. 137–139.

4

DANIEL ALBRIGHT

Early Cantos I–XLI

Here begins the great unwieldy poem, all light and mud, to which Ezra Pound devoted much of his life. It was the work of a poet too ambitious, too afraid of being cramped, to work according to a plan. Instead of a plan, Pound devised a strategy for creating a self-scrutinizing text, continually extending itself, ramifying outward, as it groped to comprehend its own prior meanings, to improvise new networks of connection, and to assimilate new material: a text shaped like a developing brain. New Cantos form themselves out of schemes to make sense of old Cantos: so the story of *The Cantos* comprises two intertwined stories, one concerning Pound's writing of the poem, the other concerning Pound's interpretations of what he had already written.

This twin story begins in 1915, when Pound was thirty years old. He was living in London, writing critical essays and reviews, shaping the modernist movement by propagandizing Eliot and other poets; and he felt that it was time to make a contribution of his own, by composing a grand poem worthy of Homer and Dante. As early as 1909, Pound told his mother that he intended to write an epic; but he was not immediately certain how to proceed. In 1915 he wrote a long poem, ultimately published in 1917 in *Poetry* magazine as *Three Cantos* – a poem quite different from any of the cantos as we know them today. It is characteristic of Pound that he had to erase the beginning of *The Cantos*, since his whole career is a structure of reinterpretation, often of repudiation, of his earlier work. The sequence of Pound's *Cantos* interrogates itself, casting off outworn versions of itself in the search for renewal.

In 1915, Pound could already present himself as the most versatile and accomplished translator in English: even today, translations of Old English tend to echo (or play off) the abrupt, overstressed voice that Pound established in 1911 in "The Seafarer" ("Known on my keel many a care's hold, / And dire sea-surge, and there I oft spent / Narrow nightwatch nigh the ship's head"); and the Chinese translations of his 1915 volume *Cathay* seemed to display a delicacy of diction new to our language. But Pound's original work was less prepossessing. He had written some fine passages in a somewhat nervously archaic idiom, as well as many of the small, tense, sometimes satirical poems, not at all archaic, that were to be collected in the volume *Lustra* (1916), such as "In a Station of the Metro" (1913). By eliminating all but the hardest kernel, through eighteen months of intense poetic work, Pound hoped to find the minimum unit of poetic expression in a haiku-like sentence:

> The apparition of these faces in the crowd:
> Petals, on a wet, black bough. (*EPVA*, 205)

But this technique, basic to the Imagist movement that Pound helped to establish, through editing the *Imagiste* anthology, was unpromising for an epic poem.

Almost as soon as the Imagist movement began, Pound sought for ways of extending the poetic image without losing its concentration. The Vorticist movement of 1914 sought ways of embodying in a poem, not just the image itself, but the *process* through which the image was conceived and transmitted: "The image . . . is a radiant node or cluster; it is what I can, and must perforce, call a VORTEX, from which, and through which, and into which, ideas are constantly rushing. In decency one can only call it a VORTEX" (*EPVA*, 207). The notion of a whirl of ideas fining themselves down, focusing on some central point, seems more useful to an epic poet than the notion of an interminable gallery of terse and disconnected images – pattern-units in the absence of a pattern. But how was Pound to write an epic in the form of a tornado?

Three Cantos (1917)

The Pound of 1915 did not want to ask himself such questions; he simply wanted to write, and to write without any particular sense of a model. His very choice of the word *canto* to describe his poem is intriguing. *Canto* is simply an Italian word for song, but in English it suggests a chunk of a single long poem, such as Homer's *Odyssey* or Dante's *Divine Comedy*. But Pound used the word ambiguously: the English sense is not quite right, for the theme of the whole, the form of the whole, the destination of the whole – none of these was determined when he began; the whole was to be a construct of the parts, and so each Canto had to claim a certain independence, a certain authority in solitude. And the Italian sense is not quite right either, for the song-like passages are intermixed with material extremely hard to sing, such as excerpts from the letters of Thomas Jefferson. The word *canto* is an impudence: an allegation of a comprehensiveness of design that was never likely to be evident – though Pound hoped that some day, somehow, it would be achieved; and an allegation of music that indeed can be heard, but only fitfully, as if the whole poem were a transcript of a radio broadcast that kept losing the proper channel, dissolving into static, or into the blare of the aggressive wrong stations occupying a bandwidth close to the faint right station.

The choice of the word *canto* arouses certain expectations in the reader, perhaps most of all that expectation that the poem is a *Divine Comedy* for the modernist age. Pound sometimes invited and sometimes resisted this. In 1915 he wrote, "I am working on a long poem which will resemble the Divina Commedia in length but in no other manner . . . it will prevent my making any money for the next forty years, perhaps" (*P/ACH*, 120); but in 1917, when Harriet Monroe was printing (contrary to his wishes) *Three Cantos* in installments, Pound wrote, "Have at last had a letter from Harriet, consenting to print the Divina Commedia, in three sections" (*P/ACH*, 223). The premise of Dante's poem, of course, is a series of interviews between a character named Dante, a tourist in the afterlife during the year 1300, and various dead souls, whose torture or beatitude takes the form of a certain expressive urgency: they boast, they exhort, they weep, they sing. There are a few passages in Pound's Cantos which closely follows Dante's premise, as in LXXII/432 when Pound meets the Futurist Marinetti. But this eerie encounter occurs in a late Canto from 1944, originally written in Italian, as if Pound could become Dante only by abandoning the English language. In the early Cantos, we behold glimpses of the torsions of hell and the opalescence of heaven, as Dante conceived them, but Pound's structural technique owes little to Dante.

Pound was reluctant to shape his poem according to classical or medieval European models; and he was also reluctant to shape his poem according to extremely up-to-date modernist models. The appearance of Marinetti in Canto LXII suggests, not only an alternate, unwritten version of the Cantos in the style of Dante, but another possible version that Pound might have considered and rejected: Cantos in the style of Marinetti. In 1915, when Pound was beginning the project, Europe was full of experiments in making language look like pictures: in 1914 Apollinaire had begun his *Calligrammes* (originally called *ideogrammes lyriques*), and Marinetti published his *Zum Tumb Tuum*. In the 1910s, Pound tended to be contemptuous of Marinetti and suspicious of the French experiments with poetic ideograms; on the other hand, he regarded Chinese as a language blessed by its pictorial specificity of meaning, and he noted with awe that the sculptor Gaudier-Brzeska was so sensitive to design that, without having studied Chinese, he could read its ideograms, through sheer power to destylize the signs into pictures (*CWC*, 31; *ABCR*, 21). The modernist hope of shaping language into typographic forms through which the eye can *see* the meaning of the text informs some passages in the Cantos, as in the phrase on the city of Arrarat inscribed inside an equilateral triangle in Canto XXXIV/171, stabilizing the city on the firm base of a visual pyramid. But such experiments are rare in the early Cantos. For the most part, neither Dante nor Marinetti, neither the old master nor the Futurist, gave Pound what he needed for his great project.

Despite Pound's unwillingness to limit his field of poetic operation by planning, *Three Cantos* did make use of a model – a model that no other poet would have chosen as the basis of a long modernist poem: *Sordello* (1840), an overwhelmingly ambitious poem by the very young Robert Browning, published at his father's expense. *Sordello* soon became a by-word for gnarled and wilful obscurity. Still, the first words given to the world from Pound's *Three Cantos* consisted of a tribute to the poem:

> Hang it all, there can be but one *Sordello*:
> But say I want to, say I take your whole bag of tricks,
> Let in your quirks and tweeks, and say the thing's an art-form,
> Your *Sordello*, and that the modern world
> Needs such a rag-bag to stuff all its thought in.   (*TC*, 53)

The ejaculative, impertinent tone of this passage is itself borrowed from Browning – but Browning's persona was only one of several features that attracted Pound to *Sordello*. Pound liked Browning's way of resurrecting the past – the historical Sordello was a thirteenth-century troubadour who eloped with Cunizza da Romana, a nobleman's wife – by means of a modern intermediary, who dramatizes himself in the act of dramatizing long-extinct characters. Indeed, Browning introduces himself to the reader as a sort of professor dressed like a clown.

Throughout the *Three Cantos*, Pound, following the Browningesque model of puppet-master, plays the genial but erratic impresario, making his pretty merchandise dance for public admiration – glances at the pomp of Italian and Spanish parades, snatches from Catullus and the story of el Cid, memories of his 1908 trip to Venice, all shot through with visions of old gods taking shape in the air. It is a self-conscious, theatrical sort of poetizing, which at last terminates in the third of the *Three Cantos*, when the poet opens an old book, Andreas Divus's Latin translation (1538) of the *Odyssey*, and gently complains about the hard work of translating, whether from Latin or Provençal:

> I've strained my ear for -*ensa*, -*ombra*, and -*ensa*
> And cracked my wit on delicate canzoni –
>   Here's but rough meaning:
> "And then went down to the ship, set keel to breakers,
> Forth on the godly sea;
> We set up mast and sail on the swarthy ship . . ."   (*TC*, 69–70)

The reader will recognize the section in quotation marks as a draft of Canto I, as it would appear in *A Draft of XVI Cantos* (1925), and as it appears today. During the eight years between the composition of *Three Cantos* and the recasting of Canto I in 1923, a tremendous reorientation had occurred in Pound's poetics; and his idea of what a Canto was had shifted so greatly that he found himself simply emancipating the translation of Odysseus's descent to Hades from all the masses of prefatory material. Pound took a flensing knife to *Three Cantos*; but in order to do so he needed to devise a clear principle for distinguishing meat from blubber.

Three Cantos is a work with deep focal field. In the foreground is the poet, the showman with his sardines; in the middle ground are exhilarating landscapes, like those Tuscan climes where "The senses at first seem to project for a few yards beyond the body" (*LE*, 152); in the background is a tissue of reminiscence of art and literature, from Botticelli to Egyptian inscription. In 1915 Pound conceived an epic as a careful mediation of a central consciousness surrounding, animating, swirling into, receding from, the brief stories and the descriptions of the text – as Joyce put it in *A Portrait of the Artist as a Young Man*, to be published the following year: in the epic "The personality of the artist passes into the narration itself, flowing round and round the persons and the actions like a vital sea".[1] Pound regarded his work as something far choppier, more discontinuous, than the old epics – as he expostulated to Browning in *Three Cantos* I,

>   You had one whole man?
>   And I have many fragments, less worth? . . .
>   Ah, had you quite my age, quite such a
>   beastly and cantankerous age?
>   You had some basis, had some set belief.   (*TC*, 54)

But Pound may have felt that the very fragmentariness of the modern age required the emollience of a clearly present core sensibility, absorbing all the fragments into a single matrix, preventing their rough edges from cutting the reader. Pound compared the *Three Cantos* to a "rag-bag"; one might also think of chunks of fruit suspended in the jello of the poet's mind.

But there were certain obvious dangers in entrusting the great project of one's life to a model of fragments stuck in a rag-bag. Any fragment, any bright pebble that catches the eye, is as good as any other, unless some method can be found for discriminating the Luminous Detail (*SP*, 22) from the general muck. And just as the contents of *The Cantos* were looking ominously random, so the coordinating sensibility, the mind of Pound, also seemed incoherent. Poggio, in Pound's dialogue "Aux Etuves de Wiesbaden" (1918), notes "They ruin the shape of life for a dogmatic exterior . . . I myself am a rag-bag, a mass of sights and citations, but I will not beat down life for the sake of a model" (*PDD*, 102). This makes a noble affirmation of a shapeless self and codeless conduct – but it seems to lead to the opposite of art, insofar as art represents selection and intensification. In 1920 Pound reviewed the list of personae in his poetry, and noted that, while Propertius, the Seafarer, and Mauberley "are all 'me' in one sense; my personality is certainly a great slag heap of stuff which has to be excluded from each of th[ese] crystalizations" (*P/F*, 42). At that time Pound was trying to decide how to proceed with *The Cantos*, and it is easy to see why he was uncertain: no single persona was inclusive enough to be the Sordello of the modernist age; but to present the whole "slag heap" was simply to present something bulging and ugly, the detritus of self instead of the informing force. The road of the *Three Cantos* leads to self-insistence, gigantism, Wagnerian opera, and general uffishness and whiffling – not the goals that Pound sought. Instead of giving up the *intaglio* method – carefully chiseled art – Pound needed to find a way of integrating epic aspirations with incisive design.

Cantos IV–VII (1919)

The Cantos got on the right path (from Pound's point of view) in 1919, when he wrote Canto IV – the first Canto that he regarded as capable of standing in the finished sequence, although it, too, was revised to some degree. Canto IV has an entirely different texture from the *Three Cantos* of 1917.

The method of the *Three Cantos* might be compared to perspective drawing, in that the reader is oriented in psychological space; but Canto IV, by contrast, is a flat field. The poet, the events, the literary allusions, all co-exist on the same plane:

> And she went toward the window and cast her down,
>   "All the while, the while, swallows crying:
> Ityn!
>   "It is Cabestan's heart in the dish."
>   "It is Cabestan's heart in this dish?"
>   "No other taste shall change this."

And she went toward the window,
　　the slim white stone bar
Making a double arch ...　　　　　　　　　　　　　　　(IV/13)

This is only a condensation of Canto IV, but it is faithful to the hard edges
of Pound's transitions: the slabs of texts abut one another without much
sense of a professor, or clown, or master of ceremonies creating a steady
context for the evolution of the pictures and stories. The last two lines did
not appear in the text until 1925 – originally the poet scarcely had any
presence in the poem. But even this final allusion to the premise of *Three
Cantos* I – the showman-poet sitting in "the old theatre at Arles" (*TC*, 57)
and conjuring visions – does not succeed in producing a graduated field
with the poet's intelligence on one plane and the stories and pictures on
another. Instead, the snapshot of poet in arena is just another pictorial
element of the collage.

Pound has cast off "Bob Browning" in favor of a different structural
model. The key to the method of Canto IV lies in the section about the
pines of Takasago and Isé: Pound has turned to the Orient to reorganize
his poem (IV/15). In an undated letter, Pound told Harriet Monroe that
the theme of the Cantos is "roughly the theme of 'Takasago,' which story
I hope to incorporate more explicitly in a later part of the poem" (*P/ACH*,
xxii). This may suggest that even during the composition of *Three Cantos*,
Pound considered the Japanese Noh play, and specifically the Noh play
Takasago, as crucial to the whole project. In *Three Cantos* Pound made
some picturesque allusions to the Noh theatre; but Canto IV suggests that
the Cantos could aspire, not simply to include pretty elements of Japanese
theatre, but to *be* a kind of Noh play.

Pound spent his winters at Stone Cottage in Sussex from 1913 to 1916,
working with Yeats on (among other things) the possibilities for finding a
Western equivalent to the classic Noh theatre of Japan. The Noh is, by
Western standards, a theatre without drama. There is rarely anything that
could be called a story; the action, which is minimal, is usually accomplished during, and by means of, the climactic dance. In the simplest plays
a travelling priest (called the *waki*), often a folklorist or a connoisseur of
landscape, meets a humble old man or old woman; after a series of inter-
rogations it dawns on the priest that what appears to be a vagrant, a
beggar, or a leech-gatherer, is actually a spirit (called the *shite*) – perhaps
the ghost of a great man triumphantly remembering the scene of a mighty
deed, or a genius loci, taking pleasure in the presence of his or her locus.
A metamorphosis is accomplished by means of a costume change and a
change of mask; there is no scenery, nothing but bridges and potted pines

and the painted pinetree that is the backdrop of all Noh plays. The dramatic action, then, is only a movement towards enlightenment: what is surrounded by material illusion at last reveals itself in its true supernatural glory, a glory that reaches its perfection in the characteristic dance of the spirit. It is an attempt to provoke a delirium of wonder.

Pound discovered in the Noh an answer to a question that had puzzled him: "I am often asked whether there can be a long imagiste... poem. The Japanese, who evolved the *hokku*, evolved also the Noh plays. In the best 'Noh' the whole play may consist of one image. I mean it is gathered about one image. Its unity consists in one image, enforced by movement and music" (*EPVA*, 209). A Noh play is unitary; it is incisive; it is an extended writing, but anti-discursive – a text with the instantaneity and direct grasp of a painting, or an ideogram. These are the very qualities to which the Cantos aspire. Motokiyo's *Takasago* takes for its "one image" the embrace of two pine trees.

> *Chorus.*
>> Though grass and trees have no mind
>> They have their time of blossoming and of bearing their fruit
>
>> · · ·
>
> *Old Man.*
>> And the look of this pine is eternal.
>> Its needles and cones have one season
>>> (trans. Pound, *P/ACH*, 114–115)

The play is an affront to time and space. The two pines are geographically apart, separated by mountain and river, and yet they clasp; the pine of Takasago symbolizes a past age, and the pine of Sumiyoshi symbolizes the present age, and yet they co-exist. Pound considered *Takasago* a nearly perfect play, and it demonstrates how the Noh theatre dismantles clock time and yardstick space in order to gesture at some evergreen eternal present, where two pine trees can incarnate themselves as an old man and an old woman, a panpsychic filed at the end of all metamorphoses.

What would it be like to be *inside* an imagist's image? Pound's *Tristan*, his 1916 attempt at a Noh drama, suggests an answer: it would be a condition where nothing is solid, nothing is determinate – a condition at the knife-edge, at the metamorphic quick, where the subway train is just about to turn into the black bough. Pound's play is a theatrical presentation of life inside Wagner's *Tristan* chord: a chord that demands harmonic resolution yet remains suspended, incapable of resolving, incapable of construing itself, at once creeping upward and diminishing ever further into its own private hypospace – an endless frustration. Because the whole spectacle is one image, the whole action is only the arbitrary spinning-out of a multidimensional stasis into a metamorphosis.

Canto IV ends with the poet sitting in an old arena because the poem is itself a kind of theatre – a composite Noh play, made up of several dissected and reassembled fragments of shape-change stories. There is the Baucis and Philemon story from *Takasago*; there is Actaeon, the peeping-Tom who spied Artemis naked in her bath, then was transformed into a stag and torn apart by Artemis's hounds; there is the lycanthrope troubadour Peire Vidal, who outfitted himself with a wolfskin out of love for a woman named Loba (she-wolf); there is Philomela, changed into a singing bird after her brother-in-law Tereus raped her and cut out her tongue – as revenge, her sister Procne killed Tereus's (and her own) son Itys, cooked him, and served the hideous meal to Tereus; there is the troubadour Cabestanh, murdered by his lord after Cabestanh slept with the lord's wife Seremonda – the lord commanded Cabestanh's heart to be served to her in a dish, and she leaped out a window to her death (*SR*, 44). Pound cunningly arrests and arranges these bright shards of narratives in such a way that they seem all part of a single incurved action: Seremonda is a second Tereus in that she eats human flesh without knowing it, but a second Philomela in that she takes to the air, swings herself out the window like a bird; Actaeon the stag and Vidal the wolf seem part of a single action, a sexual urgency that either flees or attacks, depending on the quality of desire. The Noh theatre provided Pound with a model for manifesting the approach through time and space of some whole beyond time and space – a complex that the poet inspects glint by glint, ply by ply. The pine of Takasago and the pine of Isé are, in some occult sense, intertwined at the root; and so are Philomela and Seremonda and Tereus and Vidal.

Canto IV was published in October 1919; in December of that year Pound wrote Cantos V–VII, not published until 1921. Pound was concerned about their obscurity, with reason:

> And Pieire won the singing, Pieire de Maensac,
> Song or land on the throw, and was *dreitz hom*
> And had De Tierci's wife and with the war they made:
>> Troy in Auvergnat
> While Menelaus piled up the church at port
> He kept Tyndarida. Dauphin stood with de Maensac. (V/18)

Canto V is like Canto IV, in that the world of troubadour adultery is still evoked for its glamours, and in that short segments are spliced together to reveal common themes. The singer Pierre de Maensac may be a *dreitz hom* (straight guy), but he was nonetheless devious enough to run off with De

Tierci's wife – a second Paris abducting a second Helen from a second Menelaus. But Canto V also represents an important departure in style. Even as early as Canto I – which, it must be remembered, did not yet exist, except as the coda of *Three Cantos* III – Pound liked to conjure up some secondary conjuror, such as Andreas Divus, to do the work of conjuring in his stead: indeed, Pound like best of all a sort of infinite regression of conjurors, according to which Tiresias's ghost is raised up by Odysseus, and Odysseus is raised up by Homer, and Homer is raised up by Divus, and Divus is raised up by Pound.

Benedetto Varchi in Canto V is just such a secondary intelligence, to whom Pound can appeal for help. But Varchi is not a translator, or a visionary, or a mythographer; Varchi is a historian, pondering the morality of a crime: was the murder of Alessandro de' Medici, in 1537, by his cousin Lorenzino de' Medici, *pia o empia?* – pious or impious? Was the murder a petty revenge, or a noble, Brutus-like attempt to save Florence from tyranny? With Canto V Pound enters history; and with history comes indecision, insecurity of analysis, uncertainty about events themselves. The mythic metamorphoses of Canto IV provide sharp focus and escape from pain; but history provides only blurred interpretations and endless mutation of pain. Pound admired Varchi for his impartiality, his refusal to assert more than he knew; but there is some peril in writing a poem so chaste, so reticent about assertion, that the reader is left to scratch his or her head, unable to understand either the meaning of the facts or the facts themselves.

The other novelty of Canto V is its elaboration of voice. Canto IV is a slide-projection of lovely pictures, an extension of the imagist principle of superposition. But Canto V is full of the sound of speech, from Varchi's elegant and inconclusive musings to the exclamation "Sink the damn thing!" (concerning the tossing of Giovanni Borgia's corpse into the Tiber, in 1497). Pound filled *Three Cantos* back in 1917 with all sorts of exclamations ("Hang it all" is the first phrase of the poem), but most of the exclamations are the poet's voice. But by Canto V the poet's own voice is quiet; and the silence is filled by other voices, loud or whispery. *The Cantos* will grow still more vociferous as it evolves. In Canto VI, for example, Pound tells the story of the troubadour Bernart de Ventadour: how his music seduced the wife of his patron Eblis III, how Eblis shut up his wife in prison in revenge. But Pound tells the story in Bernart's own voice; and Bernart quotes the Provençal title of the song with which he captivated the wife, "Que la lauzeta mover" ("When I see the lark a-moving," *SR*, 41). Probably Pound intended the reader to hear Bernart's leaping, subtle melody as an undertone to the words – for the Cantos, the Songs, are now beginning to fill with music. Cantos V and VI resound with intelligent or exuberant voices; by Canto VII, a Canto of old men, grave, withered, the voices have mostly dwindled to a kind of muttering, "Dry casques of departed locusts / speaking a shell of speech . . . The words rattle: shells given out by shells" (VII/26–27). The project of *The Cantos* now seems an attempt to animate a dead or dying language; to remember and re-speak the words of power, spoken long ago but still echoing in the mind.

Though Pound was reluctant to say so in public, *The Cantos* have a certain aspect of mediumship, as if a poem were a seance through which the voices of the dead could reverberate among the living. In *Three Cantos* I, Pound wrote, "Ghosts move about me / Patched with histories" (TC, 54); and often these ghosts use the poet as a kind of speaking-trumpet. In Pound's very earliest work, there is a sense that the poet must empty himself of identity, until he becomes an achromatic medium, an ectoplasm on which the souls of the great dead can take shape, as he writes in "Histrion" (1908; *CEP*, 71).

Yeats, of course, spent a great deal of time participating in spiritualist experiments, and the period of Pound's close association with Yeats coincides with the beginning of the Cantos. Pound wrote to his fiancée Dorothy Shakespear in 1913, "I read ghosts to the eagle [Yeats]" (*P/DS*, 274), and also "As for the soul being 'mixed up' I dare say we've the whole divina commedia going on inside of us" (*P/DS*, 206). When he began *The Cantos* two years later, he attended to the many voices in the mixed-up soul, to the infernal and heavenly noises all jumbled together within him.

Cantos II, VIII–XI (1922)

During 1920 and 1921 Pound evidently wrote no Cantos. Instead, he finished *Hugh Selwyn Mauberley* – a poem about an ineffectual, morbidly self-involved artist, sometimes regarded as an attempt to dispell the finesses and lethargies that prevented Pound from making much progress on the Cantos. And he wrote an opera, *Le Testament,* devising his own music for texts of François Villon. And he engaged himself with his fellow modernists, first by arranging to meet Joyce at Sirmione, then by performing his famous "Caesarean Operation" on the text of Eliot's *The Waste Land*. These experiences profoundly changed the future Cantos, and even changed Pound's relationship to the Cantos already written.

The Waste Land follows, to a degree, the model of Cantos V–VII: ragged textual surfaces imprinted with voices ("My nerves are bad to-night"; "Well now that's done: and I'm glad it's over") often juxtaposed abruptly, and interspersed with spangles hinting at a kind of remote aesthetic relief ("Those are pearls that were his eyes"; "Inexplicable splendour of Ionian white and gold"). Indeed, *The Waste Land,* even before Pound started cutting it, almost seemed more a part of the Pound canon than the Eliot canon, due to its piecemeal construction and the failure of the coordinating sensibility to coordinate the parts properly: the role that Varchi plays in Canto V, or that Pound himself plays in the *Three Cantos*, Tiresias plays in *The Waste Land.* Eliot's poem was originally titled *He Do the Police in Different Voices*, and that could also serve as a secret title of the early Cantos as well: for from Canto V onward the Cantos are a set of impersonations, as the poet's voice reels back through history and myth, trying to discover the authentic voice that can rectify the modern world, that can say what the thunder said.

The Waste Land and the Cantos are both comedies, sometimes divine comedies, sometimes hilarious comedies, sometimes sickening comedies, but in all cases the ideal reader is a comedian, an expert vocal mime who can speak the highbrow lines in a highbrow voice ("Go with your lutes, awaken / The summer within her mind, / Who hath not Helen for peer" – VIII/30), foreign accents in a cartoon voice ("Looka vat youah Trotzsk is done, e iss / madeh deh zhamefull peace!!" – XVI/74), and the Bronx cheers and backrubbing noises with idiot emphasis ("woh woh araha thumm, bhaaa" – XX/93; "thkk, thgk" – XXXIX/193). There seems to be no master voice in the Cantos, no default background voice that reliably engages when the vocal *tours de force* are complete. Indeed, even as early as 1916, Pound *talked* in the polyvocal style of the Cantos, as Iris Barry noted: "His is almost a wholly original accent, the base of American mingled with a dozen assorted 'English society' and Cockney accents inserted in mockery, French, Spanish, and Greek exclamation, strange cries and catcalls, the whole very oddly inflected, with dramatic pauses and *diminuendos*."[2] Charles Ives – an American composer with several points of resemblance to Pound – once wrote, "I think there must be a place in the soul / all made of tunes" ("The Things Our Fathers Loved," 1917). Pound's soul was made of voices, voices occasionally rising into melody.

But the typical strategy in the Cantos of 1922 – the ones then numbered VIII–XII and now numbered II and VIII–XI – is not the choppy polyphony of V–VII; instead, Pound develops two sustained voices, that of Acoetes in II and Sigismundo Malatesta in VIII–XI. This is not the method of *The Waste Land*, even though the first Malatesta Canto begins with the line "These fragments you have shelved (shored)" (VIII/28) – clearly echoing (to Eliot's displeasure) a famous line at the end of *The Waste Land. The Waste Land* will remain an abiding presence in the Cantos: a snatch of Eliot's serving-maid is heard in the line "five abortions and died of the last" (XXXVIII/187), and Pound's line "crab for an eye, and 30

fathom of fishes" (XXXIX/194) echoes an *unused* passage from the manuscript of *The Waste Land*, "Full fathom five your Bleistein lies . . . Graves'
Disease in a dead jew's eyes! / Where the crabs have eat the lids."[3] But the
Cantos of 1922 aggressively distance themselves from the procedures of
The Waste Land, as if Pound needed to differentiate his work from Eliot's
triumph. Eliot gathers fragments to shore against his ruins from all over
the place; but Pound, in the Malatesta Cantos, gathers his fragments from
one source, the battered Tempio that Malatesta labored to build.

First came the Canto about Acoetes, the humble pilot who found on his
boat a surprising passenger, the god Dionysus, first disguised as "a young
boy loggy with vine-must" (II/7); when the boat is hijacked by thugs, eager
to sell the young boy into slavery, the god reveals his power in series of
dazzling metamorphoses, first summoning from thin air the Bacchic totems
("hot breath on my ankles, / Beasts like shadows in glass, / A furred tail upon
nothingness" – II/8), then transforming the thugs into monsters ("Black snout
of a porpoise / where Lycabs had been . . . Fish-scales over groin muscles"
– II/9). Pound was (justifiably) proud of his accomplishment in this Canto;
he even thought of discarding all the previous Cantos and starting the
whole project afresh, as if the premise of *The Cantos* should be Travels
with Dionysus: as Pound mused just after finishing the Acoetes Canto, "I
dare say it wd. be easier to cut the 7 preceding cantos & let Acoetes
continue = only I dont see how I cd. get him to Bayswater" (*P/F*, 67). It
should be noted that, at least for a moment, Pound toyed with the notion
of *The Cantos* as a single voyage, evidently beginning in mythic antiquity
and continuing to modern times and familiar civilized places. Of course
Pound quickly abandoned this scheme, if he ever seriously proposed it –
though the fact that, when he published *A Draft of XVI Cantos* in 1925,
he designated the Acoetes Canto as the new Canto II shows the growing
prestige and priority of the theme of the sailor who beholds metamorphoses. It is possible that, for Pound, the many sailors of the Cantos –
Odysseus, Acoetes, Hanno the Navigator (in Canto XL) – are versions of
one sailor, their voyages the scattered traces of one voyage. Eliot noted
in the footnote to line 218 of *The Waste Land* that "Tiresias . . . is the
most important personage in the poem, uniting all the rest . . . all the women
are one woman, and the two sexes unite in Tiresias." Pound would have
resisted any attempt to smear away all distinctions from person to person, but the resourceful sailors all share a certain common tonality. Even
the Odysseus of the opening of *The Cantos* does not speak with the
pure voice of Homer: he springs from the translation of a translation,
"Done into an approximation of the metre of the Anglo-Saxon 'Sea-farer' "

(*TC*, 309) – his voice from the beginning has overtones of other farers on other seas.

As Canto II suggests, *The Cantos* is both an enchantment and a disenchantment. A disenchantment, in that metamorphosis leads ugly things to distend, flatten, bristle, grow scaly, manifest their ugliness: Lycabs with a porpoise-snout has lost his false human face, has shown what he really is. An enchantment, in that metamorphosis is the basic controlling force of human evolution. In 1921 – the year before Canto II – Pound wrote:

> Let us suppose man capable of exteriorizing a new organ, horn, halo, Eye of Horus. Given a brain of this power, comes the question, what organ, and to what purpose?
>
> But man goes on making new faculties ... You have every exploited "hyperæsthesia," i.e., every new form of genius, from the faculty of hearing four parts in a fugue perfectly, to the ear for money ... (*PDD*, 210)

Pound's ultimate hope for *The Cantos* might have been to hasten the evolution of a new human race, a race that sprouted horns, whiskers, antennae sensitive to divine tremblings in the ether.

The next Cantos – VIII–XI – turn from myth to history: from Acoetes to the landlocked Odysseus of fifteenth-century Rimini, the warlord Sigismundo Malatesta, ever harassed, ever trying to construct his private Ithaca, the Tempio. These four Cantos are the most coherent, chronologically intelligible sequence in the whole *Cantos*, until the Chinese dynastic Cantos LII–LXI. And yet they are as technically advanced as any of their precedessors.

Pound had been long experimenting with personae that were not (so to speak) whole-body personae, personae in which the poet was completely hidden by the mask: Pound was fascinated by personae in the form of half-masks, in which the poet only partly hid himself. In the year that he began *The Cantos*, 1915, Pound wrote "Near Perigord," in which the poet dramatizes the difficulty of finding out enough about the belligerent troubadour Bertrans de Born in order to adopt him as a persona: we see Pound gathering puzzling documents, bemusing himself with possible constructions of Bertrans' physical appearance, pretending for a moment to speak in Bertrans' voice, but at last watching the whole charade fall apart into "a broken bundle of mirrors" (*P*, 1926, 157). Sigismundo is Pound's most far-reaching experiment with the half-mask: Pound prints documents, sometimes in translation, concerning Sigismundo's life (a poem he wrote to his mistress Isotta; instructions concerning his generous patronage of the arts; a gracious letter he received from his son; a description of the bonfire at St. Peter's basilica, in which an effigy of Sigismundo was burnt, following his excommunication by Pope Pius II); but Pound is reluctant to feign Sigismundo's voice, and prefers to let "Sidge" speak for himself.

Much of the narrative is told in the third person, but Pound occasionally slips into the first person plural, as if the poet had enlisted in Malatesta's army:

> And we beat the papishes and fought
> them back through the tents
> And he came up to the dyke again
> And fought through the dyke-gate
> And it went on from dawn to sunset
> And we broke them and took their baggage   (XI/48)

The repeated *And* suggests the soldiers' inexorable advance. This technique, in which the poet retains a half-anonymous, tentative presence on the fringes of the poem, would persist in *The Cantos*; for example, in Canto LVI (1940), the excitable poet starts to affiliate his own voice with that of Yuentchang, taking arms against the Mongols:

> Li, Su, Tong and I
>   were four musketeers
> We were workmen in the same village
>   we were plain sojers together
> If we can take Chantong province, we can take Pekin
>   (LVI/308)

But there is a moment in the Malatesta Cantos, toward the end of Sigismundo's life, when the poet presents himself in a slightly different manner:

>   and came back with no pep in him
> And we sit here. I have sat here
>   for forty thousand years   (XI/50)

This might be the exaggeration of a footsoldier, whose hard life might seem forty thousand years long; but it also might be the voice of the poet of Canto IV, conjuring up the shadows of the fifteenth century in an old arena; and it also might be the voice of Eliot's Tiresias, who sat by Thebes below the wall, and walked among the lowest of the dead. Sometimes Pound's voice is focused through a mask; but sometimes it blurs, grows hollow with echoes, as if a whole Grand Canyon had opened around it. As Sigismundo's dreams crumble, as it becomes clear that his syncretic temple, in which the gods of pagan antiquity would be worshiped along with the Christian god, will never be finished, the poet starts to disengage himself from Sigismundo, to range for new ghosts.

The Malatesta Cantos were among the first written after Pound's opera, *Le Testament*; and in a sense they constitute a kind of opera without music.

Le Testament has a simple scenario: it is 1462, and Villon, soon to be hanged, is writing his will within hailing distance of a tavern, and a church, and a brothel. Villon, by bequeathing his poems to his friend Ythier, to his aged mother, to the decayed prostitute La Hëaulmiere, endows his otherwise mute companions with voices; so Villon's testament remembers and preserves a whole culture, in fragments of sound. Pound was by temperament an anthologist: and his books – *ABC of Reading*, *Guide to Kulchur*, *The Cantos* itself – represent human culture in a severely deleted condition, with all the boring and useless parts omitted. In this sense, *Le Testament* is the opera of mankind, with all the prose left out: tavern, church, brothel, these are the places that matter to all generations. The music is also pared to the bone: it consists typically of simple vocal lines, moving up and down in non-repetitive patterns, often without sharps or flats, often with a troubadour-like sound – indeed, Pound at one point borrowed an actual troubadour song, anachronistically, since the troubadours flourished more than two centuries before Villon. But Pound thought that the troubadours found melodic lines so sensitive to the words that they became an ideal for all future music to follow. The instrumentation is strange: the first song in *Le Testament* employs (among other things) a saxophone, a cymbal, a tambourine, a drum, a bassoon, and a cello, but these instruments do little, except occasionally to repeat a note or a series of notes from the vocal line, usually on the same pitch. The instruments seem less to accompany the voice than to alter the type-face of the voice, so to speak. As Pound wrote at the beginning of the score, "The 'orchestration' in the first part of the opera is not in the usual sense 'musical.' It is simply an emphasis on the consonantal & vowel sounds *of the words*" (YC).

Sigismundo was a contemporary of Villon, on a higher social plane, but equally engaged with sex, religion, and death. Instead of excerpts from testamentary poetry, Pound provides for his "score" the documents that constitute Sigismundo's testament – his generosity to painters such as Piero della Francesca, his consultation with Alberti on the architecture of the unfinished (but still preserved) Tempio. Instead of cello and bassoon, Pound provides cues that establish the right *timbre*, the right roughening of voice: the poet's own macho zest for combat ("we had smashed at Piombino and driven out" – X/46) or explicit judgments about Sigismundo's accomplishment, as when Pound visits what is left of the Tempio and notes, "The filigree hiding the gothic, / with a touch rhetoric in the whole" (IX/41). Perhaps this will serve as a judgment on *The Cantos* as well as on the Tempio that seems a stone metaphor for *The Cantos*. The typographical novelties of the Canto are addressed to the ear more than to the eye: the page layout is designed to influence the reader's perception of vocal tone:

ALL typographic disposition, placings of words *on* the page, is intended to facilitate the reader's intonation, whether he be reading silently to self or aloud to friends. Given time and technique I might even put down the musical notation of passages or "breaks into song."   (*L*, 322)

In Canto LXXXI there is a passage marked *Libretto* in the margin; and perhaps the whole series, from Canto I on, has an odd look because it is the word-book of an unwritten opera or *Singspiel*.

The Sigismundiad is one of the most impressive sequences in *The Cantos*, and many readers perhaps wish that Pound could have written more passages like it; but Pound was restless for new compositional methods as well as new subjects, and he moved on.

Cantos XII–XVI (1922–23)

By 1922, Pound realized that his project had outgrown the earlier Cantos, especially the *Three Cantos* written in 1915, and he needed to find a new beginning: "up to now it has been mainly hash, necessary beginning if I am to reconstruct the various ichthiosauri that I need later in the poem" (*P/F*, 63). And in 1922 and 1923 Pound wrote a burst of new Cantos and revised the old Cantos for publication – though *A Draft of XVI Cantos* was not published until 1925. Canto VI was substantially rewritten. *Three Cantos* III was stripped down to the translation of Odysseus's descent into the underworld and the flurry of images at its end, and turned into the new Canto I; the Canto VIII of 1922 became the new Canto II; and *Three Cantos* I and II were erased almost entirely, except for a few terse passages – chief among them the proclamation that anyone who helped El Cid would be beheaded – gathered up into the brief new Canto III. But Pound would keep an eye on the unused parts of *Three Cantos* for the rest of his life: when he needed an ichthyosaurus, there was always a fossil at hand in *Three Cantos*.

The final Cantos of *A Draft of XVI Cantos* show Pound ranging far in space and near in time. It is probable that he transposed Canto VIII in Canto II because it was part of mythological antiquity, and he thought that the first sixteen Cantos showed a certain tendency to lurch forward in chronological order: the present ceaselessly interrupts the past, and the past ceaseless interrupts the present, but Canto I begins with Homer, Cantos V–VI treat the Middle Ages (the troubadours and Eleanor of Aquitaine), Cantos VIII–XI treat the Renaissance (Sigismundo), and Canto XVI ends with the Great War of 1914–1918. Acoetes must come to Bayswater: what began in myth must end with the mundane. The contemporaneity of many of the Cantos of 1923 may owe something to *The Waste Land*: Pound, like

Eliot, needed modern England to serve as a terminus for the deformations
and degradations of history.

The Waste Land also seems related to the peculiar fable in the second
half of Canto XII: the Tale of the Honest Sailor, who was persuaded that
a baby had been taken out of his belly after he landed in the hospital,
drunk – the sailor then reformed himself, raised the lad and sent him to
college, and confessed on his deathbed:

> "I ain't your dad, no,
> "I am not your fader but your moder," quod he,
> "Your fader was a rich merchant in Stambouli"   (XII/17)

Pound also mused on the notion of male birth in a letter to Eliot from the
end of 1921, describing Pound's midwifery on *The Waste Land*:

> These are the poems of Eliot
> By the Uranian Muse begot;
> A Man their Mother was,
> A Muse their Sire.   (*L*, 170)

Perhaps the Cantos are also the children of a man's womb – as Pound
noted, also in 1921, "the brain itself, is . . . only a sort of great clot of
genital fluid" (*PDD*, 203). The Honest Sailor is the most trivial version
in the whole *Cantos* of the sailor-figure, Odysseus and Acoetes reduced to
the stick figure of a dirty joke; but insofar as the Cantos attempt to be
the total story of mankind, as that story impinged on Pound's intelligence
– the epic not of a particular culture but of the whole race – the Honest
Sailor, too, plays his part. Canto XII has been cited for introducing humor
into *The Cantos*. This may not be quite correct: there is much humor in
the earlier Cantos, and it is possible that the passage in Canto V about the
dreitz hom Pierre de Maensac, with its laborious and obfuscated parallelisms,
was intended to be a kind of self-lampoon. But Canto XII does tell the first
sustained joke in *The Cantos* – it is to the Cantos what the song of the
drunken Bozo is to *Le Testament*, a comic routine. Canto XII has the rich
Amurrikan voice of "Jim X . . ." (John Quinn, the New York businessman
who gave financial assistance to Pound and Eliot) to ape the sailor's low
accent; *Le Testament* has trombones to perform Bozo's farting and belching
for him.

The navigator of the Cantos takes a brief detour to China, in Canto XIII,
to hear the wisdom of Confucius, one of the first voices in the Cantos to
promote social order from a rational, secular perspective, rather than from
the sensitive man's attempt to align himself with divine energies – even
Sigismundo Malatesta was a visionary, who attempted to realize in architecture a dream of pagan gods. During the early 1920s, Pound was starting

his research into economics: and Confucius is the ancestor of all those same monetary thinkers – sane by Pound's lights – such as C. H. Douglas, whose prescriptions for reform would decorate many later Cantos. History can look for correction to some transcendental realm; or history may have a mechanism for self-correction, if the Confucian voices are properly heard.

And now, having looked from West to East, having looked from past to present, Pound was ready for hell and purgatory. Cantos XIV and XV are an immensely accelerated Inferno; Canto XVI is a Purgatorio. It is as if Pound had spent the first thirteen Cantos slowly creeping up to Dante, and then had exhausted two-thirds of the Divine Comedy in a few lines. Pound's reason for drastically foreshortening the tour of the less comfortable parts of the afterlife was perhaps a simple one: for Dante, hell is eternal and immutable, a sculptural frieze; but for Pound, hell is incapable of sustaining itself, a state that is always collapsing, a sort of liquid dung that falls through the fingers that try to grasp it. Samuel Beckett remarked of Joyce's *Finnegans Wake* that the modernist purgatory is different from the medieval: "Dante's is conical and consequently implies culmination. Mr Joyce's is spherical and excludes culmination."[4] Pound's hell is like Joyce's purgatory, an endless directionless slosh of movement, a dissolving that never quite falls into complete dissolution.

For Dante, a canto in hell entailed a teasing scene – why is this man carrying his head in his arms? – followed by a clear explanation of the crime and the punishment, as Pound paraphrases Bertrans de Born's speech in *Inferno* XXVIII, ll. 118–42:

> Goes on that headless trunk, that bears for light
> Its own head swinging, gripped by the dead hair,
> And like a swinging lamp that says, "Ah me!
> I severed men, my head and heart
> Ye see here severed, my life's counterpart." (P, 1926, 156)

But for Pound, the denizens of hell had lost most of their identities – even their names have almost eroded away:

> The stench of wet coal, politicians
> . . . . e and . . . . . n, their wrists bound to their ankles,
> Standing bare bum (XIV/61)

As Pound commented, "Even the XIV–XV has individuals in it, but *not* worth recording as such . . . [An editor] tried to get the number of . . . . correct in each case. My 'point' being that not even the first but only last letters of their names had resisted corruption" (L, 293). The dots in the passage cited above stand for "Lloyd George" and "Wilson" – whose resolution of the First World War Pound considered a loathsome capitulation to the interests of profiteers.

Pound is here operating in the mode of the Dionysus of Canto II, who transformed the slave-traders into fish: Pound squashes Lloyd George and Wilson into a fitting shape. In this extremely disarticulated place, the distinction between buttocks and head has vanished: the politicians have been (so to speak) folded in two and then flattened in a steam press. The limit of monstrousness in Pound's imagination is the displacement of sense organs – eye on buttock, tongue in anus – as the human form turns into a jumble, a plate of spaghetti. *The Cantos* makes up a poem about voices, and here human voices have turned into farts, simulations of oratory with intestinal gas, a complete disarticulation of speech. At the bottom of the *Inferno*, only a few feet from Satan himself, Dante placed Nimrod, a giant sunk to his waist in the frozen ground, babbling incomprehensible words because he had built the impious Tower of Babel and forever shattered the integrity of language (*Inferno* XXXI): but for Pound all the residents of hell are Nimrods, uttering meaningless noise, "the arse-belching of preachers" (XIV/63).

Hell is, to some degree, a bad bank. It is full of "usurers squeezing crab-lice . . . obstructors of distribution" (XIV/63) – usury, to Pound, was the attempt to create profit without increase of labor or commodities or any true value; the entropy of money. The excrementitiousness of money, a thesis dear to Freud, has rarely been presented so vividly as in Pound's *Cantos*. But hell is chiefly a bad printing press. The loudest noise in Pound's hell seems to be "howling, as of a hen-yard in a printing-house, / the clatter of presses, / the blowing of dry dust and stray paper" (XIV/61–62). The great theme of the hell Cantos is the degradation of language, both spoken and written. Through the first thirteen Cantos, Pound sought and displayed the most potent texts and voices he could find; here Pound mangles, smears, unwrites, unspeaks, the texts and voices that need to be consigned to oblivion.

Finally, in Canto XV, the tourist Pound uses a clever optical trick to escape from hell: with a mirror, Medusa's petrifying gaze is angled down to the ground, creating a solid path amid the general diarrhea. It is a proof of the power of light to resist mud. In Canto XVI, we emerge from the "hell mouth" onto a

> dry plain
> and two mountains;
> On the one mountain . . . in hard steel
> The road like a slow screw's thread,
> The angle almost imperceptible,
> so that the circuit seemed hardly to rise   (XVI/68)

The mount of purgatory climbs toward heaven at a rate so slow that it may be no ascent at all. The Canto goes on to reminiscences of those who fought in the Great War, those who died, such as Gaudier-Brzeska and T. E. Hulme, and those who lived, such as Wyndham Lewis and Hemingway. These names have not been effaced: Pound memorializes them. But the purgatory of the war kills or cripples or leaves unharmed, not according to any principle of moral consequence, but at random. It is hard to be sure whether this is a fault in Pound's ethical design of the Cantos, or whether he meant to imply that, in the twentieth century, we have reached a state beyond even the possibility of justice.

Cantos XVII–XXIII (1925)

A Draft of XVI Cantos does not finish strongly, but the ending has a certain cliffhanger quality: here is hell, here is purgatory – now where is heaven? This was a question that Pound was not prepared to answer directly. But he was full of energy to write, and the next seven Cantos followed quickly: Cantos XVII–XXIII were all written by March 1925.

Canto XVII begins with an explosion of Dionysiac energies: "So that the vines burst from my fingers . . . ZAGREUS! IO ZAGREUS! . . . the goddess of the fair knees . . . with white hounds / leaping about her" (XVII/76). But soon we are in Venice, exceedingly beautiful, with its gilt beams, its dye-pots in the torch-light, its "trees growing in water, / Marble trunks . . . The light now, not of the sun" (XVII/76). Nothing in this depiction of Venice is specifically ominous or morbid, and yet there is an undertone of the artificiality, of surrogation: marble columns have replaced tree-trunks. The placement of Canto XVII makes the reader look for paradise: but Canto XVII neither offers paradise nor refuses paradise – it simply gives something that is *like* a paradise. Substitute paradises, which will dominate the Cantos from this point on, appeared as early as *Three Cantos* III and will soon appear in Canto XX with the lotus-eaters who "Feared neither death nor pain for this beauty; / If harm, harm to ourselves" (XX/93).

Canto XX offers a rare case of a Canto for which Pound offered his own glosses and interpretation, in a letter to his father:

> Nicolo d'Este in sort of delirium after execution of Parisina and Ugo . . .
> Various things keep crossing up in the poem. The original world of the gods; the Trojan War, Helen on the wall of Troy with the old men fed up with the whole show and suggesting she be sent back to Greece . . .
> Then in the delirium Nicolo remembers or thinks he is watching death of Roland. Elvira on wall or Toro (subject-rhyme with Helen on Wall) . . . The whole reminiscence jumbled or "candied" in Nicolo's delirium. Take that as

a sort of bounding surface from which one gives the main subject of the Canto, the lotophagoi: lotus eaters, or respectable dope smokers; and general paradiso. You have had a hell in Canti XIV, XV, purgatorio in XVI etc.

(*SL*, 210)

Niccolò d'Este married a very young woman, Parisina Malatesta (a cousin of Sigismundo's), but discovered she was sleeping with his own illegitimate son Ugo – and so he had them both killed. It is not surprising that Pound would think to intercut this tale with allusions to other beautiful wives who ran off with attractive men, from Helen and Paris onward; what *is* surprising is his announcement that such affiliations are part of a psychological process, a delirium within a persona. He seems to be returning to the mode of the *Three Cantos* of 1915, with the role of the matrix-intelligence being played by Niccolò, instead of Pound himself. But Pound has taught us too well in the intervening years: we read this Canto (unless coached to do otherwise) as a flat surface, or a montage of flat surfaces, in which Niccolò and Helen of Troy and Charlemagne's brave Roland all cohabit on the same plane.

Pound evidently felt that he could establish Niccolò as a controlling sensibility, flowing over and around the rest of the material in the Canto; but he did nothing to bring Niccolò far enough into the poem's foreground to achieve that effect. And the invitation to regard Canto XX as a prince's delirium, or as a construct of dope smoking, is also an invitation to deride Pound himself. Just as it is dangerous to announce that *The Cantos* are a rag-bag, so it is dangerous to announce that *The Cantos* are a fever dream. It is odd that Pound would have chosen to interpret Canto XX, because this very Canto begins with an affirmation of the inexplicability of old texts: Pound records a visit to a Professor Lévy, the World's Leading Authority on Provençal – he asked Lévy what Arnaut's word *noigandres* means, only to be told that Lévy used to ask himself every night, " 'Now what the DEFFILL can that mean!' " (XX/90). Pound asks the questions of his readers for us.

The lotus-eaters offer a false relief from the torment of Niccolò's existence, an *Ersatz* of paradise. Paradise is one major theme of Cantos XVII to XXIII; another is economics. This set of Cantos is full of munitions-merchants and exploiters of labor; their patron saint appears near the beginning of the sequence: Kubla Khan.

It should be noted that Kubla Khan, who in Coleridge's poetry is the builder of Xanadu, appears in Pound's poetry as a debaucher of currency. Pound liked to rectify the errors of "romantical" poets: in 1959 Pound quoted genuine documents of Justinian's Constantinople ("Mr Yeats called it Byzantium" (XCVI/681), setting forth the penalties for selling wine at false measure, or for building a wall that falls down – as if Pound were show-ing that civic magnificence could be achieved honestly through a good law code, instead of existing precariously in the dreams of an ignorant poet. Coleridge's Kubla Khan had dwindled to Kubla "Kahn," as if he were an early member of Pound's Jewish Banking Conspiracy (XVIII/80).

Just as paradise is difficult to find in a welter of substitute paradises, so money is confounded by substitute money. In *A Draft of XVI Cantos*, it is usually quite easy to tell the light from the mud; but from Canto XVII evaluation, discrimination, start to become far more difficult. We are still in purgatory, though teased by gorgeous glimpses that may or may not have something to do with heaven.

Cantos XXIV–XXX (1925–28)

Between 1925 and 1928, Pound wrote Cantos XXIV–XXVII, and then published all the Cantos written after *A Draft of XVI Cantos* as *A Draft of the Cantos 17–27* (1928). Cantos XXIV–XXVII begin by recounting more of the life of Niccolò d'Este – his Odysseus-like travels through the Mediterranean, his subtlety and benevolence as a ruler – but the main theme of these Cantos is Venice: Pound, like many other poets, was attracted to the spectacle of Venice sinking into Adriatic slime as a metaphor for the foundering and decay of old glory. There is some light in these Cantos, but a great deal of mud: the degeneration of the guild spirit of good craftsman-ship, the degeneration of the painter's relation to his patron, the degenera-tion of painting itself.

But in some respects this period was more notable for Pound's explana-tions of Cantos than for the Cantos themselves. During 1927–28 Pound made the most intense effort to understand what he had done, and what he was trying to do. In 1927 he wrote to his father:

> Afraid the whole damn poem is rather obscure . . . Have I ever given you outline of main scheme ::: or whatever it is?
> 1. Rather like, or unlike subject and response and counter subject in fugue.
> A. A. Live man goes down into world of Dead
> C. B. The "repeat in history"
> B. C. The "magic moment" of moment of metamorphosis, bust thru from quotidien into "divine or permanent world." Gods, etc.   (*SL*, 210)

It is likely that Pound devised this scheme by noting that the first two Cantos displayed (1) a descent into hell and (2) a metamorphosis, in which the normal world buckles and the divine world breaks through. As for the third element, the "repeat in history," it is certainly the chief constructive principle of the Cantos: the achronological superposition of stories with common formal elements, such as married women abducted by handsome young lovers. Later in this letter Pound explicated Canto XX, and used the phrase "subject-rhyme": a fascinating term, implying that Pound has displaced the principle of rhyme from the level of phonics to the level of theme: history itself displays a structure of echoes, a sort of stanza form. As early as 1912 Pound discovered that a landscape in southern France could shape itself in the manner of a poem:

> The r[oa]d. to Celles is indeed a sort of sestina, of cusp & hills,
> of prospects opened & shut, or round trees & poplars aligned.
> sestina vs. recurrence in nature. (WTSF, 15)

A sestina is a poem in which the same six words, falling at the line-ends of each six-line stanza, reappear in a different order in the subsequent stanzas. The route's varied monotony – hills alternating with valleys, round trees alternating with tall, thin poplars – made Pound conceive the road to Celles as a kind of landscape-projection of the sestina: the even recurrence of trees and hills seemed a prosody of objects, rising and falling like the stressed and unstressed syllables of a line of poetry. In some sense the Cantos, as Pound conceived them in 1927, are to history what this landscape is to geography: a mapping of recurrence in time, *heard* as a subtle chiming, as if history were an endless troubadour song, a huge *canto*. The tripartite design of descent into "world of Dead" (hell), "bust thru from quotidien" (heaven), and "repeat in history" (our world – or purgatory) suggests that there is a whole divine comedy in every Canto, all mixed up together.

Pound's use of the word *fugue* is also fascinating. Pound's opera *Le Testament* is fugueless, almost completely without counterpoint of any sort – indeed, Pound's major musical interest so far had been the troubadour song, with its single vocal line. And he conceived the earlier Cantos either as collages of pictures or as successions of voices. But now he wanted to hear the voices in the Cantos, not as taking regular turns, but as *sounding all at once*, in an overlapping vocal polyphony. While the metamorphosis begins, the descent to the underworld continues; while the voice of Jim X . . . tells the story of the Honest Sailor, the voice of Sigismundo continues somewhere in the background. Pound strains his ear to grasp history ahistorically, as a chorus of voices all of which are co-present, contemporaneous.

But if Pound hoped that a fugal model of *The Cantos* would impart a satisfying form to the whole project, he was mistaken. As the musicologist Donald Tovey has noted, a fugue is not a form, but a texture: "The first thing to realize about fugue is that it is a medium, like blank verse, not a thing, like a rondo."[5] It requires extraordinary art to make a satisfactory fugue, but the art is a local art, an art of arranging overlaps in a pleasing manner, not a global art. It is the sort of art that a poet gifted at writing lyrical miniatures, like Pound, could employ to produce one of the longest poems in the language. Pound may have been aware, however, that the hope that *The Cantos* would become a rounded, polished, formally satisfying whole was a forlorn hope: the year after he described the tripartite scheme to his father, he wrote: "I am not going to say: 'form' is a non-literary component shoved on to literature by Aristotle . . . But it can do us no harm . . . to consider the number of very important chunks of world-literature in which form, major form, is remarkable mainly for its absence" (*LE*, 394).

In February 1928 Pound tried to explain *The Cantos* to Yeats, who remembered his explanation as follows:

> Now at last he explains that it will, when the hundredth canto is finished, display a structure like that of a Bach Fugue. There will be no plot, no chronicle of events, no logic of discourse, but two themes, the Descent into Hades from Homer, a Metamorphosis from Ovid, and, mixed with these, mediaeval or modern historical characters . . . He has scribbled on the back of an envelope certain sets of letters that represent emotions or archetypal events – I cannot find any adequate definition – A B C D and then J K L M, and then each set of letters repeated, and then A B C D inverted and this repeated, and then a new element X Y Z, then certain letters that never recur . . . and all set whirling together.　　　(*A Vision*, 3–5)

Pound was exasperated with the attention that Yeats's description received: "CONFOUND uncle Bill YEATS' paragraph on fuge . . . more wasted ink due his 'explanation,' than you cd. mop up with a moose hide" (*P/I*, 35). Yeats was not always a reliable reporter, but there seems little reason for doubting Yeats's account. Yeats's word "whirling" recalls the vorticism of the mid-1910s, when the Cantos began; Yeats's phrase "no logic of discourse" recalls many of Pound's statements on the anti-discursive qualities of the art he espoused; and the notion of a fugue has the sanction of Pound's letter to his father. What is new in Yeats's account is the concept of retrograde permutation: first A B C D, then D C B A.

Retrograde is certainly a manner of defeating chronology: if order is so arbitrary that the elements can be placed indifferently forward or backward, then time's arrow is blunted. But the Cantos were slow to emancipate themselves from clock and calendar: many sequences, including *A Draft of XVI Cantos*, show a distinct chronological structure; and, although the later Cantos are sometimes more adventurous, it is often possible to establish a sort of base-epoch for a Canto or for a sequence of Cantos.

Of course, the transposition of the terms of history itself is far more ambitious than the transposition of the terms of a cliché: it is one thing to say, "conquest exhausted by the Alsace Lorraine of Europe"; it is another thing to scramble the chronology of 4,000 years of epic events in the search for an achronological pattern. And yet there is a sense in which we can take the Cantos as a Dada project: insofar as Pound accepted a model of the Cantos based on permutation, a tendency toward acid satire would become manifest. Pound surely wanted to build stone, build a new Tempio through the Cantos, as well as to eat away the old stone of worthless things. But it is no accident that, in the late 1920s, at the very moment when he conceived the Cantos according to a somewhat Dadaist model, he wrote a series of burningly satirical Cantos – deconstructions, not constructions; and it is no accident that, at the very moment when he conceived the Cantos as a fugue, the Cantos start to resound with music more loudly than after before. Music and satire become explicit, as Pound's new model for what he had done started to influence what he was doing.

The most striking music in the whole Cantos – perhaps in all modernist poetry – occurs in Canto XXV:

> ... the flute: pone metum. ... [Lat.: put aside fear]
> Form, forms and renewal, gods held in the air,
> Forms seen, and then clearness,
> Bright void, without image, Napishtim, [Babylonian sage]
> Casting his gods back into the νοῦς [Gr.: mind]
>
> "as the sculptor sees the form in the air ...
> "as glass seen under water ...
> and saw the waves taking form as crystal,
> notes as facets of air,
> and the mind there, before them, moving,
> so that notes needed not move. (XXV/119)

The music seems to freeze before the poet's eyes into visible sine waves, vitreous, glistening, a string of swells and tapers like a necklace of translucent cowrie shells. This arrested sound-wave can be studied, like sculpture, from any angle: a reified audibility, comprehended into a breathless instantaneity of being. In a fugue all the musical material tends to be co-present; and in this Canto, melopoeia, the poetry of the musical phrase, turns into phanopoeia, the poetry that casts images before the visual imagination.

The later Cantos in this sequence become less explicitly musical, more satirical. In Canto XXVII, the Xarites – the Graces – confront tovarisch – the comrade, a plodding, strictly political man, who "wrecked the house of the tyrants" (XXVII/131) and seems unable to respond to the antique lovelinesses that hover over him; this is a Canto not about building stone, but about smashing it. In Canto XXIX, Pound presents a young numbskull named Juventus, also tantalized by glimpses of the glories beyond the earth's. This aria constitutes an all-too-close-for-comfort spoof of neo-Platonic transcendentalisms from Pound's *The Spirit of Romance* (XXIX/143; *SR*, 92) and elsewhere. The more closely Pound approaches a Dadaist model for the Cantos, the more desecrated the whole project becomes: even Pound's own holy things start to grow farcical before his acid gaze.

In 1930 Pound decided to gather *A Draft of XVI Cantos*, *A Draft of the Cantos 17–27*, and three new Cantos into a summary volume, the accomplishment of fifteen years of work: *A Draft of XXX Cantos* (1930). The last Canto in this group feels like an ending: instead of the farce of some of these Cantos preceding, Canto XXX is sober and clear. It presents the major antitheses of the Cantos – light and mud – as two great personifications: Artemis, a goddess cleansing the world of foulness, in a Chaucer-like "Compleynt . . . Agaynst Pity" (XXX/147); and Madame ΎΛΗ (Hyle, Gr. for *wood* or *matter*), who stands for the materiality of the world, all opacity, resistance to illumination, love of death; her chief worshiper seems to be Pedro, the fourteenth-century Portuguese king, who dug up the skeleton of the woman he loved and set it on the throne beside him. Pound originally told this story in *Three Cantos* II – and its position at the end of *A Draft of XXX Cantos* suggests the degree to which the whole Cantos whirligig out of the original version of 1915.

But the last part of Canto XXX is devoted, not to Artemis and Madame ΎΛΗ, but to a document about the development of the cursive type-face in 1503 – a means for turning printed books into works of art. Pound concludes this huge installment of his life's work with typography: just as Sigismundo controlled all the decoration of his Tempio, devoted to the old gods of Greece and Rome, so Pound controls the appearance of his private Tempio, the printed book that the reader holds in hand. The Cantos threatened to disperse into the fluid permutation of fleeting elements, A B C D and X Y Z; but at the end of this large sequence the project once again aspires to weight, solidity of design.

Cantos XXXI–XLI (1934)

Eleven New Cantos XXXI–XLI (1934) followed quickly after *A Draft of XXX Cantos*; after Pound clarified his method and his themes to himself, he could work faster, it seemed. One of the chief accomplishments of this series was the establishing of an eleven-canto sequence (what Pound would call a decad) as the basic chunk in which new Cantos would appear. The "major form" of this decad is simple, but effective: these eleven Cantos pivot around Canto XXXVI, the middle Canto, which has a texture far different from the five before it and the five after it.

The first five Cantos take the arch of the Venetian sequence XXIV–XXVII and transpose it to America: Pound tells the story of the flowering of genius among the early American presidents, and the subsequent decay. We hear the inquisitive, well-educated, very adult-sounding voices of Adams, Jefferson, John Quincy Adams: studying European architecture, planning canals, civilizing the Indians, finding rice and turnips adapted to the American climate. But the focus of the American shaping intelligence soon starts to blur, and little corrupt leaders – Clay, Calhoun, Webster – start to take over; soon we are in the world of child labor, mud, and mid-European stupidity, coarseness, and venality; at the end of this group, Madame ῞ΥΛΗ herself puts in an appearance, all tarted up (XXXV/175).

The transition from Canto XXXV to Canto XXXVI is one of the most startling in the whole project. Instead of heavy Jewish accents, and descriptions of heavy tolls on heavy cargoes, we have this:

> A lady asks me
> > I speak in season
> > She seeks reason for an affect, wild often
> > That is so proud he hath Love for a name . . .
> Where memory liveth,
> > it takes its state
> Formed like a diafan from light on shade . . .
> Cometh from a seen form which being understood
> Taketh locus and remaining in the intellect possible
> Wherein hath he neither weight nor still-standing,
> Descendeth not by quality but shineth out
> Himself his own effect unendingly . . .   (XXXVI/177)

This is a translation of a poem that Pound had been laboring to translate since his youth, Guido Cavalcanti's *canzone*, *Donna mi priegha*. The calm intensity of this poem makes it the axis of *Eleven New Cantos*, the still point in its turning world. Guido's *canzone* describes with extreme subtlety – indeed so subtly that Pound himself never claimed fully to understand the whole poem – the psychic processes through which Love imprints itself on the memory; how Love fills the whole mind with love, a self-generating motive force. The psychological inwardness of Canto XXXVI sets it apart; it might be conceived as a complement to all the other Cantos Pound ever wrote, in that it describes the mind's receptivity to those divine energies, those dazzles that intermit the gloom. Here we have a cool subjectivization of the gods; this Canto corresponds to the other Cantos as persona corresponds to images – a mental device for assimilating the glories at the edge of the visual field.

Canto XXXVI provides only a brief respite from " 'The fifth element: mud' " (XXXIV/166). By Canto XXXVII we are back in America, amid the snarlings and yelpings of the financiers, and their political stooges, eager to deprave the American economy by manipulating the second National Bank. And in Canto XXXVIII the munitions-sellers will return, to foment war and increase useless consumption of goods. But the last five Cantos have a different texture from the first five: instead of a fairly steady fingering-through-documents that illustrate the triumph and decline of America, the last five Cantos are riddled with rays of light, from a variety of plausible paradises. For example, Canto XXXVIII offers a peculiar glance at Marconi, kneeling before the Pope:

> (and the Pope's manners were so like Mr. Joyce's . . .)
> Marconi knelt in the ancient manner
>   like Jimmy Walker sayin' his prayers.
> His Holiness expressed a polite curiosity
>   as to how His Excellency had chased those
> electric shakes through the a'mosphere.   (XXXVIII/187)

The Pope ought to be an expert in spiritual transmission and reception – but Marconi seems to have replaced him. This whole passage is satirical, very much in the mode of *Hugh Selwyn Mauberley*: we have the press for wafer, franchise for circumcision, and radio waves for beams of divine guidance. But Pound took electromagnetic radiation (at least half seriously) as a method of conceiving the pagan gods appropriate to the limited bandwidth of the Modernist intellectual spectrum, as he elaborated in his essay "Calvacanti" (*LE*, 154). Potentially Marconi's radio-waves can stimulate divine excitements, in those who possess sufficiently sensitive antennae; but, as so often in Cantos XVII–XXX, it is not certain what is parody and what is paradise.

As the decad comes to a close, Pound orients the sequence by referring it back to the original themes of Cantos I and II: Odysseus on his way to the underworld, and the metamorphosis of "bust thru." These two are combined in Canto XXXIX, adapted from Homer's account of Odysseus's sojourn with Circe, and figured with some of Homer's original Greek. It is likely that Canto XXXIX demonstrates how the tripartite scheme of Pound's letter of 1927 was starting to control the actual substance of the Cantos written after it. Still, the Odysseus of Canto XXXIX has altered considerably from the sober, intent, troubled, "Seafarer"-like character of Canto I.

The Odysseus of the 1930s is a slangier, hipper, more casual, more cosmopolitan character entirely:

> Fat panther lay by me
> Girls talked there of fucking, beasts talked there of eating,
> All heavy with sleep, fucked girls and fat leopards,
> Lions loggy with Circe's tisane   (XXXIX/193)

Pound tended to become flippant with his major characters as his applications of the scheme of 1927 grew slightly mechanical. By 1938 Pound was calling the Homeric world "very human. The *Odyssey* high-water mark for the adventure story, as for example Odysseus on the spar after shipwreck. Sam Smiles [a writer of pop self-help books] never got any further in preaching self-reliance" (*GK*, 38). By 1955, when Pound wrote the Canto that treats Odysseus on the spar, he imagined Leucothea offering Odysseus a trade: " 'my bikini is worth your raft' " (XCI/636).

But if Odysseus is growing more amusing, Pound's devotion to pagan ideals is growing more intense. Later in Canto XXXIX, Pound writes of a headland "with the Goddess' eyes to seaward / By Circeo, by Terracina, with the stone eyes" (XXXIX/195). This passage restates Pound's "Credo" of 1930:

> Given the material means I would replace the statue of Venus on the cliffs of Terracina [a town on the Tyrrhenian sea, between Rome and Naples]. I would erect a temple to Artemis in Park Lane. I believe that a light from Eleusis persisted through the middle ages and set beauty to the song of Provence and of Italy.   (*SP*, 53)

Pound considered that belief in Venus and Mars and Bacchus had never been exterminated by Christianity, but had maintained a clandestine existence throughout the centuries, occasionally flickering into public consciousness – in the songs of the troubadours, in the heretical Cathar religion attacked by Christian armies during the Albigensian Crusade of the thirteenth century, in the Tempio of Sigismundo. From the time of *Three Cantos* on, Pound conceived the Cantos as a reconstruing of history according to pagan terms – as if Pound could recreate a liturgy for Dionysus.

But the volume *Eleven New Cantos* ends on a note of secular, as well as religious, hope:

> Ma questo,"
>   said the Boss, "è divertente."
> catching the point before the aesthetes had got there;
> Having drained off the muck by Vada
> From the marshes, by Circeo, where no one else wd. have drained it.
>   (XLI/202)

The Boss is Benito Mussolini: Pound gave a copy of *A Draft of XXX Cantos* to *il Duce*, who consented to an audience with the poet; Mussolini told Pound that he found *The Cantos* diverting. This power of discernment impressed Pound more than it has impressed others, since "diverting" is a comment that could be applied to almost any text; but Pound thought that Mussolini had recognized a fellow genius. Pound associated Circeo with Circe: for the purposes of *The Cantos*, the draining of the marshes of Circeo is equivalent to ridding the world of vile transformations; under the benign gaze of Mussolini, pigs are changing back into men. Wherever Pound looks, at the end of this most optimistic of all the batches of Cantos, he sees signs that, despite the general degradation, social virtue is taking hold in a few fortunate places: Mussolini's Italy; and a small town in Austria called Woergl (XLI/205), where the residents grew prosperous, while the surrounding towns were caught in poverty: the authorities issued their own local money, stamped with a date, which steadily lost value if hoarded and not spent. Pound thought that this measure would cure the problem of obstruction of distribution that had long bothered him: for money stamped, so to speak, with an expiration date quickly reverted to the empty paper that all paper money truly was. Money thereby lost its power of surrogation, its power to usurp labor and goods. But Pound did not yet seem much closer to a vision of paradise that was the real thing, and not a substitute.

Eleven New Cantos begins with Jefferson and ends with Mussolini. And in 1933, as he was finishing these Cantos, Pound wrote *Jefferson and/or Mussolini*, a treatise to make prose sense of the coordination between his two heroes. In this book, Pound made a remarkable connection between poetry and politics:

> The real life in regular verse is an irregular movement underlying. Jefferson thought the formal features of the American system would work, and they did work till the time of General Grant but the condition of their working was that inside them there should be a *de facto* government composed of sincere men willing the national good. When the men of understanding are too lazy to impart the results of their understanding...I don't believe it matters a damn what legal forms or what administrative forms there are in a government. The nation will get the staggers. (*J/M*, 95)

Just as Pound set up the principle of rhyme at an orthogonal to the usual axis – governing subject matter, not word-sounds – so Pound now conceives politics as an irregular motion of accents underlying the regular prosody of official laws, administrative flow-charts. Just as Pound's verses exaggerate the hesitations and accelerations that underlie normal iambic verse, so Pound's *Cantos* attempt to seize the erratic compulsive movement of the intellectual lives of Jefferson, Adams, and other wise leaders – the source of real authority in early America.

By 1934, when *Eleven New Cantos* was published, Pound had devised a new, or partly new, scheme for conceiving the Cantos: the ideogram. Pound had discovered this scheme for the ideogram in the notes of the sinologist Ernest Fenollosa – notes which Pound had used for his translations from Chinese and Japanese during 1914–16, and which he had edited and published as *The Chinese Written Character as a Medium for Poetry*. But in the 1930s Pound took new inspiration from these notes, and recommended them as an *Ars Poetica* (*SL*, 322) and an instruction in thinking (*J/M*, 22). This model of the ideal poetic act – a signifying whole extrapolated from a heap of concrete particulars – helped Pound to explain what he had done, and also provided a dominant model for the Cantos to come, which are far more ideogrammatically self-conscious than Cantos I–XLI. There is a moment, though, near the end of this sequence, when we see ideogrammatic thinking at work. In a passage that ponders African and Arab languages, Pound noted:

> Bruhl found some languages full of detail
> Words that half mimic action; but
> generalization is beyond them, a white dog is
> not, let us say, a dog like a black dog.
> Do not happen, Romeo and Juliet . . .   (XXXVIII/189)

For some folks, a rose by any other name would not smell as sweet, because there is no such thing as a rose, only particular roses. Pound was starting to dream of an English like the language described here: a language with tremendous powers of evoking concrete action, but without generalization, except insofar as the reader's mind draws unmistakable inferences from minute particulars. In his "Vorticism" article of 1914, Pound spoke of certain generalizations as " 'lords' over fact" – just as $(x - a)^2 + (y - b) = r^2$ is not a particular circle, but the general form of all circles (*EPVA*, 207). But in many of *The Cantos*, Pound pursued the ideogrammatic method so remorselessly that he, essentially, asked facts to find ways of becoming lords over themselves.

He hoped that he could present rose, cherry, rust, and flamingo, and that he could then present the idea *red* with a devastating clarity. There are occasions in the later Cantos when he did. But there are other occasions when the reader is more likely to discover, not *red*, but a thorny flamingo-leg terminating in a curlicue of scrap iron – a futile mishmash. The ideogrammatic method – like the rag-bag method, the Noh play method, and the fugal method – did not solve all Pound's problems. Instead, it created problems; but Pound's strength as a poet lay in his astonishing capacity for creating problems, without necessarily solving them.

At the bottom of the last page of *Eleven New Cantos*, Pound wrote "ad interim 1933" (XLI/206). He thought that a time would come that was no longer *in the meantime*, a time when *A Draft of XXX Cantos* would be simply *XXX Cantos*. But of course all Pound's Cantos, past and future, were to be provisional Cantos. And it is in their improvisation that their power dwells.

NOTES

1 James Joyce, *A Portrait of the Artist as A Young Man*, ed. Hans Walter Gabler with Walter Hettche (New York: Vintage International, 1993), p. 207.
2 Barry, cited by Charles Norman in *Ezra Pound*, p. 193.
3 T. S. Eliot, *The Waste Land: Facsimile and Transcript*, ed. Valerie Eliot, p. 119.
4 Beckett, *Disjecta*, p. 33.
5 Tovey, *Symphonies and Other Orchestral Works*, p. 17.

5

IAN F. A. BELL

Middle Cantos XLII–LXXI

"ad interim 1933" is the promisory note concluding *Eleven New Cantos* of 1934 in a Canto which offers Mussolini and the shade of Jefferson as potential ameliorators within the crisis of belligerency and money that for Pound constituted contemporary Europe. It is the function of the two following volumes, *The Fifth Decad of Cantos* (1937) and *Cantos LII–LXXI* (1940), to meet that promise through a negotiation of a cultural map constructed in the main by the founding of a bank, the Monte dei Paschi, in sixteenth-century Siena, the reforms instigated in Tuscany during the eighteenth century by the Grand Duke Pietro Leopoldo and his son Ferdinando (in *FDC*), the history of China (based largely on Confucian principles) through to the eighteenth century, and the career of John Adams (in *CL*). These are the presiding issues in a pair of volumes which offer a diagnosis of the corruption of Western culture by usury and seek to discover alternatives through resurrecting pre-capitalist systems of exchange, the values of Confucian thought, and the ideals of the early American Republic.

While *Cantos LII–LXXI* uses a simple bipartite structure (where the first half, Cantos LII–LXI, is devoted to China and the second half, Cantos LXII–LXXI, to Adams), *The Fifth Decad* is more various in its preoccupations. It begins with the Monte dei Paschi in Cantos XLII and XLIII where the bank is figured as an image of fiscal solidity and certainty based upon its deployment not of the abstract and speculatory structure of capitalist finance but of the produce from the immediate region (see *SPR*, 240). Pound plays upon the word "Monte" to emphasise its substantiality – "A mount, a bank, a fund a bottom" (XLII/209. cf. XLIII/219) – a substantiality which is later given additional typographical weight as the capitalized "MOUNTAIN" accompanied by a pictograph testifying to the generatively organic, rather than abstractly geometric, shape of its subject (XLII/214), "MOUNT" (XLIII/218), and "BANK" (XLIII/219).

Pound celebrates the "BANK of the Grassland" (XLIII/219) for two principal reasons. First, it marks a moment prior to the breach between use-value and exchange-value (the division which characterizes the practices of industrial capitalism) where specie is loaned to "whomso can best use it USE IT" (XLII/210) for immediate rather than speculative benefit, where the capitalized emphasis is further underlined by the parenthesis in Latin which translates as "that is, most usefully." Secondly, the bank's success depends not upon the usurious manipulation of money but upon what Pound views as "real" wealth, a "guarantee of the income from grazing" (XLIII/218). Here, the "guarantee" is that of natural order, with grass "nowhere out of place" (XLIII/219), in combination with human order – the "fruit of nature" is united with "the whole will of the people" (XLIII/218) – so that money may be freely available at little cost (the bank makes only a minimal handling charge). This union promotes what is perhaps the key term for understanding the relationship between nature, money, and "the people" offered in these two Cantos – a relationship of responsibility, or, as Pound graphs it (twice), "REE-/sponsibility" (XLIII/217 and 218) in another instance of typographical bravura in which capitalization wrenches the word's etymology to suggest the condition of thinghood in Latin.

The lexical solidity here returns us to the sustaining view of the bank as "a base, a fondo, a deep, a sure and a certain" (XLIII/219), as the ultimate foundation of a sound economy and, by its position at the beginning of this sequence in *The Cantos*, also the source of, for Pound, the right and ineluctable relation between nature, money, and human life. Canto XLIV pursues the lesson in its account of the Leopoldine reforms two centuries later – their expressions of "provident law" (XLIV/223 and 224) and catalogue of tax management (XLIV/227–8). Their support for the Monte dei Paschi continues the view of it as a source of solidity, but now given an explicit function as the Canto ends by quoting Nicolo Piccolomini, the bank's supervisor: "The foundation, Siena, has been to keep bridle on usury" (XLIV/228). Piccolomini's position prepares the way for one of the most celebrated parts of the entire sequence, Canto XLV, the "Usura" Canto, where the high declamatory voice catalogues in extraordinary and stunningly observed detail the pernicious effects of usury throughout western culture. Canto XLVI pursues the issue in more contemporary terms, linking usury to war and affirming the non-productivity of the banks which make money "ex nihil," "out of nothing" (XLVI/233 and 234, 231). Canto XLIV has already argued for the protection of productive instruments and practices from sequestration for debt (XLIV/223), and Canto XLVI reforms the argument into the short parable of the camel driver where the abstractions of monotheistic religion (always associated in Pound's mind with the abstractions of money) are contrasted with the ceremonies of sustenance based upon immediate use and need (XLVI/232).

The cultural work performed by the proclamations of Cantos XLV and XLVI, and based on the documentation gathered by Cantos XLII–XLIV, prepares for the mythic and erotic dimensions of Canto XLVII which indicate the fertile visionary world that for Pound may function as a counter to a contemporaneity broken by usury and belligerence. We need to stress, with Donald Davie, that this visionary element is *worked for* through the preceding Cantos: it is not a matter of transcendental release,[1] even if, as P. H. Smith and A. E. Durant have argued, its construction tends to suppress historical difference.[2] By comparison, Canto XLVIII is something of an oddity, a "miscellany," as George Kearns has noted, "into which the poet has crammed scraps of anecdotes, documents and historical bits"[3] – domestic reminiscences, the American Bank Wars of the 1830s, the declining years of the Ottoman empire, the carnage of World War I, early English history and the sacred places of Provence are thrown together to recapitulate the abiding tensions between the evils of interest rates and poetic/sexual creativity.

With Canto XLIX, we re-enter the tranquillity offered earlier in Canto XLVII but within an immediacy of topography eschewed by the more visionary thrust of the latter. Canto XLIX is known as "The Seven Lakes Canto" and is based upon a series of paintings and poems of river scenes in a Japanese manuscript book owned by Pound's parents. Here, the world of myth and eroticism is replaced by a clear landscape, orchestrated by the seasons, but both Cantos foreground a major theme of *The Fifth Decad* and *Cantos LII–LXXI* – the relationship between seasonal time and work, already implied in the parable of the camel driver (XLVI/232), and evident more generally (XLVII/237 and XLIX/245) as testimony to the god-like "power over wild beasts" with which each Canto ends (XLVII/239 and XLIX/245). It will be my argument that it is precisely this relationship between time and work which provides a principal lens whereby the preoccupations of *The Fifth Decad* and *Cantos LII–LXXI* are focused.

The two final Cantos in *The Fifth Decad* recapitulate and anticipate. Leopoldine reforms are re-tested against other European commercial practices of the eighteenth and nineteenth centuries in Canto L and are seen to be comparable with the ideals of the American revolution. Cantos LI recasts Canto XLV's stylized litany against "usura" into a more contemporary idiom and, just as the landscape of Canto XLIX gave figure to the visionary ethos of Canto XLVII, so here the catalogue of usury's human and cultural distortions receives graphic specificity by the marvellously sustained account of the seasonal and temporal manufacture of flies for trout fishing, a manufacture which is rendered as free from such distortions by its observances of "natural" time and work (LI/251). The account celebrates the technical skill and observational perceptiveness of a craftsmanship allied to nature during the pre-capitalist period.

Accuracy is the key-note here, and it is entirely appropriate that the Canto and the volume end with the ideograms for Ching and Ming, the "right name" (LI/252. They recur towards the end of the China Cantos in LX/333, and throughout the Adams Cantos in LXVI/382, LXVII/387, and LXVIII/400). It is equally appropriate that the first of the Chinese Cantos in the following volume, *Cantos LII–LXXI*, should repeat the lesson, "Call things by the names," after another catalogue which views labor in terms of seasonal appropriateness (LII/261). And as *The Fifth Decad* concluded with a prospective glance, so *Cantos LII–LXXI* begins retrospectively, reinvoking, again, the examples of Leopoldine reforms and the Monte dei Paschi where the "true base of credit" is "the abundance of nature / with the whole folk behind it" (LII/257).

To name accurately, based upon a notion of work within "natural" time and within an economic system that contests usury through a reliance upon nature's productivity, is the source of *The Cantos'* mystical vision expressed in terms of human government and society. Arguably, we find here the major tenet of the poem's ambition, summarized in this opening Canto as "Between KUNG and ELEUSIS" (LII/258) – a unification of Confucian management and the Greek fertility ceremonies at Eleusis celebrating the mysteries of the godhead. To place these ideas in action, Pound deploys *Cantos LII–LXXI* as an *exemplum* of the principles advanced by *The Fifth Decad*, taking a Confucian reading of Chinese history and John Adams's revolutionary America as the sites in which they operate most meaningfully; his gritty yoking of idealist thought and pragmatic politics may be read as his particular form of resistance to what he regarded as the debasements of human life within the contemporary conditions of bourgeois liberal economics – the conditions of capitalism. At the forefront of those debasements is the changed nature of work, of the time-scale by which it is measured, and Pound's notions of wealth that inform both.

The entire sequence of the middle Cantos commences with a highly specific portrait of work – that of Pound's own labors in researching Sienese history. As George Kearns observes, Pound "wants to plunge us into the act of discovery itself"[4] by registering the effort involved in the struggle to get at the necessary information, rather than providing the comfort of organized reading. This activity literalizes one of the main lessons of the sequence, that "History is a school-book for Princes" (LIV/280) where the stress is upon the work towards knowledge and not merely its reception. In this sense, it is useful to see the Sienese Cantos as, in Teresa Winterhalter's phrase, "dramatic acts,"[5] which rehearse their sailings after knowledge and so have ambitions to resist the past as somehow given and to revivify it by practical engagement in the present.

The reader, as audience in Pound's theatre, potentially, shares the search for understanding within the varieties of diverse data presented, and refutes the historiography which, as Cantrell and Swinson have noted, views history as a sequence of events which "exist objectively and can be presented neutrally."[6] But we need to be careful here: although this ambition for the active work of the poem in which the reader may share is wholly laudable, we need also to acknowledge the hardening view of authority and law which colors the middle Cantos, particularly in their presentations of China and John Adams. Consequently, we need to be sensitive to the extent to which this latter group rely upon single bodies of source for their information and so create a pressure upon the reader that encourages passivity rather than activity – as Peter Nicholls puts it, thinking of the Adams Cantos, our collaboration with the poem has a tendency to become a matter of "faith" rather than interrogation.[7]

Nevertheless, the engaged action of research provides the enabling premise of the sequence, and it emphasises also its own material – the documents on which it is based. These documents are not to be regarded as "sources of some kind of simple-minded historical truth" to be blended into the "smooth pasta of narrative summary," but as "reminders that every document has a human author and that every author is limited to his own perspective which is revealed in his style" (Cantrell and Swinson, "Cantos LII–LXXI," 117). Such a recognition of human alterability might go some way towards requestioning the authoritarian impulse that otherwise structures the presentations of China and Adams.

The archival work behind the Sienese Cantos prescribes a specific function for documents in these and the following Cantos: they become not only the foundations for the sound economic management of the Monte dei Paschi and the right forms of government in China and revolutionary America, but, as Philip Furia has argued, they are texts which transmit authority and preserve law from tyranny or merely individualistic quirks.[8] Adams's success in legal matters (including his argument for disputing royal authority in the colonies) was largely a consequence of his knowledge of the necessary documents, of British *Statutes* and of Sir Edward Coke's *Institutes of the Laws of England* for example (see LXIV/359 and LXXI/419), and Pound views such knowledge as equivalent to the textuality he admires in Confucian culture: laws become equivalent to the rites and ceremonies of the *Li Ki*, the book of observances where work is intimately allied to the times of the seasons (in LII/258–261, for example). Documents, then, testify to the work of textuality, a particular form of labor which, through the instances Pound cites, becomes associated with seasonal appropriateness, principles of continuity, and freedom from tyranny.

The pinnacle of this equation, and arguably one of the most important lines in the *Cantos* as a whole, is the line Pound finds quoted by John Adams in "Thoughts on Government": "empire of laws not of men" (LXVII/391). In part, this recapitulates the view of law put forward in the Chinese Cantos where "law" is not bent to "wanton imagination" or to the "temper of individuals" (LXII/343), but is the law of "MOU," of "the just middle, the pivot" (LIII/269). When Adams claims "I am for balance," he is urging not only the system of checks and balances in the tripartite structure of government but is associated by Pound with Confucian thought – Adams's claim is followed by the ideogram "Chung" which is the "Unwobbling Pivot" (LXX/413). But in greater part, Adams's quotation belongs to the dynastic impulse of the Cantos which is designed to maintain the Confucian reverence for the work of documents and the preservation of law.

Pound ends the Adams Cantos with Cleanthe's "Hymn to Zeus" (LXXI/421) which he translates in his note to the "Table" of contents for *Cantos LII–LXXI* to conclude "by laws piloting all things" (256), and the piloting here is the product of the dynastic temperament concerned to preserve continuity. It is a temperament that is sensitive to "the people at large" while being "not dependent on any body of men" in order to ensure a "total" form of government (LXVII/391), and it *is* dependent upon a peculiarly American form of hierarchy – "orders of officers, not of men in America" (LXVII/394). Here, Pound misquotes his source in Adams in order to humanize his point without losing its reliance upon the need for disinterestedness – "mens sine affectu" (LXII/343). Adams is comparing the American form of hierarchy with those in Europe: "In America, there are different orders of *offices*, but none of men. Out of office, all men are of the same species, and of one blood; there is neither a greater nor a lesser nobility."[9] The dynastic temperament that Pound seeks to maintain through his recovery and renewal of documents is, then, a principal factor in the conceptions of law and authority which motivate the middle Cantos: it is simultaneously representative and expressive of a hierarchy based upon technique and knowledge rather than blood – "No slouch ever founded a dynasty" (LVI/302, 307).

It is at the behest of the dynastic impulse that Pound chooses Adams as his central figure during the late 1930s rather than the Jefferson whom he used in *Eleven New Cantos* of 1934, particularly Cantos XXXI–XXXIV. This is a shift away from the singularity and exceptionalism of the hero figure (such as Odysseus or Malatesta who are instrumental in the early stages of the poem) and towards the figures who might be considered as representative and who thus provide greater access to the issues of authority and money which increasingly come to dominate Pound's thinking during the course of the decade.[10] Pound had a strong sense of his own family history, particularly as it focused upon his grandfather, Thaddeus Coleman Pound, whom he views in part as a victim of the corruption engendered by the coalition of politics and business[11] – a victim in miniature of the line of corruption Pound finds endemic to capitalist culture. It is not accidental that Pound's source for the Adams Cantos is the multi-volume *Works* which included an account of his father's life by John Quincy Adams and was edited by his grandson Charles Francis Adams, nor that a later member of the family, Brooks Adams, provided in *The Law of Civilization and Decay* (1895) a treatment of history which Pound found particularly persuasive during the late 1930s.

In 1935 Pound succinctly summarizes his shift from the "genius" of Jefferson to the Adams who displayed a Confucian respect for ancestry and lineage: "John Adams believed in heredity. Jefferson left no sons. Adams left the only line of descendants who have steadily and without a break felt their responsibility and persistently participated in American government throughout its 160 years" (*J/M*, 19). The "common rights our ancestors have left us" (LXVI/383) need protection dynastically in order to legitimize law and authority as representative and not as prey to individualistic despotic whim.[12] John Adams, allied not only to Confucian thought but to the Leopoldine reforms of *The Fifth Decad* (cf. LXII/350 and XLIV/223, 224), becomes then the socially responsible "pater patriae" who both "made us" and "saved us" on the model of the Chinese rulers for whom a care for the "Good of the empire" is "like a family affair" (LXI/337, 338).

The alliance between Adams and the Leopoldine reforms offered by the sequence takes us back to its "fund" in the account of the Monte dei Paschi (and, by extension, to the physiocratic notions of wealth Pound had explored in his earlier Jefferson Cantos, XXXI–XXXIV,[13] notions largely shared by Adams), to the archival labor and documentation that for Pound seems associated with the pre-capitalist "real" work and the "real" wealth "bottomed" in an idea of natural order and immediate use. Such association does battle with the abstractions and distortions of money under speculative capitalism, incorporated under "usury." The shift from the real to the abstract may be graphed through the etymology of the word itself which witnesses, as George Kearns has observed, "a perversion of its basic meaning, which begins in the *use* of things" (Kearns, *Guide*, 122), a shift from use-value to exchange-value. Kearns rightly points out here that

"Pound is less concerned with quibbles over interest rates than with the perversion of *use* – of a man's time, of the fruits of the earth. The usurer wants more than he can decently use, and to get it he 'stoppeth' other people's use of things" (Kearns, *Guide*, 122). In 1944, Pound will argue that "Money is not a product of nature but an invention of man" (*SPR*, 316), but this argument for money's abstractive quality is not as straightforward as it might appear because he goes on to say "what man has made he can unmake" (*SPR*, 317). Money is injurious when it is taken as a solid entity rather than as merely a representation of that solidity, as an invented abstraction from nature, but at the same time, the inventive capacity of man would seem to offer a laudable alterability.

These contradictory tendencies provide instructive ground in the middle Cantos. The sequence is littered, certainly, with instances of "natural" solidity: the pastures which fund the Monte dei Paschi where, for the first time in the poem, "money is seen as the instrument of productive activity" (Nicholls, *Politics, Economics and Writing*, 75), Adams's insistence that "property EQUAL'D land" (LXIII/351), and the craftsman's unalienated labour in producing flies for fishing in Canto LI.[14] And the sequence is littered equally with strictures against damaging such solidity. In the China Cantos, these strictures are firmly anchored by pragmatism: "Gold is inedible" instructed the emperor Hiao Ouen Ti, and halved the taxes to "Let the farm folk have tools for their labour" (LIV/277. Cf. LVI/303), and under Tai Tsong "300 were unjailed to do their spring ploughing" by the remit "Lock not up the people's subsistence" (LIV/286). John Adams had an equally pragmatic eye which saw that "foreigners have profited by the difference/between silver and bills of exchange" (LXVIII/399) during the depreciation issue of 1780, and in arguing that the depreciation of money affects only those who "have money at interest" and not "Merchants, farmers, tradesmen and labourers" (LXIX/403), he posited the stability of "real" wealth against the uncertainty of "paper" wealth. Cantos LXIX–LXXI in particular resonate with Adams's opposition to speculators and his "aversion to paper" (LXX/411).

Adams's view of wealth here belongs to the sequence's general predilection for stability rooted in natural abundance and the correct forms of government. Pound wants also to include the principle of linguistic precision as part of the equation: shortly after his rendering of Adams's views on depreciation, he adds the Ching Ming ideogram to Adams's sense of "the importance of an early attention to language / for ascertaining the language" (LXVIII/400). The full context of these lines from a letter of 1780 (quoted in Sanders, *John Adams Speaking*, 387) suggests a further view of dynasty – the tradition, stemming from Athens and Rome, of words and education which is essential for liberty and prosperity. This tradition, it is implied, ought to be a matter of governmental policy, not left merely to the accidents of the learned mind. It depends on a particular form of reciprocity maintained by Adams, again in 1780: "It is not to be disputed that the form of government has an influence upon language, and language in its turn influences not only the form of government, but the temper, the sentiments, and manners of the people."[15] Surprisingly, Pound makes no use of this passage. Even more surprisingly he neglects Adams's views on the "latitude" for differences of definition in the language of legislation which "allows a scope for politicians to speculate, like merchants with false weights, artificial credit, or base money, and to deceive the people, by making the same word adored by one party, and execrated by another" (Adams, *Works*, V, 452). Adams's choice of metaphors is strikingly Poundian in its reading of language's corruption through a joining of politics, business, and money, areas which for Pound seek to gain through speculation at the expense of solidity: for both Adams and Pound, the activity of the "swindling banks" engaged in "taxing the public for private individuals' gain" (LXXI/414, 416) provides an enabling figure for the full range of political and linguistic corruption, and the founding of the Bank of England in 1694 becomes "the decisive moment in which real property was replaced by credit as the basis of the economy" (Dasenbrock, "Jefferson and/or Adams," 515).

It is to challenge such corruption that Pound seeks solidity, a stable base for the economy that would allow real wealth to be, in David Murray's phrase, "the fixed element in a series of transformations of value."[16] But at the same time he remains committed to a world of alterability where "what man has made he can unmake" (*SPR*, 317). This contradiction is a version of the conflict that, as Thomas Gustafson has recently urged, holds true generally for the competing traditions of language and government in American thought throughout the nineteenth century – a "conflict between the need to settle the meanings of words to maintain order, community, and communication and the need to unsettle them to pursue liberty, independence and self-expression."[17] The oscillations between constitutional and revolutionary impulses, between compliance and resistance, characterize not only the overall shape of the middle Cantos (their dynastic reverence for documents which is simultaneously informed by the need to make them new, to revive their contemporary urgencies) but also the negotiations of wealth they conduct. In this latter context, we can historicize Pound's position quite closely, because in many ways that position in the late 1930s, convinced of the corrupt alliance between politics and business and of the belligerent tendencies following from that corruption – Adams is celebrated for his efforts against Hamilton (in Pound's view, a predecessor for Roosevelt) to keep America out of a war with France as a result of national debt (LXII/348 and particularly LXXI/418 which concludes the sequence. Cf. *SPR*, 308, 310) – reworks several of the determinant issues of the Gilded Age into which he was born.

Foremost amongst these issues was the debate during the 1890s over money itself between the liberals and the populists. Both sides sought a "natural" form of money, but chose radically different routes towards it where the former favored the gold standard and the latter campaigned for free silver. As several commentators have noted, Pound may be generally seen as belonging to the populist predilection for free silver,[18] but to encode him entirely in this way tells only part of the story since the liberal position held much that was attractive for Pound. Both the liberals and the populists conducted a struggle in common against the banks and the new forms of corporation they saw as being in alliance with a corrupt political system. The liberal response was to invoke notions of natural law, a return to the republican values of the early years of the century, and a plea for the "honest dollar" which had an intrinsic, fixed value based on a redemption through gold. By contrast, paper currency was seen as "unnatural" and inflationary, and silver became associated with its "fraud." Pound would have agreed with all these sentiments in principle, just as he would have admired the liberals' faith in the "independent" man in politics, unsullied by party, business, or greedy self-interest, the man equipped for the construction of an ideal ordered society under the guidance of the kind of responsible, elite government associated with Jefferson.[19] We find all of these principles in his earlier treatment of Jeffersonian America at the beginning of the 1930s in Cantos XXXI–XXXIV (see Bell, "Speaking in Figures," 158–59).

But despite all this, Pound remains resolutely opposed to the gold standard and its supporters who, as Martin Kayman observes, "obstruct economic, linguistic and epistemological liquidity by valuing precisely that opaque metal which stops the light rather than giving it form and letting it flow."[20] The liberals saw themselves as inheriting the line of the older, cleaner, values of the early republic, and regarded the gold standard as a means of securing the economy by giving notes a solid base while silver, coin, and paper were seen as a system of uncertain circulation with no promise of redemption, an inflationary tendency, and too close an association with the newer forms of commercial and industrial success. By denying this view, Pound would seem to be denying that very solidity of representation he discovers in the Monte dei Paschi. Simultaneously, Pound's own class position (an earlier affluence waning under the changes of industrial capitalism) might ally him with the liberal position where the middle classes felt threatened from both ends – by the increasing incorporation of capital and business (joined with an untrustworthy politics) and by the enormous influx of immigrants.

The "gold bugs" tended to belong to older forms of wealth, needing the stability of gold against the instability of non-redeemable paper and silver that placed power in the hands of bankers and speculators, the newer forms of wealth which made "money out of nothing." Pound's populist bent in the end objected to gold as a single system of value, determined monolithically, against which everything else could be fixed. In tune with his general resistance to all things monotheistic in society, gold for Pound belongs to the manipulations of the few for the benefit of the few, in contrast to a system where value is determined by the goods and labor available, and where wealth circulates within the community at large. Pound urges both solidity and flow in his economics, both a base in nature and a circulatory medium: his contradictory response to his populist heritage indicates his difficulties in responding to industrial capitalism during the 1930s – his idealism in prioritizing distribution over production blinds him to the real iniquities of the system he opposes (see Murray, "Pound-Signs," 76, and Kayman, "The Color of His Money," 44) – but it prompts also his focus upon *work* in the middle Cantos as perhaps the most immediate arena of capitalism's distortions.

In 1937, the year of *The Fifth Decad*, Pound quoted a phrase from Constantin Brancusi – "ONE OF THOSE DAYS WHEN I WOULD NOT HAVE GIVEN FIFTEEN MINUTES OF MY TIME FOR ANYTHING UNDER HEAVEN" – and he commented: "There speaks the supreme sense of human values. There speaks WORK unbartered" (*SPR*, 253). Here, value is found in labour "unbartered": it is measured not by money but by the time of social labour allocated to it (cf. *SPR*, 155), recalling the Jacksonian principle from the 1830s, the earlier period of America's debate about the nature of money, that "'THE REAL VALUE OF LAND IS DUE TO LABOUR'" (*SPR*, 153). Pound translates the concept of "work-money" as a "'*certificate of work done*'" to sustain the general idea that "work might serve as a *measure* of prices" on the grounds that "work cannot be monopolised" (*SPR*, 315) in direct opposition to the practices of capitalism which determine labor costs not by a measure of the work involved but by the time taken for the work's accomplishment – as David Harvey argues, "industrial time" is that which "allocates and reallocates labour to tasks according to powerful rhythms of technological and locational change forged out of the restless search for capital accumulation."[21] This is what E. P. Thompson has called "timed labour," characteristic of an industrial economy, which he opposes to time as "task-orientation," associated with a pre-industrial economy, governed by what needs to be done at specific moments (the timing of harvests or lambing, etc.), attending to "what is an observed necessity," and displaying the least demarcation between "work" and "life."[22] This latter valuation of work provides the resource for Pound's views on labour in the *Cantos* – "Begin thy plowing / When the Pleiades go down to their rest" and "When the cranes fly high / think of plowing" (XLVII/237). The instructions "Sun up; work / sundown; to rest" (XLIX/244) understand work as allied not only to the rhythms of nature but as determined by task rather than by horology (cf. LI/252, LII/258–261, LIII/271).

The Chinese Book of Rites, the *Li ki*, which organizes the main argument of Canto LII, offers the clearest model for the measurements of value by task as opposed to time – we should not be distracted by its insistence on the correspondence with the seasons because what matters here is not the seasonal cycle in its temporal sense,[23] but in the sense of the particular appropriatenesses of particular tasks organized by the accompanying rites, attending to "observed necessity" on the model of the camel driver parable (XLVI/232) and the manufacture of flies (LI/251). It is insufficient to see these oppositions solely in terms of "organic" and "mechanical" time (see Pearlman, *Barb of Time*, 167–168) because they leave the notion of "nature" largely uninterrogated and neglect the necessary issue of labor. The seasons as temporal measure *do* matter, but they need to be understood more pragmatically, as the *Cantos* understand them. When, for example, Ngan advises "Lend 'em grain in the spring time / that they can pay back in autumn," it is on behalf of a system of "equity" where tithes are "proportionate" to the "rarity or the abundance of merchandise" so that "the folk be not / overburdened" (LV/297). The equity and proportion of the tithe system here is directly opposed to the monolithic taxation system which is insensitive to the rhythms of scarcity and surplus (cf. LXI/335).

What is important about Pound's notion of labor as value, informed by task rather than clock, is the extent to which it offers release – release from the horology that otherwise organizes the working day. This is the release of "WORK unbartered" he learned from Brancusi (*SPR*, 253), and of John Adams's delight in variety, "Read one book an hour / then dine, smoke, cut wood" (LXIII/353), a delight in the rhythms of task released from pressure. The canal to TenShi is not only one of the *Cantos*' many images for the free flow of communication (possibly Pound's most strongly held belief), it is built "for pleasure" (XLIX/245), thus combining non-alienated labor and a freedom from industrial time necessary for creativity – as John F. Kasson notes, "in the less intense pace of work, all may be artists"[24] within the "spare time free from anxiety" (Murray, "Pound-Signs," 52).

Such release is the prime strategy Pound wields against the husbandry of time by the Puritanism he distrusted historically and the industrial capitalism he experienced uncomfortably. Thompson points out that "In mature capitalist society all time must be consumed, marketed, put to *use*; it is offensive for the labour force merely to 'pass the time'" where "Time is now currency: it is not passed but spent" (Thompson, "Time, Work-Discipline and Industrial Capitalism," 395, 359). The Puritan tradition, with the decline of the medieval Catholic Church (for Pound, the beginning of the usurious period) and in conjunction with the time-discipline of capitalism, literalizes the equation "time is money" whereby "time-valuation" becomes "commodity-valuation" (Thompson, "Time, Work-Discipline and Industrial Capitalism," 400–401).

In short, the antipathy of industrial time, ruled by clock not task, to possibilities for release marks Pound's most abiding concern in the middle Cantos and enables us to see that their reliance upon nature and the seasons is impelled by the specific conditions of contemporaneity – under the aegis of Frederick Winslow Taylor and Henry Ford, time is not only vastly accelerated (in the interests of more efficient output and turnover) but also compressive, thus doubly distorting both the non-alienated nature of pre-industrial labor and the availability of necessary release. David Harvey has reminded us of Heidegger's invocation of the values of pre-Socratic Greece and the power of myth in proposing a condition of "being" rather than "becoming" as his resistance to contemporary technology (Harvey, *The Condition of Postmodernity*, 209), and this provides a useful parallel to Pound's activity. Pound also seeks "being" (where space is equated with the permanent) rather than "becoming" (where time is equated with change) to try and spatialize time (detecting the permanent within process) and discovering solutions from pre-industrial cultures. While art uses space to compress time, capitalism uses time to control space, and in his concision of some 5,000 years of Chinese history, for example, we see a clear gesture against capitalist discipline. And we should note finally on this point, that Pound recognizes how time also directly informs the capitalist practice he distrusts the most, the usury which takes time ever further away from "observed necessity": "The difference between money and credit is one of time. Credit is the future tense of money" (*SPR*, 278. Cf. 315).

The endeavor of the middle Cantos, then, is to oppose the disciplinary society of a capitalist market economy (Taylorist principles of time management and Fordist systems of production) by invoking the pre-industrial models of Sienese banking, Confucian China and revolutionary America. Simultaneously, however, they register also the extent to which they are caught by the terms of their opposed subject – efficiency, pragmatism,

technique (the hall-marks of Pound's aesthetics) and the effort to natural-
ize these terms serve to display how his own practice remains firmly within
them. In part, this belongs to the *American* nature of Pound's modernity –
the artist as artisan, workmanlike and constructivist, combining beauty
and utility. The joining of form and function, as John Kasson has argued,
thinking of John Adams, is also the basis for a "republican aesthetic"
within a tradition which stresses contiguity rather than difference between
nature and technology: "To be both Nature's nation and a rapidly developing industrial power was . . . not a contradiction, but the fulfilment of
America's destiny. The natural landscape and modern technology provided the resources to complement one another" (Kasson, *Civilizing the
Machine*, 144, 174). Waste and inefficiency are here abhorred equally by
industrial capitalism and by republican/modernist notions of art, and it is
not difficult to see how the rites of the *Li ki* or Adams's celebration of a
variety of tasks can come close, in structure at least, to the exhaustion of
time for utility by seriality (of body and function) we associate with a
disciplinary society.[25]

Against the fragmentation of such seriality, the middle Cantos set
Adams as the "one man of integrity" (LXII/345), representative of "a life
not split into bits" (*SPR*, 122), through what Fredric Jameson has called
"the ideological valorization of the 'strong personality'."[26] We need to understand such ideological valorization in order to offset too idealist a reading
of the poems – or, rather, to recognize that their reverted eye has its own
history. Additionally, I think it necessary to recuperate the wisdom of
E. P. Thompson's advice: "We shall not ever return to a pre-capitalist
human nature, yet a reminder of its alternative needs, expectations and
codes may renew our sense of our nature's range of possibilities."[27]

Pound's exercise may serve as such a "reminder." Certainly he subsumes
labour under nature from the position that "labour is part of a harmony
with nature, rather than being for most men the means of their alienation
from their full humanity" (Murray, "Pound-Signs," 63), but if this is
idealistic it is also, given the textual labor that is so important an element
in these Cantos, an honorable effort towards the revivification of alternatives, however shadowy: as Jeffrey Twitchell has argued for Pound's use
of the Quattrocento in Canto XLV, "It is not that Quattrocento society
represents a realized utopia, but that it represents the end point of a
tradition in which it was possible for men to think and live outside economic values – before marketability had been turned into both a virtue
and a necessity."[28] We cannot live "outside economic values," but as an
imaginative possibility that might ameliorate the disorder of that life,
remind us of potential alterability, then to "think" it will have a human

resonance: as the cultural work with which *The Fifth Decad* begins demonstrates, the art object should be something that we think with – otherwise it becomes subject merely to wage rather than task value, to the seriality that is amongst capitalism's most damaging conditions.

If the middle Cantos are to be regarded as essaying these imaginative reminders, we need to be aware also of the ahistorical risks they take in eliding the material differences of place and time in their yoking of Siena, China, and revolutionary America (see, for example, Smith and Durant, "Pound's Metonymy," 328; Murray, "Pound-Signs," 76; Kayman, "The Color of His Money," 44). But, again, to recognize such yoking as a response to the time-scale of industrial capitalism is to recognize it not merely as illusory but as itself informed by immediate history. T. J. Jackson Lears has explored a well-developed portrait of the tendency amongst the "cultural élite" around the turn of the century to look to medieval and pre-industrial cultures for alternatives to modernity and mechanicalism,[29] and David Harvey has argued that "The ideological labour of inventing tradition became of great significance in the late nineteenth century precisely because this was an era when transformations in spatial and temporal practices implied a loss of identity with place and repeated radical breaks with any sense of historical continuity" (Harvey, *The Condition of Postmodernity*, 272).

Pound, who can be recognized in so many ways as belonging to the thought of this period, conducts his yoking of disparate periods and places exactly on behalf of his own cultivation of a "cultural élite" as his defense against war and the economics which lead to war. And it is not accidental that it was during the late 1930s that Pound was reading one of the exemplary texts from the era both Lears and Harvey negotiate – Brooks Adams's *The Law of Civilization and Decay* (1895), produced from the final stages of the "dynasty" inaugurated by John Adams. It is a text which anticipates much of Pound's intellectual furniture and is founded on the premise that with the "new era," after 1871, "the whole administration of society fell into the hands of the economic man."[30]

Brooks Adams makes a lengthy case for the causes of this decline, foremost amongst which are the manipulations of finance capitalism and the ascendancy of the economic temper in place of the martial and imaginative instincts (Brooks Adams, *Law of Civilization and Decay*, 4–7, 300–307). As a counter, a reminder of alternative needs, he posits the need for rejuvenation through "barbaric blood" (7, 299, 308) by which he means the energies that pre-date finance (as opposed to productive) capital, those of the Middle Ages. On a particularly Poundian note, Adams claims that "to the last, the barbarians married for love" and by comparison, "women seem never to have more than moderately appealed to the senses of the economic man" (299). This union of pre-capitalist energy and the focus of the female has long been a major element in Pound's thinking, and he chooses to end Canto LXX by adding "AMO" to the "DUM SPIRO" he takes from one of John Adams's letters, thereby constructing "while I breath, I love" (LXX/413). Against the incursions of industrial capitalism, the middle Cantos offer labour and passion as underwriting their reminders of alterability and alternative needs.

NOTES

1 See Donald Davie, *Ezra Pound. Poet as Sculptor* (London: Routledge and Kegan Paul, 1965), p. 159. Cf. M. L. Rosenthal, "Pound At His Best: Canto XLVII as a Model of Poetic Thought," *Paideuma*, 6 (1977), 309–321.

2 See P. H. Smith and A. E. Durant, "Pound's Metonymy: Revisiting Canto XLVII," *Paideuma*, 8 (1979), 327–333.

3 George Kearns, *Ezra Pound. The Cantos* (Cambridge: Cambridge University Press, 1989), p. 42.

4 George Kearns, *Guide to Ezra Pound's Selected Cantos* (New Brunswick: Rutgers University Press, 1980), p. 104.

5 Teresa Winterhalter, "Eyeless in Siena, or Ezra Pound's Vision through History," *Paideuma*, 21 (1992), 111.

6 Carol H. Cantrell and Ward Swinson, "Cantos LII–LXXI: Pound's Textbook for Princes," *Paideuma*, 17 (1988), 114.

7 Peter Nicholls, *Ezra Pound: Politics, Economics and Writing* (London: Macmillan, 1984), p. 132.

8 See Philip Furia, *Pound's Cantos Declassified* (University Park and London: Pennsylvania State University Press, 1984), chapters 6–8.

9 Quoted in Frederick K. Sanders, *John Adams Speaking. Pound's Sources for the Adams Cantos* (Orono, Maine: University of Maine Press, 1975), p. 355.

10 See Reed Way Dasenbrock, "Jefferson and/or Adams: A Shifting Mirror for Mussolini in the Middle Cantos," *English Literary History*, 55 (1988), 505–526.

11 See James J. Wilhelm, *The American Roots of Ezra Pound* (New York and London: Garland Publishing, 1985), pp. 23–24, and Wendy Stallard Flory, *The American Ezra Pound* (New Haven and London: Yale University Press, 1989), pp. 21–22.

12 See Daniel D. Pearlman, *The Barb of Time: On the Unity of Ezra Pound's Cantos* (New York: Oxford University Press, 1969), p. 213, and Nicholls, *Politics, Economics and Writing*, p. 126.

13 See Ian F. A. Bell, "'Speaking in Figures': The Mechanical Thomas Jefferson of Canto XXXI," in Bell (ed.), *Ezra Pound: Tactics for Reading* (London and Totowa, NJ: Vision Press and Barnes & Noble, 1982), pp. 148–186. Cf. Nicholls, *Politics, Economics and Writing*, pp. 73–74.

14 See Robert Demott, "Ezra Pound and Charles Bowlker: A Note on Canto LI," *Paideuma*, 1 (1972), 189–198.

15 John Adams, *The Works*, ed. Charles Francis Adams, 10 vols. (Boston: Little, Brown, 1850–6), VII, p. 249.

16 David Murray, "Pound-Signs: Money and Representation in Ezra Pound," in Bell (ed.), *Tactics for Reading*, p. 56.

17 Thomas Gustafson, *Representative Words. Politics, Literature, and the American Language, 1776–1865* (Cambridge: Cambridge University Press, 1992), p. 13. Cf. *SPR*, 291.

18 See Murray, "Pound-Signs," pp. 70–77; Flory, *The American Ezra Pound*, pp. 39–40; Tim Redman, *Ezra Pound and Italian Fascism* (Cambridge: Cambridge University Press, 1991), p. 66.

19 This paragraph draws upon the best single study of the subject – John G. Sproat, *"The Best Men": Liberal Reformers in the Gilded Age* (London: Oxford University Press, 1968), chapters 6, 7, and 10.

20 Martin A. Kayman, "Ezra Pound: The Color of His Money," *Paideuma*, 15 (1986), 45.

21 David Harvey, *The Condition of Postmodernity* (Oxford: Basil Blackwell, 1989), p. 202.

22 E. P. Thompson, "Time, Work-Discipline and Industrial Capitalism," in Thompson, *Customs in Common* (Harmondsworth: Penguin, 1993), p. 358.

23 See Wendy Stallard Flory, *Ezra Pound and The Cantos: A Record of Struggle* (New Haven: Yale University Press, 1980), pp. 162–163, and Jean-Michel Rabaté, *Language, Sexuality and Ideology in Ezra Pound's Cantos* (London: Macmillan, 1986), p. 90.

24 John F. Kasson, *Civilizing the Machine. Technology and Republican Values in America, 1776–1900* (Harmondsworth: Penguin, 1977), p. 228.

25 See Michel Foucault, *Discipline and Punish. The Birth of the Prison* (Harmondsworth: Penguin, 1979), p. 154. Cf. Georg Lukács, *History and Class Consciousness. Studies in Marxist Dialectics* (London: Merlin Press, 1971), p. 90.

26 Fredric Jameson, *Fables of Aggression. Wyndham Lewis, the Modernist as Fascist* (Berkeley: University of California Press, 1979), p. 109. Cf. Thomas Cody, "Adams, Mussolini, and the Personality of Genius," *Paideuma*, 18 (1989), 77–103.

27 Thompson, "Introduction," *Customs in Common*, p. 15.

28 Jeffrey Twitchell, "Art and the Spirit of Capitalism: Iconography and History in the Usura Canto," *Paideuma*, 19 (1990), 9.

29 In T. J. Jackson Lears, *No Place of Grace: Anti-Modernism and the Transformation of American Culture, 1880–1920* (New York: Pantheon, 1981).

30 Brooks Adams, *The Law of Civilization and Decay. An Essay on History* (New York: Vintage Books, 1955), p. 285. Cf. Ray Ginger, *Age of Excess. The United States from 1877 to 1914* (London: Macmillan, 1965), p. 36, and Sproat, *"The Best Men,"* pp. 172–173, 276.

6

RONALD BUSH

Late Cantos LXXII–CXVII

Introduction

The final phase of *The Cantos* began when Pound started planning the poem's paradisal conclusion. In 1944 he explained that "for forty years I have schooled myself . . . to write an epic poem which begins 'In the Dark Forest[,]' crosses the projected Purgatory of human error, and ends in the light, and 'fra i maestri color che sanno.'"[1] Seven years before, he had assumed the middle part of that progress was concluded: in 1937 he published *The Fifth Decad of Cantos* [XLI–LI] and wrote in Canto XLVI that "This case, and with it / the first part, draws to a conclusion, / of the first phase of this opus" (XLVI/233–234[2]). The crisis of impending war, however, caused him to insert an extra section on economics and politics – the China and Adams Cantos published in *Cantos LII–LXXI* (1940). It looked then like there would be one more push – one section in which, as he wrote to T. S. Eliot in January 1940, he had "29 canters to write" to match Dante's *Commedia*.[3] At that point, the coils of Pound's own political and ideological misapprehension combined with the contingencies of history to produce a more complicated and extended outcome than the one he had foreseen. Having asked the world in general and T. S. Eliot in particular whether you "think you will / get through hell in a hurry" (XLVI/231), Pound discovered for himself how difficult it was to get to the other side of "human error," rage and hardened judgment. Whether he ever reached the light is a question that different readers will answer in different ways.

From the perspective of the 1990s, it is difficult not to emphasize that Pound only partially recanted his fascist and antisemitic beliefs, which intermittently returned to haunt the poem to its close. On the other hand, forced to work through the ideological contradictions of his age through thirteen scathing years of imprisonment and another fourteen years of private distress, Pound opened himself up to moments of tragic enlightenment.

Forced by certain of his poetic procedures scrupulously to register colloquial speech and by others to maintain rigorous and programmatic openness, he recorded even what he was reluctant to accept and in the late *Cantos* left a model for dialogical discourse that poets in succeeding generations have ignored at their peril.

What follows will trace the unfolding of the later Cantos through four major publications: *The Pisan Cantos* (Cantos LXXIV–LXXXIV, begun 1945, published 1948); *Section: Rock-Drill de los cantares* (Cantos LXXXV–XCV, drawing on fragments left over from Pisa and on the Confucian translations Pound pursued after the war, substantially drafted in 1952–1954, and published in 1955); *Thrones 96–109 de los cantares*, sketched out in notebook drafts[4] from late 1954 to early 1958 and published in 1959; and *Drafts & Fragments of Cantos CX–CXVII*, beginning from fragments written as early as 1957 and published in 1968/9.

Underlying the publication history of Pound's work are the stark facts of his later life: indicted for his wartime radio broadcasts in 1943, he was temporarily taken prisoner in May 1945 by renegade Italian partisans and turned over to the Allies, then released. After reporting voluntarily to American forces, he was incarcerated, aged nearly sixty, at the US Army Disciplinary Training Center, a prison camp located near the Viareggio road just north of Pisa. From May 24 to June 15, he stayed in a concrete-floored, wire isolation cage in the open air of a fierce summer, and slept under constant illumination until he suffered acute symptoms of confusion, anxiety and fatigue. He was then transferred to an officer's tent in the medical compound, where he remained until November 16. Put without warning on a plane to Washington, he was imprisoned and immediately arraigned. On February 13, 1946, a jury after a day-long hearing took three minutes to agree with Pound's lawyer that he should be judged mentally unfit to stand trial.

It now seems all but certain, that, under great stress and as flamboyant as ever, Pound was not insane, but acceded to a political compromise out of fear for his life and in ignorance of the long-term consequences of the decision. He spent the next twelve years in St. Elizabeths Hospital, a federally mandated detention center for insane prisoners, where visits by the literary elite of several continents and the care of his wife Dorothy mitigated but never fully relieved the stress of his confinement. At first his conversation with visitors was limited to fifteen minutes under the supervision of a guard. Later he was permitted to speak with visitors on the grounds, eventually until the evenings. In Peter Makin's pithy description, for twelve years he was denied the power "to shut out the television, the smell, the wraiths of madmen drifting in and out, the occasional screams and the endless chatter." In the middle of this period, Makin notes, Pound wrote to Archibald MacLeish that "'The little and broken-up time that I get (with no privacy and constant interruption and distraction) makes impossible that consecutive quality of feeling so important to me.'"[5]

On April 18, 1958, a changed political climate obtained Pound's release. Pound then sailed to Italy to reside with his daughter Mary in Brunnenburg. For a brief but turbulent period he struggled with the claims of the several important women in his life and suffered the first of a long string of renal problems and minor strokes. Within a year Pound had left Brunnenburg, and a short time later he reconciled with Mary's mother Olga Rudge, and lived out his seventies and eighties with her in a small house in Venice. He died in Venice on November 1, 1972.

Interacting with the often contradictory stylistic and ideological premises of his poem in progress, these events would condition all four final volumes of the *Cantos*. After strongly affirming hierarchy and natural order in the thirties, Pound, especially in the *Pisan Cantos* and *Drafts & Fragments*, rediscovered his early sympathies for the bohemian and the outcast. Whether because he had himself become an imprisoned renegade or because of an insurgence of the irrepressible iconoclasm of his youth, this dissonance drove him to compose poetry charged with powerful internal conflict.

The Pisan Cantos: Background

To understand the background of Pound's Paradiso, it is essential to re-member the way his ideological and political beliefs had been transformed between 1919 and 1939. In the 1920s, like so many others who experi-enced the economic and social unrest then roiling France, Italy and Ger-many, Pound shifted his affiliations from anarchist bohemianism to a fixation on strong and patriarchal cultural forms. As Eva Hesse has pointed out, before he moved from London to Paris in 1921 he had espoused "a down-right rejection of the bourgeois conception of family, [but] from his early forties to his early seventies he gradually went over to advocating [a patriarchalism that] passes for Confucianism."[6] By the late thirties Pound was condemning the most cherished of his cultural heroes. In *Guide to Kulchur* the *Odyssey* had become merely an "adventure story . . . preaching self-reliance," and Pound transferred his praise from "the maritime adven-ture morals of Odysseus [and] the loose talk of argumentative greeks" to Rome ("the responsible ruler") and "the need for coordination of indi-viduals expressed in Kung's teaching."[7]

Inevitably *The Cantos*, Pound's poem of cultural values, absorbed these changes, and not just in subsequently published installments. Realigning earlier work with new ideology, Pound repackaged earlier poems steeped in the anarchism of the 'teens in his first collection of Cantos (*A Draft of XVI. Cantos*, 1925), which took its keynote from what a recent critic has called the "stereotypical male-writ-large" world of Sigusmundo Malatesta.[8] Then in *A Draft of XXX Cantos* (1930), he made important alterations to earlier Cantos, most dramatically to Canto VI, a text in 1919 sympathetic to turn-of-the-century feminism but in 1929 refashioned to celebrate the quasi-mystical sexual powers of Guillaume of Aquitaine and Cunizza da Romano.[9] After 1930, not only parts but the whole of *The Cantos* seemed to express Pound's growing fascist inclinations. *Cantos LII–LXXI*, published in January 1940, concerned the dynastic successes of emperors in China and the Adams family in the United States. Written in a hurry – the Adams section in only five weeks – the volume was a last desperate attempt to hold up a vision of ordered government before Europe exploded. Along with the diplomatic mission that Pound took upon himself in 1939, when he flew back to Washington and attempted to persuade his numerous carefully cultivated correspondents in the US Congress to prevent a war driven by Western capitalism, he regarded the volume as a necessary detour in a crisis.

Disheartened by having failed to prevent the onset of the war, Pound in 1939 pronounced himself eager to get his poem out of "dead matter and negations" and into its Paradiso; he envisioned starting with Scotus Erigena, whose philosophy he had begun taking notes on in the thirties.[10] On October 24, 1939, in reply to T. S. Eliot's query as to where the Cantos were going, he spoke "about writin' more cantos [. . .] If you wuz to find me a nice TEXT of Scotty the Oirishman (index name Scotus ERIGENA, nut Dunce kotus), I might get through another FOUR canters in six months."[11] He also buttonholed George Santayana, like himself expatriated in Italy, and expressed his desire to "tackle philosophy."[12]

Pound's resolve, though, lost its energy in the confusion of the war. Between 1940 and 1944 he wrote a flurry of fragments, only two of which are substantial enough to mention: a typescript dated "Undici Dec. XX 1941" concerning the Confucian virtues of the governor; and a sequence dating from 1943 memorializing Pound's frightened journey from a disintegrating situation in Rome to the haven of his daughter's foster family in the Tyrol after the Italians, having deposed Mussolini on July 25, 1943, surrendered to the Allies on September 8.[13] (The Germans quickly retook the city and installed Mussolini as the puppet head of the Salò Republic.) In hindsight, both of these sequences anticipated Pound's writing at Pisa, especially the second, which laments a world in ruins and seeks consolation in a landscape suffused with Greek and Confucian presences.

Then, unpredictably, Pound began to write again, beginning with two Cantos he had never envisioned. By the end of May 1944, the war had turned definitively against the axis, and Pound and his wife Dorothy, forced to flee their flat in Rapallo, moved into an excruciating *ménage à trois* above the city on the cliffs of Sant' Ambrogio in the home of Pound's lifelong companion Olga Rudge. It was here, in the midst of running friction between the two women he loved, that Pound read the news that many of his sacred places had been blasted. The worst came on Sunday June 4 when he read that bombs had severely damaged his touchstone of Renaissance civilization, the Tempio Malatestiano in Rimini.[14] From then on, Pound's state of mind, strained by his domestic relations, swung between phases of defiant denial and passivity bordering on the sense of an afterlife.

The defiance appears in the Italian Cantos LXXII and LXXIII, whispered about for years and now published both in the most recent New Directions collected *Cantos* and in Mary De Rachewiltz's Mondadori *I Cantos*.[15] When the Allied push through Italy was stalled for the winter, Mussolini made what was to be his last public speech. It was a stirring appeal for a reversal of the Axis fortunes that had seemed doomed since Montgomery's victory in Africa, and it ended with a call for a "riscossa," a counter-attack. Mussolini delivered his speech on December 16, fourteen days after the Futurist poet and ardent fascist Tomaso Marinetti died, and the combination of the two events spurred Pound into writing. But, as he had since 1943 been translating a selection of his earlier work into Italian in the company of his daughter Mary, he attempted his new Cantos in an Italian that incidentally enabled him (in Canto LXXIII) to echo Mussolini's "*riscossa*."[16]

These Cantos, only now beginning to be read,[17] are vitally important for understanding the writing that followed them. Canto LXXIII represents the exultation of Guido Cavalcanti, returned from the sphere of Venus to witness the heroism of a young girl who sacrificed her life for her country by leading Canadians who had raped her into a minefield. Canto LXXII is longer, and required more work. It depicts the appearance of Marinetti's spirit, who asks to appropriate Pound's body so that Marinetti can continue to fight in the war. Marinetti, though, is first displaced by Pound's friend Manlio Torquato Dazzi, and then by the ferocious figure of Ezzelino da Romano, the early thirteenth-century Ghibilene whom Dante sees boiling among the tyrants of *Inferno* XII. It is in Ezzelino's suitably enraged voice that Pound calls for the damnation of treacherous Italian peacemakers and for the revenge of the monuments at Rimini.

Having drafted the two poems in a pencil notebook along with still more Italian Cantos, Pound published a fragment of Canto LXXII and all of Canto LXXIII in the *Marina Republicana* (a newspaper associated with his friend Ubaldo degli Uberti) in January and February of 1945.[18] Even before they saw print, Pound had gone on with Italian sequels – the poems Pound referred to when he wrote to his daughter at Easter 1945 that he had made numerous notes for more Cantos but had decided not to use them. Yet, as Mary de Rachewiltz adds in her account of his letter, the drafts contain visionary moments her father was to draw upon that summer and fall.[19]

Pound's abandoned Italian Cantos included manuscripts and multiple typescripts for two partially achieved cantos, "74" and "75," both of which grew out of Canto LXXII and absorbed the extended preparations for a Paradiso that Pound had already made. One of their recurrent characters is Ezzelino da Romano's sister, Cunizza, whom the troubadour Sordello courted, and who (Pound believed) spent her old age in the house of Guido Cavalcanti when Dante was a boy. Dante had placed much-married Cunizza in the sphere of Venus in the ninth canto of his *Paradiso*, and, twenty years before Pisa, Pound, meditating on the mystical precisions of Guido Cavalcanti's *Donna mi pregha*, had begun to imagine the reasons why. In the late thirties in *Guide to Kulchur*, he characterized Cunizza as the woman whose "charm and imperial bearing [and] grace" had been responsible for the last glow of Provençal song and for the transmission of the culture of mystical philosophy and Romanesque architecture to the young Guido and the younger Dante.[20]

Pound's winter 1945 drafts rehearsed these suggestions in an Italian derived partly from Dante and Cavalcanti and partly from colloquial speech. They are set among the natural beauties of Sant' Ambrogio, from whose cliffs they register the disintegration of Italy. In one of his holograph manuscripts, Pound speaks of hearing "the ancient voices" (*"le vetuste voc[i]"*) louder than ever before (*"più che mai prima"*), "clear and more frequent" (*"chiare e più sovente"*)." As the world falls apart around him, he reassures himself that these ancient voices represent a paradisal bedrock in human experience that cannot be destroyed.

Pisa: 1945

Pound's Italian verses, written in January and February 1944, were in his head when, in late June and early July his incarceration at Pisa gave him time and motive to continue. Once out of the cage and in a tent in the Center's medical compound, he acquired a packing crate table, a pencil and four or five inexpensive writing pads. He had intended to continue the translations into English of Confucius's *The Great Digest, The Unwobbling*

Pivot, *The Analects* and *The Classic Anthology* he had begun in Rapallo, and he had managed to bring with him materials including Legge's bilingual edition of the Confucian texts and a small Chinese dictionary. But, now terrified that his breakdown might be causing him to lose his memory, he also set about composing new Cantos.

Pound's Pisan holograph manuscript incorporated much of the Italian drafts in an unfolding visionary quest for internal peace. Both the manuscript and Pound's typescript revision begin with the salutation now occupying lines eleven and twelve of Canto LXXIV: "The suave eyes, quiet, not scornful, / rain also is of the process," and telescope a vision of the *stil-novisti* beloved with a mystical reading of Confucius very like the one that concludes his contemporary translation of *The Unwobbling Pivot*: "The *unmixed* functions (in time and space) without bourne. This unmixed is the tensile light, the Immaculata. There is no end to its action."[21] Pound's "suave eyes" initiate a poem which is intent upon the redeeming energies of light and reason and which proceeds through intuitions of "la luna" to the healing power of "pale eyes as if without fire" in Canto LXXX and to unexpected forgiveness of blindfolded eyes in Canto LXXXI. Like Cunizza's eyes in the Canto LXXV typescript, the latter are "in costume" and "senz' ira" – without "anger." In the *Pisan Cantos* they herald a final crisis, when, reappearing in Canto LXXXIII after a dark night of the soul in Canto LXXXII, the eyes "pass and look from mine," effecting a miraculous return of compassion and peace.

Pound did not discover in the Pisan landscape the apparitions that he now celebrated: they are (in several senses) translations. Nevertheless as he recast and elaborated his Italian verses into English he suffused his wartime visions with an apprehension of natural process so intensely felt that critics of the poem were convinced the one had grown out of the other. Quite deliberately, Pound orchestrates his symbolic sequence with a series of finely drawn observations of the quotidian world, so that the atmospherics of the light and the goddesses seem to be one with the solidity of ordinary creatures:

> if calm be after tempest
> that the ants seem to wobble
> as the morning sun catches their shadows (LXXX/533)

The result is a kind of twentieth-century *Walden* in which, as Forrest Read put it in an early but still remarkable essay, "purification of [the poet's] will" follows first upon powers released by natural observation and then upon a discovery of the "paradisal energies which move nature."[22] The whole effect is grounded in the everyday, as Pound signals when, near the end of Canto LXXVIII, he remarks, "as for the solidity of the white oxen in all this / perhaps only Dr. Williams (Bill Carlos) / will understand its importance, / its benediction. He wd/ have put in the cart" (LXXVIII/503).

A second and perhaps more enduring part of *The Pisan Cantos'* appeal appears continuous with its symbolic texture but in fact draws on quite different sources of style and value. Driven by a terror of losing his memory and perhaps even his identity, Pound extemporized a poetic idiom nervous and flexible enough to articulate the moment-by-moment shiftings of a diary/reminiscence. Receiving the first of his poems in the mail, his wife Dorothy immediately recognized them to be the realization of an autobiographical work they had talked about years before.[23] Yet, as Pound explained in a "Note to [the] Base Censor" he wrote to assure the camp authorities that his typescripts were not encoded sedition, there was something more involved as well. Interspersed with his memories, Pound recorded interruptions from the life of the camp around him. In Pound's words, "the form of the poem and main progress is conditioned by its own inner shape, but the life of the D. T. C. passing OUTSIDE the scheme cannot but impinge, or break into the main flow. The proper names given are mostly those of men on sick call seen passing my tent."[24]

Superimposing diary and reminiscence upon visionary poetry, Pound required new generic models for his work. Even modulated into the key of symbolist reverie, the totalizing epic of *The Divine Comedy* would not fully suffice. And so he adapted for his purposes the lyric and episodic *Testament* of Villon, taking his cue especially from lines from stanza XXIX: "Where are those laughing comrades / that I was with in former days, / who sang so well, talked so well / and so excelled in word and deed? / Some are dead and stiff – / nothing now remains of them: / may they find peace in Paradise, / and may God save the rest."[25] In the very first lines he wrote at Pisa – lines that memorialize the hanging, on July 2, 1945, of Louis Till – Pound invoked Villon's gallows setting. From that point on, the *Testament's* loose lyric progression proved ideal for recording the flow of his day-by-day memories, perceptions and activities. Probably it also reinforced an openness toward his fellow inmates that counteracted Pound's rage and anxiety: speaking in Villon's voice, Pound movingly acknowledged the sometimes mortal suffering of the people around him.

Pound's Pisan imitation of Villon subtly altered his poem's ideological coordinates. Against the hierarchical pull of Confucian epigram and the morality of Dantescan epic, Pound's swerve toward Villon identified the poem with the outcast instead of the governor, the renegade instead of the policeman, the bohemian instead of the courtier. Indeed, Pound seems to have been made uncomfortable enough by what he had previously written to try to disguise it. Ultimately, however, he reinforced his original impulse. This happened near the end of his composition when Pound was convinced he had finished. Having written his wife Dorothy that "I have done a Decad 74/83, which dont seem any worse than the first 70," Pound received a letter from her in October saying that J. P. Angold, a correspondent and promising poet, had died. In the same letter she also mentioned the pending deaths of several fascist collaborators.[26]

Pound was sufficiently moved by this news to compose a coda to the sequence he had completed, and he began with a cry of grief. Before he knew it the new Canto (LXXXIV) had turned into a bitter farewell to "il Capo [Mussolini], / Pierre [Laval], [and] Vidkun [Quisling]" (559). In effect, this unforeseen conclusion reframed the sequence, and Pound completed the job by moving ten angry and as yet unplaced lines to the beginning of Canto LXXIV.[27] As difficult as it is to believe, the dramatic of *The Pisan Cantos* was an afterthought. Pound's elegy to Mussolini announces a much more political and programmatic poem than the one he thought he had completed:

> The enormous tragedy of the dream in the peasant's bent shoulders
> Manes! Manes was tanned and stuffed,
> Thus Ben and la Clara *a Milano*
>   by the heels at Milano
> That maggots shd/ eat the dead bullock
> DIGONOS, Δίγονος, but the twice crucified
>   where in history will you find it?
> yet say this to the Possum: a bang, not a whimper,
>   with a bang not with a whimper,
> To build the city of Dioce whose terrances are the colour of stars.
>
>   (LXXIV/445)

However belated, Pound's last-minute revisions made what remained vibrate in a different way, and made it more difficult for readers to hear the contradictions of his text. The Mussolini lines send *The Pisan Cantos* on their way bristling with self-protective hostility and hurtling toward Canto LXXXIV. Tuning our ear to them, we hear not openness or generosity but only what one critic has called a "proud and intransigent ... stoicism" that helps Pound "to control and order" his chaos and his despair.[28]

Section: *Rock-Drill de los cantares*: 1946–1955

After the trauma of his relocation and brush with execution, Pound became habituated to his bizarre new life at St. Elizabeths – inmate of an insane asylum yet also an international celebrity visited by America's aspiring poets and the world's literary elite. Perhaps inevitably, his work entered a period of consolidation and retrenchment. Starting in 1948, his lifelong friends and publishers, James Laughlin at New Directions and T. S. Eliot at Faber & Faber, brought out volumes of his collected *Cantos, Selected Poems, Literary Essays* and *Translations*, hoping to rehabilitate and restore Pound's reputation and to improve his chances for release. The project encountered a major setback in 1949, when a Library of Congress committee that included Eliot, Allen Tate and others awarded *The Pisan Cantos* the first in a series of projected Bollingen prizes and provoked a storm of abuse from a public that was not yet ready to honor a man under indictment for treason. Forced to defend the claims of art against political judgment, Pound's supporters fixed the terms of a period of formalist criticism that lasted for a generation and more.

Inside St. Elizabeths, Pound's new work mirrored the tensions of his age. He could hardly forget that his influence in the world of affairs had been destroyed. His defiance fueled also by resentment at being unable to defend himself in court, he went about justifying himself and produced a series of belligerently mandarin poems. What Eliot or Tate implied about the deficiencies of post-war mass culture by the elevated tone of their criticism, Pound incorporated into a fable about Confucian wisdom. Meanwhile Pound worked assiduously at his Confucian translations, more convinced than ever that they were the key to perpetuating the best of the fascist world view.[29]

What his Confucian studies meant to Pound in such circumstances can be seen in his succeeding Cantos. Against the grain of the Villon-related passages of *The Pisan Cantos*, he produced two volumes of a Paradise as mystified and authoritarian as anything he had composed in the thirties. The only element of counterpoint seemed to come from a subsidiary translation, of Sophokles' *The Women of Trachis*, published in the *Hudson Review* in late 1953. The ghastly sufferings of Herakles, martyr of love and good faith, appeared regularly in the *Cantos* and came to figure the apparently interminable agon of Pound himself.

In a notebook written in the beginning of his internment in Washington, D.C. (possibly 1946), Pound layed out a plan for "Cantos 85–100 in brief" that began:

> Bellum cano parenne –
> to which Troy but a flea-bite
> between the usurers
> & the man who wd do a good job

[. . .]
Thrones
          belascio or topaze
Something
          (Erigena)
god can sit
     on
     without having it squish
          ———

Make it New
     from T'ang to Ocellus
"To keep some of the
non-interest bearing national debt
     in circulation
          as currency"
T.C.P.[30]

The note, which would guide the composition of most of *Rock-Drill* and *Thrones*, stubbornly resurrects ideas Pound had first formulated in 1940. Once again Pound's focus is on an eternal war between "them" and "us" – between the usucratic West and a few intelligent resisters (Erigena, the emperor T'ang, the neo-Platonist Ocellus, and Pound's grandfather Thaddeus Coleman Pound) who by careful observation of the natural order rediscover and transmit an eternal wisdom about human affairs. Pound included a version of this exordium for the transition between the published versions of Cantos LXXXVI and LXXXVII ("Bellum cano perenne . . . / between the usurer and any man who / wants to do a good job" – (LXXXVI–LXXXVII/588–89), but its insistence can be felt from the very opening lines of the new work. Canto LXXXV, which Pound began to draft in a notebook in September 1952 associated with his translations of the Confucian *Odes*,[31] begins with a Chinese character for spirit or intelligence Pound extracted from the Confucian History Classic (the *Chou King*).[32] Almost immediately, using words translated from Seraphin Couvreur's French and Latin edition, it adds: "Our dynasty came in because of a great sensibility" (LXXXV/563). As Massimo Bacigalupo, probably *Rock-Drill*'s most perceptive reader, has commented, the phrase "our dynasty" along with (a few lines later) the line "our science is from the watching of shadows" positions the poetry as the speech of "a member in a community of initiates." Hence the tone of the sequence, so different from the vacillations of Pisa. Speaking with an initiate's certainty (and with a conviction that his conclusions are based on the observations of occult "science"), Pound shades toward what Bacigalupo calls "sectarian obtuseness." That is, in the purportedly "objective" world of *Rock-Drill*, there seems to be "no place for exceptions and qualifications: every statement is desperately peremptory, impermeable to all objections." This obstinacy "follows upon, and compensates for, the precarious status . . . of Pound's discourse, which proceeds warily one step at a time, from one small fact to the next, and cannot admit any hesitation, doubt, or self-irony, for then the whole shaky poetic-ideological edifice would collapse."[33] Whence the appropriately pugnacious title of *Rock-Drill*, which, incorporating the name of Jacob Epstein's famous avant-garde sculpture of the teens, is a more direct reference to the title of Wyndham Lewis's 1951 review of Pound's *Selected Letters*.[34]

Yet the style of *Rock-Drill* possesses a kind of hermetic toughness that (for better or worse) did not lack admirers (for example, the Charles Olson of the later *Maximus* poems). As Bacigalupo notes, Pound's transcription of sources becomes gnomic, nodal, "shrinking to small bits of mosaic" – "irreducible atomic facts" that in their syntactic simplicity recall "primitive thought" rather than "Pisa's discourse-in-progress."[35] And whether we agree that the style represents simply a "naked transcription of [Pound's] arduous and at times arid mental condition,"[36] there is no doubt about its appropriateness in a sequence designed to articulate the divinings of a magus.

Section: Rock-Drill begins with two Cantos (LXXXV and LXXXVI) which endorse the *Chou King*'s claim that governments have always risen or fallen according to their observance of mystical truths about human nature. Vital to this primary theme is the corollary figure of the heroic resister. Since "We flop if we cannot maintain the awareness" (LXXXV/577), culture continues largely due to the efforts of individuals who in ignorant times "Risked the smoke to go forward" (LXXXV/579). In Cantos LXXXVII–LXXXIX, the focus of these linked concerns is American. Drawing on Thomas Hart Benton's memoir, *Thirty Years' View: A History of the Working of the American Government for Thirty Years, from 1820 to 1850* (2 vols., 1854, 1856), Pound selects an incident in the life of John Randolph that occurred on the site of Pound's own imprisonment to suggest the power of a decent individual to rectify the nation's honor. The testimony is all the more important because Randolph has been forgotten by posterity.

The center of gravity of *Rock-Drill*, however, can be found in Cantos XC to XCV, which comprise an elaborate celebration of the rites and arcanum of an initiate into the earthly paradise of love. Unfolding from Erigena's contention that (XC/626) "Ubi amor, ibi oculus" (where there is love there is sight), Pound weaves and reweaves variations on the experience of a lover cleansed in spirit, disciplined in attention and expert in expression. The paradigm here is "Amphion!" (XC/625), whose musical response to a magical communication with the natural world calls forth the constructions of civilization and culture. And the center of the mantra is a figure of the beloved incorporating (in Canto XC) the Cunizza of the *Pisan Cantos* but now imagined as a resplendent queen ("La Luna Regina," (XCII/639). As Canto after Canto returns to encounter her presence, Pound seems to rise out of his despair.

In *Rock-Drill*, however, such moments, deliberately conflated with initiation rites, are less *cris-de-coeur* than stylized and calculated ceremonies. They forego emotional poignancy for a cold, Byzantine shimmer. Hence what seems to be a cry torn from extremity in Canto XC ("from under the rubble heap / m'elevasti") turns into Canto XCIII's purposeful cultivation of darkness ("not yet! not yet! / Do not awaken"). Only the kind of concentrated awareness that arises out of confused experience can produce illumination. Only thus does real knowledge come into being. In America, long before Pound Emerson had also contended that no two can "know the same in their knowing" (XCIII/651); knowledge is after all a function of personal vision working upon the world. Hence, Pound's homage in *Rock-Drill* to persecuted but holy wanderers, such as the mystic sage Apollonius of Tyana. Finally Pound's sages blur into one – Odysseus as the neo-Platonics imagined him: the shipwrecked figure of *Odyssey V*, destined for miraculous redemption. *Rock-Drill* ends with that crisis.

Thrones 96–109 de los cantares: 1955–1959

Pound transitions from *Rock-Drill* to *Thrones* at the moment when Odysseus achieves land, releases the instrument of his salvation – the veil of Ino-Leucothea – and watches his savior as "the wave concealed her, / dark mass of great water" (XCVI/671). Instead of exploring the drama of such a moment, however, *The Cantos* immediately turn elsewhere, paying less attention to the introspection of Odysseus at the Pheaecian court than to the Phaecian setting itself – the magically ordered and aesthetically brilliant kingdom against which Odysseus rediscovers his suffering humanity. In *Thrones*, Phaecia stands as the first in a series of charmed societies whose archetype is Byzantium.

The last two Cantos of *Rock-Drill* had in fact begun to associate the state of mind of the confirmed initiate with the mystical harmony that holds together an ordered society. In Canto XCIV, for example, the wanderer Apollonius is placed both in opposition to the king who tries him and in parallel with lawgivers such as Confucius and Coke, Justinian and Antoninus. The same Canto also speaks of "AMOR" and the path of illumination that leads "Above prana, the light, / past light, the crystal. / Above crystal, the jade!" Each is both "Beyond civic order" and part of its essential foundation (XCIV/654).

Pound maintains the link between magus-wanderer and magus-lawgiver throughout *Thrones*, but allows the lawgiver first prominence. As he explained to Donald Hall a few months after *Thrones* was published, "the Thrones in Dante's *Paradiso* are for the spirits of the people who have been responsible for good government. The thrones in the *Cantos* are an attempt to move out from egoism and to establish some definition of an order possible or at any rate conceivable on earth . . . *Thrones* concerns the states of mind of people responsible for something more than their personal conduct."[37]

Following this program, Pound assembles a palimpsest of legal codes from the breadth and depth of human civilization. Yet, with some exceptions his exempla are not the great Solons themselves – Justinian, say – but transmitters of wisdom in a dark time, after a great culture has collapsed under the pressures of perfidy, decadence and war. So we find Canto XCVI concerning itself with the darkness following the fall of classical Rome, vividly evoked by floods "in the Via Lata" (the modern Via del Corso). First Pound gives us the civilization of the eighth-century Lombards as recorded by Paul the Deacon's *History of the Lombards* (edited in volume 95 of Migne's *Patralogiae Latina*). Then he turns to Byzantium as registered by a revision of Justinian's institutes – *The Book of the Eparch of Leo the Wise*, translated into French in 1893 by Jules Nicole. Cantos XCVIII and XCIX draw from a Neo-Confucian Chinese text (*The Sacred Edict*) written in 1670 AD but (like the Eparch's Book) edited in the age of Western orientalism – by F. W. Baller in 1892.[38] Canto CV shifts back in time and space to St. Anselm's *Monologium* and *Proslogium*, which in Pound's reading argue "the compatability of faith and reason" in late eleventh-century France and England and prepare the way for the Magna Carta and English liberty.[39]

Back in the east, Canto CVI cites from Lewis Maverick's edition of *Economic Dialogues in Ancient China: Selections from the Kuan-tzu*. Concluding, Cantos CVII–CIX, heavily influenced by Catherine Drinker Bowen's 1956 biography of Sir Edward Coke, *The Lion and the Throne*, allude to Coke's *Second Institutes of the Laws of England* and to the monumental struggle between Coke and James I in which the rights guaranteed by the Magna Carta were specified and broadly expanded.

Behind each of these tableax, however, stands a much more familiar prototype. As Pound admits almost offhandedly,

> "Constantinople" said Wyndham "our star,"
> Mr. Yeats called it Byzantium   (XCVI/681)

An aestheticized image of Byzantium very close to the one memorialized by Yeats animates both the subject and the treatment of *Thrones*. For however much Pound believes himself to be creating an ideogram of wise leadership, only with difficulty can one glean from his texts the clear outlines of legal or administrative policy. These Cantos concern themselves not with the ordinary life of society but with the gem-like clarity of an idealized moment when the whole of culture has become a work of art. The substance of *Thrones*, though, is so abbreviated as to be unreadable, causing even such appreciative critics as Bacigalupo to speak of an "unyielding" "coriacious" verse, "which is all the time approaching silence, the unrelated rock splinter."[40] As a means to transmit the distilled wisdom of the ages, the truncated and gnomic style of *Thrones* is inappropriate to the point of absurdity. Only by remembering the volume's beginnings in *Rock-Drill* does one realize the purpose of its hermetic procedures.

Even in Canto XCVI's charming tableau of the tabulary, Pound comes to rest on an image of ritual silence. The tabulary, having disciplined himself by study and habit, graduates to the more searching discipline supplied by incense at his consecration, showing "how his thought shd/ go." Pound's lawgivers, initiates of the inner recesses of the secretum, are similarly associated in these Cantos with a recurring movement, beginning in Canto XCVI, resurfacing in Cantos XCVII, CI and CII, and culminating in Canto CVI, in which rites of love are affiliated with hermetic symbolism. At issue here is the naming of that which anchors human value. As in all the Cantos since the Pisans, Pound focuses on the eyes of the beloved. And as was the case in *Rock-Drill*, a Byzantine intricacy pervades his supplication:

> copper and wine like a bear cub's
>   in sunlight, thus Atalant
> the colour as *aithiops*
>   the gloss probably
>   *oinops*
> as lacquer in sunlight
>   haliporphuros,
>   russet-gold   (CII/750)

This sequence is at once an encounter with the white goddess and an etymological excursion on the nuances of her name. By Canto CXVI, the encounter has become, in its dense concentration, haunting and compelling. (In comparison, Canto XC's incantation seems stagey.) Not the least part of its power lies in Pound's finally acknowledged delight in the vocation of word-smith: part tabulary, part symbolist master. Long half in love with the nineties' faith in the power of words to create reality, here Pound writes with the proud assurance of one who has scrupulously followed the advice of his mentor:

> And as Ford said: get a dictionary
> and learn the meaning of words.   (XCVIII/709)

Despite its peculiar virtues, *Thrones* was not well received by contemporary reviewers nor does it currently have a passionate following. This resistance stems to a certain extent from the deliberate recalcitrance of Pound's procedures, but unresolved problems in the sequence's composition also play a part.

Thrones began as an unhesitating continuation of *Rock-Drill*. Even before the earlier sequence was published in 1955, Pound had gone on with new Cantos. He focused first on the *Sacred Edict* material. Several notebooks of 1954 and 1955 block out sections of Baller for Cantos XCVIII and XCIX while simultaneously drafting lines to be used in the more lyric Canto CII.[41] Then in early 1956 Pound doubled back to Paul the Deacon and began assembling material for the more miscellaneous Cantos XCVII and C. At about that time he also started working on what became the St. Anselm Canto CV (he also envisioned a Canto on St. Ambrose), and substantially drafted Canto CVI. With Canto CI roughed out in the last half of 1956, he had blocked out a sequence that began with Paul the Deacon, swelled out to two unusually full Cantos on *The Sacred Edict*, found a lyrical focus in Cantos CI and CII and concluded with the visionary Canto CVI.[42]

In the second half of 1956, Pound became fascinated with Joseph F. Rock's anthropological monographs on the religious lore of the Na Khi culture of highland China.[43] By mid-1957 he had interpolated some of this material into drafts for Canto CI, CIV, and CVI, and by the summer of 1957 he used it to redraft the *Sacred Edict* Cantos XCVIII and XCIX. His additions, though, achieved a kind of pyrrhic success. The new material was unmistakeably powerful, and enriched the atmosphere of the ceremonial Cantos. However, some of the Na Khi legends that attracted Pound were anti-Confucian: they grew out of the experience of a people who had been forced to conform to Confucian marital practices, and their power had precisely to do with the force of protest against an oppressive civil order. Pound would, in *Drafts & Fragments*, come to understand the nature of this material, and would artfully redeploy it with impressive results. In 1957, however, the Na Khi images displaced *Thrones'* center of gravity, and Pound, having pried open Cantos CI and CVI to treat the Na-Khi ceremonies more fully, seemed to realize as much. Reacting to the pull of the elegaic, he hesitated to go farther.

Then in the later summer of 1957 still another subject intruded. Note-books dating from August 1957 contain Pound's first extensive treatment of Sir Edward Coke, whom he had before this mentioned only in passing.[44] Charmed by Bowen's biography of Coke, Pound saw immediately that the English jurist provided an Anglo-American counterpart to the medieval documents in Canto XCVI and a postscript to the paean to Western liberty he had begun in Canto CV. Using Bowen and Coke's *Institutes*, he drafted three more Cantos: CVII, CVIII and CIX. But these additions, which might have been the making of *Thrones*, in fact dragged the volume down. Pound tried to remake Coke as a compound of Confucius and himself – both legislator and rebel, a man of great sensibility and enormous stub-bornness. Drafted in enthusiastic haste, the new Cantos never quite got Coke in their sights but wouldn't let him go. They prolonged *Thrones* for nearly twenty pages beyond the volume's logical conclusion and destroyed the proportions of an eleven-Canto sequence of the kind Pound had crafted with increasing skill from *Eleven New Cantos XXXI–XLI* (1934) to the *Pisan Cantos* and *Rock-Drill*.

Nor is it clear that left to his own devices Pound would have quit even with Canto CIX. This last includes a sequence that associates the Magna Carta – the basis for Coke's consolidation of English law – with an incident in 1715 in which a Wadsworth ancestor of Pound preserved a copy of the Connecticut Charter from royal confiscation (CIX). In a subsequent typescript Pound went on with this material in a short new Canto marked "Canto 110 (or 111 or 112)."[45] Clearly he was thinking of extending *Thrones* in this direction. But as had happened with the *Pisan Cantos* in 1945, the unexpected intervened.

After years of futile behind-the-scenes manipulation, pressure by James Laughlin, Robert Frost, T. S. Eliot and others in 1958 suddenly succeeded in effecting Pound's release. On April 18, he was set free, and on July 1 he sailed for Italy accompanied by his wife Dorothy and a young admirer, Marcella Spann, and with the typescripts of the not quite finished *Thrones* in his luggage. That summer he finalized the sequence, whose proofs he read in June and July 1959.[46] In the meanwhile, he envisioned a succeeding volume of Cantos beginning with the Connecticut Charter story and with a full treatment of the Na Khi.

Drafts & Fragments: 1958–1972

Landing in Genoa and still accompanied by Dorothy and Marcella, Pound arrived on July 12, 1958 at Brunnenburg, the home that his daughter Mary with her husband Boris de Rachewiltz and their two young children had prepared to receive him. Mary had married against her mother's advice soon after the war, and the ensuing family quarrel helped to estrange Pound from Olga. Meanwhile Mary and Boris had reclaimed a ruined castle in the Italian Tyrol. With the help of visiting artist friends, by 1958 it had become an imposing setting to welcome a septuagenarian poet. Yet despite its grandeur, the castle proved inauspicious. Set deep in the mountains, it began to resonate with the melancholy legends of the Na Khi.

Shielded for over a decade from problematic personal decisions, in the fall of 1958 Pound faced a series of competing personal claims amid the first signs of faltering health. Though he appreciated his daughter's generosity, life at the castle bored him and the mountain air made it difficult for him to breathe. He also had somehow to negotiate the feelings of Dorothy, Mary, and (in the background) Olga, all of whom wondered about the continued presence of Marcella. Pound would not do without Marcella, and took her (often with Dorothy or Mary) to revisit the landscapes of his poetic life. In late September they travelled to Venice and Torcello, and in January and February to the towns of Lake Garda. And as Pound insisted on his desire to keep Marcella near him, their difficulties recapitulated in a minor key the situation of the 1910s, when Edwardian conventions had postponed his marriage to Dorothy. This time, though, the long-suffering Dorothy had become one of the obstructors of an ill-defined arrangement of old age, and the outcome was far from simple.

In these circumstances, Pound went on with *The Cantos*. Temporarily putting the Connecticut Charter material aside, he concentrated on a longer typescript based on lines he had drafted in his notebooks the previous December in Washington.[47] Alternating between the Na Khi material and economic history, the fragment had contained one personal passage. It started with the cry of a beach bird and the memory of a highly charged moment, possibly involving Dorothy but more likely Marcella, on a Virginia beach in June. Onto this memory, the passage grafted the eyes of the heroine of a Na Khi suicide romance edited by Rock. In the tale, a representative girl, forced to give up her lover and marry a man chosen by her parents, chooses to hang herself. The Na Khi, a non-Confucian tribe, had once countenanced easy sexuality and free marital choice. When they were forced to emigrate to Confucian China the old customs were condemned, and many young people chose to kill themselves rather than submit to the new ways. Their tragedies were turned into romance, and the rituals that emerged from the poetry concerned souls of the departed young women that were said to inhabit the wind. The manuscript Pound brought to the Tyrol steeped itself in this history, but turned from the sombreness of the suicide romance ("will you walk with the earth's root") to another, more positive, ritual, the ²Muan ¹bpo, said to connect man, earth and heaven.[48]

Though the point of the suicide in Pound's early draft is its illumination, elaborating the manuscript in Italy Pound amplified its melancholy lyricism with an undertone of the growing friction at the Castle and a premonition of ongoing illness. His increasingly elegaic tone also speaks of the failing health of two old friends – his college fiancée, Hilda Doolittle (H.D.), who from a sanitorium in Switzerland in 1958 had sent him a memoir of their time together (*End to Torment*, later published in 1979; Doolittle would die in 1961); and William Carlos Williams, once also in love with Hilda, who had suffered a serious stroke in October 1958 and would die in 1963. The glory and sadness of all this imposed itself on Pound as he composed. Though he twisted and turned the political material in other parts of the typescript, his heart was no longer in the themes of *Thrones*, and he finally abondoned much of it.[49]

Meanwhile, Pound transformed the young Na Khi suicide into the focus of *Drafts & Fragments*, generalized near the end of Canto CX into the simplicity of a more traditional figure:

> A wind of darkness hurls against forest
> the candle flickers
> is faint
>
> Lux enim –
> versus this tempest.   (CX/801)

He also thickened his emotional subject with the suddenly resurgent voice of the Herakles of *The Women of Trachis*. In *Rock-Drill* and *Thrones*, Pound tried to draw consolation from the sense of destiny that Herakles achieved in his suffering. At LXXXVII/591, C/734, and CIX/ 792, he alluded to the blaze of light that "The play [is] shaped from" (LXXXVII/591), in the midst of which the dying Herakles exclaims: "What splendour! It all coheres!" In 1959 the relevance of Herakles' shirt of flame (the product of a husband's unfaithfulness and a wife's affection twisted from its natural course by possessiveness and an enemy's treachery) proved almost too much to bear. Distraught by the suffering caused by his divided affections, in *Drafts & Fragments* Pound endowed a Herakles-like voice with lamentation suitable to the Na Khi suicide ("No man can see his own end," CXII/807) and a continuing insistence that "it coheres all right /

even if my notes do not cohere" (CXVI/817) – all it takes is "A little light, like a rushlight / to lead back to splendour" (CXVI/817).

Pound's determination to celebrate light amid the gathering darkness first enters *Drafts & Fragments* in the form of a reminiscence of the happiness he had enjoyed in Venice in that fall. ("Hast' ou seen boat's wake on sea-wall, / how crests it? / What panache? / paw-flap, wave-tap, / that is gaiety," CX/797.) Nevertheless, such moments only make the sombreness of the suicide more intense. In Canto CX, Pound introduces the latter with an epitaph from the Francesca episode of *Inferno V* ("che paion' si al vent'"). And before anything else he invokes the haunting figure of the young Madonna in the apse of the Cathedral at Torcello. The final reincarnation of the intercessor who had visited him in 1945 on the cliffs of St. Ambrogio, after the hieratic images of *Rock-Drill* and *Thrones* she appears again as a moon-waif, abandoned and seeking refuge. Her survival deep in the silent lagoon creates an image of a delicate, vulnerable and compassionate beauty "From time's wreckage shored" (CX/801).

Finally, Canto CX subtly but inexorably reorders the emphases of the St. Elizabeths draft discussed above. It is not the Ceremony of Heaven but the ceremonies surrounding the suicide that now seem most important. And Pound's questions become more than perfunctory. Do you know, he asks the girl in the story, that the black tree on which you will hang yourself is dumb, and that your courage will be never spoken? Are you aware of the darkness and silence to come? Still clinging to beauty and joy, Canto CX does not smooth over death, nor disconnect it from the forces of the surrounding wind.

Stylistically, the tone and articulation of *Drafts & Fragments*, unlike those of *Rock-Drill* and *Thrones*, seem genuinely noncoercive. As Pound moves toward Canto CXVI's confession that "my errors and wrecks lie about me [CXVI/816]," his writing regains some of the humility of the Villon-related verses at Pisa. All of *Drafts & Fragments* partakes of this new tentativeness, but it is perhaps easiest to see in "From [Canto] CXV":

> The scientists are in terror
>   and the European mind stops
> Wyndham Lewis chose blindness
>   rather than have his mind stop.
> Night under wind mid garofani,
>   the petals are almost still
> Mozart, Linnaeus, Sulmona,
> When one's friends hate each other
>   how can there be peace in the world?   (814)

This is an elegy for Wyndham Lewis, who had died in 1957, and appropriately its opening celebrates his courage. Pound memorializes Lewis's 1951 decision to accept certain blindness rather than submit to an operation that might impair his mind. But, as Timothy Materer points out, "the tone of the elegy darkens" in the lines[50] that follow the opening as Lewis's rebarbative resistance aligns with the night wind against the peaceful petals of the garofani (carnation) flower. Hence what had started as Pound's affirmation of Lewis's energy turns into a questioning of Lewis's hate, and youth's diversions appear all the more wasteful from the perspective of "a blown husk that is finished" (CXV/814). Lewis's disputations over time and space in *Time and Western Man* provided no answers, and Pound suggests his own categories were no more adequate ("In meiner Heimat / where the dead walked / and the living were made of cardboard") (CXV/ 814). Hauntingly, Lewis returns, becoming one of "the dead" who continue to "walk."

"From CXV" shows Pound's revived power to mime the twisting stages of thought and feeling, and speaks of the difficult and painful development of *Drafts & Fragments* as a whole. The most evocative and poignant of *The Cantos*, their genesis was the most problematic. In the early Spring of 1959, Pound, continuing to chafe at life in Brunnenburg, settled down with Dorothy and Marcella in Rapallo. Meanwhile he wrestled with the fragments he was composing, rearranging and rearranging in a vain attempt to integrate the Na Khi and political material he had brought over from Washington. By May, he had set aside early versions of Cantos CX and CXI and drafted a Canto CXIII in which jealousy and possessiveness were major themes. Canto CXIV, written mostly in June and July 1959, continues these preoccupations, remembers "good guys in [Pound's] family," and amplifies Pound's meditation on isolated and beleaguered excellence. Later in the summer, Pound composed a long confessional precursor ("115") of "From CXV" after unpacking a batch of Wyndham Lewis letters. Then, when the understanding between Pound, Dorothy and Marcella began to break down, Pound composed Canto CXVI and a Canto "117" he later decided not to retain. The latter adverts explicitly to the unhappiness Pound had caused, exclaiming "I have been a pitiless stone – / stone making art work / and destroying affections." Yet at least in one typescript of "117," Pound ended on a note of exultation:

> Till suddenly the tower
>   blazed with the light of Astarte
> @ Genova the port lay below us.
>   Miracolo di Dio

Then in the autumn of 1959, Pound found himself no longer able to go on. Dorothy's diary records that on September 26, Pound was "in a fuss – re M[arce]lla" and that on the 27th Dorothy was "exhausted." By the next day, Dorothy's attorney Arthur V. Moore was relaying to James Laughlin that "Dorothy ... is having a very worrying time indeed, and she feels that he is really too difficult for her alone, and that the young Texan Secretary [Marcella] says she is returning to the U.S.A. I gather E.P. changes his mind so often, and worries – and now says he wants to go back to Brunnenburg to die, and has suicidal spells."[51] The same day Moore wrote his letter Pound set off for Brunnenberg. Dorothy would follow on October 4.

What happened after that comprises one of the most fascinating stories in the annals of textual study. Not much improved in January, 1960, Pound with his daughter's encouragement went to stay in an apartment in Rome that belonged to his old friend Ugo Dadone. (Dorothy went back to Rapallo.) At the end of February, after two rocky months, he was visited by the young poet Donald Hall, who had come to interview him for *The Paris Review*. For four days, Hall treated him like a hero and eagerly sought out news of the continuation of *The Cantos*. Though an admirer, Hall had been annoyed and perplexed by *Thrones* and was eager to see Pound break out of the style of their condensed political discourse. He picked up on Pound's intermittent interest in writing a Paradiso, and on Pound's moments of self-doubt. Pound read him from the manuscripts he had so far composed. Hall enthused, and (as a back-door method of paying Pound for the interview) asked Pound to send fragments to *The Paris Review* for publication.

Hall's pressure was responsible for Pound's pushing on with poems he was not eager to reread, and for substantive revisions Pound made and later questioned. In preparing a manuscript for Hall, Pound condensed his sequence radically. On one hand he resisted Hall's eagerness to have a Paradisal ending, and he cut Cantos "114" and "115" drastically. ("114" would later be largely restored, and many of the "paradisal" parts of the original "115" would later reappear in the final fragments.) On the other hand, the same revisions underscored the introspection of the sequence in a way that confirmed and even exceeded Hall's expectations.[52]

True to his word, Hall retyped the sequence, sending one copy to James Laughlin and another copy to Pound. Pound answered a first set of editorial queries about the Cantos and about Hall's interview, then stopped responding. Hall was frantic. He wanted to finalize production of the cantos and the interview for *The Paris Review*, but that now seemed impossible. He proceeded only after September 24, 1961, when Laughlin wrote Hall that Dorothy had sent him a corrected interview, which Pound had started to edit but, in Dorothy's words, "about halfway through" his "concentration g[ave] out."[53]

Hall then worked as quickly as he could. In Summer–Fall 1962 (vol. 7, no. 28), the Pound issue of *The Paris Review* appeared, containing among other things, Hall's smoothed over interview and two Cantos – "*from* Canto 115" and one of the "Canto 116" variants.

Meanwhile, over the next five years and with some help from Pound, James Laughlin placed other canto fragments in periodicals. By 1967 parts of all the cantos between CX and CXVI had appeared. For the most part these were variants of the revisions that Pound had made for Hall and that Hall had copied for Laughlin. There were, however, two substantive exceptions, and both of these involved "paradisal" fragments from the more confessional earlier version of "From CXV."[54]

These difficulties came to a head in 1967, and once again Hall bore responsibility. Hall had lent a student a copy of his retypings, and two borrowings later it had been retyped and mimeographed into a pirated text – "Cantos 110–116," "printed and published by [Ed Sanders at] the FUCK YOU / press at a secret location in the lower east side."[55] At that point, apparently with little sense of the textual dislocations that had occurred, James Laughlin decided to put out his own text "fast . . . to try to stop some more piracies." "It was on the basis of this piracy," Laughlin wrote in the same letter, "that I was able to persuade Ezra to do some work in putting these Drafts & Fragments into shape."[56]

When New Directions wanted to bring out a revised text of *Drafts & Fragments of Cantos CX–CXVII* in 1968/9, Pound at first witheld his authorization. According to his daughter, Mary de Rachewiltz, to remedy the situation caused by the piracy, she and Laughlin struggled to get Pound's permission.[57] After they thought they had failed, Pound finally acquiesced (perhaps because Laughlin forced his hand), and his signature ("23 Aug 1968 / Venezia") and corrections can be found on a set of New Directions galley proofs now at the Houghton Library, Harvard.

Nor was Pound's prolonged ambivalence missing from the New Directions text. Building on the Hall version, Pound's revision for Laughlin restored important features of his earlier sequence: the long pre-Hall "114," for example, and more interestingly a conclusion that contained two 1941 fragments and a "Notes for CANTO CXVII et seq." made up of two fragments ("For the blue flash"; "M'amour, m'amour") descended from the pre-Hall "115" and one ("La faillite") from the first typescript version of Canto CXIII. Pound could not bear, it seems, to omit these (however qualified) affirmations of light, love and natural order.

Nor even then was the sequence finalized. The same year (1969) that New Directions printed its version of *Drafts & Fragments*, a magazine entitled *The Anonym Quarterly* published a "CANTO 120" that presumably was to follow the three fragments of "CXVII et seq." In fact "Canto 120" was a slightly revised version of lines from the pre-Hall "115":

> I have tried to write Paradise
>
> Do not move.
>   Let the wind speak.
>   that is paradise.
> Let the Gods forgive what I
>   have made
> Let those I love try to forgive
>   what I have made.

The *Anonym* publication raised several portentous questions. If these lines were to conclude *The Cantos*, they made a major difference. A recantation of sorts, they more accurately represent an affirmation. Out of the dialectic, out of the search, they announce the natural site of wisdom. In this light, Pound's decision to publish "Canto 120" reinforced the resurgence of the three "CXVII et seq." fragments. All four passages reconfirm the mystical portions of earlier parts of the poem and resist the skepticism of the 1960 Hall-related revisions.

What happened next made things more puzzling still. Three weeks after Pound's death in November 1972, James Laughlin inserted "Canto 120" into an obituary notice New Directions placed in *The New York Times Book Review*.[58] Then in a 1972 reprinting of the 1970 collected *Cantos*, New Directions placed "Canto CXX" at the conclusion of the poem, capping the mysterious but apparently inevitable return of the excised paradisal material. Peter Stoicheff, whose insightful account of the history and significance of Canto CXX I have been following, notes that Laughlin justified his decision on the basis of copyright alone, because no copyright had been recorded in the Library of Congress for either of the poem's serial appearances. Stoicheff, however, quite rightly goes on to speculate that this, like so many of the other interventions that altered *Drafts & Fragments*, represents more than an accidental event. The decision to end the 1972 text with "Canto CXX" was a substantive editorial act, involved interpretative and aesthetic matters, and corresponded "in its own way to what [an editor] vainly hoped Pound intented, or to what [he] thought *The Cantos* requested in the absence of its author."[59]

Nor did the evolution of *Drafts & Fragments* end in 1972. Widely circulated in the collected *Cantos*, "Canto CXX" was greeted by some as

a small miracle. As Pound released his grip on the poem, his readers –
including not only the friends who thought they were helping to complete
the poem as he would have wished, but also the detractors who were glad
to have *The Cantos* end as they expected – instinctively supplied a reflex
Pound himself had (for a while) outgrown. At the same time, another
group of readers, including editors at Pound's English publishers, Faber &
Faber,[60] rejected the new conclusion. The result was that New Directions
was forced to rethink its 1972 decision and to experiment with an alternate one, so that, in Stoicheff's words, "we have been given, over the last
twenty-two years, at least six" significantly different versions of both *Drafts
& Fragments* and the conclusion to the *Cantos*.[61] These included, in the
New Directions 1995 printing (824), the following:

> That her acts
> Olga's acts
> of beauty
> be remembered.
>
> Her name was Courage
> & is written Olga
>
> These lines are for the
> ultimate CANTO
>
> whatever I may write
> in the interim.
> [*24 August 1966*]

Pound's irresolution, however uncomfortable, reinforced the dominant
virtues of *Drafts & Fragments* and ironically won over more readers than
the fierce determination of his political verse. Along with the idiom of
the *Pisan Cantos*, which through Robert Lowell had influenced the
so-called confessional school of poets, the evocative shards of *Drafts &
Fragments* confirmed Pound's reputation for a new generation. Whether or
not he limned a coherent Paradise, and whether or not he relinquished his
enthusiasm for Italian fascism, Pound entered the phantastikon of the late
sixties as an iconoclastic poet whose experimental procedures signified, in
Allen Ginsberg's words, "no less than the whole alteration of human
consciousness."[62] Without the Cantos he began to write in 1945, he would
be known today as a fellow traveler of the Eliot of *The Waste Land* who
self-destructed, like so many others, on the ideological reefs of the 1930s.
Instead, Pound remains as influential as he is controversial, an outcast who
lived long enough to doubt his strongest convictions and make haunting
poetry of the remaining disarray.

NOTES

1 See "An Introduction to the Economic Nature of the United States," reprinted in Ezra Pound, *Selected Prose: 1909–1965*, ed. William Cookson (London: Faber and Faber, 1973), p. 137.

2 All references to the *Cantos* will take the form of Canto / Page Number, with the page numbers keyed to the thirteenth printing of the New Directions *Cantos of Ezra Pound* (New Directions: New York, 1995).

3 January 18, 1940. Cited in Tim Redman, *Ezra Pound and Italian Fascism* (Cambridge: Cambridge University Press, 1991), p. 194.

4 Selections from Pound's poetic notebooks at the Beinecke Library, Yale University, will be referred to below using notebook numbers assigned in *A Catalogue of the Poetry Notebooks of Ezra Pound*, comp. Mary de Rachewiltz, ed. Donald Gallup (Yale University Library: New Haven, 1980).

5 See Peter Makin, *Pound's Cantos* (London: Allen and Unwin, 1985), pp. 252–253.

6 Eva Hesse, "The End of *The Cantos*," in Harold Bloom (ed.), *Ezra Pound* (New York: Chelsea House, 1987), p. 32. For a more comprehensive account of Pound's ideological evolution, see Ronald Bush, "Excavating the Ideological Faultlines of Modernism: Editing Ezra Pound's *Cantos*," in George Bornstein (ed.), *Representing Modernist Texts: Editing as Interpretation* (Ann Arbor, MI: University of Michigan Press), pp. 67–98.

7 Ezra Pound, *Guide to Kulchur* (1938; rpt. New York: New Directions, 1952), p. 38.

8 Eli Goldblatt, "Gender Matters in Pound's *Cantos*," *Journal of Modern Literature*, 16, 1 (Summer 1988), 52.

9 For a discussion of the ideological implications of Canto VI's revision, see Bush, "Excavating the Ideological Faultlines of Modernism," pp. 71–77.

10 The following discussion has been excerpted from my " 'Quiet, not scornful'?: The Composition of *The Pisan Cantos*," in Lawrence S. Rainey (ed.), *A Poem Containing History: Textual Studies in The Cantos* (Ann Arbor, MI: University of Michigan Press, 1997), pp. 169–211.

   Pound's comment about "dead matter" comes from a letter of November 3, 1939 to Douglas McPherson. See *The Letters of Ezra Pound 1907–1941*, ed. D. D. Paige (New York: Harvest, 1950) p. 328. Pound also wrote of his plans for one more volume to Lulu Cunningham in 1939 in a letter quoted by Charles Norman in *Ezra Pound* (New York: Macmillan, 1960), p. 376. Both letters are cited by Humphrey Carpenter in *A Serious Character: The Life of Ezra Pound* (London: Faber and Faber, 1988), p. 575.

   Pound had featured Erigena prominently in Canto XXXVI, and in the late thirties had worked through some of the Erigena in the *Patralogia Latina*. His notes in the Beinecke Library at Yale (Pound Archive, Series III, folder 2681) can be dated from a provisional sketch of the Chinese Cantos they include. For a discussion of the significance of Erigena in Pound, see Peter Makin, "Ezra Pound and Scotus Erigena," *Comparative Literature Studies*, 10, 1 (March 1973), 60–83; and Carpenter's *Life*, p. 578.

11 Cited in Redman, *Ezra Pound and Italian Fascism*, p. 194.

12 In a letter to Santayana in December 1939, cited in Carpenter's *Life*, p. 576.

13 A page of this last was transcribed and published by Christine Froula in *The Yale Review*, 71, 2 (1982), 161–164.

14 On the news of the Tempio's destruction, see Lawrence Rainey, *Ezra Pound and the Monument of Culture* (Chicago: Chicago University Press, 1991), pp. 212–213; 329–331.

15 See *Ezra Pound: I Cantos*, trans. with notes Mary de Rachewiltz (Milan: Mondadori, 1985), pp. 825–835; and the 1995 New Directions *Cantos*, pp. 425–441.

16 See *I Cantos*, p. 1,566. On Mussolini's speech, see Rainey, *The Monument of Culture*, pp. 331–332. Rainey's account has been confirmed by the first notebook drafts of Cantos LXXII and LXXIII, recently made available among the Olga Rudge manuscript material at the Beinecke.

17 For commentary on Cantos LXXII and LXXIII (some of it preliminary), see Massimo Bacigalupo, "The Poet at War: Ezra Pound's Supressed Italian Cantos," *The South Atlantic Quarterly*, 83, 1 (Winter 1984), 69–79; Barbara C. Eastman, "The Gap in the *Cantos*: 72 and 73," *Paideuma*, 8, 3 (1979), 415–427; Carpenter's *Life*, pp. 637–640; Rainey, *The Monument of Culture*; Eva Hesse, *Ezra Pound: Die Ausgefallenen Cantos LXXII Und LXXIII* (Zurich: Arche, 1991); Robert Casillo, "Fascists of the Final Hour: Pound's Italian Cantos," in Richard J. Golsan (ed.), *Fascism, Aesthetics, and Culture* (Hanover Press of New England, 1992); and Massimo Bacigalupo, "Ezra Pound's Cantos 72 and 73: An Annotated Translation," *Paideuma*, 20, 1–2 (1991), 11–41.

18 Lines 9–35 of Canto LXXII were published with editorial help by Uberti as "Presenza di F. T. Marinetti" in the *Marina Repubblicana* for January 15, 1945. Canto LXXIII appeared in the same journal as "Cavalcanti–Corrispondenza Repubblicana," February 1, 1945. The young girl's story came from a newspaper article in the *Corriere della Sera*, October 1, 1944. See Rainey, *Ezra Pound and the Monument of Culture*, pp. 243–247.

19 See *I Cantos*, p. 1,569. Translations of Pound's typescripts of the Italian Cantos "74" and "75" have now been published by Massimo Bacigalupo. See "Ezra Pound's Cantos 72 and 73," pp. 30–40. Facsimiles of the original Italian (including a page 74/S which Bacigalupo omits) can be found in Bush, "'Quiet, not scornful.'" I have included transcripts and translations of still other Italian Cantos in "Towards Pisa: More from the Archives about Pound's Italian Cantos," *Agenda*, 34, 3–4 (Autumn-Winter 1996/7), 89–124.

20 *Guide to Kulchur*, pp. 107ff, and for commentary, Peter Makin, *Provence and Pound* (Berkeley: University of California Press), pp. 199ff.

21 Ezra Pound, *Confucius* (New York: New Directions, 1969), p. 187.

22 Forrest Read, "The Pattern of the Pisan Cantos," *Sewanee Review*, 65, 3 (Summer 1957), 400–419, esp. p. 405. Read has been more recently supplemented by the extended readings of Massimo Bacigalupo, *The Forméd Trace: The Later Poetry of Ezra Pound* (New York: Columbia University Press, 1980) and Anthony Woodward, *Ezra Pound and The Pisan Cantos* (Routledge and Kegan Paul, 1980).

23 On September 25, 1945, Dorothy, still unsure that Pound would ever receive her message, wrote that "Should this reach you. – You may imagine that I am thinking of you all the time: but I do not worry all that time. I only hope captivity is not proving bad for your health, & that you are able to work at

some writing or other. The moment perhaps for those 'memories'?" The word "memories" here has Dorothy's quotes around it, and points to the fact that the two of them have already discussed the possibility of a serious work about Pound's life. Which explains why, on October 13, having seen parts of Cantos 74, 75 and 76, she writes with something of the satisfaction of a prophet confirmed, and then with an uneasiness about private experience that mirrors Pound's own: "Of course," she exclaims, "all these last, apparantly, scraps, for cantos, are your self, the memories that make up yr. person." But she adds: "Is one then only a bunch of memories? i.e. a bunch of remains of contacts with the other people?" (Letters at the Lilly Library, Indiana University. For permission to read and quote them, thanks are extended to Dorothy's executor, Omar Pound.)

24 The typescript of Pound's "Note to Base Censor" was collected with the other Pisan typescripts in the Beinecke Library, Yale, and was reproduced as "A Prison-Letter" in *The Paris Review*, 28 (Summer Fall 1962), 17.

25 As translated by Anthony Bonner in *The Complete Works of François Villon* (New York: Bantam, 1960), p. 33.

26 Pound's mention of his "Decad 74/83" is dated October 2, 1945 (letter at the Lilly Library in Indiana). In a letter of October 4 he instructed Dorothy to send "72 or 74 to 83" to T. S. Eliot.

Dorothy's letter about Angold, also at the Lilly Library, arrived sometime after October 4, and on October 8 Pound began Canto LXXXIV.

27 The new opening was affixed to the beginning of an almost final typescript at a moment that can be precisely determined. Pound had written an "incipit" next to "Canto ?74" above the first page of what he intended as his setting typescript, and which still began, "The suave eyes, quiet, not scornful." *After* that he affixed the page beginning "The enormous tragedy of the dream." And only then did he indicate that this extra page would be page "1" and renumber the next set of pages 1–9.

28 Peter Nicholls, *Ezra Pound: Politics, Economics, and Writing* (Atlantic Highlands: Humanities Press, 1984), p. 166.

29 For an excellent account of the progress and political coloring of Pound's Confucian translations, see Mary Paterson Cheadle, *Ezra Pound's Confucian Translations* (Ann Arbor, MI: University of Michigan Press, 1997).

30 From Notebook 69 in the numbering of *A Catalogue of the Poetry Notebooks of Ezra Pound* (see p. 59).

31 From Notebook 71 in the numbering of *A Catalogue of the Poetry Notebooks of Ezra Pound* (see p. 61).

32 See Seraphin Couvreur, *Chou King, Les Annales de la Chine* (rpt. Paris: Cathasia, 1950), p. 295, and for commentary Carroll F. Terrell, *A Companion to the Cantos of Ezra Pound*, vol. II (Berkeley: University of California Press, 1984), p. 467.

33 See Bacigalupo, *The Forméd Trace*, pp. 234, 240. This book remains the standard commentary on *Rock-Drill* and *Thrones*. See also however, the relevant chapters of Makin, *Pound's Cantos*; James J. Wilhelm, *The Later Cantos of Ezra Pound* (New York: Walker, 1977); and George Kearns, *A Guide to Ezra Pound's Selected Cantos* (New Brunswick: Rutgers University Press, 1980).

34 See the *New Statesman and Nation* for April 7, 1951.

35 Bacigalupo, *The Forméd Trace*, pp. 232–233.

36 *Ibid.*

37 From the interview Hall conducted in 1960 and published in the *Paris Review* in 1962. The interview was subsequently collected in the second series of *Paris Review Writers at Work* volumes and then with Hall's associated recollections in *Remembering Poets* (New York: Harper and Row, 1978).

38 See Bacigalupo, *The Forméd Trace*, for the provenance of this text, which even in Chinese was the product of an intricate transmission: The *Sheng Yu* or *Sacred Edict* is, he explains,

> a summary of Confucian . . . ethics . . . written by the great K'ang-hsi (1670), and [includes] a commentary appended by Yung Cheng; Wang-iu-p'u, "salt commissioner" of Shensi, translated it from the literary (Uen-li) to the colloquial tongue. [The text Pound consulted was] . . . F. W. Baller's 1892 edition . . . an unassuming little book which includes the Uen-li text and Wang's colloquial rendering, the latter with English translation, and which the editor intended as an introduction for fellow missionaries to the language and culture of China. (Bacigalupo, *The Forméd Trace*, p. 372)

39 See Terrell, *A Companion to the Cantos of Ezra Pound*, II, p. 683. Terrell quotes a Pound interview with D. G. Bridson: "You can be damn well thankful to St. Anselm, because all your liberties back before 'Maggie Carter' as they used to call her in the law schools in America – I mean the fight between him and William Rufus, the dirty bandit – all your liberties come out of that."

40 Bacigalupo, *The Formed Trace*, p. 333.

41 See Notebooks 90 and 91 in the numbering of *A Catalogue of the Poetry Notebooks of Ezra Pound*, dated November 1954–January 1955 and January 1955–February 1955.

42 For Cantos XCVI, XCVII and C, see Notebooks 93, 94, 95 and 96 in the numbering of *A Catalogue of the Poetry Notebooks of Ezra Pound*, dating to March of 1956. For the St. Anselm and St. Ambrose jottings, see Notebooks 98, 99, 100, and 105. For early drafts of Canto CI, see Notebooks 101 and 102.

43 See especially Notebook 101, which contains Dorothy Pound's manuscript notes on Rock's *The Ancient Na-Khi Kingdom of Southwest China* (1947), II, p. 337.

44 See Notebooks 111–113, dated August 1957–March 1958.

45 This typescript was based entries in Notebook 113 dating from December 28, 1957 and was sent to Professor Norman Holmes Pearson from St. Elizabeths on January 22, 1858 with a note: "Just a little one, before we git on to Linnaeus." The typescript and note are to be found in the Pound Archive at the Beinecke Library, Yale, Box 71, Folder 2754.

46 Dorothy Pound refers in her diaries, now in the Lilly Library, to Pound's reading proof on June 21 and July 7, 1959.

47 See Notebook 112, dated November 1957–July 22, 1958. The typescript can be found in the Pound Archive at the Beinecke Library, Yale, in Box 71, Folder 2757.

48 For the suicide story, Pound's source is Joseph F. Rock, "The Romance of K'A-^{2}ma-^{1}gyu ^{2}mi-gkyi, A Na-Khi Tribal Love Story," *Bulletin de l'Ecole Française d'Extreme-Orient*, 39 (1939), 1–152. The source of the Ceremony of

Heaven is Rock's "The ²Muan-¹pbo Ceremony, or the Sacrifice to Heaven as Practiced by the Na-Khi," *Monumenta Serica*, 13 (1948).

49 For a fuller account of the composition of *Drafts & Fragments* and especially of the development of Canto CX, see Ronald Bush, "'Unstill, Ever Turning': The Composition of Ezra Pound's *Drafts & Fragments*," *Text*, 7 (1994), 397–422. The essay also appears in *Ezra Pound and Europe*, ed. Richard Taylor and Claus Melchior (Amsterdam: Editions Rodopi, 1993), pp. 223–242. See also Peter Stoicheff, *The Hall of Mirrors: Drafts & Fragments and the End of Ezra Pounds Cantos* (Ann Arbor, MI: University of Michigan Press, 1995).

50 See Timothy Materer, "A Reading of 'From CXV,'" *Paideuma*, 2, 2 (Fall 1973), 205.

51 From Dorothy's diaries at the Lilly Library, Indiana University. Moore's letter is dated September 28, 1959 and is quoted in Carpenter, *Life*, p. 860.

52 For Hall's own history of these and subsequent events, see his *Remembering Poets*. For a detailed discussion of the revisions here summarized, see Bush, "Unstill, Ever Turning," section I.

53 Dorothy's words as quoted by Laughlin in a letter to Hall, September 27, 1961 (Letter in the Houghton Library at Harvard). See also Hall, *Remembering Poets*, p. 181.

54 For a more detailed discussion, see Bush, "Unstill, Ever Turning," section II.

55 For a more complete account, see Peter Stoicheff, "The Composition and Publication History of Ezra Pound's *Drafts & Fragments*," *Twentieth-Century Literature*, 32, 1 (Spring, 1986), 78–94, esp. pp. 88ff.

56 To Robert Gales, September 9, 1968, cited in Peter Stoicheff, "The Interwoven Authority of a *Drafts & Fragments* Text," Rainey (ed.) *A Poem Containing History*, pp. 213–231; see p. 215.

57 In conversation with the author, July 16, 1991.

58 *New York Times*, November 26, 1972, p. 42.

59 From Stoicheff, "The Interwoven Authority," p. 221.

60 Cf. a letter that appeared in the *TLS* for August 20, 1976, in which Peter du Sautoy of Faber & Faber wrote that Faber in its edition of the *Cantos* chose not to reproduce "the 'Canto 120' that appears in the New Direction edition as we did not feel certain that these lines were what Pound intended to come at the end of the long poem" (p. 1,032).

61 From Stoicheff, "The Interwoven Authority," p. 221.

62 From an interview in *Allen Verbatim*, quoted in Marjorie Perloff's essay, "The Contemporary of Our Grandchildren: Pound's Influence," in George Bornstein (ed.), *Ezra Pound among the Poets* (Chicago: University of Chicago Press, 1985), p. 206.

7

PETER NICHOLLS

Beyond *The Cantos*: Ezra Pound and recent American poetry

"There they are, you will have to go a long way round / if you want to avoid them": these lines from Basil Bunting's poem "On the Fly-Leaf of Pound's Cantos" have a slightly ominous tone, preparing us for the complications which haunt the reception of Pound's work in America.[1] You can't avoid *The Cantos*, says Bunting, if you are in any sense committed to the art of poetry – at least the work you will need to do for yourself which Pound has already done for you will be immense – yet there are at the same time reasons why you still might want to avoid the poem. Tellingly, perhaps, Bunting's poem carries the dateline 1949, the year in which Pound, now confined in St. Elizabeths, received the Bollingen Prize for poetry. The award – for *The Pisan Cantos* – was bound to provoke controversy: was it acceptable to give this type of recognition to a man who had espoused fascism and antisemitism, or could the remarkable lyric beauty of the new sequence be judged apart, as something transcending political error?

It is within this quite explosive context that we have to consider the nature of Pound's influence on a younger generation of writers.[2] Indeed, the ambivalence which is hinted at in Bunting's lines makes the whole issue of influence complicated, especially if we assume it to connote forms of anxiety and concealment as it famously does for Harold Bloom. My own sense of the impact of *The Cantos* on subsequent writing is rather that the poem has acted very much as a kind of force-field or matrix, presenting a textual world which other poets have inhabited in their own different ways. From this point of view, the negotiations with *The Cantos* that are of most interest tend to have less to do with anxiety than with conscious strategies of emulation and resistance. What is especially striking is the extent to which younger poets have felt Pound's work as a forceful presence, often in an almost occult way. In Bunting's poem, *The Cantos* is compared to the Alps – "Sit down and wait for them to crumble!" – and this idea of the poem's monumentality is a common refrain amongst younger American poets. Robert Creeley, for example, writes that for his generation "the fact of Ezra Pound and his work is inescapable, no matter what the particular reaction may be."[3] Pound is "inescapable" because of both the complexity and breadth of his legacy. Like many of his generation – one thinks of Robert Duncan and Charles Olson – Creeley emphasizes the practicality of that legacy: Pound, he says, "gave a very succinct and clear and utterly unmistakable body of attitudes for reading poetry."[4] Even more important, Pound's poetry and criticism suggest avenues yet to be explored. "Pound," Creeley explains, "has given so many possibilities just in his work that it will be a long time indeed before they're exhausted."[5] This sense of *The Cantos* as an epic to be mined by generations to come is also what Duncan has in mind when he celebrates the Poundian project as "the adventure of a poetics to come that is not done with."[6]

If Pound's influence is in some sense different from that of T. S. Eliot or William Carlos Williams it is perhaps because his writings have become the seedbed of a whole range of different poetries. In offering a counter-tradition to the one associated in America with Eliot and the New Critics, Pound's work has suggested different paths to different poets. This is perhaps why writers have rarely rejected him out of hand for the political content of his work. Unattractive as that has often seemed, later poets have still found themselves able to learn from him, extrapolating stylistic and epistemological techniques which they have pursued to very different ends.

Indeed, to retain my earlier idea of a force-field, we might be surprised by the extent to which American poets have quite self-consciously allowed their work to be somehow embraced by, even contained within, particular versions of the Poundian project. And this in itself gives one good reason for thinking about modernism as a mode rather than as an epoch, for the new poetry which is sometimes called "postmodern" was actually formed within a cultural ambience in which Pound remained a powerful symbolic presence.[7] The dust from the Bollingen Prize controversy gradually settled, but Pound would continue to hold forth as resident sage at St. Elizabeths hospital where, until his release in 1958, young poets flocked to venerate or argue with him.[8] Literary history likes its chronology cleancut, as a progression from one tendency to another, from modernism to post-modernism. But things tend to be more complicated than that, and if we are going to speak of Pound as a high modernist we must also remember that some of his most important volumes appeared as late as the fifties and sixties (*Section: Rock-Drill*, 1955; *Thrones*, 1959; *Drafts & Fragments*, 1969). For many of the key poets of this period, then, Pound's work was still very much a live issue. Would he finish *The Cantos*? Was the poem irretrievably damaged by his political errors? Was a full recantation likely or possible?

The presence of Pound in Washington during the fifties, then, could fairly be described as troubling, and the sense of his magnetic pull – both attractive and repellent – is everywhere in reminiscences of the period. As Olson's record of his visits to Pound eloquently shows, the poet invited both sympathy and disagreement, affection and outrage. From within the circle of writers who exhibited this type of complex response one finds some reluctance to criticize Pound which is partly due to a sense of personal indebtedness. For Pound had constructed what he called his own "Ezuversity," an agenda for learning which offered an exciting alternative to the conventional map of Western culture, excavating forgotten or suppressed poetries and pushing out into non-Western societies such as China and Japan.

If Pound's poetry and criticism were, in Creeley's word, "inescapable," it was thus in part because they supplied what one can only call an education. From the fifties to the seventies, those who submitted to Pound's influence had their intellectual horizons set by his work. That could mean anything from believing wholeheartedly in his economic analysis to following his advice on European cuisine. Pound's influence was as multifarious as it was, in a particular sense, deliberately amateurish. Ever the pragmatist, he managed to convince many of his readers to break with traditional academic constraints and protocols. You did not have to be an expert to read Provençal love lyrics; you could tackle them with perseverance and a good dictionary. Pound thus hammered away at the secure lines of demarcation and professionalization in academic culture, redefining knowledge as everyday practice and possibility. Creeley, for example, has noted that he was "intrigued by Olson's reference to *The Cantos* as 'a walker' – something you could take a walk into daily, and have as experience of daily possibility."[9]

We may now begin to get a sense of the double nature of Pound's influence, at once enabling, as in that comment by Olson, and also prescriptive, authoritarian even. It is interesting, too, that the matter of "influence" is one with which Pound himself was intermittently preoccupied. As I have argued elsewhere, we can think of at least three main approaches to influence in his work, and these also characterize principal tendencies in his own writing.[10] In the very early poems, Pound frequently conjures up writers from the past as *personae* or masks for himself. The recurring trope is of the writer's self invaded or possessed by another: in the poem "Histrion," for example, he writes, "the souls of all men great / At times pass through us, / And we are not / Save as reflexions of their souls."[11] The passivity of this kind of metempsychosis then yields to a much more active relation to past cultures as Pound explores the medium of translation. We now find forms which *juxtapose* past and present, the writing process itself construed as a kind of *re*-inscription which allows past and present languages to exist in tension with each other. That is the mode of the early Cantos, up to, roughly, the extended China and Adams sequences written in the thirties. But Pound's direct engagement with the pressing political and economic questions of his day and, specifically of course his support for Mussolini's regime, could not long postpone the emergence of a polemical axis to the poem. Once the diagnostic tendency had been fully established it was only a matter of time before "history" would mutate into a more programmatic narrative of right or wrong choices. With the partial exception of the Pisan sequence, *The Cantos*, in short, would succumb to exactly the kind of rhetorical insistence against which Pound had long campaigned in his criticism. In the later parts of the poem, "influence" would become a tricky term indeed, with tropes of self-exposure and vulnerability consorting with an often coarsened didacticism.

These three phases give an idea of the complexity attaching to a reading of Pound for writers who were keen to learn from his example. Certainly, his achievement in opening poetry to a range of different knowledges and in embedding the poetic act within a complex historicity would shape much of the significant writing to come. And in a sense it was the range and flexibility of that poetic which allowed younger writers to use Pound against himself, as it were, to develop serial and collagiste forms which avoided the judgmental closures which dogged the final stages of *The Cantos*. In these negotiations with Pound, then, formal and political matters were very closely entwined: younger writers wishing to resist the pull of his politics looked to Pound's intricate explorations of sound and syntax as a resource from which to create non-totalizing and essentially un-Poundian poetic structures.

The publication of *The Pisan Cantos* in 1948 played a key role in making such options available to younger writers. Pathos, regret, debility, and yet the same old Poundian energy and fire, intransigence, even: these were the immediately striking aspects of the new section, but beyond the drama of its occasion the intricately sounding echo chamber of *The Pisan Cantos* was a rich repository of new devices. Most notable was an extreme fluency of transition: more than at any other previous point in the poem, Pound uses rhythm and syntax to bind together radically different tones and registers.

> Light tensile immaculata
>   the sun's cord unspotted
> "sunt lumina" said the Oirishman to King Carolus   (449)

The allusion to the cosmology of Scotus Erigena in the third line ("sunt lumina"), for example, moves from the reverential Latin phrase to the idiomatic, slightly irreverent "Oirishman", shifting tones within the space of a single line. On a larger scale, the sense of floating elements only occasionally brought to definitive focus (as, for example, in the Chinese ideogram which precedes this passage) implies patterns of order which remain latent, summoned periodically by verbal echo and rhythmic refrain. Here as elsewhere in the sequence the dominant motif is one of *return*, the return of the gods, the return of the past as memory, and in line with this Pound deploys an array of rhythmic signatures and parallelisms which enact the mind's movements backwards and forwards across time. The visual images are sharp and striking ("the ideogram of the guard roosts", the "dark sheep in the drill field" [448]), but more consistently notable is Pound's attention to sound-patterning and forms of musicality. These features are largely responsible for holding disparate elements together in the present tense of the mind's process, with rhythmic phrases unfolding as the measure of thought and memory rather than as predetermined forms. Of course, the provisionality and openness of the writing here painfully reflect Pound's actual dilemma in the death cells at Pisa, though the foregrounding of textual effects and allusions inhibits to a remarkable degree the kind of transparency we associate with conventionally confessional poetry.

As we move into the Cantos written during Pound's subsequent confinement at St. Elizabeths, however, a desire for synthesis and closure becomes clearer and more rhetorically enjoined. Pound continues to draw on an almost infinite number of "luminous details," as he calls them, though the writing increasingly lays claim to some original ground which will guarantee their inter-relatedness. So, in the opening lines of Canto XCVIII, for example, we find him presenting a range of different knowledges, some factual and verifiable, like Byzantine interest rates, others secret, founded in faith, like the primitive vegetation rites to which, apparently, the wearing of black shawls for mourning was originally connected. As we read, the individual allusions constantly invoke a larger narrative order to which the fragment may ultimately be referred. The important thing for Pound is that relations can then be traced, that one thing may lead meaningfully to another, and that these emerging connections will provide the foundation for clear moral judgment and – by extension – for properly directed political action. Perhaps the trickiest thing about *The Cantos* – and especially about these late sections – is that a radical fragmentation of syntax belies the drive toward the ideational *coherence* on which Pound's model of social order increasingly depends.

Pound's sense of his own failure in *The Cantos* is famously registered in Canto CXVI – "I cannot make it cohere," he writes. One way of understanding developments in recent American poetry is to see how unattractive that particular model of "coherence" would quickly become. Take the so-called Objectivist poets, for example, Louis Zukofsky and George Oppen. Zukofsky was in touch with Pound in the twenties, and it was Pound who encouraged Harriet Monroe to run a special Objectivist issue of *Poetry* magazine in 1931. Zukofsky's introductory essay, "Sincerity and Objectification," shared the Poundian commitment to "clarity of image and word-tone" and emphasized the musicality of writing: "Writing occurs which is the detail, not mirage, of seeing, of thinking with the things as they exist, and of directing them along a line of melody."[12] The talk of clarity and melody was reminiscent of Pound's poetic theory around the time of Imagism, though the term "Objectivism" notwithstanding, Zukofsky was actually more interested in making the poem an object – a "rested totality" – than he was in writing about objects.[13] Already this idea of objectifying the poem implied a certain resistance to understanding which ran counter to Pound's investment in "direct presentation" and accuracy.

Perhaps not surprisingly in view of his own experiments in automatic writing, it was William Carlos Williams rather than Pound who grasped this aspect of Zukofsky's poetics. Responding to "Poem Beginning 'The',"" Williams noted that "It escapes me in analysis (thank God) and strikes against me a thing (thank God). There are not so many things in the world as we commonly imagine. Plenty of debris, plenty of smudges."[14] Zukofsky had certainly learned from the exploration of ellipsis and musicality in Pound's work, and after 1929–30 *The Cantos* would stand for him as a model of technical insight: "The devices of emphasizing cadence by arrangement of line and typography have been those which clarify and render the meaning of the spoken word specific."[15] Yet his own long poem "*A*" lacks any pretension to overall design comparable to the Dantescan ascent of *The Cantos*, and the pleasure Zukofsky takes in puns, phonetic play, and multiple ambiguities entails a fundamental move away from the Poundian criteria of linguistic precision. And where Pound finally bemoans his poem's lack of "coherence", Zukofsky is fascinated by the aspects of his poem which seem to elude his control. As he puts it in "*A*"-12: "Each writer writes / one long work whose beat he cannot / entirely be aware of. Recurrences / follow him, crib and drink from a / well that's his cadence..."[16]

The divergence of "*A*" from *The Cantos* can be explained, then, in various ways – there were political differences between the two men, exacerbated by Pound's increasingly belligerent antisemitism, and Zukofsky's loss of confidence in left-wing politics midway through "*A*" shifted the poem away from the defiantly public modes of *The Cantos*.[17] Yet it was not just that Zukofsky's poem became more domestically focused and more hermetic in style, it was also – as in those lines about "recurrence" – that he turned away from the didactic and interpretive idioms of *The Cantos*, away from (as fellow Objectivist Carl Rakosi called him) "the Olympian; Pound."[18]

The same uneasy mixture of admiration and aversion colors George Oppen's relation to Pound. The two men had met in Rapallo in 1930, and Oppen's first volume of poems, *Discrete Series* (1934), carried Pound's endorsement on its jacket ("I salute a serious craftsman, a sensibility which is not every man's sensibility and which has not been got out of any other man's books"[19]). The abbreviated but highly focused poems of *Discrete Series* acknowledged the clarity of Pound's imagist poems, but their urban detail and intricate discontinuities made them altogether less static and remote than the poems of *Lustra*. Oppen and Pound lost touch soon after, with Pound in Italy and Oppen in exile in Mexico to avoid FBI harassment. Then in 1969 they met again by accident in the offices of New Directions in New York. It was an emotional encounter which led Oppen to write a poem called "Of Hours."[20] It is a characteristically difficult text, the meeting with Pound framed by a series of different, sometimes displaced concerns, but perhaps what is most striking is the poem's elliptical quality by which Oppen resists giving the past (Pound's past) a simple legibility. Indeed, the poem implies that this assumption that history can somehow be made transparent is perhaps the main source of Pound's "error." The poet is familiarly addressed, as "Old friend," but at the same time Oppen foregrounds gaps and opacities, resistances to readability ("Holes   pitfalls open / In the cop's accoutrement") as if Pound's attempt to order and police his poem is somehow undermined from within. Indeed, if the "sap" of his legacy is "not exhausted" it is because of his poem's resistant musicality ("Movement / of the stone") rather than because of the truths it claims to present. Recalling the fissured landscape of his own wartime experience, Oppen sees himself as son to Pound's father, brother to a sister, friend to a friend, but most conclusively as a Jew marooned in "the rubble of Alsace." The sheer brokenness of the writing gestures toward Pound's ultimate failure to overcome his egotism – "What is it you 'loved'," asks Oppen in a sharp reminder of Pound's "What thou lovest well remains," and the "old poet" is finally glimpsed walking homeward, alone and "unteachable."[21]

Yet Oppen, of course, does not want to teach, and the fractured forms of his own poetry provide spaces of encounter and recognition which are intended to acknowledge the contradictory claims made upon us by being at once "singular" and "numerous" (his major poem-sequence is titled "Of Being Numerous").[22] Sincerity, for Oppen, is not so much a true account of one's inner feelings (manifest, then, Pound would say, in precise verbal formulation), as it is an acceptance of what *exceeds* the self. Hence Oppen's attempt to transcend what he calls in "Philai Te Kou Philai" "a ruined ethic / bursting with ourselves" (*CP*, 76). "The self," he warns us in "World, World – ," "is no mystery" (*CP*, 143) but there is instead "a force of clarity, it is / of what is not autonomous in us" (*CP*, 185). This "clarity" reveals a grammar of shared social relations rather than the authoritative word of one man or, as Pound calls himself in *The Pisan Cantos*, "ego scriptor" (LXXVI/458).

Oppen's attempt to establish poetry as a medium of relationship rather than of hierarchy and authority is paralleled in the work of writers such as Robert Creeley and Charles Olson, Allen Ginsberg and Gary Snyder, and can also be observed in the writings of some of the so-called Language poets. "We describe our time as one in which relationships rather than the hierarchies to which these might refer, are dominant," says Creeley.[23] Younger poets would thus continue to explore the implications of Pound's "ideogrammic method," with its rapid shifts and unexpected contiguities, but they would do so with an eye more to kinship and equivalence than to Pound's Dantescan *"sense of gradations.* Things neither perfect nor utterly wrong, but arranged in a cosmos, an order, stratified, having relations one with another."[24]

Robert Duncan's work is of special interest in this respect, since his habit of reading Pound as primarily a romantic writer allows him perhaps more than any other poet of the period to inhabit Pound's visionary world.[25] Duncan, who first read *A Draft of XXX Cantos* in 1937 and visited the poet at St. Elizabeths ten years later, identified closely with the "cult of romance" which Pound had traced "from Apuleius to Dante."[26] Yet Pound's achievement was not simply to have reestablished contact with a suppressed and occult tradition: "it is his genius," said Duncan, "that even when he presents flashes of eternal mind – veritas, claritas, hilaritas – he does not sublimate but remains involved, by defect, in the agony of the contemporary."[27] The magical air of Pisa, breathed alike by prisoners, goddesses and figures from Pound's past, was for Duncan the pure expression of this enchanted weaving together of the eternal and the contemporary: "It is the marvellous of *The Pisan Cantos* that reassures me. Even after a lifetime of struggle for publication and importance, because of his love for poetry, for song and for romance, Pound dwells in the innermost enchantment of the mind. He has been initiated into a world transformd [*sic*] and inhabited by spirits" (*ASP*, 14).

Where his friend Charles Olson would learn from Pound the historian, Duncan chose to follow the "sublime and ecstatic voice" of Pound the mythologist (*ASP*, 91), seeking, like him, the return of the gods. The relation of that "return" to Pound's intimate understanding of sound and rhythm underlay Duncan's intense response to *The Pisan Cantos*:

> That one image may recall another, finding depth in the resounding is the secret of rime and measure. The time of a poem is felt as a recognition of return in vowel tone and in consonant formations, of pattern in sequence of syllables, in stress and in pitch of a melody, of images and meanings. It resembles the time of a dream, for it is highly organized along lines of association and impulses of contrast towards the structure of the whole. The same impulse of dream or poem is to provide a ground for some form beyond what we know, for feeling *"greater than reality."*[28]

The technique of the "grand collage" which Duncan learned from *The Cantos* may operate according to different premises from Pound's – for Duncan it is mystical rather than quasi-scientific[29] – but it is based on one of Pound's most important insights, namely that "All ages are contemporaneous" (*ASP*, 99), and that "the contemporary opens upon eternity in the interpenetration of times" (*ASP*, 124). Yet, for Duncan, myth is not so much a repository of essential knowledge as it is a means of establishing relationship, so that mythic contemporaneity becomes the ground for what he calls "the community of the poem" (*ASP*, 170), the poem as an expression of "the communality we have with all men, our interdependence everywhere in life."[30]

Duncan's "A Poem Beginning with a Line by Pindar," for example, demonstrates how an almost exclusive attention to the mythic registers of *The Cantos* can generate a reading which stresses the collective dimension of Pound's poem as "the tale of the tribe."[31] Duncan's vistas are unembarrassedly democratic ones, aiming to "strike again the naked string / old Whitman sang from," and quotations from *The Pisan Cantos* are deployed as exemplars of sincerity and "candor," with Duncan's frank homage to Pound implicitly standing against the ironic modes then fashionable in mainstream poetry.[32] For Duncan – and this is where we can see the use of Poundian techniques *against* certain aspects of Pound's own work – the crucial feature of mythopoeia and its effect of simultaneity is its openness, its lack of an end-in-view. According to Duncan, what is sought is "the suspension of conclusions at the point of decision, so that all decision moves forward toward a totality that is pending, rather than reinforcing the prejudice of an established totality" (*ASP*, 93). Poetry is "a pouring forth of thought, not a progression but a medium of thought"

(*ASP*, 77). Here Duncan touches upon one of the most influential and problematic aspects of Pound's poetics, for like other poets of his generation, Duncan finds in *The Cantos* the promise of a radical openness which might allow "ego scriptor" to yield to "the I that we all are,"[33] but it is a promise in part betrayed. For the ideogrammic method also has a teleological or pragmatic dimension which, in Duncan's view, leads to various forms of closure. The aim of his own poetics, partly coincident with Olson's in this respect, is a writing "as meaning realized as it was 'made' or 'discovered' in the process of invention and experiment" (*ASP*, 139). Not so much, then, the reduced "piths and gists" of Poundian wisdom, but rather "a communication below the threshold of language," a "language like the murmuring of bees" (*ASP*, 19), inchoate, emergent, "a field in which we see the form of the poem happening" (*ASP*, 66).

The idea of the poem as "field" derives from Olson's influential essay on Projective Verse. Like Duncan, Olson constructs his poetics as an "attack ... on the 'completed thought', or, the Idea ... ," proposing "Projective Open or Field verse versus Closed."[34] This new poetics is unashamedly indebted to Pound: it reiterates the older poet's attack on abstraction (which Olson associates with "discourse") and looks instead to the phonetic and ideographic "as impetus and explosion in our alphabetic speech" (*HU*, 18). Following the Poundian concern with history, Olson fashions his concept of Projective Verse as a means of making poetry "again carry much larger material than it has carried in our language since the Elizabethans" (*HU*, 61). So too, Olson's emphatic attention to the functions of the breath as the basis for poetic measure (*HU*, 53) has its origins in "The revolution of the ear, 1910, the trochee's heave" (*HU*, 53). Yet where Pound's poetic and ethical commitments converge in an ideal of "the welding of word and thing,"[35] Olson (as Joseph Riddel puts it) "identifies speech with performance, with the 'act' that shatters representation."[36]

It is through this conception of the "act" that Olson attempts to distinguish his own poetics from Pound's (a distinction finally not without personal and intellectual difficulties, as is clear from the poem "I, Mencius, Pupil of the Master ..."). It is not simply that Olson comes to lament the limits of Pound's historical consciousness, his confinement within "the Western box,"[37] but that *The Cantos*, in its ambition to be "a poem including history", had ultimately reduced the past to an assemblage of static data.[38] As Barrett Watten has observed, "[f]acts are never points of rest for Olson," and "The event of the poem is less history than the present being constructed in the work; perhaps this *is* the only way that history can be known."[39] Where the late Cantos seem at times to veer toward mere antiquarianism, Olson takes from philosopher Alfred Whitehead the idea that "events are absolute only because they have a future, not from any past", concluding that "History is to want to."[40] The emphasis, then, is on the "field" of the poem, on history as process ("what you find out for yourself ['*istorin*']" [*HU*, 97]), and one result of this shift away from Poundian "history" is that the poem frees itself from dependence on some external ground or on what Olson calls, in a critique of both Pound and Duncan, "some outside concept and measure of 'wisdom'" (*HU*, 67). Historical materials are thus to be configured by the force-field of the present moment rather than by the pressures of belief or ideology: "The objects which occur at every given moment of composition (of recognition, we can call it) are, can be, must be treated exactly as they do occur therein and not by any ideas or preconceptions from outside the poem" (*HU*, 56).

Olson's *The Maximus Poems* attempts to bring this new history into being, focusing on the poet's home town, Gloucester, Massachusetts. Olson has no Dantescan map to follow, and although the poem concerns itself with nothing less than "a total placement of man and things among all possibilities of creation,"[41] it is always the present tense of perception that his writing struggles to enact. In contrast to the intense cultural regard which motivates *The Cantos*, Olson's objective is something simple, primitive, even: "There are no hierarchies, no infinite, no such many as mass, there are only / eyes in all heads / to be looked out of."[42] "Primitive," though, in a specialized sense: "not ... in that stupid use of it as opposed to civilized. One means it now as 'primary', as how one finds anything, pick it up as one does new – fresh/first" (*HU*, 96).

Olson's work is at once inside and outside the Poundian paradigm. His emphasis on the "primary" is intended to situate the poetic act as somehow "pre-cultural" and no longer complicit with the notions of social hierarchy on which *The Cantos* deliberately rests. As Olson suggested to Creeley, "Ez's epic solves problem by his ego: his single emotion breaks all down to his equals or inferiors (so far as I can see only two, possibly, are admitted, by him, to be his betters – Confucius, and Dante.)"[43] For Olson, as in a different way for Duncan, the impulse to order and hierarchy is supplanted by a commitment to openness and chance: "He sd, 'You go all around the subject.' And I sd, 'I didn't know it was a sub-/ject.' He sd, 'You twist' and I sd, 'I do'."[44] At the same time, though, Olson's commitment to the voice and to the "phallic energies" (*HU*, 23) associated with it cannot altogether avoid the Poundian trap of "ego." As Language poet Charles Bernstein observes:

> Olson's overly literal insistence on breath and place too often distracts from the enactment of line and location as facts primarily of a text ... The heroic

stance translates into a will to dominate language rather than let it be (heard) . . . In short, the 'humanist' claims of the heroic help evade the responsibility for creating a prosody not based on received idealizations of speech and the willful man.[45]

With the ascendancy of Language poetry in America, Olson's literary stock has fallen. As Bernstein's comment suggests, this is in part because of a reaction against the "willful" tendencies of the Olsonian voice and the masculinist fantasies they generally project. Poet Susan Howe has observed that "the feminist issue may do away with interest in Olson by the young,"[46] and we are reminded that the same tendencies in Pound's work have made his impact on women poets relatively insignificant. Certainly, after Olson there has been a widely shared distrust of any aesthetic which covets forms of heroic authority. It is as if one counter-poetics has required another, for many poets who still appreciate Pound's rejection of a comfortable "mainstream" writing have found it necessary to develop techniques in critical tension with those of The Cantos. Extreme examples are the aleatory writings of John Cage and Jackson MacLow, each of whom has used "mesostic" procedures to disrupt the controlling patterns of Pound's poem. Cage's Writing through the Cantos (1982) and MacLow's Words nd Ends from Ez (1989) variously use Pound's name as a kind of "seed string" by which to draw out words from The Cantos.[47] The effect is of a sort of literal dissemination of Pound throughout his poem, with the letters E, Z, R, A and P, O, U, N, D occurring in alternate lines, but absorbed into the collage of languages which comprises the text. Cage's poem, for example, reduces the whole of The Cantos to a few pages of text exploiting the sheer heterogeneity of the poem's language to generate lines which at once dissolve propositions into a mesh of single words, and open them to often ironic implications they had not had before. So we find lines such as "Printed sOrt fU dyNasty Dynasty", which quite by chance points up "nasty" in "dynasty" and reminds us that this is precisely the kind of snap judgment Pound was making increasingly during the thirties. Or again: "toPaze a thrOne having it sqUsh in his excelleNt Dum / sacro nEmori von humboldt agassiZ maR wAy," where the chance reworking of Pound's jokey definition of a throne as "something God can sit on / without having it sqush" (LXXXVIII/581) now serves as an example not of precision but of its opposite.

These moves against Poundian criteria of accuracy and control are also to be found in the work of writers who drew on French Surrealism for new possibilities. Where Oppen, Zukofsky, Rakosi and Olson had all lined up, with Pound, against Surrealism, John Ashbery and Frank O'Hara looked to France for very different models from those proposed by Pound. Where he had originally stressed the line from Gautier through Laforgue (a line exemplifying verbal clarity and irony), Surrealism allowed a writer like Ashbery to connect with a literary tendency which, having one origin in the work of Gertrude Stein, offered exciting alternatives to the moral investments in "history" and reference which were of fundamental importance to the Poundian project.

Take, for example, Ashbery's early volume, *The Tennis Court Oath* of 1962, often considered his most radical work and highly regarded for that reason by Language poets such as Susan Howe, Barrett Watten and Bruce Andrews. In this volume, Ashbery clearly taps one vein of the tradition running through Dada and Surrealism for which, in Watten's words, "language and psyche [are] a kind of vast reservoir for collage."[48] It is the *principle* of collage which is important here, rather than the materials themselves. In what seems almost a parody of Poundian modernism, Ashbery tends to choose trivial, often banal texts on which to work (here once again we observe the non-hierarchal principle at work in post-Poundian writing). Critic John Shoptaw's account of the poem "Europe" and its debt to a children's story called *Beryl of the By-plane*, for example, tells us much about Ashbery's methods of composition but it doesn't really help us to understand the poem any better.[49] Indeed, Ashbery's characteristic use here of ellipsis (the "leaving out business"[50]) and the pseudo-declarative sentence not only block immediate understanding but assert its impossibility, even its undesirability.

This is a poetry of "how it feels, not what it means," as Ashbery puts it in the later *Houseboat Days*,[51] a poetry in which "thought" is not something to be articulated but rather something that is encountered in the making of the poem ("I always begin at zero," says Ashbery, "and discover my thought by writing"; compare Language poet Lyn Hejinian's related observation, that "where one once sought a vocabulary for ideas, now one seeks ideas for vocabularies"[52]). It is this aspect of *The Tennis Court Oath* which now seems so prescient, so indicative of things to come. For the reordering of priorities denies us the forms of identification we assume from conventional lyric at the same time as it also blocks the sort of hermeneutic impulse encouraged by *The Cantos* or *The Maximus Poems*. Take the first stanza of "Leaving the Atocha Station," a celebrated or, depending on how you look at it, an infamous example of Ashbery's new style. Ellipses and typographical spaces produce moments where sense simply fails, and in that failure we are meant to discover both pleasure and a certain eerie foreboding of incompletion. For poems like this (to adapt what Charles Bernstein has said of Clark Coolidge) "refuse . . . the syntactic ideality of the complete sentence, in which each part of speech operates in its definable place so that a grammatic paradigm is superimposed on the actual unfolding of the semantic strings."[53] If there is something a little too cute about some of Ashbery's periphrastic moves here – "tar grams" for "cigarettes," for instance – any attempt to transcode the lines confronts us with an unrelenting banality (as in Shoptaw's interpretation of the "blind dog" lines as "While reading the newspaper . . . and smoking . . . we watched the seeing eye dog dig up a tulip garden for a buried bone").[54] It is the rapidity of the transitions – often, as for the Language poets, a result of suppressing transitive verbs in favor of passive constructions and unhooked participles – which would make this volume so significant for later experimental writers.

Poetry thus sets its face against what Bruce Andrews calls "communicative competence" and in doing so repudiates any notion of linguistic "transparency."[55] It is here that Ashbery's attraction to certain types of Surrealism allows him to develop a powerful alternative to Pound's poetics. What is at issue is not so much a question of dream imagery as a sense of the anti-referentiality of some Surrealist language. This is Surrealism as, for example, William Carlos Williams had understood it in the thirties: "Surrealism does not lie. It is the single truth. It is an epidemic. It is. It is just words."[56] That view of Surrealism not as a poetics of the inner life but as a practice of *writing* is the one which helps us to understand how "Surrealism" could become a sort of portemanteau word for an alternative non-image based poetics in America running from Gertrude Stein to the Language writers ("It is simple," wrote Williams. "There is no symbolism, no evocation of an image."[57]).

There is, of course, straightforwardly Surrealist imagery in Ashbery's poems ("the spoon of your head," and so on, the kind of thing exploited by the more "orthodox" of Breton's American followers such as Kenneth Patchen and Charles Henri Ford). Yet the line of development in which we might situate Ashbery is closer to what has frequently been called "literary Cubism," a tendency best represented by one of his favourite poets, Pierre Reverdy. It was Reverdy who gave Breton the original definition of the Surrealist image as "a pure creation of the mind. It cannot be born from a comparison but from a juxtaposition of two more or less distant realities."[58] But where Reverdy differed from Breton was in the latter's refusal of any conscious "juxtaposition": "In my opinion," he wrote, "it is erroneous to claim that 'the mind has grasped the relationship' of two realities in the presence of each other. First of all, it has seized nothing consciously."[59] The difference in emphasis is finely caught in Kenneth Rexroth's account of Reverdy's work:

Poetry such as this attempts not just a new syntax of the word. Its revolution is aimed at the syntax of the mind itself. Its restructuring of experience is purposive, not dreamlike, and hence it possesses an uncanniness fundamentally different in kind from the most haunted utterances of the Surrealist or Symbolist unconscious.[60]

The "restructuring" of which Rexroth speaks is primarily a praxis of writing, not of recollection; and it is here that we can begin to discern a sort of faultline which separates the canonical works of Anglo-American modernism – *The Waste Land*, *The Cantos*, *Paterson*, "A" – from what Rexroth calls "literary cubism." In the great modernist works, he suggests

as in Apollinaire's "Zone," the elements, the primary data of the poetic construction, are narrative or at least informative wholes. In verse such as Reverdy's, they are simple, sensory, emotional or primary informative objects capable of little or no further reduction. Eliot works in *The Waste Land* with fragmented and recombined arguments; Pierre Reverdy with dismembered propositions from which subject, operator and object have been wrenched free and re-structured into an invisible or subliminal discourse which owes its cogency to its own strict, complex and secret logic.[61]

So in place of the unconscious as an absent scene to be represented we have this "secret logic" which, for Ashbery, entails a constant movement between "meaningfulness" and "randomness."[62] The terms Rexroth uses here – "dismembered," "wrenched" – point up the violence which shadows this act of poetic "reduction," a violence which in *The Tennis Court Oath* attends both the literary echo and the twisted references to "ordinary" speech. What results is a certain linguistic *opacity*, which is to be distinguished from the referential *difficulty* or, as Ashbery puts it in an essay on Reverdy, "the eternal dead weight of symbolism and allegory" he finds in Eliot, Pound, Yeats and Joyce.[63]

Perhaps what is most striking, then, about *The Tennis Court Oath* – and this is what has made it a crucial reference point for the Language poets – is its practice of courting unreadability.[64] In this respect Ashbery situates himself in a tradition which begins with Mallarmé but which on the face of it might also seem to include the late Pound, of whose *Section: Rock-Drill* Donald Davie, for example, wrote that "The mere look of Canto 85 on the page . . . announces it as 'unreadable'."[65] Yet, as we saw earlier, the reader's role in *The Cantos* is in part to restore a certain readability to the text by discerning deep-lying connections. For many writers after Pound, however, it would be important to see the condition of unreadability not as just a hermeneutic device of deferred disclosure but rather as (in Lyn Hejinian's word) a "generative" mode.[66] For the Language writers, transparency and readability are closely aligned with forms of oppressive authority. To quote Hejinian again: "The open text, by definition, is open to the world and particularly to the reader. It invites participation, rejects the authority of the writer over the reader and thus, by analogy, the authority implicit in other (social, economic, cultural) hierarchies."[67] Somewhat paradoxically, the "openness" of a text and its modes of readability will depend upon the work's resistance to meaning; hence Hejinian's notion of seeking ideas for vocabularies rather than vocabularies for ideas. "Thought" is not to be articulated as "content" but is rather encountered in the making of the poem. And just as the writer finds her thought by writing,[68] so the aim is to keep "the reader's attention at or very close to the level of language."[69] The result of this double objective is a writing which strives to prevent the integration of linguistic items into higher grammatical levels, a writing which ostentatiously parades its constituent elements, phonetic and graphic, at times reducing words to a rubble of morphemes. This extreme emphasis on what Bernstein calls "writing centred on its wordness"[70] disrupts forms of narrative and dialectic, substituting for the temporal closure of the sentence a verbal matrix of cross-connected time-schemes.

This move away from a poetics founded on Pound's ideal of a "welding of word and thing" also entails a conception of "writing *as* politics, not writing *about* politics."[71] In different ways, the poets associated with L=A=N=G=U=A=G=E explore writing not as a vehicle of expressive authority, but as a medium in which social relations are constructed and managed. Pound's hierarchy of voices now breaks down, as does any clear division between public and private idioms. As Barrett Watten notes of Steve Benson's performance work, it "casts the shadows of lyrical self-consciousness in Ashbery and O'Hara into the light of public discourse."[72] The watchword for this poetics might well be Bakhtin's: "The word in language is half someone else's."[73] As Watten puts it,

> the performer acts out a continually reflexive encounter with his language, trying to hear what it is saying and respond verbally at all points. The total self-involvement can only undermine its own authority; the other is rendered intact, but it is simultaneously the speaking subject that is the other.[74]

In different ways, Language writers such as Hejinian, Bernstein, Perelman and Susan Howe explore this "otherness" attaching to the speaking subject. The aim is a "poetics of the nonegocentric,"[75] a poetics in which "the very conditions of self-reflection bind us to grammars we share with other people."[76] In one sense, this is a project which tacitly defines itself by reference to the "failure" of *The Cantos*, though even as it does so it acknowledges radical possibilities latent in the poem. As Bernstein notes, the "complex polyvocal textuality" of *The Cantos* constantly threatens to break through the rhetorical constraints Pound sought to impose upon it.[77] For the writers associated with $L=A=N=G=U=A=G=E$, it is precisely those literary effects which Pound tried unsuccessfully to banish from his poem which are most valued: Bernstein lists them as "indeterminacy, fragmentation, abstraction, obscurity, verbiage, equivocation, ambiguity, allegory."[78] Herein (ironically) lies the possibility of a writing which situates itself outside the hegemonic codes of standard English in order to allow other voices to speak.[79]

What, finally, of the Poundian commitment to the epic as "a poem including history"? The work of Susan Howe is perhaps most eloquent testimony to the continuing role of the poet-as-historian, though her texts also argue the need for a fundamental reformulation of Poundian principle.[80] Howe clearly believes with Pound that the poetic medium offers a means by which to reactivate a "history" long since atrophied under the dead hand of the academy. Yet, for her, poetry offers not a medium for dealing with historical "facts," but rather a kind of "counter-memory," as she calls it, which will resist successful assimilation to the order of discourse. Howe's history, in contrast to Pound's, is always uncertain: it will not quite become what Jean-François Lyotard has called "memorial history," it will not allow us to *forget* the original traumatic event by erecting the psychic defense of a normalizing narrative. "One forgets," says Lyotard, "as soon as one believes, draws conclusions, and holds for certain."[81]

The thrust of Howe's poetics is thus firmly against cognitive and narrative modes of historical understanding, against any secure position of knowledge from which we might view the past. History is grasped instead as a force which invades the poet, and, as in Freud, there is always a tension in Howe's writing between this memory of a past which, as she puts it in *Pythagorean Silence*, "never stops hurting" '[82] and its belated inscription in a language somehow disfigured by it. "This tradition that I am part of," she explains, "has involved a breaking of boundaries of all sorts. It involves a fracturing of discourse, a stammering even. Interruption and hesitation used as a force. A recognition that there is another voice, an attempt to hear and speak it. It is this brokenness that interests me."[83]

Much is contained for Howe in that idea of hesitation, a word, as she notes, "from the Latin, meaning to stick. Stammer. Hold back in doubt, have difficulty in speaking."[84] The failure to speak fluently thus becomes a sort of strength as it sets up a resistance to conceptuality and dialectic, embedding a kind of violence at the heart of poetic language. Stammering keeps us on the verge of intelligibility, and in her own work Howe's emphasis on *sound* is coupled with an habitual shattering of language into bits and pieces. "The other of meaning," she tells us, "is indecipherable variation,"[85] thus gesturing toward a writing which constantly courts the non-cognitive in its preoccupation with graphic and phonic elements.

This type of opacity far exceeds the particular unreadabilities of *The Cantos*. For Howe, the blasting of a segment of the past out of the continuum of history produces a condition of language which is in a particular sense anti-metaphorical: words do not become figures for things but remain stubbornly themselves. If poetic language thus becomes cryptic, it is perhaps because "history," if not felt as literally traumatic, appears partly unreadable in the wake of modernism. Where Pound could find the key to past iniquities in, say, the manipulation of Byzantine interest rates, "history" for Howe is registered less as a phalanx of facts than as an indeterminate force which produces opacities and distortions within our means of expression. History, in this sense, is what she calls a kind of "ghost writing" which perpetually refuses to become transparent, a writing of gaps and traces which keeps us poised between opacity and readability.

We have travelled some way beyond *The Cantos*, perhaps, but it is hard to imagine the work of any of the poets I have discussed without Pound's problematic poem as a reference point. Indeed, *The Cantos* retains its Alpine prominence partly *because* it fails to achieve the kind of coherence Pound desired for it. It is that gap between intention and achievement which has allowed contemporary writers to continue to read the poem as a source of new possibilities. As Bernstein puts it, "the success of *The Cantos* is that its coherence is of a kind totally different than Pound desired or could – in his more rigid moments – accept. For the coherence of the 'hyperspace' of Pound's modernist collage is not a predetermined Truth of a pancultural elitism but a product of a compositionally decentered multiculturalism."[86] Such a reading may indeed save *The Cantos* from the simple charge of "error" and allow us to re-discover it as (in Duncan's words) "the adventure of a poetics to come that is not done with."

NOTES

1 Basil Bunting, *Collected Poems* (Oxford: Oxford University Press, 1978), p. 110.
2 Anyone writing about the general question of Pound's influence will be indebted to Christopher Beach's admirable *ABC of Influence: Ezra Pound and the Remaking of American Poetic Tradition* (Berkeley and Los Angeles: University of California Press, 1992). See also K. L. Goodwin, *The Influence of Ezra Pound* (London: Oxford University Press, 1966) and Marjorie Perloff, *Dance of the Intellect. The Poetics of Indeterminacy: Rimbaud to Cage* (Princeton, NJ: Princeton University Press, 1981).

3 Robert Creeley, *The Collected Essays* (Berkeley and Los Angeles: University of California Press, 1989), p. 25.

4 Robert Creeley, *Contexts of Poetry: Interviews 1961–1971* (Bolinas, CA: Four Seasons Foundation, 1973), p. 14.

5 Creeley, *Contexts of Poetry*, p. 90.

6 Robert Duncan, *A Selected Prose*, ed. Robert J. Bertholf (New York: New Directions, 1995), p. 90. Further references to *ASP* will be given in the text.

7 For the distinction between "mode" and "epoch," see Jean-François Lyotard, *The Postmodern Condition: A Report on Knowledge*, trans. Geoff Bennington and Brian Massumi (Manchester: Manchester University Press, 1984).

8 See especially Charles Olson, *Charles Olson and Ezra Pound: An Encounter at St. Elizabeths*, ed. Catherine Seelye (New York: Grossman, 1975). E. Fuller Torrey, *The Roots of Treason: Ezra Pound and the Secret of St. Elizabeths* (New York: McGraw-Hill, 1984) is contentious but contains useful information.

9 *Contexts of Poetry*, p. 160. Olson's reference is in his *Mayan Letters*, ed. Robert Creeley (London: Cape, 1968), p. 29.

10 See my *Modernisms: A Literary Guide* (Berkeley and Los Angeles: University of California Press, 1995), pp. 167–179.

11 Pound, *Collected Early Poems*, ed. Michael King (London: Faber & Faber, 1977), p. 71.

12 Zukofsky, "Sincerity and Objectification," *Poetry*, 37, 5 (February 1931), 272, 273.

13 Cf. *The Selected Letters of George Oppen*, ed. Rachel Blau DuPlessis (Durham and London: Duke University Press, 1990), p. 47: "'Objectivist['] meant, not an objective viewpoint, but to objectify the poem, to make the poem an object. Meant form."

14 Williams, *Selected Letters*, ed. John C. Thirlwall (New York: McDowell, Obolensky, 1957), p. 94. See also Peter Quartermain, *Disjunctive Poetics: From Gertrude Stein and Louis Zukofsky to Susan Howe* (Cambridge: Cambridge University Press, 1992), p. 102.

15 Zukofsky, *Prepositions: Collected Critical Essays* (London: Rapp and Carroll, 1967), p. 139.

16 Zukofsky, *"A" 1–12* (New York: Doubleday, 1967), p. 220.

17 See the discussion in Bob Perelman, *The Trouble with Genius: Reading Pound, Joyce, Stein and Zukofsky* (Berkeley and Los Angeles: University of California Press, 1994), pp. 170–216.

18 Carl Rakosi, *The Collected Prose* (Orono, ME: National Poetry Foundation, 1983), p. 42: "The Olympian; Pound; *he* deals the cards, contained and imperturbable."

19 Pound's "Preface to *Discrete Series* (1934)" is reprinted in the George Oppen issue of *Paideuma*, 10, 1 (Spring 1981), 13.

20 *The Collected Poems of George Oppen* (New York: New Directions, 1975), pp. 210–212. Further references to *CP* will be given in the text.

21 In an interview of the same year, Oppen made the point more directly: "Pound's ego system, Pound's organization of the world around a character, a kind of masculine energy, is extremely foreign to me." Interview with L. S. Dembo, *Contemporary Literature*, 10, 2 (Spring 1969), 170.

22 For a more detailed discussion of this question, see my "Of Being Ethical: Reflections on George Oppen", *Journal of American Studies*, 31, 2 (1997), 153–70.

23 Creeley, *The Collected Essays*, p. 170.

24 Pound, *Selected Prose 1909–1965*, ed. William Cookson (London: Faber & Faber, 1973), p. 120.

25 Cf. Duncan, quoted in Beach, *ABC of Influence*, p. 145: "my ties to Pound, Stein, Surrealism and so forth all seem to me entirely consequent to their unbroken continuity from the Romantic period."

26 Duncan, "From the Day Book, – excerpts from an extended study of H.D.'s poetry," *Origin*, 10, 2nd series (July 1963), 16. The reference is primarily to Pound's *The Spirit of Romance*.

27 Duncan, "The H.D. Book: Chapter 1," *Coyote's Journal*, 5/6 (1966), 19.

28 Duncan, "The H.D. Book: Chapter 4," *Tri-Quarterly*, 12 (Spring 1968), 82.

29 Noted in Beach, *ABC of Influence*, p. 174. For the notion of "grand collage," see Duncan, *Bending the Bow* (London: Cape, 1971), p. vii: "in this realm of men's languages a poetry of all poetries, *grand collage*, I name It, having only the immediate event of words to speak for It."

30 Duncan, "From the Day Book," p. 41.

31 Pound, *Guide to Kulchur* (1938; London: Peter Owen, 1966), p. 194.

32 Duncan, *The Opening of the Field* (1960; New York: New Directions, 1973), pp. 64, 65.

33 Duncan, "From the Day Book," p. 44.

34 Olson, *Human Universe and Other Essays*, ed. Donald Allen (New York: Grove Press, 1967), p. 95. Further references to *HU* will be given in the text.

35 Pound, *The Selected Letters 1907–1941*, ed. D. D. Paige (London: Faber & Faber, 1950), p. 158.

36 Joseph Riddel, "Decentering the Image: The 'Project' of 'American' Poetics?", in Josue V. Harari (ed.), *Textual Strategies: Perspectives in Post-Structuralist Criticism* (London: Methuen, 1980), p. 351.

37 Olson, *Mayan Letters*, p. 90. Olson is commenting on Pound's *Guide to Kulchur*.

38 See Beach, *ABC of Influence*, p. 88.

39 Watten, *Total Syntax* (Carbondale and Edwardsville: Southern Illinois University Press, 1985), pp. 149, 134.

40 Olson, *The Special View of History*, ed. Ann Charters (Berkeley, CA: Oyez, 1970), pp. 16, 28.

41 Olson, *Proprioception* (Bolinas, CA: Four Seasons Foundation, 1965), p. 16.

42 Olson, *The Maximus Poems*, ed. George F. Butterick (Berkeley and Los Angeles: University of California Press, 1983), p. 33.

43 Olson, *Mayan Letters*, p. 26.

44 Olson, *The Maximus Poems*, p. 72. See also "The Twist," *ibid.*, pp. 86–90.

45 Bernstein, *Content's Dream: Essays 1975–1984* (Los Angeles: Sun & Moon Press, 1986), p. 329.

46 Howe, *The Birth-mark: Unsettling the Wilderness in American Literary History* (Hanover and London: Wesleyan University Press, 1993), p. 180.

47 MacLow explains that he "used a 'diastic' word-selection procedure, using the name 'Ezra Pound' as a 'seed string' through which words and 'ends' (i.e., fragments of words ranging from all but the first letter to only the last) were drawn from the poet's *Cantos* while I read through them." "Poetic Vocabularies: A Conversation between Barrett Watten and Jackson MacLow," *Aerial*, 8 (1995), 109. For excerpts from *Words nd Ends from Ez*, see MacLow,

Representative Works: 1938–1985 (New York: Roof Books, 1986), pp. 320–325. Cage's text is included in Paul Hoover (ed.), *Postmodern American Poetry* (New York and London: Norton, 1994), pp. 21–26.

48 Watten, *Total Syntax*, p. 40.

49 John Shoptaw, *On the Outside Looking Out: John Ashbery's Poetry* (Cambridge, MA and London: Harvard University Press, 1994), pp. 57–63.

50 Ashbery, "The Skaters," in *Rivers and Mountains* (New York: Ecco Press, 1977), p. 144.

51 Ashbery, "Saying It to Keep It from Happening," in *Houseboat Days* (1977; Harmondsworth: Penguin Books, 1978), p. 29.

52 Ashbery quoted in Shoptaw, *On the Outside Looking Out*, p. 6; Lyn Hejinian, "If Written is Writing," in Bruce Andrews and Charles Bernstein (eds.), *The L=A=N=G=U=A=G=E Book* (Carbondale and Edwardsville, IL: Southern Illinois University Press, 1984), p. 29.

53 Bernstein, *A Poetics* (Cambridge, MA and London: Harvard University Press, 1992), p. 60.

54 Shoptaw, *On the Outside Looking Out*, p. 44.

55 Bruce Andrews, "Misrepresentation (A Text for *The Tennis Court Oath* of John Ashbery)," in Ron Silliman (ed.), *In the American Tree* (Orono, ME: National Poetry Foundation, 1986), p. 521.

56 *A Novelette* (1932), in Williams, *Imaginations* (New York: New Directions, 1971), p. 281.

57 *Ibid.*, p. 299.

58 Quoted in André Breton, *Manifesto of Surrealism* (1924), in Richard Seaver and Helen R. Lane (trans.), *André Breton: Manifestoes of Surrealism* (Ann Arbor, MI: University of Michigan Press, 1972), p. 20.

59 Breton, *Manifesto of Surrealism*, pp. 36–37.

60 "Introduction" to Kenneth Rexroth (trans.), *Pierre Reverdy: Selected Poems* (New York: New Directions, 1969), p. vii.

61 Rexroth, *Pierre Reverdy*, pp. vi–vii.

62 Interview with Ashbery (1974), quoted in Helen Vendler, "Understanding Ashbery," in Harold Bloom (ed.), *Modern Critical Views: John Ashbery* (New York: Chelsea House, 1985), p. 185: "In the last few years I have been attempting to keep meaningfulness up to the pace of randomness . . . but I think that meaningfulness can't get along without randomness and that somehow they have to be brought together."

63 John Ashbery, "Reverdy en Amérique," *Mercure de France*, 344 (January/April 1962), 111 (my translation).

64 There is a growing body of commentary on the work of the Language writers. See, for example, Marjorie Perloff, *Poetic License: Essays on Modernist and Postmodernist Lyric* (Evanston, IL: Northwestern University Press, 1990), Linda Reinfeld, *Language Poetry: Writing as Rescue* (Baton Rouge: Louisiana State University Press, 1992), Hank Lazar, *Opposing Poetries*, 2 vols. (Evanston, IL: Northwestern University Press, 1996).

65 Davie, quoted in Humphrey Carpenter, *A Serious Character: The Life of Ezra Pound* (London: Faber and Faber, 1988), p. 813.

66 Cf. Jacques Derrida, "Living On: Borderlines," trans. James Hulbert, in Harold Bloom *et al.* (eds.), *Deconstruction and Criticism* (New York: Seabury Press,

1979), p. 116: unreadability "does not arrest reading, does not leave it paralyzed in the face of an opaque surface: rather, it starts reading and writing and translation moving again. The unreadable is not the opposite of the readable but rather the ridge [*arête*] that also gives it momentum, movement, sets it in motion."

67 Hejinian, "The Rejection of Closure," in Bob Perelman (ed.), *Writing/Talks* (Carbondale and Edwardsville: Southern Illinois University Press, 1985), p. 272.

68 Cf. John Ashbery, quoted in Shoptaw, *On the Outside Looking Out*, p. 6: "I always begin at zero and discover my thought by writing."

69 Ron Silliman, *The New Sentence* (New York: Roof, 1987), pp. 63–93.

70 Bernstein, *Content's Dream*, p. 32.

71 Bruce Andrews, "Poetry as Explanation, Poetry as Praxis," in Hoover (ed.), *Postmodern American Poetry*, p. 669.

72 Watten, *Total Syntax*, p. 114.

73 M. M. Bakhtin, *The Dialogic Imagination: Four Essays*, trans. Caryl Emerson and Michael Holquist (Austin: University of Texas, 1981), p. 293.

74 Watten, *Total Syntax*, pp. 113–114.

75 Bernstein, *Content's Dream*, p. 298. The reference is to Creeley's work.

76 Charles Altieri, "What is Living and What Is Dead in American Postmodernism: Establishing the Contemporaneity of Some American Poetry," *Critical Inquiry*, 22, 4 (Summer 1996), 787.

77 Bernstein, *A Poetics*, p. 123.

78 *Ibid.*, p. 124.

79 See Bernstein, "Poetics of the Americas," *Modernism/Modernity*, 3, 3 (1996), 1–23 for a discussion of poetry and multiculturalism.

80 For an expanded discussion of Howe's notion of "history," see my "Unsettling the Wilderness: Susan Howe and American History," *Contemporary Literature*, 37, 4 (Winter 1996), 586–601.

81 Lyotard, *Heidegger and "The Jews,"* trans. Andreas Michel and Mark Roberts (Minneapolis: University of Minnesota Press, 1990), p. 10.

82 Howe, *The Europe of Trusts* (Los Angeles, CA: Sun & Moon, 1990), p. 26.

83 Howe, "Encloser," in Charles Bernstein (ed.), *The Politics of Poetic Form: Poetry and Public Policy* (New York: Roof, 1990), p. 192.

84 Howe, *My Emily Dickinson* (Berkeley, CA: North Atlantic Books, 1985), p. 21.

85 Howe, *The Birth-mark*, p. 148.

86 Bernstein, *A Poetics*, pp. 122–123.

8

RICHARD TAYLOR

The texts of *The Cantos*

Our general understanding of textual criticism, its aims and procedures, has changed rather dramatically over the past twenty years or so, and it is no longer possible to consider the texts of *The Cantos*, or of any other major modernist work, without first reviewing, at least in outline form, relevant theoretical perspectives. Earlier views held that authors are isolated, unified, and integral personalities, and that they naturally work toward the creation of an end-product. In fact, no one lives in total isolation as a self-contained and consistent integer. Writers normally exist in a world of friends and family, as well as of colleagues and business associates. It is also difficult to assume that they never change their minds or points of view. More importantly, authors are in constant contact with literary tradition, the innumerable works of existing literature which form and influence them, not to mention their experience of both current and historical events.

Of course, writers set out to produce poems, novels, plays, etc., but there are two possible models for the process. The first contends that the most important moment in the creative process is the initial flash of inspiration and that subsequent rewriting, the working-out of an idea into final form, compromises the tension which gave birth to the work by moving further and further away from it, perhaps even censoring or repressing it. The other model holds that the original conception is little more than a rough sketch which must be elaborated upon, filled out, even reshaped in a more clear-headed, craftsmanlike way, perhaps even by persons other than the originator. In both cases attention is focused on the process of creation, the development and transmission of the text, rather than the end-product or work that first finds its way into print.

Authors often start out with notes and then write a draft or drafts which is/are copied over and corrected, as well as revised any number of times, before arriving at a publishable version. At some point the authorized text

161

is then sent to a publisher/editor who may ask for substantive revisions and most certainly will attempt to standardize spelling, punctuation, grammar, and even syntax, as well as choose typeface, design page-layout, and generally determine the physical characteristics of the published book. All of this has a significant effect on shaping the reader's response to the work over and above the meaning of the words themselves. When agreement is reached between author and editor(s), the revised text (now called setting copy) is ready for printing.

Before computer technology was available, a printer had then to set or compose type; that is, copy over the text as submitted in order that it be mechanically reproduced. Accidental errors now enter the picture as it is nearly impossible to copy a complex text perfectly. Proof sheets would then be printed for both author and editor, who correct them, but more often than not during the process of rereading, new questions as to wording, etc. would be raised, resulting in further authorial revisions as well as editorial emendations. Indeed, the author may even be moved to rewrite substantial portions of the work and, once again, editors and printers come into play, admitting even more chance of further changes and errors. The point is that the very process of publication is actually one of socialization, and any number of outside influences directly affect the text as originally submitted. The degree to which this happens in any particular case obviously has an important bearing on our perception of the work.

The story, of course, does not stop when the first printing appears. Major literary texts are published over and over again during an author's lifetime, and, of course, even beyond. Over the course of years and as they either develop or decline, authors also change their minds as well as their world view, and they may well alter their aesthetic values. As a work is revised for republication, its history obviously repeats itself, but there is also the possibility of unauthorized editions, either pirated by unscrupulous editors or those sanctioned by family and legitimate copyright holders (such as the author's usual publisher), but without the knowledge or participation of the actual author. In this later case interference in authorial decisions may go well beyond unauthorized changes and typographical errors. Works or versions which an author wishes to suppress might be republished, or drafts and fragments which had been rejected and abandoned in the course of writing, not to mention work in progress which in the author's judgment was not yet ready for publication, might find their way into print. Serious readers, therefore, should be aware of a text's history and the authority of any given version in relation to other existing texts.

It often happens that toward the end of a working life, well-known authors collaborate in the preparation of a revised or collected edition and such publications used to be acclaimed as definitive texts. They were especially prized because they were considered to embody the author's "final intentions." In cases where no retrospective edition existed, the next most authoritative text was taken to be the last edition approved by the author. The unspoken assumption underlying such views espoused the single, integral work or end-product which takes precedence over all other versions, and in every case accepted the author's latest judgement as preferable to earlier ones. It goes without saying that the author's intention was also conceived of as being singular and unchanging. In cases where either the creative power or health of an author was in decline, such a policy was obviously counterproductive, and scholarly editors who addressed themselves to the problems of textual criticism might then choose what they believed to be the most "authoritative" text as the basis (copy text) for a critical edition. The aim of such an editor was to achieve an ultimate version which was as free from unauthorized alteration as from accidental error. The greatest problem, of course, lay in determining "final intentions," not to mention unravelling the social interaction of actual book production and making decisions based on literary interpretations where necessary.

Critical editions of this type tended to eclecticism, not to mention reliance on the aesthetic judgement (literary taste) of the editor because it was believed that no single text was entirely authoritative, and editors were free to choose readings from differing versions, conflating them into a new whole, a text in which every word had actually been written by the author at one time or another, but had never appeared together in that particular combination or form. Such a practice was justified by saying that the role of the editor was to recover the "work," a hypothetical entity to which all known versions contribute.

> In this sense, the work may be the form traditionally imputed to an archetype; it may be a form seen as immanent in each of the versions but not fully realized in any one of them; or it may be conceived of as always potential, like that of a play, where the text is open and generates new meanings according to new needs in a perpetual deferral of closure.[1]

There is, however, an alternative concept to the one which maintains that the text is sanctioned by the author: singular, considered, and contained. The other, and more current view, is that the text is inherently incomplete, open, unstable, and subject to endless re-making by readers, performers or audiences. Indeed, for some theoreticians the question arises as to whether the text exists at all apart from the reader's creative act of interpretation. Reader-centered, rather than author-centered, criticism has become a norm, and editors now entertain renewed respect for the historicity of each individual version.

> In *Scholarly Editing in the Computer Age* [Peter Shillingsburg] sketches four main orientations towards literary forms: historical, which emphasizes the accurate presentation of documents as they existed historically or might ideally have existed; aesthetic, which relies finally on the editor's taste; authorial, which emphasizes authorial versions of a text over nonauthorial ones; and sociological, which emphasizes the social nature of text production and does not grant complete authority to the author alone.[2]

All four orientations should be employed when reading, but the exact weight and balance given them depends very much on knowing something about the nature of the text at hand, and more particularly, the course of its development and transmission. Ezra Pound's *Cantos* are necessarily subject to indeterminacy and instability both because of the great size and complexity of the surviving body of textual materials and the checkered history of attempts to revise and correct the text, as well as vexing questions of non-authorial intervention which have arisen over the years. The work as we now have it is over 800 pages long and has presented monumental problems for publishers/editors, printers, and proof-readers. Not only is it fragmentary in style, but the poem also employs more than twenty languages and contains innumerable quotations from both reliable and unreliable sources, as well as references to a great many historical persons and events. Pound himself was not always interested in factual accuracy nor in consistency of presentation, and the process of creation stretches from at least 1915 to 1968. During that period individual cantos were written and published in periodicals as well as anthologies. They were then revised and gathered into volumes, which like periodical publications appeared in various countries, and were finally brought together in collected editions (now entitled *The Cantos*), first published in New York (1948) and London (1950). The process of creation continued, and four more gatherings of cantos were published separately before being added to the existing collections. The first publication of the Italian Cantos ("LXXII–LXXIII") in book form took place eleven years after the author's death (November 1, 1972), and they were not included in the collected edition until 1986.

The following outline provides a scheme of major gatherings in volume form, but does not account for the occasional change of title:

A Draft of XVI Cantos. (Paris, 1925)

A Draft of the Cantos 17–27 (London, 1928)

A Draft of XXX Cantos (Paris, 1930; New York, 1933 & 1940; London, 1933)

Eleven New Cantos, XXXI–XLI (New York, 1934; London, 1935)

The Fifth Decad of Cantos (London, 1937; New York, 1937)

Cantos LII–LXXI (London, 1940; New York, 1940)

The Pisan Cantos (New York, 1948; London, 1949)

Section: Rock Drill (Milan, 1955; New York, 1956; London, 1957)

Thrones (Milan, 1959; New York, 1959; London, 1960)

Drafts & Fragments (Iowa City, 1968; New York, 1969; London, 1970)

Cantos LXXII & LXXIII (Washington DC & Toronto, 1973; Milan, 1983)

The first two gatherings of cantos listed above were limited, *de luxe* publications as were the first editions of *Section: Rock Drill, Thrones*, and *Drafts & Fragments*. The first 210 copies of *A Draft of XXX Cantos* were published in Paris on special paper and numbered (ten were signed), while the first edition of *Cantos LXXII & LXXIII* was mimeographed and published privately in order to secure copyright. The second edition was a limited, *de luxe* printing.

Multiplying the number of separate publications over longer periods, of course, gave the author more time to revise and correct texts which had already been much reworked. In every case transfer to collected editions gave rise to further revision (authorial), emendation (editorial), and printing error (accidental). Nor did efforts to correct the texts end with Pound's death. As early as August 5, 1939, the author had suggested that Faber & Faber might bring out a collected edition to be entitled either "Septuagint" or "Seventy One,"[3] but the war intervened, and then there was the sensation of the treason trial followed by the scandal of the Bollingen Prize for *The Pisan Cantos*. Pound reminded T. S. Eliot that he had made the same suggestion in 1935 when *A Draft of Cantos XXXI–XLI* was in press: "If no plates of XXX exist/ I probably shd/ consider revisions in that part/ IF plates exist, the revisions can wait till 1950 or whenever D/v. etc." [Faber & Faber] Eliot acknowledged Pound's proposal of a collected edition on October 19, 1945 when considering the publication of cantos written at Pisa. [Lilly: Pound, II]

The overview of publication history for the collected editions which follows, distinguishes between volumes of *The Cantos* in which the text was either altered significantly or enlarged, and reprintings of an already established text. The New York editions were published by New Directions and the London volumes by Faber & Faber. The contents of each is given by canto number in Arabic numerals within parentheses.

New Directions		Faber & Faber	
1948	(1–71), 74–84), rpt. 1951 [2 states], 56, 58 [with errata sheet], 60, 64.	1950	(1–71) [pages numbered consecutively]
1965	(85–95 added), rpt. 1966.	1954	(1–71, 74–84) [with errata sheet], rpt. 1957.
1970	(96–117 added), rpt. 1971 [titles Romanized, pages numbered consecutively].	1964	(85–109 added), rpt 1968
1972	(120 added), rpt. 1973, 75, 77, 79, 81, 83.	1975	[1976] (120 excluded) [ND sheets]
1986	(120 untitled & included in 117; 72, 73 & Fragment 1966 added at end)	1981	(120 included) [ND sheets]
1989	(72 & 73 in numerical order, full repagination)	1989	[ND sheets]

Since corrections were entered silently at various stages, ranging from one or two changes to 138 in the New Directions edition of 1970,[4] it cannot be assumed that texts listed as reprints of a given edition are identical to that of the first edition or, for that matter, to any other text in the same series. The situation was rendered even more complex by the fact that two very different versions of the poem were in circulation from 1950 to 1975; at which point, and for purely economic reasons, Faber & Faber decided to take unbound sheets from New Directions and abandoned their own edition.

The differences between the American and British versions are easily explained and there is a good deal more to the story than the imposition of a publisher's house style or rigor of copy editing. Publishing schedules at New Directions were usually under great pressure because it was difficult to estimate future sales with any accuracy, and printings were very often rushed affairs. In the 1950s and 1960s, print-runs were also kept to a minimum because it was believed that a "definitive" edition would be soon to hand.

British sales were not so extensive, but they were much steadier, and prior planning was possible. London also had the advantage of printing the first collected edition (1950) by the offset method (photo-reproduction) which allowed changes to be made by stripping in the new word(s) or line(s) and photographing the corrected page, not to mention the introduction of consecutive page numbers. New Directions was still using the original metal plates which could not be easily altered. More importantly, however, Faber & Faber was nearly two years behind in getting out a collected edition, and that contained only the first seventy-one cantos. It was not until 1954 that *The Pisan Cantos*, which was selling slowly but steadily, could be included in the collection. The time-lag gave Pound ample opportunity to re-read his text, correct, rethink, and revise. With the demise of the Faber edition, we have lost important aspects of the historical text, and this should make us aware of how important it is to read *The Cantos* in a wider perspective, to engage in a radical reading that does not adhere to the linearity and specificity of a particular document, but includes the multiplicity of variant readings over longer periods of time. Serious readers now respond to the different discursive acts of various texts and especially to their more hidden implications. However private the discourse, the text is not so much a "material thing" as it is an event or set of events in which certain communicative interchanges are experienced.[5]

A variorum edition, therefore, is the ideal vehicle for a serious reader of *The Cantos*, an edition based on the present collected edition and including all variant readings, line by line, from setting copy for the first (possibly periodical) publication of each canto to the latest printing. Such a compendium is being prepared, using the 1975 New Directions publication as a base text, but completion of the project is still some years away. No privilege is to be given to any particular reading and the authenticity of variants will be documented by quotations from letters between author, literary agents, lawyers, publishers, editors, printers, friends, and family, concerning the publication of various texts.

Ultimately all texts are collaborative events, but some authors participate more willingly than others in the process. A text may well evolve in ways which the author could not have foreseen, let alone "intended." One must distinguish between what might be considered a single, integral work (the 1975 New Directions edition, for example) and an extended series of historical documents presenting very different versions, for the most part authorized by the poet, although authority and sometimes even authorization might have been shared among a larger number of people.

The publication history of those cantos which were published in selected editions either in New York or London, offers another striking case in point, and more readers make their acquaintance with Pound's *Cantos via* selections rather than a complete text. The following outline gives an overview of major editions and reprintings:

New Directions	Faber & Faber
	A Selection of Poems (1, 2, & 45), 1940, rpt. 1942, 45, 46, 50.
Selected Poems (from 1–84), 1949, rpt. 1950.	*Selected Poems* (from 1–94), 1975.
– (from 1–94), 1957; rpt. 1959, 60, 62, 63, 65, 66, 67, 68, 69, 70, 72, 74, 76, 77, 79, 80, 83, 85, 86.	– (from 1–117), 1977.
Selected Cantos (from 1–117), 1970; rpt. 1971, 72, 73, 75, 77, 79, 81, 83, 86.	*Selected Cantos* (from 1–109) 1967; rpt. 1969, 74.
	– (from 1–109) 1987 [type reset].

From an unpublished letter written by Eliot to Ann Ridler, it is obvious that neither he nor Pound was wholly responsible for *A Selection of Poems.* "Thank you very much for your Ezra Pound selection which seems to me very satisfactory and has saved me a great deal of trouble. I have made a few alterations[. . .]. Finally I have added *Cantos 1* and *45* which Pound said he wanted and *Canto 2* to please myself." [R. A. Gekoski]

In the same way, the choice of material to be included in the New Directions edition of *Selected Poems* was very much a collaborative affair. Laughlin wanted to offer the public good poetry at a bargain price ($1.00), and the selection was made by the American poet, John Berryman. Pound was not particularly happy with the results and protested more than once about the length and arbitrariness of those from *The Pisan Cantos*. He advocated using a sixteen, rather than a thirty-two page sheet, reducing the selections accordingly.

Of course to make half the book Cantos. is flagrant violation of the agreement: and E.P. is not in the least pleased by that fact. It also, etc. wd/ be improved by cutting at least three galleys from the Pisan lot. But not if it means delay. NO the hash made of Pisans is too filthy to pass. I acceded to request to put in a FEW bits of cantos/ you have the thing HALF cantos/ BUT the PISAN chunk is just a mess of snippets/ and CANNOT stand as is. Better omit the whole of it. at any rate it is not in scale with the rest. and to print it with invisible dots for breaks is LOW. I haven't energy to do selecting. but the ONLY possible alternative to TOTAL and preferable omission is to put in one or two coherent bits. Not a lot of breaks in the sense. [James Laughlin]

On March 28, 1949 Laughlin responded:

Many thanks for fixing up the proofs of the SELECTED volume, and your comments have been suitably digested. Let me explain how it came about that so much CANTOS material was included in the selection. We have originally planned that the CANTOS would only occupy 20% or 25% of the book at the most, and Berryman was aware of that. However, as he got into the selection, he told me that he kept finding passages that were so marvelous that he simply couldn't leave them out. Thus by the time the selection reached me, it was almost 30% CANTOS already. But when I looked through it myself, I noted that he had given no representation at all to certain very important themes, such as the Italian, the Chinese and the Old Yankee. So I felt that suitable chunks of these epochs had to be added to give a rounded picture. Then when I looked over what he had chosen from the Pisan Cantos, I found that it was nothing but a tiny little collection of snippets. If you think it is snippity now, you ought to have seen what it was like when Berryman turned it in. In many instances he had picked out single lines from here or there or little short paragraphs that had no connection with nothing at all. These were, it is true, very beautiful lines, but by themselves they were awfully lonely. I then set about trying to give them some fat on the sides of their bones, with the results that you have seen. I agree with you that the volume, as it now stands, is overweighted with CANTOS, and I have asked the printer to give me a page count of how the thing is going to form up when he pages it, and after I have this, I will see what can be done about cutting down the representation for the CANTOS. [James Laughlin]

Pound later objected to at least one passage, which was thrown out, but approved the inclusion of China and Adams material and found the strength to correct page proofs. The volume was reprinted in 1950, and soon after, preparations were underway for a serious revision. Most of the work was done by Hugh Kenner, then Professor of English Literature, University of California at Santa Barbara, who not only weeded out misprints but also made suggestions as to rectifying what he considered to be unfortunate cuts.[6] Not all of the suggestions he outlined in a letter to Robert MacGregor of New Directions (January 15, 1957) were actually carried out, however.

What you should include from ROCKDRILL is 91 down to the bottom of page 73: "So hath Sibile a broken isette." Much more immediate appeal than 92. After all you're not committed to a whole canto. Second choice, 93, beginning near top of p. 88 ("The autumn leaves blow from my hand") to end of page 92. Third choice. 90 intact; and 92 would be my fourth choice. If it were a case of leaving out, I'd leave out XV–XVI, pages 118–123 of Selected Poems, on ground that componants there exhibited were represented elsewhere. [New Directions, New York]

MacGregor wrote to Pound on January 21, 1957:

We would also like your permission to include some short passages from SECTION: ROCK DRILL. We suggest Canto 91, from the beginning down to the bottom of page 73: "So hath Sibele a broken isette." If we have room we would like also to include from Canto 93, beginning near the top of page 88 with, "The autumn leaves blow over my hand," to the end of page 92. [Beinecke: Pound, I]

Hayden Carruth, a freelance author and editor who was also working on the volume, participated in the decisions, but the final compromise was largely determined by practical factors as MacGregor informed Kenner on March 20, 1957: "it turned out that we couldn't add pages to the book without making it another kind of a project and much more expensive [. . .] We took slightly different parts from SECTION: ROCK DRILL than you first suggested, mainly because they would fit as far as space was concerned." [New Directions, New York]

In the end, XV and XVI were omitted and selections from LXXIV, LXXVI, and LXXX altered, while passages from XCI and XCII were added, and an acknowledgement to both Kenner and Carruth was included on the back of the title page. Later, when the edition was taken over by Faber & Faber (1975), the shape of selections from *The Cantos* underwent still further changes. The London edition of 1977 was extended by including selections from XCVIII, CVII, CX, and CXVI and all of CXV from *Drafts & Fragments* (1969).

The history of *Selected Cantos* is even more problematical in that there was a marked difference between the two editions from the very beginning. The story begins in a visit to Pound made by J. Laughlin and reported to Eva Hesse, Pound's German translator and a considerable scholar of modern poetry in English, in a letter of September 14, 1964. Peter du Sautoy of Faber & Faber was also convinced of the need for a new selection from the whole poem (Cantos 1–109) to be made by the author himself. A marked up copy of the Faber edition indicating the poet's choices and including a few minor corrections, by the way, reached London in 1965 and was published two years later exactly as outlined by the author. In 1970 New Directions brought out its own edition which was based on Pound's list of selections to be included, a list which was identical with that supplied to Faber & Faber. No corrections were stipulated, however, as New Directions intended to set up type from their own collected edition which differed in a great many individual readings from the London text. Faber, of course, was using offset methods of reproduction and so could include corrections while avoiding the introduction of typographical error. Twenty-eight lines from XVI (19–46) were inadvertently omitted from the first New York edition and they were not reinstated until the fourth reprinting in 1975. The text of the American edition differed in other significant ways from that of Faber & Faber and not merely because of the many variations in wording (substantives) and punctuation (accidentals), etc.

Because of the compressed setting, a few extra pages were available to the publisher, and Pound's selection was extended by the addition of the final seventy-eight lines of LII which was originally represented by lines 50 through 79. The first 107 lines of LXXXIII were also added although that canto had not been designated by the author, nor had CXV and CXVI which were also included. These last two cantos had not yet been published when Pound made the selection in 1965 and although he authorized the later publication, as well as actively participating in the project, *Drafts & Fragments of Cantos CX–CXVII* (1969) came into being only in order to protect the copyright.

In 1967 a pirated version of work in progress had been mimeographed and stapled together in New York City; a number of copies were actually sold before the "edition" was suppressed, but the intervention of outside legal and economic factors played as great a role in the history of publication at this point as did the commercial and aesthetic judgement of publishers and editors. By 1970 the poet was so withdrawn and indifferent to the world of affairs that New Directions acted unilaterally. On April 10, 1970 Laughlin wrote to Hesse, who had long been much involved, along with others, in gathering possible corrections for the collected edition of *Cantos*:

> I also enclose a copy of the little publisher's Note which I have written to explain our additions to the Faber text of "Selected Cantos." I did not think it was honest not to mention our additions in some way. But, as you requested, I have not mentioned you by name as the source of them. Nor have I referred to the fact that we have made certain corrections to the Faber text, I think that is just too complicated to explain, and few people except the experts will notice it. [James Laughlin]

Once again, however, practical considerations forced a change in their earlier decision. On July 14, 1970 Laughlin wrote:

> In paging up the "repros" for the "Selected Cantos," from Mardersteig's handsome composition I discovered that I had "goofed" in my calculations, and we were a page long. Accordingly, the best thing to do seemed to be to eliminate the "Cthonian" passage which you had added from Canto 82. I'm sorry about this, as I thought it was an excellent suggestion, but it proved to be the easiest out to make, both for length, and coming late in the book, so that there were fewer folios to repaste. [James Laughlin]

As we can see from Laughlin's reply to du Sautoy, Faber & Faber were not altogether pleased by editorial interference with the original text, but they obviously did use the precedent as rationale for extending their 1977 edition of *Selected Poems* to include even more material from *Drafts & Fragments*:

> I think you are quite right to chide me a little for having made additions to Ezra's basic selection for our "Selected Cantos," I may have overstepped the proper licence of a publisher. But I felt there were good reasons for doing so, at least as far as we were concerned. First of all, there are such lovely bits in the "Drafts and Fragments," and, on top of that, with our new Mardersteig composition for the book, we had a few blank pages, but I just couldn't see leaving them blank. So far I have had no "blast" from Ezra for doing what I did, since I put in the little note in the front of the book explaining exactly what I added to his basic selection. [James Laughlin]

However well-intentioned, the addition of 280 lines does change both the shape and tenor of the work, and the result can hardly be acknowledged as the author's original intention. We cannot know whether he might have agreed to the additions as he never had the opportunity to make the decision. Indeed, that particular text, as was so often the case, underwent changes which he could not have imagined, and we are again forcibly reminded that the particular reading text we have in hand does make a great difference in our apprehension of and response to the poetry.

Even though the London *Selected Cantos* is obviously preferable to the New York edition, both are more faithful to the author's reading of the epic than the choices made by Berryman (as modified by Laughlin and Pound) for *Selected Poems*. In any case none of the selected editions contains texts that fall within a direct line of descent for any particular canto and they do not always carry the authority of collected editions which continued to evolve and change. Before going on to consider the relationship between the editions published by New Directions and Faber, not to mention the efforts to "correct the text," it might be helpful to give a stemma (family tree) of development for Canto I. The following scheme includes both periodical and book publications, as well as acknowledging the radical revision of July 1923 when the first three cantos were largely rewritten.

The texts of *The Cantos*

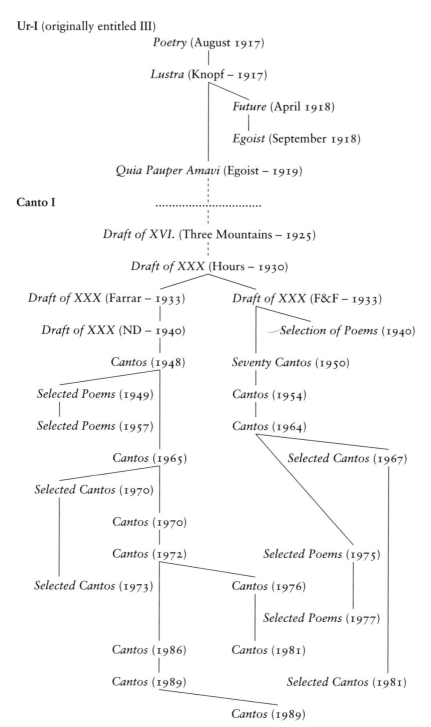

Ur-I (originally entitled III)

Poetry (August 1917)

Lustra (Knopf – 1917)

Future (April 1918)

Egoist (September 1918)

Quia Pauper Amavi (Egoist – 1919)

Canto I

Draft of XVI. (Three Mountains – 1925)

Draft of XXX (Hours – 1930)

Draft of XXX (Farrar – 1933)   *Draft of XXX* (F&F – 1933)

Draft of XXX (ND – 1940)   *Selection of Poems* (1940)

Cantos (1948)   *Seventy Cantos* (1950)

Selected Poems (1949)   *Cantos* (1954)

Selected Poems (1957)   *Cantos* (1964)

Cantos (1965)   *Selected Cantos* (1967)

Selected Cantos (1970)

Cantos (1970)

Cantos (1972)   *Selected Poems* (1975)

Selected Cantos (1973)   *Cantos* (1976)

Selected Poems (1977)

Cantos (1986)   *Cantos* (1981)

Cantos (1989)   *Selected Cantos* (1981)

Cantos (1989)

Unfortunately, the time is not yet ripe for making a detailed comparison of readings between the New York and London printings of the various collected editions, but something of their relationship in Pound's view can be gleaned from his unpublished correspondence. On May 4, 1949 Laurence Pollinger, Pound's literary agent in London, wrote to Dorothy Pound: "About three weeks ago Faber wrote that they would like to publish a collected edition of Ezra's CANTOS up to but excluding PISAN CANTOS [. . .] They have no standing type of the CANTOS so this is really a new book." [Lilly: Pound, II]. Pound wrote in the margin: "O.K. as new set up let us correct errors." By June 11, the collected Cantos were already in press and on the sixteenth Pollinger reported to Dorothy Pound that "[t]he corrected copy of SEVENTY CANTOS is just here and is being handed to Eliot" [Lilly: Pound, II]. Production difficulties ensued which seriously delayed publication, and a number of people suggested further emendations, notably John Drummond, friend and translator, and Peter Russell, poet and critic. Realizing that extensive revision would be an expensive proposition, the production department at Faber & Faber advocated limiting the number and incorporating them in an errata sheet. Pound, on the other hand, began to worry that corrections would further delay publication as he had in 1946 when Dorothy Pound wrote to Laughlin (July 31): "yesterday E. said to photograph his pencilled-in ideograms if it would hurry up the printers of the last cantos – it would at least add an interest anyway" [James Laughlin], but a good many changes were also made to the Faber edition, including the addition of Chinese ideograms in the blank spaces at the end of several cantos. Laughlin was also interested in correcting the New York edition and Pound wrote to him in July 1950:

> Yes send on the "battered copy," I will keep corrections down to one or two main points, and as many outrages to the greek as I can spot or remember. and add the DAWG ideogram, and the other correct. Can yu foto from the debased Faber edtn/ of Pisans?[. . .] There are also EIGHT large and handsome ids/ to fill in spaces at end of the 52/61 Chinkese cantos BEEyewteefully done and soup-lied to Faber for their new ed/ wot they keep DEElaying..[. . .] the new ids/ EmPHAsise the main points of the doctrine an Jas/ MaZwell Embellish with 'em. The other change is in p/ 15yr/ edtn/ Canto IV. taking the Catullus back to HarryStopHerKnees [Aristophanes], whaar Cat[ullus]/ mebbe got it, anyhow the greek shows the real way Cat/ wd/ hv/ tookd it fer graunted the Epithalamium wd/ be sung. Recon the choon stayed thaaar right down into the middle ages. [James Laughlin]

Pound was anxious that the notes for LII–LXXI should precede the section in forthcoming Faber editions, but type was never reset, and he did agree to prepare an errata sheet for the 1954 printing. Other hands were also at work, and David Bland of Faber & Faber wrote to Russell on January 21, 1954:

> Thank you very much indeed for your help in this matter and for identifying "Wemyss". We had suspected that there might be many other mistakes, and in fact we are altering the transposed pages which you mention. Pound himself has supplied a short list of errata, but this does not include either of the two major corrections which you mention. I think it might be a good plan to add these to the slip, but I suppose we ought to refer the matter to Pound himself before doing this. [Faber & Faber]

Pound was interested not only in revising the text but also in providing a useful and scholarly apparatus. On July 14, [1954] he wrote to Norman Holmes Pearson, Professor of English Literature at Yale University who was then helping to coordinate corrections to the text, which included an oft repeated *cri de coeur*:

> Of course if some frosh/ wanted to be USEFUL, he cd/ make an INDEX of proper names (and even subjects) in the Cantos. save gramp/ making memos on back leaf. Question of what edition/ Fabers new 84 has some corrections/ and a eroter list/ (emended by office punk, to take life out of it. But it is such a lousy firm, they prob/ wdn't add the index, so better stick to Nude Erections (chordee rather) paging. Faber STILL got the rays ideogram, and notes on China Adams section in wrong place/ despite request. [Beinecke: Pearson, Pound]

It would be impossible to contend that one or the other of the collected editions was superior. Each had its own advantages as well as failings. The Faber text has unfortunately been discontinued and its authoritative readings are not represented in the present version. Over the years much has been made of the superiority of the London edition, but when preparing the *Selected Cantos* in 1965, Pound wrote to Laughlin (September 1), "For your information more misprints in Faber, than in N.D." [James Laughlin] As late as December 21, 1971 Laughlin shared some of his doubts with Kenner:

> As you say, Faber did go pretty far in changing things in their resetting of the later sections. I'm glad that we made the decision to photograph the Mardersteig settings, which presumably followed Ezra's own instructions, even though the type doesn't exactly match. But I still feel that in these pages there are certain words or phrases which are "runovers," that is, dropped below the line where they belong at the right side, rather than meaningful placements in terms of a visual pattern. [New Directions, Norfolk]

The answer to this and many other problems awaits careful collation of published versions with the actual setting copy, not to mention proof sheets and correspondence with publishers, editors, printers, and other interested parties.

Yet another question which arises when considering the authority and "correctness" of the text has to do with stylistic uniformity and the accuracy of both quotations from other sources and historical detail. Throughout his working life Pound's approach to the problem was fairly consistent. Laughlin, for example, wrote the following to Achilles Fang, Professor of Chinese at Harvard University, on July 19, 1950:

> Very tactfully I enquired of Ezra whether he would like to have you suggest certain changes for the new printing of the Cantos, with respect to the spelling and date errors in the Chinese Cantos. Here is his response, which I quote to you verbatim: "No need to correct Chinese Cantos – they are not philology, all the funny spellings indicate tradition, how the snooz got to your-up [;] some latin, some by Portergoose, some by frog [. . .] when it comes to tradition – yes, thank Fang for any precisions, but, there is also another point, even where diagrames (romanj) fer Ez himself to study, and work on theory that changes of dialect, etc. – do not affect melodic coherence – this not dogma, it is conjecture." [James Laughlin]

A few years later [Spring 1953 or 1954] Pound mentioned the subject to Laughlin again: "Fang ain't to make changes in TEXT, but if he deigns, he can supply a lot of pretty IDEOgrams fer the margin [. . .] all for the disTANT future, not fer the present emission" [James Laughlin] Writing to his son-in law, Boris de Rachewiltz, on August 16 [1954], he reiterates the point: "I do not think Spelling of chinese names of ANY importance/ No spelling will ever content everyone/ so shd/ leave 'em as in orig/ wop edtns/" [New York Public: Berg, Pound].

The poet's preoccupation with page design, typography, and uniformity are all represented in his correspondence with Vanni Scheiwiller who published first editions of both *Section: Rock Drill* and *Thrones* in Milan. On November 25, 1954 Pound wrote:

> Cantos 90–95, the difference in spacing between the lines has an importance for placing of the text on the page perhaps TWICE that which is the only possibility on a typewriter/ ought to be reduced to 1 1/2. NOT as here, twice that. Hudson exaggerated in the first proofs of 85. I think that the Arabic numbers 85 without *CANTO 85* would be preferable to the Roman numerals LXXXV/ when one reaches LXXXVIII/ too much. but I leave it to Mardersteig [. . .] in every case I want to see proofs in final form, or nearly final/[. . .] For clarity I have written the Greek quotations very big/ they needn't be so large when printed/ font size as used by Faber in 84 Cantos. don't be upset that Leocothoe is written in two ways/ Leucothoe. It's OK. Kádmon's daughter, all the same. I amuse myself with the BIG Greek dictionary the

accents occur in so many different ways that not even a fusspot would dare pontificate about the choice [. . .] 90/5 musicality etc/ indicated by typography. therefore disposition of verses etc. more complicated [. . .] whether the 88 should be centered or on right/? etc/ how would a great printer manage it, let's hear HIS opinion/[. . .] Later/ because of the large ideogram LING, Canto 85 and the Egyptian verse/ I think that the numbers would be better at the left than in the middle.

Apart from the fanciful spelling and grammar of the original Italian, it is interesting to note how impervious Pound was to questions of formality and accuracy as well as how ready he was to leave certain decisions for others to make. A letter to Scheiwiller dated June 21, 1955 confirms the point with even greater emphasis:

Proofs arrived/ many thanks for assiduous care/ especially where you have found errors. but in some places QUOTATIONS are not grammatical exercises. Donna che VOLGO (quoted from a Canzoni). later "Tolgo"/. "Volge" falsifies/ other points of minor importance the latin words should keep their relationship with an absent context/. Canz/ dell fortuna/ Io son la donna che VOLGO. Fixed spelling belongs to certain periods not to others. Certain cases are not worth changing type already set. etc. But very many thanks for the correction of errors, Hudson, for example, was on the verge of spoiling a line by abandoning the dialect of the original. I hope they will keep my corrections. and not insist on dictionary spelling [. . .] Where I have nothing against it, I have left your emendations or corrections. Thanking you, Variation Leocothoe, Leucothea/ done intentionally. do as you like/ but as far as I'm concerned it is not worth bothering Mardersteig in order to make Riccardus and Richardus uniform, etc. because in the Middle Ages such uniformity was NOT observed. The concepts of the poets from early centuries are a bit falsified when the texts are Renaissanced etc.. But I am not fanatical in asking for this diversity in each case. do as YOU like, except in cases where I have inked in preferences.

Fortunately, almost every decision and alteration in the text can and will be documented, as well as revisions of prior decisions which can be seen in Laughlin's letter to Hesse of May 9, 1966:

Our latest printing of the "Cantos" still has the Arabic numerals for 85 to 95, but this is only because this is a temporary printing, in which we are offsetting from "Rock Drill", and I know that Ezra wants them to be Roman numerals throughout, because he told me so the last time I saw him. We will get them all that way eventually when we make a proper revision and resetting of the text. [New Directions, Norfolk]

Pound not only changed his mind from time to time about page design and typography, not to mention variant readings, but he also revised quotations to fit in with his metrical scheme. Kenner reported to Laughlin in a letter of October 27, 1955: "[w]hen I asked Ez in May 1950 why he used the spelling 'brododaktulos' he said he could not recall any reason except that it sounded better" [Beinecke: Pound, I]. In the same way the preparation of each new publication encouraged revision as he confirmed in a letter of April 23 [1955] to Ingrid Davies: "One ALWAYS improves ANYthing if forced to retype. Gtly annoyed at NOT having spare carbon of Cantos 88/9. BUT did improve paragraphing when forced to prepare same for Hud/" [Harry Ransom: Pound, Davies]. He wrote again on November 7:

> Literary item, Canto 96 sweated into let us hope correct form and transmitted. Must have added 46 or thereabouts commas, faked two gk. accents, no longer having text of whatever they were quoted from/ and the suffering reader may console herself with the thought that the blasted author will HAVE to look up some of the gk/ himself in future, BUT then it is all stuff he wd/ like to look up if there is NO other way of recalling wot the HELL it refers to. [Harry Ransom: Pound, Davies]

Although he was well aware of his own deficiencies – "I am the WORST proof-reader natr/ ever let liv. so loathe the physical action of reading I do NOT see anything if I know it is supposed to be there" [February 9, 1995?/ Beinecke: Pearson, Pound] – he did want a "Definitive Cantares" reset by Mardersteig, although he left the actual work to others. For example, he wrote the following to Pearson (January 24, 1957): "What wd/ be useful is an index saying what canto and what line something appears in [. . .] Of course a good text, lines numbered by 10/s/ with Fang's proper chinese names in margin/ that I wd/ look at" [Beinecke: Pearson, Pound]. Unfortunately, a reset and thoroughly revised edition was never published, but the corrected text brought out by New Directions in 1970 incorporated many of Pound's desired corrections as governed by views outlined by Kenner in a letter to Laughlin of October 15, 1968:

> My opinion is that one should leave Ezra's text alone unless one is *quite* sure his intention does not surpass one's perception. He frequently feeds one language through another, as in the Jap spellings in *Cathay*, to indicate a chain of transmission. Which is to say that while I have no special knowledge of the details you mention in 113, I should be inclined to back your inclination to tell *New Yorker* to leave 'em alone. Better the author's error, if errors they be, than someone else's. [New Directions, Norfolk]

In a letter to Laughlin Hesse later concurred, and in a long, detailed examination of problems arising from her translation of *Drafts & Fragments* which outlines a number of possible errors and traces them through earlier Cantos (June 18, 1975), she concludes: "These many small slips should I think be considered as reflecting the element of human error in the *Cantos* as a dimension of the poem; nothing much is gained by correcting them" [New Directions, Norfolk].

Concerted efforts toward correcting the Cantos had been going on for some long time, however. Fang had offered to work on the Chinese Cantos and Pearson shared the queries and annotations collected by his graduate students with the common goal of a "definitive" edition. Pound welcomed the idea in a letter of March 11 [1953], so long as he was free to accept or reject suggested changes [Beinecke: Pearson, Pound]. He even outlined a methodology for gathering possible corrections at Yale and proposed a committee to Kenner who reported the names to Laughlin on December 20, 1953: "Kenner, Pearce, Pearson, Emery, Paige, Davenport, OP, Fang, Idlet" [Beinecke: Pound, I]. After the publication of *Section: Rock Drill* (1955) Hesse became increasingly involved, and Mary de Rachewiltz, Pound's daughter, contributed lists to the common pool which derived from translation exercises with her father. Robert Mayo, editor of *The Analyst* (1953), and John Edwards, who edited the *Annotated Index* (1959), were consulted, and Reno Odlin sent in a number of queries and suggestions. Views differed as to which existing texts were the most accurate, not to mention on-going conflicts between concepts of historical accuracy and creative revision as well as those of uniformity of presentation and the acknowledgement of variable traditions. There was a consensus of opinion, however, that many of the corrections offered were doubtful and all queries should ultimately be referred to the author.

There can be no doubt that Pound wanted a corrected and copper-bottomed text. On December 28, 1955 Laughlin wrote to Eliot:

> He told me lots of fascinating things about the structure of the Cantos which I had never known before. He says now that there will be between 100 and 120 of them, probably 112, and there is every indication that he is working hard on them. At some point, he wants us to do a completely new edition of them because there are so many variations and errors in our present texts. [James Laughlin]

On January 29 [1956] Pound complained to Pearson:

> Some urge toward a correct edtn/ of Cantares/ WITH Fang's ideog/s in margin of Chink Canters, still keep on finin errors/ Faber qt/ gk/ Canto 39 p. 202 three errors. Damn all I cant spend my time readin what I HAVE writ/ got to pay some attention to the FURTHER devilupment of the poEM. [Beinecke: Pearson, Pound]

Efforts to complete the project continued into 1963, but had already peaked around 1958 when a new edition seemed imminent. Throughout this period New Directions had been limiting their print-run and only corrected the most obvious errors. More problems arose, however, than were solved, and the successful completion of the exercise seemed further off than ever. Even Pound's enthusiasm waxed and waned. On June 17, 1958 MacGregor wrote to Fang:

> J. Laughlin is just back from Washington and reports that Pound seems quite exhausted with the decisions of life, and he thinks it would be a mistake for me to send him questions about the revisions in the new printing. I am going ahead, therefore, and getting a few changes in hand, as well as the errata list and then I will just tell him what I am doing. [New Directions, New York]

On September 9 [1959] the poet was again ready to tackle the problems and wrote to Pearson:

> everyone I suggest to do work seems disqualified to receive practical support. My last suggestion was fellowship to do thesis on actual articulation of at least some of the sources of canto facts ANDH/ not as retrospect but as FIELD for further clarification of history/ such as in Rouvere on Medici Bank. Would there be any chance of a grant or fellowship for ME, to sort out such books as Memorie Istoriche, La Zecca e la Moneta di RIMINI. Bologna 1789. Salmasius, etc. The, I suppose unique, greek with latin translations, of Martial done for Lorenzo dei Medici in 1480. etc. [Beinecke: Pound, I]

No grant was forthcoming, nor was an application for support from the Bollingen Foundation for a scholarly project to establish a corrected text of *The Cantos* pursued (1963). It was, of course, rather late in the day to co-ordinate the disparate searches and studies that had already taken place or to settle on a single base text to which all other versions might be compared. From the correspondence now available Pearson seems to be the only scholar who specifically mentions the need to go back to setting copy. On November 19, 1963 he wrote to Laughlin:

> Hugh's suggestion of a formal committee and a grant is a sound one – given at least three contingencies: (1) that Ezwroh really assist (there[,] even a little help is better than none, and he does seem to be in an amiable mood; (2) that Mary [de Rachewiltz] would assist, for the mss are left to her; (3) that the mss of the Cantos at Brunnenburg would be made available at some point or other. Nothing can be more important than the establishment of the text of the cantos, which was my aim when I thought I had Ez pen on it. He agreed to answer queries, but soon lost interest, & was often quixotic. We agreed also to designate the lineage in terms of true lines versus run-overs because of the size of the page, so that a definitive lineation could be determined. but he never did get to this; and I admired his determination to plan ahead rather than to contemplate and revise. The problem of correcting actual factual

mistakes is a difficult one. The problem of correcting his frequent Greek and Chinese characters seems more pedantic to him than to others. Gradually I came to rely on Mary [de Rachewiltz] and the excuse of her translations to solve the problems with him as she came to them. These problems will probably always remain, but need be no bar. I am happy to help in any way that seems best suited to the goals and the tactics of arriving at them. I am happy to go to Ezra, but would have no confidence in complete and definitive results. [Beinecke: Pearson, Pound]

In the end Pearson silently withdrew from the project, and Kenner's views as outlined to Laughlin in a letter of December 17, 1963 underline its lack of feasibility:

no one seems to realize how far your fifth printing and the Faber Seventy Cantos can have crept apart. I'm pretty sure, for instance, though I can't be certain without access to Faber copies, that the English text of the Lerici has been set from one of the Faber versions, whereas Mary [de Rachewiltz] made her translation from a New Directions copy! The sheets of EP's corrections which you sent me as from Olga [Rudge, M. de R.'es mother] illustrate another kind of lost labour; Ezra was going through your second printing, though at least some of those errors were caught midway through your second printing.[. . .] Mary got rid of a lot of [the errors of fact or trans-criptions committed by EP or a typist] in Lerici by simply going back to the sources, and prevailing upon EP to accept her findings. I take it Eva has been doing work of this kind, too. And lots of other people have, also. I should follow the principle that many of the errors are just plain errors: for instance the unpronounceable Greek word on the first page of XXII (corrected in Lerici), where the printer has mistaken a capital Upsilon for a gamma. But there are lots and lots of borderline cases that should be referred to EP. [New Directions, New York]

Earlier, Laughlin had written to Hesse (October 30, 1963):

I guess Ezra has never really cared about such details. Perhaps this is because in old manuscripts and texts things are spelled so many different ways, and he feels that if the general meaning gets through, that is enough. Neverthe-less, I do feel that we must do our best to try to make things right for him. I think that it is a very good idea that you should "vet" the final corrections list, even after Kenner has been over it, careful as he is. I wish there were some way that we could all get together, the whole "correction committee," and then send a delegate to Ezra to work out the final answers to problems. [New Directions, Norfolk]

The different lists of problematical readings which had been accumu-lated from various sources over so long a time, were finally conflated by Laughlin and entered into a copy of the New Directions collected edition.

The "committee" never met, but Laughlin visited Pound in Venice and later reported to Jay Martin (November 15, 1965):

> The Task of getting things corrected has advanced not at all because Ezra just cannot concentrate on the corrections suggested by various experts. I tried to get answers when I saw him in Venice last January, and it was painful. He would stare at the page where the correction was marked for a long time, without answering and then just start turning pages aimlessly. [New Directions, Norfolk]

Progress toward a "definitive" edition had been undermined from the beginning by contradictory intentions and inconsistent methods; it was ultimately doomed, however, by Pound's indifference. The plan failed, but the process of emending the text continued, and according to Barbara Eastman, some 236 changes were incorporated in the printings from 1970 to 1975.[7] The majority of them, however, can be traced to corrections authorized by Pound himself.

Other changes were also introduced at that time, or after, and they are obviously more problematical, not to mention the questions which have arisen over the authorization of *Drafts & Fragments* (1968). Both Peter Stoicheff and Ronald Bush take the view that Pound was at best a very reluctant participant in the effort to publish that volume,[8] and there is no doubt that the publication was spurred on by a pirated edition of work in progress (*Cantos 110–116*. New York: FUCK YOU/ Press, 1967). The story has already been told in some detail, but the shifting pattern of Pound's intentions certainly deserves more documentation. Up to the point of his release from St. Elizabeths he had been in a highly creative phase and on December 5 [1958] wrote to Pearson: "Cantos won't be finished until my demise, shd/ always reserve possibility of death-bed swan" [Beinecke: Pearson, Pound]. He seems to have been preoccupied very much with work in progress and wrote to Eliot on January 12 [1959]:

> There are some fragments of Cantos 110–116, that I wd/ like you to guard from destruction if necessity arises. one line at least that: Wyndham accepted blindness rather than risk having his mind stop. I DO need a few months to work in. An amiable photographer so relieved to hear that the Cantos are a failure, and that they or A canto hadn't a form that I cd/ define at that particular moment in state of exhaustion. Of course that will go out as authorized, timeless, universal. You might at least note that there are at least elements of form, progress, design. [Faber & Faber]

From a letter written to Laughlin on November 24 [1959] it is clear that Pound did plan to publish work in progress: "Nor shd/ later Cantos be released until Thrones has had time to operate" [James Laughlin]. As early as December 31, 1959 Kenner commented to Laughlin: "I heard a rumour a while back that Canto the last was to be 117, on which reckoning one more volume should do it" [New Directions, Norfolk]. Long before the 1967 piracy which led to the publication of *Drafts & Fragments*, a number of periodical publications from work in progress were authorized by Pound himself:

Periodical	Canto
Threshold ([Spring?] 1962)	CXV
Paris Review (Summer/Fall 1962)	From CXV, CXVI
Agenda (March/April 1963)	Notes for CXI
National Review (10 September 1963)	From CX, *From* From CXII, *From* CXIV, *From* From CXV, Notes for CXVII et seg. [a]
Agenda (December/January 1963/ 1964)	[Reprinted from *N.A.*]
Agenda October/November 1965)	From CXV

Different versions of the variously named poems were published as well as selections therefrom, but they were all released by Pound himself, or at least with his blessing. Elsewhere I have asserted that the *Threshold* version of CXV was selected from among Pound's papers by his daughter and sent for publication while he was undergoing treatment at a private clinic in Merano,[9] but it now appears that earlier the poet had given a copy of the same text to Desmond O'Grady who had been commissioned to pass it on to Professor Roger McHugh of University College, Dublin, a guest editor of *Threshold*. Laughlin had suspected all along that O'Grady had functioned as intermediary and so held the lines taken from that text and later entitled CXX as published in *Anonym* (Spring? 1969) to be authoritative. From the specific comment in the letter to Eliot quoted above, and the fact that different versions or excerpts were published so many times, the importance of CXV in Pound's mind cannot be doubted, and that eventually leads to the controversy over the various "endings" ascribed to *The Cantos*.

Interim, there were also a number of unauthorized periodical publications:

Periodical	Canto
Poetry (October/November 1962)	CXIII
Niagara Frontier Review (Fall 1965/ Spring 1966)	CX, CXVI
Anonym (1969)	CXX

Laughlin supplied the editor of *Poetry* with a text for their fiftieth anniversary issue[10] but the history of the other two publications remains something of a mystery. The pirated pamphlet, *Cantos 110–116*, (1967), falls between the *Niagara Frontier* and *Anonym* publications, and certainly impelled the authorised version of *Drafts & Fragments* (1968). On March 1, 1968 Laughlin wrote formally to du Sautoy:

> The cable above mentioned had chiefly to do with the possibility of a book of "Canto fragments." I had written Ezra about the piracy here, and pointed out that if we could do an official book, even a limited edition, it might help stop more of that sort of thing. His reply indicates that he sees some merit in this plan, and now he has asked me to send him copies of all the texts of the fragments which I have, so that he can look them over, and I have done so. [New Directions, New York]

A few days later (March 6, 1968) he wrote more spontaneously to Kenner:

> Ezra seems to be a little bit more peppy lately. I've had several notes from him, and I believe he is actually bestirring himself to try to put the "Canto Fragments" in shape for a temporary book, hopefully to head off any more piracies like the disgusting ED Sanders mimeographed effort, did you see that? A shameful business. [New Directions, Norfolk]

The effective relationship between publisher and text, however, is made clear in a Laughlin letter to J. P. Lippincott & Co. of May 7, 1968:

> As you know, ever since that miserable Sanders piracy of Pound's "Canto Fragments." I have been pushing Ezra to try to get the material that he has completed so far in shape so that we can publish a proper book here and get some decent copyright protection for it. I now hear from him in Venice that the work is proceeding, though it is slow, because his eyes are in bad shape. It sounds as though what we will get will be about twenty to thirty pages of the portions of Cantos 110 to 117 which he has completed. So I think we will have to have some title such as "A Draft of Cantos 110 to 117." There is precedence for this title as the first 30, when they were first done here, were titled "A Draft of Thirty Cantos." Were it not for the acute copyright problem, I would say that a limited edition was indicated for this, but I feel it is important to get the book out widely so as to stop more piracies. So I guess I will have a very small book and David will just have to figure out some way to make it "bulk." It could be suggested that this material could simply be added at the back of the big "Cantos" volume, the way we will be doing with "Thrones." now that that is out of stock as a separate book, but this could not happen quickly enough, for our copyright purposes, since we have nearly a two year supply of the big "Cantos" in hand, and also it would not get the special edition that we want to head off piracy. I couldn't really put it into this catalogue anyway because I wouldn't know how to describe it till I see what I get. Sorry I didn't know about this the other day, when we had our meeting, so that we could discuss the problem. I just

learned this morning that he was actually working on getting the stuff in shape, pursuant to my request. I hope this won't make too many complications for you all down there, please let me know if you think of a better way to handle it. [New Directions, New York]

At the same time and with Pound's participation, Laughlin was attempting to place revised or uncopyrighted texts in various periodicals. Most noticeable, perhaps, is the revision of the pirated CXVI and the first periodical publication of "Notes for CXVII et seq."

Publication	Canto
American Literary Anthology.	
New York, 1968	CXVI
Stony Brook (Fall 1968)	CXIV
New Yorker (30 November 1968)	*From* CXIII
Sumac (Winter 1969)	Notes for CXI, Notes for CXVII et seq. [c]

Pound did submit setting copy for *Drafts & Fragments* as well as answering editorial queries and correcting proof sheets. He also elected to incorporate an earlier fragment under Laughlin's eventual title, "Addendum for C." Explaining the problem to Kimberly Merker, who was editing the Stone Wall Press limited edition, Laughlin lamented (June 27, 1968): "If he wants now to attach it to Canto 100, that gives us a bit of a problem with our title. I hope we can persuade him just to have it at the back, among the fragments, with some indication that it eventually belongs with Canto 100" [New Directions, Norfolk]. When *Drafts & Fragments* was added to the collected edition in 1970, the last line of the text as authorized by the poet was "To be men not destroyers."

As early as June 6, 1962, however, Laughlin had commented to S. D. Newberry:

I know from talks that I had with Ezra about two years ago that he has never placed any fixed limitation on the number of Cantos which there might eventually be. Once he thought there would only be a hundred, but now he is well past that, and I don't think he has any other exact number in his mind. He has, however, written the final "ending," which he says should be tacked on wherever he stops. [New Directions, New York]

In the meantime Pound's work in progress had been distilled into *Drafts & Fragments*, but the publication in *Anonym* of a seemingly new poem, caused some confusion. In good faith the text was added to the collected edition in 1972, but later William Cookson, editor of *Agenda*, wrote to Laughlin (June 13, 1973) that "I also had a letter from E.P. himself saying no permission had been given to *Anonym*" [New Directions, New York].

There seems to have been no denial, however, that the verses were authentic, and a letter from Pound does survive in the Cookson archive dated August 15, 1970 which responds to a request for publishable manuscripts and acknowledges the existence of a poem entitled "CXX": "Here are some notes, parts of which have been used in later drafts, which you may find useful[.] I haven't 120 here." So far no pre-publication text from Pound's hand has turned up.

The 1986 edition of the collected cantos added CXX to "Notes for CXVII et seq." and omitted the title, while the Italian cantos, LXXII–LXXIII, and verses entitled "Fragment 1966" were also added at the end of the volume. The fragment in question is the text that Laughlin had referred to as early as 1962 (see above), but it is not possible to accept either of these texts as the "endings" of Pound's long poem containing history.

It certainly matters a great deal just which edition or printing of *The Cantos* one reads. The texts vary enormously and now that the Italian Cantos have been inserted in chronological and numerical sequence (1989), the pagination of the volume's second half no longer corresponds to that of existing critical works. There are many problems to be overcome, but aside from the loss of authorized readings from the former Faber edition, the present text is not at all so overwhelmingly corrupt as is often maintained. The final lines of the text as actually authorized by the poet remain: "To be men not destroyers."

NOTES

1 D. F. McKenzie, *Bibliography and the Sociology of Texts* (London: The British Library, 1986), p. 29.
2 Michael Groden, "Contemporary Textual and Literary Theory," in George Bornstein (ed.), *Representing Modernist Texts, Editing as Interpretation* (Ann Arbor, MI: University of Michigan Press, 1991), p. 271.
3 Unpublished letter to T. S. Eliot, Faber & Faber Archive. The location of further unpublished letters will be given in the text within square brackets after each quotation.
4 See Barbara Eastman, *Ezra Pound's Cantos: The Story of the Text, 1948–1975* (Orono, ME: National Poetry Foundation, 1979), p. 35.
5 See Jerome J. McGann, *The Textual Condition* (Princeton, NJ: Princeton University Press, 1991), p. 21.
6 See unpublished letters of March 24 and April 3, 1953, Lilly Library, Pound II.
7 See Eastman, *Ezra Pound's Cantos*, pp. 35–36.
8 See Stoicheff, "The Composition and Publishing History of Ezra Pound's Drafts and Fragments," *Twentieth Century Literature*, 32, 1 (Spring 1986), 78–94 and Bush, " 'Unstill, Ever Turning'," The Composition of Ezra Pound's Drafts & Fragments," in R. Taylor and C. Melchior (eds.), *Ezra Pound and Europe* (Amsterdam: Rodopi, 1993).

9 See "Reconstructing Ezra Pound's Cantos," in Jacqueline Kaye (ed.), *Ezra Pound and America* (London: Macmillan, 1992), p. 143.
10 Taylor, "Towards a Textual Biography of The Cantos," in Lawrence Rainey (ed.), *A Poem Including History: The Cantos of Ezra Pound* (Ann Arbor, MI: University of Michigan Press, 1997).

9

MASSIMO BACIGALUPO

Pound as critic

Ezra Pound published some seven books that can fall under the heading Literary Criticism. The majority of these were collections of previously printed essays: *Pavannes and Divisions* (1918), *Instigations* (1920), *Make It New* (1934), *Polite Essays* (1937). None of these has remained in print, having been replaced by T. S. Eliot's excellent selection *Literary Essays* (1954), and by William Cookson's *omnium gatherum*, *Selected Prose* (1973). These anthologies contain some of Pound's better known and more important critical writings. But they are necessarily uneven, for they have not been conceived as a single effort by their author.

A more unified picture of Pound the critic emerges from the books and pamphlets that he envisaged and brought forth as a whole. These are *The Spirit of Romance* (1910), *How To Read* (1931), *ABC of Reading* (1934), *Guide to Kulchur* (1938), *Carta da Visita* (1942). The two last are devoted only in part to literature, but this is characteristic of the uncompartmentalized way Pound worked. In fact, *Jefferson and/or Mussolini* (1935) could be added to the list of books of criticism that were created as wholes. These unified volumes make for exciting reading because they move with their own momentum, in a somewhat improvisational fashion, from day to day, and often refer to their writing in process by place and date. They are one form of intellectual journal kept by Pound – the other being *The Cantos*, which also appeared as unified sections often written over a short period of time.

The Spirit of Romance (1910) covers the ground from Ovid and Apuleius to the Latin poets of the Renaissance, devoting most of its attention to the Troubadours and Dante and his circle. Other chapters offer comments on the Chanson de Geste, the Cid, François Villon, Lope de Vega and Camões. Pound had studied these writers in college and had been imitating them and using them as characters in his early poems, so he was going over familiar territory with the new perspective of his year in London and of his acquaintance with several notable writers, Yeats being the chief influence.

At one point, cavalier fashion, Pound writes: "Yeats gives me to understand that . . ." (*SR*, 50) – so, as it were, making a public exhibition of his familiarity with the internationally acclaimed Irish poet.

But in general *Spirit* is a controlled and understated book by a promising young writer who has a flair for finely turned phrases, who loves such obscure practitioners of the art as Arnaut Daniel, the technician, but also identifies with the outcast Villon – as he was to do again in *Mauberley*: "He passed from men's memory in *l'an trentiesme / De son eage*." This preference for the outcast and the obscure was to remain constant in Pound's prose and poetry. Propertius, Mauberley, Sigismondo, are all embattled figures who have been treated poorly by contemporaries and posterity, misinterpreted and forgotten. They are projections, sometimes ironic, of Pound's view of himself as victim, forced into exile and poverty by a materialistic society.

Spirit of Romance was to remain one of Pound's principal sourcebooks for his poetry. The Dante references as late as *Drafts & Fragments* are the same that first appeared here (Paolo and Francesca in CX, Geryon in CXI, "To 'see again'" in CXVI). The book has a pleasantly relaxed surface, and though still Edwardian in its kind of literary "appreciation," is often humorous and mischievous in tone. Occasionally, it is a little tremulous, grandiose, and gushing, as in the final comments on Dante ("my mind is not yet ripe, nor is my pen skilled" – p. 163). This unevenness of tone is one of the more conspicuous traits in all of Pound's work, and is often used to advantage. The reader is made to laugh, and before he knows it he gets a punch in the midriff appealing to his emotions. He capitulates to the canny poet.

When Pound reprinted *Spirit of Romance* in 1932, he inserted a new chapter 5, "Psychology and Troubadours: A Divagation from Questions of Technique," originally published in 1912 as an essay in G. R. S. Mead's spiritualist periodical *Quest*. Here Pound suggests tentatively that the Troubadours may have been into some kind of mystical cult connected with the Albigensian heresy, that Paganism may have survived in Provence, and speaks of eroticism and visionary experiences. This was in keeping with the milieu of Mead, whose interest in Simon Magus is mentioned in a footnote, and with Yeats's spiritualism. The essay is of great interest as an early sketch of Pound's "religion." The myth of Albigensian eroticism, mysticism, and art, and of a neo-pagan Provence is nothing less than a keystone of *The Cantos*, where it recurs from IV (the Cabestan–Ityn and Vidal–Actaeon parallels) to XLVIII and XC ("the room in Poitiers where one can stand casting no shadow"), and climaxes in *The Pisan Cantos*, Pound seeing the defeat of Mussolini's Italy by Roosevelt and Churchill's armies as a new Albigensian crusade: "Manes! Manes was tanned and stuffed / Thus Ben and la Clara *a Milano*" (LXXIV).

Pound's religious opinions inclined to the heretical precisely as his literary tastes inclined to the outcast *poètes maudits* of the Villon kind. Thus he was happy to discuss in the later essay "Cavalcanti" (1928, reprinted in *SE*) the possibility that the Italian poets were also using a secret heretical code, and for a while was particularly attracted to Guido Cavalcanti as possibly more heterodox than Dante. But then Dante was also an exile, so he could be safely chosen as a model.

"Psychology and Troubadours" thus becomes one of Pound's central texts, opening up a field to be developed chiefly in the "Postscript" (dated 1921) to *The Natural Philosophy of Love*, "Medievalism" (part of "Cavalcanti," 1928), and *Guide to Kulchur* (the chapters on Dante's *Paradiso*). Pound's interest in literature is largely existential, a search of models for his own work both in the way of form and of content. He tends to fantasize and project his inclinations on remote texts, the obscurity of which allows lots of latitude for such overinterpretation. By the time his religion had become a kind of worship of light, he translated some Confucian classics and felt quite free to insert such passages as the following: "The *unmixed* functions [in time and in space] without bourne. This unmixed is the tensile light, the Immaculata. There is no end to its action" (*The Unwobbling Pivot*, 1947). Confucius and Cavalcanti can become part of the same myth, of the tradition of "the room in Poitiers." This is the main story line of *The Cantos*.

The Spirit of Romance was followed in Fall-Winter 1911–12 by a series of articles in A. R. Orage's London weekly, *The New Age*, largely devoted to Cavalcanti and Arnaut Daniel, and to questions of technique: *I Gather the Limbs of Osiris*. The title, which Pound (as he was often to do subsequently) does not stop to explain in the course of the series, suggests that there may be more than meets the eye to these technical matters, that is the "religion of mysteries" of "Psychology and Troubadours." Yet *Osiris*, Pound's first contribution to *The New Age*, does not stray from literary criticism, though Pound proposes to redefine the field by availing himself of "luminous details." The reader will be spared the drudgery of (Germanic) scholarship, he will only get the kernels that go to the heart of the matter, which may be a certain fact of history or a text that changes the course of literature. Apart from the instances Pound gives ("the particular slide in our microscope," as he calls them – *SPR*, 39), his notion of "luminous details" is basic to his criticism and to his poetry, both in their lapses (we often disagree about the importance of the details and even about their factual truth) and their strengths. "A few dozen facts of this nature give us intelligence of a period . . . These facts are hard to find. They are swift and easy of transmission. They govern knowledge as the switchboard governs an electric circuit" (*SPR*, 22–23). It is easy to see how Pound, believing this, thought he could encompass all that was valuable in human experience in 100 or 120 cantos – in fact, one could probably do it in smaller compass. Another noteworthy point is the difficulty of access to such details. Pound came to believe that they are hidden for reasons, and saw himself as the bringer of light who would finally show in his writings what civilization is all about and how to overcome obscurantists who impede the coming of paradise on earth. For, if these facts are "swift and easy of transmission," once they have been divulged action cannot but follow. In this way the poet as critic and historian may bring about changes in society.

As my quotations show, Pound often favored technical language from mathematics, physics and chemistry. Already in *Spirit of Romance*, poetry is said to be "a sort of inspired mathematics, which gives equations, not for abstract figures . . . but for the human emotions" (p. 14). The same idea was to be developed a decade later by T. S. Eliot's concept of the "objective correlative" as "a set of objects, a situation, a chain of events which shall be the formula of that *particular* emotion" ("Hamlet," 1919). Eliot is speaking here of a sort of "luminous detail," but unlike Pound he is limiting its applicability to the field of expression, of art, that should be impersonal, conveying emotions through objective "formulas." It was only Pound who played with the idea that the readers of *The Cantos* would get the "real" Sigismondo and Sordello – that poetry and history could be one and the same.

Both Pound and Eliot use leitmotifs, i.e. the repetition of phrases and images to connect and sum up different situations. For example, "Those are pearls that were his eyes" in *The Waste Land*, Eliot's most Poundian work, and "in the gloom the gold" in Cantos XI, XVII, XXI. Pound's leitmotifs, however, are mostly historical, not symbolic. They are "luminous details" which recur endlessly with little change, variously juxtaposed, throughout his texts. This is in accordance with his premises, for if the details contain important truths, then all one can and has to do is repeat them in new combinations until all their implications have been discovered. But apart from the theory, it would seem that Pound's reliance on catch-phrases and quotations was peculiarly related to his way of thinking. The world presented itself to him in set-phrases, hard bits of mosaic or "ideogram" that could not be broken up into their constituents. So it is no surprise that there is a continuous spill-over between his correspondence, essays, poetry and recorded conversation. All of these "verbal manifestations" (a favorite formula) are but variant versions of the world according to Pound – a rather eccentric but nevertheless fascinating one. It should also be mentioned that the basic model of Pound's writing is always the spoken word. Whether he indites a canto, a letter, or an essay, it is always a voice which begins to speak and shift from one tone to another. The concentration and care of the exposition may vary, yet the materials and mannerisms are the same. The term "canto" is significant in this respect, for it stresses the factor of orality, the voice, which is equally capable of anecdote, invective, and song.

I Gather the Limbs of Osiris is a seminal text that shows us Pound just before the modernist revolution. It is brilliantly written, with the felicity and sweep of Pound's best prose and poetry. Besides such out-of-the-way "details" as Daniel and Cavalcanti, Pound offered the *New Age* reader a more traditional curriculum: Homer, Dante, Chaucer, and Shakespeare (he even mentions Milton next to Yeats as "great masters of rhythm"). Of the four major European writers he listed, Pound noted characteristically that "each of these men constructed some sort of world into which we may plunge ourselves and find a life not glaringly incomplete" (*SPR*, 30). He added that Homer and the others all profited from "the virtues of many forerunners and contemporaries." The concept of a major work of art as an encompassing, total, experience, the end product of a complex gathering of forces, is clearly relevant to *The Cantos*, a poem which could appropriately be called *I Gather the Limbs of Osiris*. In stressing technical aspects, *Osiris* also points the way to the Imagist poetics Pound was to define within a few months of writing his series "in illustration of 'The New Method' in scholarship." Accuracy of expression is stressed throughout: "Technique is the means of conveying an exact impression of exactly what one means in such a way as to exhilarate" (*SPR*, 33). Hackneyed poetic themes are amusingly ridiculed (*SPR*, 35). Yet one of the articles is devoted to "Virtue," which is the Renaissance *virtù* or essential personality of the writer, that which makes him memorable, thus reminding us of Pound's continued fascination with strong poetic personalities like Bertran de Born or François Villon. Powerful art is born from profound conviction: "Only that man who cares and believes really in the pint of truth that is in him will work . . . to find the perfect expression" (*SPR*, 34) – and will keep his audience's attention.

While it is true that Pound rarely indulges in biographical criticism, and in his constant concern with individual texts points the way to the developments of New Criticism, on the other hand he is attracted to personalities. The close of "Provincia Deserta," one of his crucial poems, expresses this clearly in connection with the troubadours: "I have walked over these roads; / I have thought of them living." At the end of *The Cantos* he repeated this with a small but poignant variation: "In meiner Heimat / where the dead walked / and the living were made of cardboard" (CXV/ 814). The search through the past is supposed to give life to a diminished present. He had said as much at the end of his first volume, *A Lume Spento*: "Make-strong old dreams lest this our world lose heart" (*CEP*, 52).

Pound's quarrel with his "beastly and cantankerous age" ("Three Cantos," I) is prominent throughout his writing, particularly in the major poems of the London years, *Propertius* and *Mauberley* ("The age demanded an image / Of its accelerated grimace"). He was accused by his fellow-Vorticist Wyndham Lewis of being "a man in love with the past." Yet these were also the years in which Pound became one of the more vocal exponents of modernisation, so much so that he made a public repudiation of his earlier and "softer" work ("Salutation the Second"). This mode of recantation followed by self-justification was to become a favorite one with Pound. He was to use it again in some of his most widely admired works, *Mauberley* and *The Pisan Cantos*, and again in Canto CXVI.

In February 1912 Pound published "Prolegomena" in the second issue of Harold Monro's *Poetry Review*, the principal organ of the Georgian poets. This included his "Credo" concerning rhythm, symbols, technique, and form. The essay stressed "that precision which I miss in the Victorians" and which one can find instead in "Daniel and Cavalcanti," condemned the "blurred" and "messy" nineteenth century, and prophesied a new poetry, "harder and saner," with fewer adjectives: "austere, direct, free from emotional slither" (*LE*, 12). "Prolegomena" is also noteworthy for its tone, especially the opening description of Lake Garda and the lackadaisical poet Pound really would like to be – a passage which points the way to "Three Cantos," I (1917) and, more importantly, to the insouciant tone and content of *Propertius* (1919). It is important to bear in mind that Pound's criticism is not only a poet's criticism, but essentially part of a larger process of writing, and appealing as such. A rhetorical performance, it tells a story and persuades the reader by poetic means. This is not to say that all of it is of equal value. Some of it, as some of Pound's poetry, is as good as anything contemporary.

October 1912 saw the launching of Harriet Monroe's *Poetry, a Magazine of Verse*, of which Pound was a correspondent from the start. He published there in the March 1913 issue the manifesto "A Few Don'ts by an Imagist." He offered a definition of the Image as "that which presents an intellectual and emotional complex in an instant of time," and added somewhat misleadingly that he was using "complex" "in the technical sense employed by the newer psychologists" (*LE*, 4). Readers of *Osiris*, however, can recognize the "luminous detail," which is of easy communication and which holds the key to a larger field (or complex) of knowledge. The image is possibly such a detail in the precinct not of history but of "intellectual and emotional" perception. Pound provided examples of this in the poems printed in the April 1913 issue of *Poetry*, among them "In a Station of the Metro" – but also "Salutation the Second," with its recantation theme.

The three principal tenets of Imagism were defined as "direct treatment, economy of words, and the sequence of the musical phrase" (*LE*, 4). Pound elaborated on these in his "Dont's," naming as safe examples Dante, Sappho, Catullus, Villon, Heine, Gautier, and Chaucer, but also "as much of Wordsworth as does not seem too unutterably dull." He referred adversely to "Milton's rhetoric" (*LE*, 7), continuing a long anti-Milton campaign, later joined by T. S. Eliot.

Eventually, Pound collected "Prolegomena" and "Dont's," with additions, under the heading "A Retrospect" (*PD*, 1918). He added a few pages about his more recent enthusiasms, especially James Joyce, T. S. Eliot, and Wyndham Lewis, and a paragraph, "Only Emotion Endures," listing "the few beautiful poems that still ring in my head." Here, we see again the appeal to the personality of the critic and the writer. Pound sheds his imagist theories to tell us what he really likes. Or, as he was to put it more beautifully in the *Pisan Cantos*: "nothing matters but the quality / of the affection – / in the end – that has carved the trace in the mind" (LXXVI).

Pound's use of short favorite quotations as examples of poetic excellence is reminiscent of the "touchstones" presented by Matthew Arnold in "The Study of Poetry" (1880) – and some of the poets are even the same. This use of the quotation as "luminous detail" is shared by Eliot, who is very apt at selecting telling passages in his essays as well as in his poetry. Both Eliot and Pound, however, often use quotations without indicating the source, in an allusive way, even in titles: *A Lume Spento*, *Ara Vos Prec*. Both of the latter phrases come from Dante, but they are taken out of context and used symbolically, also for their exotic sound. Since Dante was surely widely read in Victorian England and America, it could be said that the choice of tradition does not vastly change with modernism, what changes is the use that is made of tradition. Those same writers who were taken as examples of an orderly world-view, as teachers of a rigorous and ordered art, have become a handful of quotations in remote languages thrown at the reader for their sound-value, for their associations. Pound and Eliot always speak of "order" as a positive, but their work parallels and portrays the breakdown of an orderly and hierarchical idea of culture.

In "The Serious Artist," an important series of articles published in autumn 1913, Pound described the scientific function of the arts as providers of data for the study of man. Hence the paramount importance of accuracy, and the virtues of prose. Pound notes Stendhal's observation on the failure of poetry in "clarity," as an instrument of thought, and counters this with the precise psychological insights in the *Odyssey* and the *Cid*. Poetry, he maintains, can and should be a means of "communication between intelligent men" (*LE*, 55). Besides, it is "more highly energized" than prose. The poetry vs prose debate is central to Pound's criticism. His two masters in London were William Butler Yeats, the archetypal poet, and Ford Madox Ford, who thought of poetry as marginal and who was personally close to some major prose writers of the turn of the century: Stephen Crane, Joseph Conrad, and Henry James.

Pound's notion of the arts as performing a scientific function derives, through Ford, from the theories on the Naturalistic novel advanced by Emile Zola and followed by Guy de Maupassant, though for Ford the ultimate artist-as-scientist was Gustave Flaubert. Pound followed Ford's directions and became a life-long admirer of Flaubert, "his true Penelope," as he called him in *Mauberley*, that is, the faithful model to whom the dedicated poet can always turn. Flaubert was known as someone who, unlike his slipshod Naturalist followers, had poured heroic efforts into every paragraph of his work, and had carefully eliminated his "personality" from the objective and poetic "data" he offered. In the "Preface" to his *Collected Poems* of 1913, Ford quoted the image of John the Baptist's head from the end of Flaubert's *Hérodias*, and commented that "such exact, formal, and austere phrases can to certain men give a pleasure beyond any other" – a pleasure rarely given by poetry. As if in answer to Ford's strictures, Pound cited the very same words in "The Serious Artist," next to a series of "touchstones" from Dante, Villon, Cavalcanti, and "The Seafarer," claiming that the "passionate simplicity" of the verse, though "perfect as fine prose is perfect," had more to offer, namely "the passionate moment." The difference between prose and poetry, Pound maintained, was that prose seeks its subject, whereas poetry records the revelation of a subject: "The poetic fact pre-exists" (*LE*, 54).

"Passionate simplicity" is a phrase with Yeatsean associations, and we know that Pound spent time in the winter of 1913–14 at Stone Cottage with his Irish mentor. He was apparently playing the ideas of the two men against each other. He concluded, in "The Serious Artist," with a compromise, claiming for "the greatest poetic passages" an "orderliness," a "quiet statement that partakes of the nature of prose and is yet floated and tossed in the emotional surges" (*LE*, 54). The definition is significant, because some of Pound's best poetic effects are in fact reached by understatement, by a fine intermixture of deep emotion and deep control.

Pound clarified some of these ideas in his review of Ford's *Collected Poems* (*Poetry*, June 1914), where he had praise for "On Heaven" (in the same issue of *Poetry*) as "the best poem yet written in the 'twentieth-century' fashion" (*LE*, 373). But perhaps his clearest expression of what he had learned from Ford came in a January 1915 letter to Harriet Monroe: "Objectivity and again objectivity, and expression: no hindside-beforeness, no straddled adjectives ... no Tennysonianness of speech; nothing – nothing that you couldn't, in some circumstance, in the stress of some emotion, actually say" (*L*, 49). That is, he advised against inversions and generally poetic mannerisms. And essentially he wanted writing to follow natural speech. This advice was not always easy to follow for a poet who had been educated in the old school and had become familiar as a boy with the King James Bible. So at his most personal and modern, in *The Pisan Cantos*, he does not hesitate to write "What thou lovest well remains" (LXXXI/540). He clearly loved the old language more than he knew or wanted, and it remained with him.

Pound's discovery of the merits of prose in 1912–13 prepared him to appreciate the crucial modernist works that came to his attention in 1914: James Joyce's *Dubliners* and *Portrait of the Artist*, and T. S. Eliot's "Love Song of J. Alfred Prufrock." Joyce in particular was (especially in *Dubliners*) the pupil of Flaubert; Eliot, on the other hand, took off, as he was to say a decade later, from the poetry of Jules Laforgue and Jacobean drama. Pound was not familiar with these areas, but could quickly appreciate the striking unpoetic city-images of Eliot's poem. Eliot in turn adopted the satirical and urbane tone of Pound's *Lustra* in the poems written after arriving in London in 1914 ("Aunt Helen," "Mr. Apollinax," etc.) The two poet-critics were to work very closely and facilitate the work of each other until 1922 and beyond.

After the renovation of the Imagist phase, 1914 brought the radical modernization of Vorticism. Pound, Eliot, Joyce, and Lewis, "the men of 1914," aged respectively 29, 26, 32, and 30, were ready to revolutionize the arts, and had the talent and energy lacked by Ford Madox Ford, who for his part could be said to have modernized Pound, and whose novel *The Good Soldier* was serialized in the first issue of *Blast* (June 1914). When England declared war on Germany on August 8, this seemed to confirm the need for a radical reassessment of European civilization. This they proceeded to offer variously in *Ulysses*, *The Waste Land*, *Propertius*, *Mauberley*, and *The Cantos*. Pound's response to the war was already expressed in the poems he published in *Poetry*, March 1915, among them "The Coming of War: Actaeon," and the poignant "Provincia Deserta" and "Exile's Letter." It could be said that the war made of Pound a major poet.

The war years were also very active for Pound the critic. About half the pieces included by T. S. Eliot in *Literary Essays* date from 1914–1918. Having largely broken the ground in his pre-war work, Pound was now promoting individual writers and adding a few past masters to his pantheon. Eliot directed his attention to Jules Laforgue, a minor French symbolist, and the result was Pound's "Irony, Laforgue, and Some Satire" (*Poetry*, November 1917), a masterly article written in mimetic Laforguian style. In turn, Pound got Eliot to read the French critic Remy de Gourmont and the poems of Théophile Gautier, and the result was, partly, Eliot's influential essays in *The Sacred Wood* (1920), and his *Poems* (1920), many of them written, like *Mauberley*, in Gautier's quatrains. Pound's contacts with such artists as Lewis and Gaudier precipitated his lively and moving Vorticist memoir, *Gaudier-Brzeska*, but also his envisioning a new "Renaissance," the subject of a 1915 series of articles for *Poetry*, partly about the Italian Quattrocento.

In this period his interests were somewhat redirected from the Middle Ages to the Classics and the Renaissance. Two series of articles for the London *Egoist*, "Notes on Elizabethan Classicists" and "Translators of Greek" are substantial additions to the Pound source-book, in fact the latter includes what was to become Canto I. Since some of Pound's most original writing borders on translation (*The Seafarer, Cathay, Confucian Odes*), he is clearly interested in his precursors, from Andreas Divus to Marlowe to Edward Fitzgerald to Swinburne (always a favorite poet of Pound's, highly praised for his classicism in a 1918 attack on Edmund Gosse's biography). In *Propertius* the speaker presents himself as a masterly translator: "I who come first from the clear font / Bringing the Grecian orgies into Italy, / and the dance into Italy" (*P*, 205). Pound saw himself as a Swinburnian translator-liberator from the servitude to custom, especially in sexual matters.

Gourmont and James were the subjects of two long essays written immediately after the war, and perhaps the presiding figures (with Gautier) behind *Mauberley*. In James Pound stresses two aspects: the "hatred of personal intimate tyrannies" and his reliance on "the authenticity of his impression" (*LE*, 299), that is, two factors prominent in Pound himself. He gladly quotes James's strictures on Baudelaire (*LE*, 308), a poet whose classic status Pound, unlike Eliot, was unable to appreciate. In an important footnote, he tackles once again the question of the relative status of poetry and prose, claiming that "Most good prose arises, perhaps, from an instinct of negation; is the detailed, convincing analysis of something detestable . . . Poetry is the assertion of a positive, i.e. of desire, and endures for a longer period" (*LE*, 324). This is a curious misreading of James, given his love for many of his characters and their passion for life and knowledge, but is characteristic of Pound's antagonistic status. He was to stress again, when championing Joyce's *Ulysses* in 1922, the novel's satirical aspects rather than its celebration of life. At any rate, to poetry he reserved the realm of the affirmative.

Pound's extremely fruitful London period came to a close with his removal to Paris in 1921, and later to Rapallo in 1925. The war years and their immediate aftermath seem to have left him exhausted, uncertain of his direction, and the twenties were a far less productive decade than the previous one. Most of his energies went into new cantos, largely dealing with the Italian Renaissance, into research for his peculiar paleographic edition of Cavalcanti (1932), and into the little magazine *The Exile* (four issues, 1927–28). Towards the end of the decade, having by then settled in Rapallo to his satisfaction, he began writing more purposefully. "Medievalism" (*Dial*, March 1928), an off-shoot of his work on Cavalcanti, celebrates the benefits to be derived from "a decent climate" like Italy's, and "the Mediterranean sanity," which eschews fanaticism and asceticism, and which according to Pound prevailed before 1527, in the age of the great cathedrals and the great poems by Dante and Guido. This is Pound's version of Eliot's "dissociation of sensibility" (occurring between Donne and Milton), and is reminiscent of the Pre-Raphaelites and of John Ruskin's idealization of the Middle Ages.

As Eliot in "Ash-Wednesday" (1930), so Pound in *A Draft of XXX Cantos* (1930) sought to recover "the radiant world where one thought cuts through another with clean edge, a world of moving energies" (*LE*, 154). "Medievalism" is a companion text on the philosophy of *The Cantos* and on Pound's vision of Italy. In the close it even mentions "the rose that [the] magnet makes in the iron filings," an image to be developed in *Guide to Kulchur* (ch. 23), and finally and most memorably in *The Pisan Cantos* (LXXIV). It is clear that when Pound writes about these visionary states he is drawing on the same sources as in his poetry. Another 1928 *Dial* article, "Dr. Williams' Position," is of interest chiefly for its defense of formlessness and inconclusiveness, on the grounds that many "very important chunks of world-literature" lack structure, or can be summarized as "BEGINNING WHOOP and then any sort of a trail off" (*LE*, 394). Here Pound rationalizes his problems with *The Cantos* – the absence of any general pattern being particularly evident in the Cantos of the 1920s. As for Williams, Pound does little but express, somewhat condescendingly, his admiration for his work, but quotes no examples. He also insists, surprisingly, on Williams's point of view being European.

Pound's critical faculties show to advantage in the articles on "How to Read" he contributed to the *New York Herald Tribune* in 1929, and collected in a pamphlet in 1931. This is the most condensed and forcible summary of his critical opinions on different kinds of writing and on the essential curriculum. He offers his definition of "great literature" as "language charged with meaning to the utmost possible degree," reminiscent of Imagist condensation and of his own allusive practices, and sorts out writers in six classes: inventors, masters, diluters, writers in the style of the period, belles lettres, and starters of crazes. A Poundian example of each class would be Cavalcanti, Homer, Virgil, Donne, Longus, Gongora. It is the third class that Pound particularly dislikes, and to which he would assign Petrarch and Milton; each of the others has its merits, and I suppose he would himself aspire to the status of "master," i.e., one who, "apart from [his] own inventions," is "able to assimilate and co-ordinate a large number of preceding inventions" (*LE*, 23). *The Cantos* seek to be such an assimilation.

In the chapter on "Language" Pound produces his handy distinction between three kinds of poetry: Melopoeia, which is poetry as music (canto), Phanopoeia, which is poetry of the visual image, and Logopoeia, defined as "the dance of the intellect among words," a poetry of irony, quotation, and allusion that Pound associates with Laforgue and T. S. Eliot. In *Carta da visita*, Pound granted Eliot preeminence in Logopoeia, or irony, while claiming to surpass him in Melopoeia, the musical art of Homer (*SPR*, 321). Later sections of *How to Read* discuss individual authors, the merits of prose vs. poetry, and the essential reading list: Confucius ("in full"), Homer, Ovid, Catullus, Propertius, the Troubadours, Dante and Cavalcanti, Villon, Voltaire, Stendhal, Flaubert, Gautier, Corbière, and Rimbaud. The list combines lyricism and a great deal of criticism of civilization, showing us that Pound, though relaxing on his Rapallo seafront terrace, was as much concerned as ever with his battle against tyranny. This explains his next move, precipitated by the world-crisis of 1929, into politics and economics, and into a poetry more concerned with contemporary issues (the middle Cantos).

Reviewing *How to Read* in 1932 Ford Madox Ford remarked jokingly that what set out to be a "*vade mecum* of the reader of verse-poetry" ended up as "the final ... passport to glory of the *prosateur*" (*P/F*, 106), proving his (and Stendhal's) point that prose had gotten the upper hand since the eighteenth century. Most of the men listed by Pound wrote prose or an equivalent, long poems by Homer and Dante being to Ford only rhythmical narratives: "The mere fact that all the writers there recommended must ... be read in translation makes [the list] a recommendation to prose." Actually, one of the points Pound had restated in his articles was the importance of verse translation, claiming that "English literature lives on translation." As for recent developments, he pointed out that "apart from Yeats, since the death of Hardy, poetry is being written by Americans ... In fact, there is no longer any reason to call it English verse" (LE, 34).

How to Read is Pound's noteworthy return to literary criticism after several less productive years. At this time he began to contribute notes in Italian to little-read periodicals, *L'Indice* and *Il Mare*, and this brought the stimulation of contact with a literary milieu, albeit provincial. Young people like Basil Bunting and James Laughlin sought him out in Rapallo, where he ran a one-man university for the young and willing, providing them with reading matter and instruction. In this happy period he found a form for *The Cantos*, that of the "decad" or sequence built around one theme with a kind of sonata-form (Jefferson, Siena), and wrote quickly some of his liveliest books, *ABC of Economics*, *Jefferson and/or Mussolini*, and *ABC of Reading*.

ABC of Reading (1934) is intended as a text-book expansion of *How To Read* , but (as usual in Pound's pamphlets) becomes an experiment in writing, very personal and unpredictable, and a treasure-throve for readers of *The Cantos*. Here Pound gives his first major exposition of "the ideogrammic method or the method of science," referring to Ernest Fenollosa's theories on Chinese picture-writing, a writing that is poetic and scientific insofar as it is not abstract but based on concrete images. This comparing of individual "slides" rather than relying on general statements is what Pound had been doing from the start. In fact he reprints the five passages of poetry (or touchstones – Dante, Cavalcanti, Villon, Yeats, *The Wanderer*) he had juxtaposed in "The Serious Artist," as an "example of ideogrammic method used by E.P. . . . in 1913 before having access to the Fenollosa papers" (*ABCR*, 96). Thus it is worth remembering that the formulation of the ideogrammic method came rather late, but that it fitted Pound's constant interest in presentation and juxtaposition, both in his prose and in his poetry, and his passion for strong contrasts and cuts. The *ABCR* is brilliantly written, contains many sharp observations, and offers an ample annotated anthology of favorite passages, including Donne's "The Ecstasy" and Boyd's "Fra bank to bank" ("the most beautiful sonnet in the language" – *ABCR*, 134). Pound reveals an extraordinary admiration for Chaucer, whom he finds more European than the Elizabethans, and endowed with "a deeper knowledge of life than Shakespeare" – a forerunner of internationalist modernism. Other selections are idiosyncratic (Gavin Douglas) and unexpected (Rochester, Butler's *Hudibras*), always instructive.

After the casting about of the 1920s, Pound's prose and poetry benefited from the political and economic tensions of the 1930s, that provided him with a sense of mission, a mission which he took seriously enough but from which he could occasionally take a holiday, to write sketches like "Mr. Housman at Little Bethel" (1934, *LE*, 66–73), a delightful attack on Housman and on his concept of poetry as a harmless pastime. Collecting his principal literary essays in *Make It New*, he added a preface, "Date Line," in which he restated his belief in the importance of language and, consequently, of literature to society, for "language alone can riddle and cut through the meshes" (*LE*, 77). He distinguished "at least" five categories of criticism, all of which he had practiced: discussion, translation, "exercise in the style of a given period," musical setting of a poet's words (his *Villon* and *Cavalcanti*), new composition (Eliot's *Sweeney Agonistes* as a criticism of Seneca, *Propertius* as criticism of the Latin poet). He added, wisely, that "the function of criticism is to efface itself when it has established its dissociations," and provided a spirited defense of his enquiries into little-explored areas. With a perceptible sense of urgency he spoke of the men of the times, Stalin, Roosevelt, the economists Douglas and Gesell, above all Mussolini, "male of the species." *Make It New*, with its title from the Confucian *Ta Hio* he had translated in 1928, is described as a contribution to "a new Paideuma," with reference to Leo Frobenius' theory of *paideuma* (or culture) "as general and overreaching, overstressing the single man." An aside reminded the reader of the existence of "a gamut of perception" of a visionary kind available only to a few. Thus Pound stated in a few pages his platform for the thirties and spoke of a feeling of rejuvenation: "the chronicler's old sap moves again." His political judgments were to prove wrong, and the "male of the species," Mussolini, was to carry him along nearly all the way to his bloody end ten years later (1945), but Pound's hopes as well as their ruin were to leave a lasting impression and animation in his work. It is as if war and its coming gave life to his writing, in 1910–20 as well as in 1933–1945.

The position outlined in "Date Line" is developed to book length in *Guide to Kulchur*, a volume largely devoted to philosophy, ethics, economics, history, music and religion, the ultimate do-it-yourself of Ezra Pound the "village explainer," as he is called mischievously by Gertrude Stein in *The Autobiography of Alice B. Toklas*. At the time Pound's village was Rapallo, and *Kulchur* comments on local events in early 1937, when it was written – a Bartok quartet performed in the town-hall (ch. 19) or Gerhart Münch's transcription of Francesco di Milano's *Song of the Birds* (ch. 23). The latter leads Pound to consider the process of transmission of "the *forma, the immortal concetto*," bringing in quotations from Yeats and Gautier. He is approaching one of the principal articles of his creed, the existence of a unified pattern that the adept can discover under the bewildering multiplicity of phenomena, the essential pattern being ultimately related to Venus and "the mysteries."

Kulchur is an impressive monologue in fifty-eight usually brief chapters, one man's account of the world as he knows it, sometimes cryptic, at the limit of solipsism (as *The Cantos* are), but mostly fresh and vigorous. In some passages Pound allows himself the luxury of self-doubt, reviewing his experimental past, and seems to envy the straightforwardness of Thomas Hardy, who is juxtaposed "ideogramically" with Dante's *Paradiso* in chapters 51 and 52, "as obscure as anything in my poetry." Pound's willingness to put everything in the balance, the sense of his cantankerous but fundamentally sincere and appealing personality, is what keeps this "book of yatter" (as he calls it – *K*, 292) together, and in fact makes it one of his most rewarding. While he partially lost his sense of balance in the following years, and wrote the arid China–John Adams Cantos and the often hysterical Rome Radio broadcasts, he recovered the emotion and ironies of *Kulchur* in *The Pisan Cantos*, that poem in the form of a prison-journal, hence similar in construction to Pound's journal-like prose volumes, experiments of writing in time as these are. Even the chapter-form of *Kulchur* is reminiscent of the sequence of *The Cantos*.

After *Kulchur*, Pound continued to write notable critical essays, such as the obituary for Ford Madox Ford (*P/F*, 171–74). *Carta da visita*, as the title suggests, was an attempt to put Pound's world in a nutshell for Italian readers, and shows him on the threshold of the Pisan revelations, worshipping at the shrine of the goddess of Terracina, Aphrodite. His post-war translations, especially the *Confucian Odes* with their free rehandling of the English lyric tradition and their cryptic notes referring as often as not to some quotation in *The Cantos*, document a continuing critical concern. And at the end of his writing life, in his mid-seventies, Pound put a lot of energy into an anthology of world poetry, *Confucius to Cummings*, which shows that he went on readjusting his canon (Donne, for example, is omitted), and includes, in the form of brief notes, many pointed additions and corrections, as well as a few thoughtful pages on Hardy and Ford ("Appendix I").

Pound is the author of some of the liveliest and most perceptive literary criticism of the modern period. His definitions of the kinds of poetry and writers, and of the related concepts of "image," "vortex," and "ideogram," are permanently useful. Though sometimes repetitive and reductionist, his criticism has the merit of being always direct and to the point, not labored and self-regarding, favoring the plain style ("to get it across e poi basta" – Canto LXXIX/506). Humorous and unimpressed by established reputations, it warns readers against taking criticism (and literature) too solemnly, and at its best encourages us to judge books for ourselves. Discussing the main thrust of his writings in a letter to James Laughlin (1949), Pound quipped: "In fak wot DO they say, over 40 years, and 40 vollums Ezept: Wake up and live" (EP/JL, 180).

Pound's interest in other cultures and languages has brought attention to writers and traditions that would have remained specialized subjects. His criticism was the opposite of Euro-centric, and he believed that literature could only be understood in relation to painting, music, economics, etc. His insights have often influenced later scholars and writers. In Italy, for example, major poets have acknowledged that their perception of Dante has been made new by Pound and Eliot. It is true that Pound often irritated the learned by pretending to a scholarship that he did not possess, notably in his 1932 edition of Cavalcanti. However, by presenting photographs of the codices in which Guido's text is preserved, he suggested that readers should not be content with modernized versions, inevitably implying interpretation, as in the case of modernized Shakespeare texts. Thus Pound anticipated recent trends in textual theory and practice.

Pound's criticism will continue to be read not only for its compact and witty style, its perceptions and reading tips, and the light it casts on the poetry, but also for the daring spectacle of creativity in action which it offers. The prose is of one piece with the verse. As Pound wrote in *Guide to Kulchur* (unwittingly echoing Wordsworth on the literature of power versus the literature of knowledge): "Properly, we shd. read for power. Man reading shd. be man intensely alive. The book shd. be a ball of light in one's hand" (K, 55).

10

MING XIE

Pound as translator

In Pound's *oeuvre*, it is often difficult to distinguish between what is translation or adaptation and what is original composition. For Pound there seems to be no fundamental distinction between the two. More than a mere preparation to stimulate his own creative faculties, translation served as an "adjunct to the Muses' diadem" (*HSM*) and assumed an importance seldom found in other modern poets. Pound's translations stimulated and strengthened his poetic innovations, which in turn guided and promoted his translations. Pound's poetics is essentially a poetics of translation and he has largely redefined the nature and ideal of poetic translation for the twentieth century. This essay will try to present a roughly chronological outline of Pound's major translations and to highlight some of the most salient features of his involvement with translation in relation to his fundamental concerns as a modern poet.

Pound embarked upon the career of poetry with the determination, as he recalled in 1913, that he would try to know what was counted as poetry anywhere by finding out what part of poetry "could *not be lost* by translation" and also whatever was unique to each language.[1] He claimed that he began this comparative examination of European literature as early as 1901 (*LE*, 77), and in 1915 he again defined his Goethean conception of world literature as involving a criticism of excellence "based on world-poetry" (*LE*, 225). For this purpose he ranged far and wide in his linguistic and literary studies to find out the best that had been written "in as many languages as I could git under my occiput" (*EPS*, 137). From 1901 to 1907 at the University of Pennsylvania and Hamilton College, Pound studied, among other subjects, English, Latin, German, French, Italian, Spanish, Provençal, Anglo-Saxon, and Greek. He specialized in Romance languages and received in 1906 a Master of Arts degree from the University of Pennsylvania.[2] Pound's command of the Romance languages was secure and solid, although even in this area his scholarship has sometimes been impugned. His grasp of the other languages (especially Greek and German) was considerably weaker ("I shall have to learn a little greek to keep up with this" he admitted in Canto CV/770). Later he also acquired knowledge of a few more languages (notably Chinese) which, however, remained rudimentary. Pound often paid little attention to the grammar of a foreign language and tended to focus his attention on meanings and equivalences. "The case of the scholars against Pound as a translator," as G. S. Fraser has observed, "is that he perpetually shows signs of not knowing properly the languages he is translating from."[3] Pound's early training in Romance philology and academic scholarship, coupled with his adventurous autodidacticism and his passionate desire to make past and foreign literature accessible and vital again, accounted in large part for his "creative translations."

"Belangal Alba" (1905), known to be the first translation Pound published and one of his very earliest poems, was actually the translation of a dawn-song written in medieval Latin with Provençal refrains from a tenth-century manuscript.[4] Between 1908 and 1910 Pound made extensive translations from the Provençal of Arnaut Daniel, Bernart de Ventadorn, Bertran de Born, Arnaut de Mareuil, Peire Vidal, and others, moving from what he called "merely exegetic" (SR, 106) or "make-shift" (LE, 115) translation to more creative and "interpretative" (LE, 200) versions. These first attempts at translation produced some of Pound's first convincingly original personae (for example "Marvoil" and "Na Audiart") which fall in "the domain of original writing" (LE, 200).[5] Pound was evidently fascinated by the very nature of troubadour poetry itself: the name *trobaire* itself comes from the Provençal verb *trobar* ("to invent, to find"), which ultimately descends from the Latin *tropus*, related to the Greek *trephein* ("turning" of thought or expression).[6] Translation was conceived by Pound to be such an inventive "turning" of previous material, of what one has found, a *translatio* which in Aristotelian rhetoric is also metaphorical translation. Thus very early in his poetic career, the troubadours provided Pound with a model of poetic originality through innovative translation. Translation, or the *activity* of translation, assumed a prime importance in Pound's conception of the essence of poetic art.

First published in 1911, "The Seafarer" was one of Pound's first major personae. Ever since its appearance it has been the object of both attacks and defences and its status as accurate translation has been much disputed. But in a well-informed and cogently argued essay, the Old English scholar Fred C. Robinson has convincingly shown that Pound had been a serious student of Old English (at Hamilton College he was the favourite student of Professor Joseph D. Ibbotson who taught him Anglo-Saxon) and that he had a more impressive knowledge of Old English and its poetry than was often supposed.[7] Robinson's findings can thus finally dispel any doubt about the seriousness and integrity of Pound's version, which is "the product of a serious engagement with the Anglo-Saxon text, not of casual guessing at Anglo-Saxon words and of passing off personal prejudices as Anglo-Saxon poetry" (Robinson, " 'The Might of the North'," 220). In both his characterization of the poem as a "lyric" and his omission of its final section as the Christianizing addition of clerkly monks, Pound was following through on the standard scholarly interpretation of the day. His intention was simply to recover what he perceived to be the real, original Anglo-Saxon poem and he believed that his version was as close as any translation can be (*SPR*, 39).

However, there is no denying the fact that in his version Pound consistently excluded any references to a transcendent God or other religious sentiments which are an integral part of "The Seafarer's" meaning, even without the ending cut by Pound who translated only 99 lines of the original 124. In line 41 for example, "dryhten" can mean secular lord or king, or religious God (a point much debated in modern Old English scholarship), but "Dryhten" in line 43 is commonly regarded by scholars as a reference to a religious God. A number of alleged howlers are in fact the result of certain textual decisions that Pound made on the basis of the then current state of Old English scholarship. They are thus strictly speaking not philological errors but part of Pound's deliberately secular interpretation and presentation of the poem. Professor Robinson has shown that many of Pound's choices and guesses are often plausible and defensible in context (for example translating *byrig* in line 48 as "berries" rather than "town", since *byrig* can be two separate words with the same spelling, meaning either "town" or "mulberry trees"), in some cases perfectly legitimate (for example translating *englum* in line 78 as "English" rather than "angels", since *englum* can mean either "English" or "angel"), and in a few places even inspired and prescient (for example, "alone" for the Anglo-Saxon *sylf* in line 35 which usually means "myself"). Pound took scholarship seriously and respected the integrity of the Anglo-Saxon text. Where his version is "often loose and inventive", it is "inventive within the limits of what he took to be faithful, philological translation" (Robinson, " 'The Might of the North'," 223).

Pound's use of archaisms and inversions is deliberate, since he wanted to adapt his English to the Old English as closely as possible, not trying to assimilate the original to contemporary language. In the opening lines, for example,

MÆg ic be me sylfum soðgied wrecan,
siþas secgan, hu ic geswincdagum
earfoðhwile oft þrowade,

May I for my own self song's truth reckon,
Journey's jargon, how I in harsh days
Hardship endured oft.   (*CSP*, 76)

Pound tried to recreate the verse movement of the Anglo-Saxon by closely approximating its sound-effects and alliterative stress patterns. Thus we notice Pound's deliberate choice of "reckon" to render both the sound and sense of *wrecan* ("to utter" or "to express"), and the forced alliteration provided by "jargon" in the second line which is nevertheless a successful imitation of the original cadence. The process of translating is closely and self-consciously interwoven with the textual reality of the poem in all its minutiae of rhythm and sound-pressures, so that Pound's language cannot but be heavily affected by the experience of the Anglo-Saxon poem, whatever distortion might have resulted in the process. This is Pound's method of a *heuristic* translation: the new version is justified to the extent that it can direct the reader's attention to certain intrinsic qualities of the original, while at the same time bringing about the equivalent effects of these qualities in a new poem. Such translation is based not so much on "The Seafarer" as a source-text of translation, as on "The Seafarer" as a *poem*, a poem that has been strongly made and can be re-made with a directly matching strength. The process of translation is thus one of closely studying the forces of the original "through their effects" (*LE*, 93), in order to "show where the treasure lies" (*LE*, 200) and to make the reader see more deeply into and indeed see through *to* the original poem (*LE*, 209). Though Pound's alliterative effects are sometimes overdone and obtrusive, his main interest in the poem is its essential music and its prosodic movement which he believed to be the embodiment of the poem's secular heroism in the face of physical harshness, solitary exile and spiritual anguish. These motifs of personal alienation and heroism came to have a major importance for Pound's later development, and the idiom of "The Seafarer" was to reappear in Canto I in a translation from Homer's *Odyssey*.[8]

Pound was essentially an appropriative translator. The act of translation is for him to respond to the *virtù* of the translated – what Pound called, translating Cavalcanti, the "forméd trace" (Canto XXXVI/178) – and to relive these traces and make them one's own. Translation is thus a concatenation of tensions between a foreign poem as model and the translating poet in his own circumstances. A prominent example of this strategy is Pound's *Homage to Sextus Propertius*. First published in 1919, it immediately created a furore and was greeted with adverse criticisms, notably from the Latinist William Gardner Hale who accused Pound of committing dozens of ignorant errors. But many of the alleged howlers were, as in the case of his previous "The Seafarer," Pound's serious and deliberate attempts to achieve certain ironic effects and as such were part and parcel of his presentation of Propertius. Whether it is technically a translation at all has been, and will likely remain, a much disputed matter, even though many passages in it have been judged to be accurate and successful translations. Pound was afterwards forced to insist that "there was never any question of translation, let alone literal translation. My job was to bring a dead man to life, to present a living figure" (L, 148–149). Pound's version is certainly based on, and inspired by, Propertius; though not easily classifiable, it nevertheless belongs to a genre somewhere between paraphrase, imitation, and adaptation. It is literally a "homage," a persona, Pound's own response to Propertius, including the process of how and why he arrived at his particular response. As such it is a work of "criticism by translation" (LE, 74) and seeks to define the true qualities of Propertius' ironic wit, pathos and mockery, qualities which were again central to Pound's *Hugh Selwyn Mauberley* published a year later in 1920.[9]

In his search for new models of poetic innovation, Pound had been briefly fascinated by the concision and suggestiveness of Japanese *haiku* forms, and by mid-1913 he was still roaming far and wide. His chance encounter in late 1913 with the posthumous papers on Chinese and Japanese literature of Ernest Fenollosa, who had been an Imperial Commissioner of Art in Tokyo before his death in 1908, was thus both timely and invigorating.[10] Pound had been entrusted with these materials by Fenollosa's widow who had read and liked some of Pound's poems. Pound immediately started working on the Japanese Noh plays, influenced in this choice by Yeats's own interest in poetic drama. But Pound seemed more interested in the aesthetics of form in Noh, rather than its religious aspects which were traditionally associated with Buddhism and Shintoism, since he was never sympathetic, and later was even hostile, to Buddhism as a religion. For Pound a Noh play presents a single image of life, a "Unity of Image" (T, 237), in the same way that Dante's "*Divina Commedia* is a single elaborated metaphor of life" (SR, 87). This unity of image is not just verbal; it is also pre-eminently spatial, a symbolic and hieratic spectacle bound by dancing rituals and stylized gestures. This anti-naturalist minimalism had a great appeal to Pound, who preferred those spirit-plays with little or no dramatic action, in which the progression toward spiritual enlightenment reveals a supernatural glory in the midst of mundane existence. Some of the muddles and deficiencies in Pound's versions are traceable to the often unsatisfactory conditions of Fenollosa's notes and fragments. For example, *Sotoba Komachi*, as Pound translated it, is only two pages long whereas the Japanese original is much longer. *Hagoromo*, an otherwise excellent version, is handicapped by Pound's heavy prose rendering of the ending. Pound handled very well the more lyrical passages in these plays when he was not closely bound by the dramatic structure of the originals. Some passages are beautiful specimens of limpid lyricism, as in *Nishikigi*, perhaps the most successful of all his Noh versions.[11]

However, Pound's interest in Noh was quickly overtaken by his discovery of Fenollosa's Chinese materials, and he believed he had found "a new Greece in China" (*LE*, 215). But it is important to note that well before the discovery of Fenollosa, Pound had already adapted a number of Chinese poems contained in Herbert Giles' *History of Chinese Literature* (1901), such as "Liu Ch'e" and "Fan-Piece, for Her Imperial Lord" which Pound published in *Des Imagistes* in early 1914. The methods which he had tried to work out from Giles' late-Victorian versions had been quickly incorporated into a canon of examples for the reform and rejuvenation of English poetry. These new Imagistic principles were in turn thought by Pound to be confirmed by his subsequent discovery of Fenollosa.

The immediate result that came out of Fenollosa's Chinese materials was *Cathay*, a booklet of fourteen Chinese poems published in April 1915. The selection and arrangement of these poems in sequence were all Pound's own: a controlled pattern of aesthetic sensibility and experience. The poems of *Cathay*, as specimens of Imagism, are translatable to the extent that emotional effects can be greatly intensified if the relation between images be allowed to remain obscure. Since in Pound's view *phanopoeia* can be translated almost entirely without loss or distortion (*LE*, 25), the Chinese imagery is easily brought over in *Cathay*, while most of the rhythmic tone-inflections are Pound's own imposition. But his muted and hesitant rhythms often fail to convey the sharper and more staccato movement of the Chinese, and he did not pay much attention to the often rigid verse forms of the original. This is partly due to Fenollosa's tendency in his notes to sight-translate the Chinese ideograms. But in any case these peculiar textual and technical features of Chinese poetic convention were not central for Pound, who believed that the only thing that mattered was the translation of "content" (*INS*, 4) or "subject matter" (*LE*, 247).

Strictly speaking, however, the question whether Pound's versions were faithful to the Chinese originals need not be relevant, since he did not know any Chinese at the time and relied solely on Fenollosa's Japanese-mediated notes which were themselves one remove from the Chinese. Fenollosa's desultory notes are often inaccurate and have sometimes led

Pound astray (in the well-known example of "The River Song," Pound conflated two different poems); yet Pound was often able to penetrate through the literal surface of these cribs to grasp the integrity of a poem as a whole and then to transmit his insight and understanding into the artifice of a new medium, thus enabling the structure of feeling to generate itself, organically, according to its own inner compulsion and momentum. What emerges at the end of this process becomes a new creation in its own right: a Poundian poem. Pound no doubt must have considered himself fortunate to be able to transpose and appropriate freely according to his own interests and principles. The seemingly unpromising task of trying to make over a body of Chinese poems into English seemed to contribute positively to his awareness of the expressive potentialities of his own English. The poems of *Cathay* should indeed be read as English poems in their own right, perhaps among the most successful of all Pound's works, though it is more often as translations that they have aroused admiration or provoked criticisms.

The language of *Cathay* was colloquial, prosaic and contemporary; it did not try to cast the original Chinese in correspondingly archaic or antiquarian English, as was often Pound's practice. *Cathay* is an example of a strong tendency in Pound to regard translation as not historical, but contemporary or timeless. Yet in a paradoxical sense, Pound's versions seem to come nearer to the real qualities of Chinese poetry, because he has largely stripped away most of the supposed or fictitious qualities that late-Victorian poetic treatment (by James Legge, Herbert Giles, and so on) had imposed upon classical Chinese poetry. But the success of *Cathay* is also largely due to Pound's tacit and skilful reliance upon a stylized evocation of China with which he could expect his Georgian or Edwardian readers to be familiar. The use of Chinese landscape, for example, seems to provide a powerful confirmation of the kind of "otherness" which Western readers tacitly identified with an emotional coding linked to understood conventions of feeling in Chinese art and poetry. Such correlation of landscape and feeling can be seen even in such a short poem as "Separation on the River Kiang":

> The smoke-flowers are blurred over the river.
> His lone sail blots the far sky.
> And now I see only the river,
> The long Kiang, reaching heaven. (*CSP*, 147)

Here, Pound seems to have understood very well the emotional pictorialism of Li Po's poem and builds his version around the two crucial images "blurred" and "blot." The word "blot" lends a certain ironic touch, an irony which is absent in both the Chinese (孤帆遠影碧空盡) and Fenollosa's notes. It makes a mark on the clear sky; a smudge of ink, itself, becomes indistinct by being moistened by river-mist ("smoke-flowers") – an adroit allusion to Chinese landscape-painting technique. By emotional implication, the vision is also "blurred" by tears of parting, so that the underlying feeling is not directly mentioned. "And now I see only the river ..." The words *now* and *only* are the markers of remoteness, parting, desolation: again, the presentation of subjective emotion is entirely oblique.

However, as its title indicates, the appeal of *Cathay* is largely its exoticism, evoking a poeticized imaginary realm with nineteenth-century Tennysonian associations. But Pound's interest was not merely antiquarian: he recognized the importance of the culturally distant and unfamiliar. In the end the so-called simplicity and ordinariness of *Cathay* may be deceptive, since the Western reader is asked to reconstruct by vicarious projection the social and moral ambience of the Chinese poems, by virtue of a dialectic interaction between the strange and the familiar. The resulting pathos and nuances of irony are thus made all the more powerful for being subdued and implied. T. S. Eliot had insisted that the appeal of the *Cathay* poems owed less to their exoticism than to Pound's own poetic development. Yet these translations were precisely what enabled Pound to exploit tensions and ironies only realizable within the framework of vicarious envisagement.[12] More importantly, Pound clearly understood that, barbarous as was the fate of some individuals, the Chinese poems implied an imperial culture, complete and ordered, whereas the Anglo-Saxon "Seafarer," a poem he translated a few years earlier, was not the product of an empire but of a more truly primitive state of social development. The idiom of *Cathay* has many nuances which could be called "civilized," not so much a matter of tribal or even individual loyalties as *social* values within an imperially ordered frame. Pound's concern with the paradigmatic frame of an entire culture was to be fully evident in his later translation of the *Shih Ching* anthology. Such an understanding also paved the way for his increasing engagement with Confucian thought between the wars.

Apart from the poems of *Cathay*, the most important discovery for Pound was perhaps Fenollosa's notes and draft fragments on "The Chinese Written Character as a Medium for Poetry," which Pound edited and published as an essay in 1918. The central tenets of Fenollosa's thinking in this respect are two-fold. Firstly, the Chinese ideogram is metaphorical, not abstract, since the ideogram is composed of concrete things and vivid pictures. Secondly, the Chinese sentence, made up of such ideograms, represents the processes and operations of nature; it denotes a "verbal idea of action" and a transference of energy (*CWC*, 9, 12). This verbal action involves the perception of dynamic relations in process. Taken together these two emphases are directly opposed to what Fenollosa (and Pound) took to be the characteristic Western habit of abstraction. The visual aspects of the ideogram had a great appeal to Pound, but he was more interested in the process of perception and definition that lies behind the pictorial analogy. Though clearly aware of the fact that most Chinese ideograms, especially the later ones, are wholly or partly phonetic, Fenollosa nevertheless tended to emphasize the primitive pictorial nature of a very limited number of the most basic ideograms. In particular, Fenollosa was fascinated by the ways in which primitive ideograms generated their meanings out of their constituent parts, which were themselves pictures of real things and objects. This etymological, compositional theory of the ideogram, from which Pound derived his "ideogrammic" method, had an enormous impact on his thinking about poetry and other cultural matters, and on the writing of *The Cantos*.

In our present context, this etymological method can be seen at work in Pound's translations of Confucian texts and of the *Classic of Poetry*. In all he translated three of the "Four Books" of canonical Confucianism. His *Ta Hio* (1928), a translation of *The Great Learning*, was in its first version mainly a close transposition of a nineteenth-century French version by Guillaume Pauthier. In the later revised version, Pound conducted a kind of semantics, what he thought to be the key notions of Confucianism, such as "sincerity," "will," "virtue," which, by using Fenollosa's ideogrammic-etymological method, he analyzed into their individual components and then constructed a new composite meaning in the light of the overall significance of the text he was translating. He gave these key concepts his own often highly idiosyncratic interpretations. But some of these amplifications and explanations are at best far-fetched and merely fanciful and have no direct basis in Chinese etymology. For example, Pound translated the opening sentence of *Ta Hio* (大學之道在明明德在親民在止於至善) as

> The great learning [...] takes root in clarifying the way therein the intelligence increases through the process of looking straight into one's own heart and acting on the results; it is rooted in watching with affection the way people grow; it is rooted in coming to rest, being at ease in perfect equity.
>
> (Confucius 27–28)

Here, the crucial phrase *ming ming tê* (明明德 "understanding the inborn luminous virtue") becomes "the intelligence increases through the process of looking straight into one's own heart and acting on the results," because the character *tê* (virtue) has "eye" and "heart" components in it. The phrase *ch'in min* (親民 "renewing the people") is rendered as "watching with affection the way people grow," because the character *ch'in* also has an "eye (seeing)" component. Pound was fascinated by the "eye" component in both these ideograms perhaps because he was reading back into Confucius a metaphysics of celestial light and intelligence which he had already found in Scotus Erigena, Grosseteste and Cavalcanti (Confucius 20). And this mystical metaphysics of light was then linked by Pound to the necessity for precise terminology and proper rectification of names as the basis for moral and political reform. We can discern Pound's gradual identification, especially towards the end of the 1930s, of Confucianism with a "totalitarian" social and political ethic. This totalitarian interpretation is most pronounced in his translations of *The Great Digest* and *The Unwobbling Pivot*, yet it is not overtly social or political but given a neo-Platonic metaphysical basis, especially the neo-Platonic vision of light.[13] Fenollosa had already convinced him that the Chinese language was essentially metaphorical and, indeed, the language of nature; thus, the Confucian ethical and political discourse built on such a language came to have an enormous moral authority for Pound. In his later translation of the Confucian *Analects*, parts of which were finished at St. Elizabeths Hospital, Pound assumed the persona and voice of Confucius the Master talking, in a language jazzed up by racy and terse American slang, to his disciples.

It was largely Pound's growing interest in Confucianism before and after the Second World War that led him to translate all the 305 poems in the earliest anthology of Chinese poems, *Shih Ching* or *The Classic of Poetry*, which he entitled *The Classic Anthology defined by Confucius* (1954). His renderings are not scholarly translations, like those previous English translations on which his versions are largely based, but are bravura re-creations of the ancient Chinese poems. His earlier preoccupation with the troubadour melopoeia or the union of *motz et son* reappears, especially in the section of "Folk Songs," and there are many virtuoso re-creations in imitation of the Chinese musical effects, thus redressing the imbalance of concentrating on phanopoeia in *Cathay*, partly because Pound came to have a greater appreciation of Chinese sound-effects and prosodic patterns. But again, he often used his method of "etymological" dismantling and amplification to translate what he took to be key words in some of the poems, in order to highlight the concrete images in the original. However, as L. S. Dembo has acutely observed, Pound's pseudo-etymological readings often indicate his propensity to "lyricize" the original Chinese.[14] In Ode 42, for example, a modest country maid in a traditional folk song becomes a "Lady of azure thought" (*CAC*, 20), because the ideogram *ching* in *ching nü* (靜女 "quiet lady") contains the *ch'ing* component

(青 "blue" or "green"). Thus Pound virtually identified her with the mystical lady of light in Cavalcanti's "Donna mi Prega."

However, Pound's great originality in the *Classic Anthology* was the use of a full range of Western forms and genres to suggest parallel or equivalent poetic structures of feeling and response: there are a whole variety of Western modes and forms and other numerous allusive echoes and familiar cadences from Western poetry, mainly English poetry of the fifteenth to seventeenth centuries. The convincing independence and internal coherence of Pound's versions represent not so much a faithful translation of individual *Shih Ching* poems, as an anthology in English that can stand side by side with the original Chinese collection. In spite of this, perhaps because of this, the Western parallels and analogues seem to enable what is alien and untranslatable to stand out more sharply. The fact that it is a complete translation of an anthology, reputed to be compiled by Confucius himself (hence Pound's title), is thus in itself highly significant, for what is translated is for Pound a fully integrated and coherent paradigm of an entire culture.

Roughly contemporary with the *Classic Anthology* was Pound's translation of Sophocles' *Trachiniae*. First published in 1953, *The Women of Trachis* was the result of his growing appreciation of Greek tragedy, and of Sophocles in particular. Although at first he did not think highly of any Greek tragedy, since he disliked the rhetorical and moralizing tendencies in Greek plays, Pound nevertheless admired what he called "Sophoklean economy" (*LE*, 36n). His choice of *Trachiniae* for translation and his high opinion of it can be largely explained by his perception of the essential similarity between the play and Noh drama both in form and spirit.[15] His translation was, as he recalled, largely prompted and inspired by re-reading Japanese Noh plays. Following Fenollosa, Pound referred to the "God-Dance" of the Noh as the closest formal analogue of the *Trachiniae* (*WT*, 3). He cut out and condensed whatever he considered to be merely rhetorical in the *Trachiniae* and modeled his version on the economy of the Noh. He was interested in "the poetic part of a drama" with the prose part omitted (*L*, 3). But not all the cuts are justified: one of the most important moments of the play in which Heracles is carried wearing his shirt of pain (lines 971–92 of the original) was altogether omitted.

Pound's interpretation of the play shifts the focus from the heroine Deianeira, whom scholars usually consider to be the central character, to Heracles, whom he took to be the embodiment of the play's essential meaning. By interpreting the play's structure to be the progressive revelation of the gods' plan and thus subordinating everything else to the divine will of Zeus, Pound builds up to a powerful climax towards the close

when the two prophecies concerning Heracles' life and death come together, so that Heracles may be finally revealed to be "the Solar vitality"
(*WT*, 4) that he truly is – a symbol of noble serenity and heroism. But the
dominant focus on Heracles may be seen as an over-emphasis on what
H. A. Mason has called "the male principle in heaven and on earth, in
Father and Son," unduly neglecting "the female principle in the Wife and
the Goddess of Love" which is the "binding-in effect" in Sophocles' original.[16]

What is remarkable about this version, especially in the dialogues, in
Pound's masterly handling of modern colloquial language, and in some
cases modern American slang, to suit the nuances and tones of a live
human speaker, and to achieve an authentic quality of actual speech. But
the version as a whole is marred by certain stylistic inconsistencies, the
effects of which are not always deliberate. The slang idioms Pound adopted
for the dialogues sometimes hover uncertainly between colloquial ease and
crude whimsicality, though some early critics unduly took Pound to task
for mixing and blurring class distinctions in the speeches. This is perhaps
Pound's parodying of what he imagined to be the speech of the socially
underprivileged: it is not a realistic representation of how slang or dialects
are spoken. But what he was trying to do in using slang was, as Donald
Davie suggests, not to translate into colloquial American but into "a special
dialect that corresponds to the special artificial Greek of the original."[17]
Indeed, Pound's deliberate use of a pseudo-colloquial style aimed precisely
to make the reader feel the remoteness and alienness of the Greek play,
much as the Noh plays are exotic and strange.

When he translated what he called "the key phrase" for which the
whole play exists,

> Come at it that way, my boy, what
> SPLENDOUR,
>
> IT ALL COHERES.   (*WT*, 50)

Pound was most likely thinking of the Noh play as a "Unity of Image."
The symbolic image of light is Pound's favourite, and it serves here as a
unifying force for the whole play, a moment of sudden illumination. Heracles
also serves Pound as a new persona having a deep personal resonance.
This epiphanic light was to return in Canto CXVI as a charged metaphor
for the meaning of his own entire life even though he cannot "make it
cohere." This Sophoclean translation, coming after the Second World War,
articulated for Pound a tragic dimension which he increasingly identified
as inherent in his own personal history.

The example of *The Women of Trachis* is highly significant, for it shows
that translation is for Pound *sui generis* interpretation and criticism,

because translation reveals the fundamental (and often hidden) structure of the original work. Yet the textual aspects of the original were often not important for Pound, even though he might have *intended* each of his translations to be a scholarly one; what mattered for him was to decide what "the *implication* of the word" was (*SL*, 271; original italics) and what significance he perceived to be "inherent in the original text" (*LE*, 235). Pound's is not a scholarly model of translation with philological accuracy as its highest goal; as he said of his *Cathay* versions, Fenollosa had wanted them translated "*as* literature not as philology" (*SL*, 214; original italics). Pound's two primary aims in translation are to achieve "fidelity to the original" in both "meaning" and "atmosphere" (*SL*, 273). "Atmosphere" seems to encompass the totality of the original work, so that it is not so much the external reproduction or transposition of the original, as the tactful articulation or modulated restitution in a new parallel structure, as far as possible, of the originary *intentio* – a translation of "accompaniment" (*T*, 17). At least in intention Pound wanted to let the original shine out more fully through and against the medium of translation, so that the original and translation may constitute a harmonious, symbiotic continuity (hence Pound's often expressed fondness for bilingual editions of translation). But in practice Pound's translations, as independent English poems in their own right, often tend to substitute or replace the original.

What Pound tried to do in *The Women of Trachis* is also closely linked to the restorative function of translation: it attempts to restore to the modern world certain vital perceptions and values (the ideal of heroism, for example) in the ancient original which he believed to have been lost. Similarly, with the Cavalcanti translations, Pound wanted to reach back to the intellectual vigor and precision of a pre-Shakespearean idiom, in order to recover a lost and in his view better tradition, had Cavalcanti rather than Petrarch been adopted as a model (*LE*, 153–54).[18] And there is no other way to retrieve, or to use Pound's own word "revivify" (*LE*, 224), these classics except through creative translation, through "mak[ing] it new" (Canto LIII/265). Translation of a classic text thus conceived, in the only way conceivable, is a creative effort which "reveals the classic work as at one and the same time forever alien and yet, mysteriously, *abordable*" (Mason, "Creative Translation," 247). The translator is thus in the true sense of the word an interpreter (Latin *interpres*, "intermediary," "go-between"), though Pound was often fond of using the words "traducer" and "traduction" which come from the Latin *traductio*, "leading across." For Pound, however, to translate is not necessarily to modernize. The "new" in "make it new" does not necessarily mean "modern" or "contemporary";

rather, it means the re-grounding of the original work in a contemporary sensibility in order to achieve, paradoxically, an historical understanding of the original now newly situated in a later historical moment by the translator. Thus *The Women of Trachis* can be seen as a kind of cultural and historical "super-imposition": while Pound's version is fundamentally based on Sophocles' Greek it is also filtered through the model of Noh.

It is in *The Cantos* that we see Pound's engagement with translation at its most complex. *The Cantos* contain numerous translations, from Homer's *Odyssey*, *The Sacred Edict* and other Chinese texts (mostly from previous European translations) to Richard of St. Victor, Ovid, Propertius and Frobenius. Interwoven with these are many of the images and motifs from Pound's previous translations: the troubadours, Cavalcanti, Old English "Seafarer," Noh plays, *Cathay* poems, Confucian texts. The whole sequence of *Cantos* starts with translation: Canto I is a rendering of the Nekyia section of Homer's *Odyssey*, not directly from the Greek, but from the Medieval Latin version by Andreas Divus, and then not into modern English but into the archaic idiom of the Anglo-Saxon "Seafarer." Indeed, behind Canto I stands "The Seafarer," both in thematic structure and poetic diction, and the whole medieval paradigm which Pound discovered as the link between Old English, ancient Greek, Provençal, Renaissance Latin, and Pound the modern poet (*MIN*, 33).[19] Pound clearly recognized the temporal gaps between these different layers of language and epoch, between the translator and the translated, and that the only way to bridge these gaps was to create a kind of overlaying *lingua franca* by juxtaposing these various idioms and making them interact.

The Cantos as a whole is indeed an epic of translation, with its multilingual, intertextual web of cultures and epochs, existing simultaneously in various modes of translation (as well as allusion, imitation, adaptation, quotation, and even parody). In *The Cantos* Pound translated or quoted from no less than fifteen foreign languages. This, together with the allusiveness of Pound's text, no doubt creates enormous difficulties for even the most well-informed and best linguistically equipped reader. But Pound once advised a new reader of his *Cantos* to "skip anything you don't understand and go on till you pick it up again": "All tosh about *foreign languages* making it difficult. The quotes are all either explained at once by repeat or they are definitely *of* the things indicated" (*SL*, 250–251; original italics). Pound's translations or equivalents of foreign phrases are sometimes followed by playful quips that seem to pre-empt those who would think his translations inaccurate ("this is a mistranslation"; "no, that is not textual," Canto XCIX/730, 732). What seems to matter for him is not so much translation from one language or culture into another as the metamorphic passage or inter-traffic *between* them. This is Pound's method of "ideogrammic" translation of what he perceives to be vital cultural fragments and values. It aims to suggest a "compendious" (*ABCR*, 101) coalescing of facts and ideas belonging to different cultural traditions to form a universal *paideuma*, a term borrowed from Leo Frobenius and defined by Pound as "the tangle or complex of the inrooted ideas of any period" (*GK*, 57).

A short passage from Canto LXXXVI may serve as an example of Pound's method of ideogrammic translation:

> non coelum non in medio
> but man is under Fortuna
> ? that is a forced translation?
> La donna che volgo
> Man under Fortune,

CHÊN

(LXXXVI/586)

Here, the first line is a quotation from Séraphin Couvreur's Latin version of the Chinese *Shu Ching* (The Book of History) in the context of an admonition to the wise ruler: the idea that Heaven deals impartially with everything. This idea of *ming* (命 "fate") Pound translates as "but man is under Fortuna" and then evokes the Goddess of Fortuna found in Cavalcanti and Dante ("La donna che volgo," the lady who turns, being an allusion to "Canzone to Fortune" which Pound had attributed to Cavalcanti and translated many years ago in *The Spirit of Romance*). Despite his half-joking question as to whether it is "a forced translation," Pound evidently wants the reader to compare and link these two ideas and to perceive that both the Chinese idea of heavenly justice and the European Goddess of Fortuna are efficacious in human affairs (individual or governmental). The ideogram *chên* denotes for Pound the thundering action from Heaven signifying divine punishment for corrupt government and for deviation from the process of natural justice. This ideogram reappears in Canto XCI:

> Now Lear in Janus' temple is laid
>
> timing the thunder   (633)

where Shakespeare's King Lear is invoked to reiterate the idea of retributive justice, as Lear himself understands it in the thunderstorm scene about the punishment of others' sins and crimes and about his own punishment for rejecting his daughter. Thus Pound's presentation of the idea gains much poignant force which resonates across two different cultural traditions; yet the meaning of the translated or quoted material remains fluid and open to interpretation. Blanks or gaps between various fragments are to be filled and interpreted by the reader, who is asked to understand a given idea through cumulative definition across individual cantos and in relation to other ideas ("by repeat"). *The Cantos* thus progressively constitute an internally allusive and self-cohesive frame of associative meanings and equivalences. But the new contexts of ideogrammic juxtapositions, invoking heterogeneous traditions, also necessarily point to different directions and cultural roots.

The importance of translation is for Pound closely connected with the self-imposed discipline of exile, with the ecumenical aspiration to be at home in as many languages and cultures as possible. Pound felt compelled to go beyond the Western tradition to construct an inclusive cultural *paideuma*. As he said of his mentor Fenollosa, "the exotic was always a means of fructification" (*CWC*, 3) in any cultural renaissance. His friend T. S. Eliot, except for his interest in the *Upanishads* and Indic thought, did not deliberately seek outside the Western-Christian tradition and criticized Pound's interest (shared by I. A. Richards and Irving Babbitt) in Confucian philosophy as "a deracination from the Christian tradition."[20] More to the point, however, is Pound's tendency to disregard real differences and historical contingencies and to play down the otherness of remote or alien traditions and thought-patterns. This is evident in his assumption that ideas and notions from different traditions may *rhyme* with each other (*SPR*, 98); but his suggestion of parallels between cultures is often weak and sometimes far-fetched (in the China Cantos [LII–LXI], for example). Pound's assumption of parity bespeaks what L. S. Dembo has called the "apocalyptic" conception of translation: Pound believes that after apprehending and seizing in the mind the Platonic essence of a given work the translator can, and indeed should, seek to embody his understanding in an "equivalent" (Dembo, *Confucian Odes*, 2). Pound's conception of translation is premised on the assumption of a simple *mimesis*, a correspondence between an essential reality and its various manifestations in different languages and cultures. For Pound, the cultural tradition or *paideuma* that really matters is precisely constituted by what will translate, by what must be fundamentally translatable. Since for Pound no single language is complete (*ABCR*, 34) and "It can't be all in one language"

(Canto LXXXVI/583), the plurality of languages constitutes a single system of equivalences and universals which makes translation both possible and necessary. Thus translation enables the poet to have access to trans-cultural and trans-historical universals while at the same time making it possible for the poet to effect original transformations in a given local language. But on the other hand, translation does not mean the simple transference of stable and definite meanings from one language or culture to another; instead, equivalences are to be arrived at interpretatively. Despite his belief in Platonic equivalents, the meaning (or essence) of a given work or culture exists for Pound only to the extent that it is accessible and retrievable through the "essential medium" of translation, with reference to the needs and concerns of the present. Thus translation is by necessity disruptive, distorting and transformative. Pound's acute awareness of the need for a cultural *paideuma* makes it imperative for him to graft and appropriate fragments from various traditions to form a new hybrid, a pattern of universal significance. But these disparate metonymic fragments, shorn of their specific and historical contexts, tend to become only "writerly" *discourse*, subsumable into a synchronous pattern of textuality which invites transformation and appropriation. The essence may seem ever elusive; yet the work of translation must go on. Translation, as Pound noted in 1918, is apt to be "a thankless and desolate undertaking" (*LE*, 268).

Appendix: A brief bibliographic list of Pound's principal translations in chronological order

Translations from the troubadours: translations from Arnaut Daniel, Bernart de Ventadorn, Bertran de Born, Arnaut de Mareuil, Peire Vidal, and others, were mostly made between 1908 and 1910, and published in *Personae* (1909), *Exultations* (1909), *The Spirit of Romance* (1910) and periodicals. For recent editions, see Charlotte Ward (ed.), *Ezra Pound, Forked Branches: Translations of Medieval Poems* (Iowa City: Windhover Press, 1985) and Charlotte Ward, *Pound's Translations of Arnaut Daniel: A Variorum Edition with Commentary from Unpublished Letters* (New York and London: Garland, 1991).

"The Seafarer": first published in 1911 in *New Age*, and can be found in *The Translations of Ezra Pound*, edited with introduction by Hugh Kenner, enlarged edition (London: Faber and Faber, 1970).

Translations from Cavalcanti: *Sonnets and Ballate of Guido Cavalcanti with Translation and Introduction by Ezra Pound* (Boston: Small, Maynard and Company, 1912) [bilingual edition]; the authoritative edition is David

Anderson's *Pound's Cavalcanti: An Edition of the Translations, Notes, and Essays* (Princeton: Princeton University Press, 1983).

Translations from Japanese Noh plays: some of these first appeared in abbreviated form during 1914–15 in *Poetry, Quarterly Review,* and *Drama,* and later published with more translations as *"Noh" or Accomplishment: A Study of the Classical Stage of Japan by Ernest Fenollosa and Ezra Pound* (London: Macmillan, 1916 [*i.e.* 1917]).

Translations from Chinese poetry: *Cathay: Translations by Ezra Pound. For the Most Part from the Chinese of Rihaku, from the Notes of the Late Ernest Fenollosa, and the Decipherings of the Professors Mori and Ariga* (London: Elkin Mathews, 1915).

"Homage to Sextus Propertius": first published partially in *Poetry* and *New Age* in 1919, and as a whole in *Quia Pauper Amavi* (1919); it has been reprinted with "a number of minor changes authorized by Pound himself" in a collated text together with "the Latin text of Propertius' work which Pound used for translation," in J. P. Sullivan's *Ezra Pound and Sextus Propertius: A Study in Creative Translation* (Austin: University of Texas Press, 1964), 114–171.

Confucian translations: *Ta Hio: The Great Learning Newly Rendered into the American Language by Ezra Pound* (Seattle: University of Washington Book Store, 1928); *Confucius: The Unwobbling Pivot & The Great Digest translated by Ezra Pound, With notes and commentary on the text and the ideograms, together with Ciu Hsi's "Preface" to the Chung Yung and Tseng's commentary on the Testament* ([Norfolk, Conn.: New Directions], 1947); "The Analects", first published in 1950 in *Hudson Review.* The above versions underwent various revisions and have been conveniently collected in *Confucius: The Great Digest, The Unwobbling Pivot, The Analects* (New York: New Directions, 1969).

Translation of the Chinese *Shih Ching: The Classic Anthology Defined by Confucius* (Cambridge, MA: Harvard University Press, 1954).

Translations from Sophocles: *Women of Trachis* was first published in 1954 in *Hudson Review,* and reprinted as *Sophokles: Women of Trachis: A version by Ezra Pound* (London: Neville Spearman, 1956); an earlier version of Sophocles' *Electra,* translated in 1949 with a collaborator, is now published as *Sophocles: Elektra, a version by Ezra Pound and Rudd Fleming,* edited and annotated by Richard Reid (Princeton: Princeton University Press, 1989).

Some of the above translations (e.g. Cavalcanti, Arnaut Daniel, "The Seafarer", *Cathay,* Noh plays), together with other miscellaneous translations (from Egyptian, Latin, Indian, French, Italian poetry), are conveniently collected in Kenner's edition of *The Translations of Ezra Pound.*

For complete bibliographic information on most of Pound's translations, see Donald Gallup's *Ezra Pound: A Bibliography*, revised and updated edition (Charlottesville: University Press of Virginia, 1983).

NOTES

1 Pound, "How I Began," *T. P.'s Weekly*, 21 (1913), 707; original italics.
2 For more details about Pound's study of foreign languages early in his career, see Noel Stock, *The Life of Ezra Pound* (London: Routledge & Kegan Paul, 1970), pp. 12–27, and Humphrey Carpenter, *A Serious Character: The Life of Ezra Pound* (London: Faber & Faber, 1988), pp. 46, 50–51.
3 G. S. Fraser, *Ezra Pound* (Edinburgh and London: Oliver and Boyd, 1960), p. 64.
4 See Donald Gallup, *Ezra Pound: A Bibliography*, revised and updated edn (Charlottesville, 1983), p. 225.
5 For the Provençal translations, see Stuart Y. McDougal, *Ezra Pound and the Troubadour Tradition* (Princeton: Princeton University Press, 1972) and Peter Makin, *Provence and Pound* (Berkeley: University of California Press, 1978).
6 James J. Wilhelm, "Pound and the Troubadours: Medieval and Modern Rebels," in Marcel Smith and William A. Ulmer (eds.), *Ezra Pound: The Legacy of Kulchur* (Tuscaloosa: University of Alabama Press, 1988), pp. 113–114.
7 Fred C. Robinson, " 'The Might of the North': Pound's Anglo-Saxon Studies and 'The Seafarer' ", *The Yale Review*, 71 (1981–82), 199–224.
8 On Pound's translation of "The Seafarer," see also Michael Alexander, *The Poetic Achievement of Ezra Pound* (London: Faber & Faber, 1979), pp. 63–79; Melvin D. McNichols, "Survivals and (Re)newals: Pound's 'The Seafarer' ", *Paideuma*, 20 (1991), 113–127; and Vilas Sarang, "Pound's *Seafarer*", *Classical Philology*, 6 (1973), 5–11.
9 For critical discussions, see J. P. Sullivan, *Ezra Pound and Sextus Propertius: A Study in Creative Translation* (Austin: University of Texas Press, 1964) and Daniel M. Hooley, *The Classics in Paraphrase: Ezra Pound and Modern Translations of Latin Poetry* (London and Toronto: Associated University Press, 1988).
10 Fenollosa's notebooks and manuscripts on Chinese and Japanese literature are in the Pound/Fenollosa special collection at the Beinecke Rare Book and Manuscript Library, Yale University. For the Fenollosa–Pound relationship, see Laurence W. Chisolm, *Fenollosa: The Far East and American Culture* (New Haven: Yale University Press, 1963); Achilles Fang, "Fenollosa and Pound," *Harvard Journal of Asian Studies*, 20 (1957), 213–238; and Wai-lim Yip, *Ezra Pound's Cathay* (Princeton: Princeton University Press, 1969).
11 For an evaluation of the Noh versions, see Nobuko Tsukui, *Ezra Pound and Japanese Noh Plays* (Washington, DC: University Press of America, 1983).
12 For a fuller discussion, see Ming Xie, "Elegy and Personae in Ezra Pound's *Cathay*," *English Literary History*, 60 (1993); 261–281.
13 For the relation between Pound's Confucian translations and his political views, see Mary P. Cheadle, "The Vision of Light in Ezra Pound's *The Unwobbling Pivot*," *Twentieth Century Literature*, 35 (1989), 113–130.

14 L. S. Dembo, *The Confucian Odes of Ezra Pound: A Critical Appraisal* (Berkeley: University of California Press, 1963), p. 48.

15 See Richard Ingber, "Ezra Pound's *Women of Trachis*: A Song for the Muses' Garden," *Amerikastudien*, 23 (1978), 131–146.

16 H. A. Mason, "Creative Translation: Ezra Pound's *Women of Trachis,*" *The Cambridge Quarterly*, 4 (1969), 257–258.

17 Donald Davie, *Ezra Pound: Poet as Sculptor* (New York: Oxford University Press, 1964), p. 236.

18 See David Anderson, "A Language to Translate Into: The Pre-Elizabethan Idiom of Pound's Later Cavalcanti Translations," *Studies in Medievalism*, 2 (1982), 9–18.

19 See Georg M. Gugelberger, *Ezra Pound's Medievalism* (Frankfurt am Main: Peter Lang, 1978), p. 166.

20 T. S. Eliot, *The Use of Poetry and the Use of Criticism* (London: Faber & Faber, 1964), p. 132.

11

REED WAY DASENBROCK

Pound and the visual arts

Ezra Pound wrote a good deal of art journalism and criticism, participated actively in one art movement, Vorticism, and wrote extensively in his poetry and prose about the effect chosen instances of art, particularly Italian Renaissance and modernist art, had on his sensibility and thinking. Aside from his 1916 book, *Gaudier-Brzeska: A Memoir*, his writing on art has been collected in *Ezra Pound and the Visual Arts* (1980), and most of the details of his varied interests in the visual arts have been carefully studied by a number of different critics.[1] This essay is not one more detailed study of an aspect of Pound's interests in the visual arts as much as a synoptic overview of those interests. What, if anything, links and renders coherent Pound's varied interests in art? More importantly, what motivated Pound's interest in the visual arts?

Pound's interest in the visual arts offers a significant contrast to his interest in music. There are, of course, some similarities between the two interests. His opinions about music and painting were both widely divergent from received notions, both in his praise of modern artists such as Henri Gaudier-Brzeska and George Antheil, and in his intemperate dismissal of Rubens and Rembrandt and the entire solo piano repertoire. We have not quite known how to learn from Pound's consciously eccentric views without adopting all of them, but for me the value of Pound's criticism is at both extremes of the range, rarely in the middle (fortunately, he is rarely in the middle). Pound's outrageous dismissals of widely accepted masterpieces always has a value in provoking thought – why is Pound wrong about Rubens or Chopin? Or is he? Do we admire Rubens – if we do – simply because we have been told to, simply from intellectual inertia? And the results of asking those questions are valuable enough even if we do not come to share Pound's judgments. More valuable yet are Pound's enthusiasms, for I think it fair to say that Pound aimed to provoke interesting dissents with his dissents but assents with his assents. By and large this is our response: we do not have to agree with his condemnation of Petrarch, Chopin and Rubens to come to appreciate Cavalcanti, Vivaldi and Agostino di Duccio as he did (and as few did before him).

Despite these similarities between Pound's art criticism and his criticism of other arts, there are also instructive differences. *Ezra Pound and Music* shows that his writing on musical topics was far more prolonged than his writing on the visual arts. The bulk of his writing on both topics was done in the years 1917–1921, when he earned a living writing for *The New Age* about art under the pseudonym B. H. Dias and about music under the pseudonym William Atheling. But in the subsequent years, Pound's interest in music deepened, as is shown by his theoretical writing of the 1920s, most notably *George Antheil and the Treatise on Harmony*, his composition of two operas, *Le Testament de Villon* and *Cavalcanti*, and his work organizing concerts in Rapallo in the 1930s which led to writing about those concerts and about another new interest of these years, the photoreproduction of musical scores. In contrast (and this is an insufficiently noticed contrast), *Ezra Pound and the Visual Arts* contains little more than fragments written after his move to Rapallo in Italy in 1924. Though at least part of this contrast can be explained by the fact that Rapallo was not a center of contemporary art in the way Paris and London were, I think it significant that the turn to explore the monuments of the past – as seen in the Malatesta Cantos – was continued after 1924 in literature in his work on Cavalcanti and in music in his work on the photoreproduction of old scores but not in the visual arts. Nor was his concern with contemporary art sustained. For example, the book on Wyndham Lewis's art which Pound planned as early as 1916 and mentioned periodically in correspondence with Lewis, was never written. After 1924, he continued to cite artists and works of art as touchstones or exemplars of civilization, but there is virtually no discussion of works of art *qua* art in the way there was in the decade from 1914 to 1924. This requires an explanation which it has not received.

To begin with, we need to remember that Pound believed in the superiority of direct acquaintance with art over any theorizing about it. Hence, in the *ABC of Reading*, Pound praises the good sense of the public interested in art because people go to see paintings before they read criticism: "For every reader of books on art, 1,000 people go to LOOK at the paintings. Thank Heavens!" (*ABCR*, 23) But he also believed in the superiority of the direct acquaintance of those with experience in the creation of the art under discussion. This position helps validate the authority of his literary criticism, as Pound was, of course, both a poet and a critic of other poets. He comparably tried to assert his insider expertise everywhere, rarely sitting on the sidelines in anything, including, most notably, economics and politics. The visual arts is, however, an exception to this pattern, virtually the only exception. Pound's acquaintance with Brancusi in Paris seems to have led to his attempting some stone sculpture in his Paris apartment in emulation of Brancusi,[2] but I don't think this was more than a momentary impulse. Pound, therefore, wrote about art as an outsider, as someone who had not mastered the tools of the trade. Pound was well aware of this, telling us in *Gaudier-Brzeska*, "I do not believe that there is any important art criticism, any important criticism of any particular art, which does not come originally from a master of that art" (*GB*, 20). According to Pound's own theories, this restricts the authority of his art criticism since he was not a master of any of the visual arts.

This apparent paradox helps explain the nature of Pound's interest in the visual arts. It is only a slight overstatement to say that Pound was not interested in the visual arts in themselves; to put it more accurately, he was not interested in them *for* themselves. What attracted Pound to the visual arts was their social and public nature, particularly in contrast to the far more private and interior world of poetry. Painting and sculpture were made to be seen, seen primarily in public spaces, and Pound was always very interested in the public-ity of art and sculpture. From the moment of Pound's arrival in London in 1908, he was anxious to make his mark on the London scene. But none of the poetic movements with which he was affiliated, the "forgotten school of images of 1909" and the far more important Imagism of 1912 and 1913, attracted any substantial public hearing or response.

In contrast, these were the years in which modern art attracted an enormous amount of attention and commentary, attention that centered primarily around a series of exhibitions. In London, the key exhibition was the "Manet and Post-Impressionism" exhibition of 1910 organized by Roger Fry, which gave London a remarkably belated introduction to the works of Cezanne, Gauguin, and Van Gogh and was the first occasion works by Picasso and Matisse were exhibited in London. It is presumably this exhibition that led to Virginia Woolf's famous pronouncement that human nature changed in 1910, and it is presumably this exhibition to which Pound was responding in his poem "L'Art, 1910." It is easier to quote this poem in its entirety than attempt to summarize it:

L'Art 1910

Green arsenic smeared on an egg-white cloth,
Crushed strawberries! Come, let us feast our eyes.

(*P*, 1990, 18)

This poem, perhaps the shortest dramatic monologue on record, places the poet or speaker and his interlocutor at an exhibition. The speaker is responding primarily to the dramatically heightened and often clashing palette of post-impressionist painting (I imagine a Fauvist painting here, though not a great deal depends on this identification), the bright greens and reds unsoftened by any sense of "finish" and in sharp contrast to the canvas which can also be seen, as in Cézanne's paintings where not every inch of canvas is painted. The language registers the shock value these paintings had at the time (the "green arsenic," the strawberries are "crushed" and "smeared"), but it is obvious that the speaker enjoys the outrageousness and expects his interlocutor to share in his enthusiasm. He may not want to eat the picture with its arsenic green but his eyes feast nonetheless.

But this show was only the first in a series of widely publicized modernist exhibitions in London and elsewhere. In New York, the famous Armory exhibition of 1913 aroused a comparably heated response, a response the London-based Pound would have read about even though he did not see the exhibition. During these years, everyone was talking about modern art, whether to denounce it or laud it to the skies. For anyone interested as Pound in how to win a hearing for his art, the dramatic success of these exhibitions must have been both exciting and a little frustrating.[3] How could poetry get in on the action?

It was the Italian writer Filippo Tommaso Marinetti, one of the crucial but least appreciated major influences on Pound, who showed him the way.[4] Poetry could get in on the action by taking part in movements linking literature to the visual arts. Marinetti had begun Futurism as a movement of poets in 1909, but Futurism quickly transformed itself into a movement primarily in the visual arts, in which Marinetti played the role of theoretician, stage manager and impresario more than that of writer. Pound was attracted less by the art of Futurism, which following Wyndham Lewis's lead, he criticized as a kind of Impressionism, than by its success at attracting attention and by the fact that the writer Marinetti was its leader. And it was with the example of Marinetti before him that just over a year after the first Futurist Exhibition in London, Pound joined together with Wyndham Lewis, probably the greatest English painter of his generation, to form their own art movement, Vorticism.

Pound did not quite manage to be the Marinetti of Vorticism, as Lewis – unlike Boccioni or Balla or Severini – was quite capable of being his own theoretician and impresario.[5] Nor did Vorticism have quite the impact on the world that Futurism had. The great Vorticist event was the publication of the first issue of *Blast* in June 1914, and *Blast* – despite its debts to

Apollinaire's writing and to the Futurist publication *Lacerba* – remains an impressive and original achievement, one of the greatest issues of any magazine ever published. But six weeks after the publication of *Blast*, a much bigger series of blasts began in the form of World War I. Despite the appearance of a second "war" issue of *Blast* in 1915, this signalled the end of Vorticism as a cohesive movement. Henri Gaudier-Brzeska went off to the trenches and was killed in action in 1915, while Lewis served in the British Army, first as a bombardier and then as a painter recording the war effort. With the departure of Vorticism's two major artistic talents for the trenches, Pound found his role in Vorticism changing, from theoretician and critic to agent, art dealer and, after Gaudier's death, de facto executor. He worked hard to publish Lewis, helping to place his first published novel *Tarr* both in England and the United States and see it through the press; he organized a Vorticist exhibition in London in 1915 and one in New York in 1917; and he did what he could to collect Gaudier's art and promote it. It was in this essentially retrospective cast of mind that he wrote *Gaudier-Brzeska: A Memoir*, which gathered the independent essays he wrote about Vorticism from 1914 to 1916 together with personal reminiscences of Gaudier, but a far better account of what he was actually doing in these years can be found in his correspondence with John Quinn, published as *The Selected Letters of Ezra Pound to John Quinn 1915–1924*. Quinn was an American lawyer who did most of the work organizing the Vorticist exhibition in New York in 1917 as well as bankrolling *The Little Review*, defending it in court against obscenity charges over Lewis's "Cantleman's Spring Mate" in 1917 as well as collecting manuscripts including those of *The Waste Land* and *Ulysses*. He was also the first great American collector of modern art, collecting not just the Vorticist art Pound urged upon him but also a great collection of French art including Seurat's *The Circus* and more than fifty Picassos.[6] Because of what he was able to accomplish, Quinn took on considerable importance in Pound's personal pantheon. It was not just that Quinn was virtually the only patron Vorticism had; more importantly, for Pound, he was an ideal patron because he was concerned – like Pound – with getting money in the hands of artists rather than – as most investment in art does – enriching middlemen and "art profiteers."[7]

But it is important here to note the sequence, which is that Pound articulated the ideal to which he felt Quinn corresponded well before the arrival of Quinn on the scene. Even before his involvement with Vorticism and with Quinn, Pound felt that modern poetry was on the verge of a Renaissance if it could find patronage. This search for patronage was part of what led him to champion links between poetry and art, and it is a crucial part of the reason for his initial exploration of the visual arts. The public nature of art meant that it demanded patronage, and Pound also quickly perceived the rather greater availability of patrons in the art world. At the same time, this interest also led him to explore the parallel between the modernist era and that period which for Pound best exemplified patronage of the arts, the Italian Renaissance.

This explains one of the most curious features of Pound's prose during the period of Vorticism (1914–1917), since references to the Italian Renaissance sprinkle his writings on Vorticism, while references to vortices and modern art are found throughout his discussions of Renaissance Italy. If Pound is asserting a parallel – whether actual or merely wished for – between the periods, it is not really between the artists – since he was fully aware that modernist art breaks in many ways with the tradition inaugurated by the Renaissance – as much as between the social conditions of the two periods. Pound is, of course, looking out for himself and his own chosen *métier* as well, as what he admires about the Renaissance Princes who were his exemplary patrons was their support of a range of artists and thinkers, including poets and scholars Pound identified with such as Lorenzo Valla.

This cluster of concerns is expressed as early as 1912–1913 in the series of essays collected as "Patria Mia" and received its most complex articulation in the Malatesta Cantos, the section of *The Cantos* written in 1922–23 focusing on Pound's favorite Renaissance patron, Sigismundo Malatesta.[8] Critics such as Hugh Kenner in *The Pound Era* have done a marvellous job of evoking the art brought into being by Malatesta, including work by Agostino di Duccio, Piero della Francesca and Alberti, but Pound's emphasis in the actual cantos is not on the activity of the artists but those of the patron. It is less that Pound thought that Malatesta was more important – though I think he might have maintained that – but that it was Malatesta whom Pound's era was particularly in need of. We had our Alberti's and Piero's, in Brancusi and Wyndham Lewis and others – even if Gaudier-Brzeska was already dead – but the social conditions that led to "the numerous vortices of the Italian Renaissance" were missing in the modern era. For Pound, John Quinn was the closest approach to a Malatesta or a Medici, but the amount Quinn was able to achieve with his comparatively limited resources just drive home for Pound how far short of the Renaissance the modern era was. What – Pound must have asked himself – could he and his friends have accomplished with the support of some of those in the modern world with the resources of a Medici instead of a comfortable but not rich lawyer who died of overwork in 1924 at the early age of fifty-four?

This pattern of emphasis in Pound's prose and in the Malatesta Cantos corresponds, I would suggest, to Pound's particular interest in the arts. His interest was above all in the conditions that gave birth to great work in all the arts, and for him one key was successful and intelligent patronage. As Pound wrote in his first letter to John Quinn of 1915:

> if a patron buys from an artist who needs money (needs money to buy tools, time and food), the patron then makes himself equal to the artist: he is bringing art into the world; he creates.
>
> If he buys even of living artists who are already famous or already making 12,000 per year, he ceases to create. He sinks back to the rank of a consumer.
>
> A great age of painting, a renaissance in the arts, comes when there are a few patrons who back their own flair and who buy from unrecognized men ... If you can hammer this into a few more collectors, you will bring in another Cinquecento. (*EPVA*, 278)

But it is clear enough in this discussion of patronage that Pound is not talking just about the visual arts. Given the material and public nature of the visual arts, one could study the operation of patronage there in great detail, but – Pound firmly believed – the lessons one could learn from the visual arts could also be applied to other arts as well, particularly poetry.

After Pound moved to Rapallo in 1924, his daily contact with artists diminished, but this only served to cement a tendency in place since the end of Vorticism as an organized movement. Pound – without any artists to play Marinetti for and without a Malatesta to support any he did find – turned instead to examining why we had no Sigismundo Malatesta now that we really needed him. The open-ended structure of the Malatesta Cantos did not suggest a particular diagnosis or solution even if it did present the problem, but across the 1920s as Pound completed the early Cantos, he began to formulate some answers. Italy looms large in his answer, as always, and his characteristic strategy is – as always – one of contrast. But the explicit contrast here is less between Renaissance Italy and the modern world than a contrast internal to Renaissance Italy. The single most sustained section of the early Cantos is the Malatesta Cantos, Cantos VIII–XII, but the second most sustained section is Cantos XXIV–XXVI, which could be called the Venetian Cantos. These are a far less studied part of the poem, but they offer a close parallel to the Malatesta Cantos, since they concern themselves with how patronage operated in Venice in the *cinquecento*, a century after Malatesta.

The two sets of cantos, though not adjacent, demand comparison. Now it is important to remember that Pound vastly preferred *quattrocento* to *cinquecento* art, so in comparing Agostino di Duccio and Titian, Pound is investigating what he would consider a perceptible decline. *Cinquecento*

Venice was a far richer and more substantial place than Malatesta's Rimini, so one might assume that Venetian patronage could be a model to learn from and imitate. It is for Pound a model to learn from but not one to imitate, for the thrust of these cantos, particularly Canto XXV, is to show how badly the purchasing of art in Venice was managed. He shows this – using his method of the luminous detail – by telling a story about how Titian in effect swindled the Venetian state and did not paint a painting he was commissioned to do.

What is the difference between Malatesta's Rimini and Titian's Venice? What happened in the intervening century was that art became a commodity, and its values were increasingly falsified by those of the marketplace, which led artists to practice the same kind of commercial chicanery that other businessmen do. Pound's point is that plutocratic societies such as Venice do not buy good art even though (or perhaps because) they can afford it. The most memorable expression of this comes years later in Canto XLV, the Usury Canto, but there is not anything in Canto XLV that is not between the lines in Cantos XXIV–XXVI or rather between the contrast between the bloated plutocracy of Venice (made up of both artists and patrons alike) and the enterprising, energetic creative community of Rimini (made up of artists and at least one patron alike). Moreover, the critique of plutocratic patronage in Cantos XXIV–XXVI is a critique of the practices of Pound's time as much as it is one of Venice in the *cinquecento*. The Venice of Titian's time, in its very richness and commercialization, is reminiscent of the modern world, where commercial values have thoroughly infiltrated the art world. And what Pound disdains about the relation between Titian and the government of Venice is precisely what he disdains about the art world wherever it is corrupted by commercial and market forces.

Pound's comparison of Malatesta's Rimini and Titian's Venice thus points back to the modern world, with the rich American collectors of Pound's time from Frick to Mellon playing the role of the modern Venetians. Pound had little direct contact with that world, since he was not of the same class or background. Like us, he knew this world mostly through reading the novels of Henry James. But his lack of direct acquaintance with this milieu did not prevent Pound from expressing his low opinion of it; what bothered him about American collectors was both that their money had not gone to support living artists and that in his view they had not even bought very good art. As he put it in his very first letter to Quinn, "As to fake Rembrandts etc. I carried twenty 'Rembrandts', 'VanDykes', 'Velasquez' out of Wanamakers private gallery at the time of his fire some eight years ago, ... My god! What Velasquez!" (pp. 20–21). Like the

Venetian government, the contemporary American collectors had been swindled in and by the art market. But this is not to assign all Americans (aside from John Quinn) the role of latter-day Venetians, for Cantos XXI and XXXI link one American, Thomas Jefferson, to Sigismundo Malatesta as rulers committed to promoting the arts. But where has the Jeffersonian legacy gone? Across the 1920s, particularly after Quinn's death, Pound became increasingly convinced that this Jeffersonian legacy was moribund in America but was alive and well in contemporary Italy. Specifically, he increasingly felt that Benito Mussolini incarnated the spirit of leadership and energy he praised in Malatesta and Jefferson.

The connection Pound asserted between Malatesta and Mussolini has been discussed by a number of critics, and the political ramifications of that parallel take us well beyond the scope of this essay.[9] But my point here is to stress the role the visual arts played in the evolution of Pound's political thinking. He damned the modern world in the first place for its indifference to art, and he identified an indolent and insular plutocracy as responsible for this indifference. They were the powerful few who could have made a difference for good if they wished, and it is in his vision of patronage that his critique of plutocracy, of irresponsible power, takes shape. By the time he comes to see Benito Mussolini as the Sigismundo Malatesta of our time, however, his concern with patronage has clearly modulated into something else. Yet the mark of the Renaissance princes Pound admired was their ability to gather the best and the brightest around them, a meritocracy inside an autocracy if you will, and Pound saw something of the same thing happening in fascist Italy.

Nor is this a completely idiosyncratic perception on Pound's part. One of the aspects of Italian fascism we have never fully recognized was the extent to which it identified with forms of artistic modernity. Pound's old friend Marinetti was an early and long-lasting supporter of Mussolini; Gabriele D'Annunzio was identified closely enough with fascism – despite his strained personal relationship with Mussolini – to have been called the John the Baptist of fascism; and Mussolini's Minister of Education was the distinguished philosopher Giovanni Gentile. In this respect, fascism at least in its early period offered a sharp contrast not just to the Nazi attack on cultural modernity but also to the plutocratic West Pound was in recoil from.[10] One did not find Wyndham Lewis, E. M. Forster, and Bertrand Russell – or anyone of their stature in English culture – playing important roles in the government, and Pound was convinced that separation was bad both for culture and for government. Italy seemed to offer a contrast, not just in the Renaissance but in Pound's time, and Pound's analogy between Sigismundo Malatesta and Benito Mussolini, thus, may not imply that he saw Mussolini as a patron of the arts as much as a patron of the leading minds of contemporary Italy.

In keeping with this redirection of analogies away from the visual arts, we should not imagine Pound paying any very close attention to the visual arts in fascist Italy. He kept in touch with Marinetti and visited the Venice Biennale regularly, discussing it for example in correspondence with the *New English Weekly* in 1935 (*EPVA*, 215), but that is about it. Had Pound been dedicated to the visual arts primarily for their own sake, as most of us have tended to assume, then he might have been more likely to recognize the artistic mediocrity of the fascist Futurist artists Marinetti gathered around him in the 1930s, a group with none of the intensity or talent of the initial group. But since his interest was so much less in the arts themselves than in the social status accorded the arts, he was perhaps taken in more easily by the superficial respect paid to the arts by Mussolini and his cohorts. As always, Pound's interest in the visual arts was a mirror for his own art, and the Pound who had descended to the point of being so flattered by Mussolini's offhand comment about *The Cantos*, "ma questo é divertente" (but this is amusing), to put it in *The Cantos* as the opening of Canto XLI is not likely to have critically inspected the actual production of fascist culture. It is less clear to me how he could have overlooked the pseudo-monumental ghastliness of fascist architecture, but all of this goes to show that Pound may have been right in insisting that his criticism lacked authority since he was not a master of the visual arts.

But one can look at this another way, which is to step back from the details of Pound's cult of Mussolini and ask what it was that Pound hoped for from Mussolini. What Pound hoped from Mussolini was a return to the close relation between art and power, between artists and patrons, that he found in the "vortices" of the Italian Renaissance. And we can admire Pound's attempt to break down the autonomy and isolation of the aesthetic even if we find his hopes for Mussolini radically misplaced. Pound goes back to the Renaissance as a way to sidestep and displace the dominant Romantic way of thinking about the artist and society in which there is a necessary opposition between the isolated and heroic artist and the society indifferent to genius. For Pound, the relation between the artist and society is not at all constant, nor is it always one of opposition. The right person in a position of power can call great art into being and thus in a sense can be as much a creator as the artists themselves. And this belief in the importance of the right kind of ruler for art was an important factor in Pound's cult of the great ruler which led him to support and idolize Mussolini.

The major role the visual arts played in his work thus was as a stimulus to his burgeoning social awareness. His theorizing about the importance of patronage was one step on the long road from aestheticism to fascism. This was a road taken by others of his generation, but it was left to Pound to find the most unusual route. Only for Pound could Sigismundo Malatesta be an intermediate step between Lionel Johnson and Benito Mussolini, and even as we deplore the final direction of Pound's journey, we must remain amazed by and indebted to the richness and variety of his wanderings. Pound is Odyssean here, as always, and his Odysseus is the man Dante put in hell for his impiety and intellectual curiosity. Lacking the surety of Dante's system of judgment, we both condemn and applaud but are never lukewarm. That is also the way Pound was and the way he wanted his readers to be.

NOTES

1 Among these, I would note Donald Davie, *Ezra Pound: Poet as Sculptor* (1964), rpt. in *Studies in Ezra Pound* (Manchester: Carcanet, 1991), pp. 11–209; my own *The Literary Vorticism of Ezra Pound and Wyndham Lewis: Towards the Condition of Painting* (Baltimore: Johns Hopkins University Press, 1985); Michael North, *The Final Sculpture: Public Monuments and Modern Poetry* (Ithaca: Cornell University Press, 1985); and much of Hugh Kenner's *The Pound Era* (Berkeley: University of California Press, 1971).

2 Ford Madox Ford tells about this in *It Was the Nightingale* (1933; rpt. New York: Ecco, 1984), p. 283.

3 The story of these London years have been told often enough; W. C. Wees's *Vorticism and the English Avant-Garde* (Toronto: University of Toronto Press, 1972) and Richard Cork's two-volume *Vorticism and Abstract Art in the First Machine Age* (Berkeley: University of California Press, 1976) do the best job of telling the history of Vorticism.

4 Marjorie Perloff's *The Futurist Moment: Avant-Garde, Avant Guerre, and the Language of Rupture* (Chicago: University of Chicago Press, 1986) was the first major study of Pound to move beyond Pound and Lewis' stress on how they differed from Futurism to see the fundamental affinities between Futurism and Vorticism. Chapter 5, "Ezra Pound and 'The Prose Tradition in Verse'," argues convincingly for the influence of Futurist manifestos on Pound's writing, including *The Cantos*. Marinetti appears in Canto LXXII; for a discussion of this, see my *Imitating the Italians: Wyatt, Spenser, Synge, Pound, Joyce* (Baltimore: Johns Hopkins University Press, 1991), pp. 186–189, and Robert Casillo, "Fascists of the Final Hour: Pound's Italian Cantos," in Richard J. Golsan (ed.), *Fascism, Aesthetics, and Culture* (Hanover: University Press of New England, 1992), pp. 98–121.

5 Lewis' own writing of this period is collected in Walter Michel and C. J. Fox (eds.), *Wyndham Lewis on Art: Collected Writings 1913–1956* (New York: Funk & Wagnalls, 1969).

6 Quinn's amazing art collection was broken up after his death, but Judith Zilczer's *The Noble Buyer: John Quinn, Patron of the Avant-Garde* (Washington: Smithsonian, 1978) is informative about Quinn's collection; this is a

catalogue for an exhibition at the Hirschhorn in 1978 which gathered together some of Quinn's collection.

7 Timothy Materer's introduction to *The Selected Letters of Ezra Pound to John Quinn 1915–1924* (Durham: Duke University Press, 1991) stresses this well.

8 The most thorough study of the Malatesta Cantos is Lawrence S. Rainey, *Ezra Pound and the Monument of Culture: Text, History and the Malatesta Cantos* (Chicago: University of Chicago Press, 1991).

9 These issues are explored in more depth in chapter 8 of my *Imitating the Italians*.

10 I sketch this contrast and discuss the attraction of fascism for modernist intellectuals in "Paul de Man, the Modernist as Fascist," in *Fascism, Aesthetics, and Culture*, pp. 229–241.

Marinetti's own work has begun to attract more attention in recent years. Recent discussions in English include a special issue of *Modernism/Modernity*; Andrew Hewitt, *Fascist Modernism: Aesthetics, Politics, and the Avant-Garde* (Stanford: Stanford University Press, 1993); Alice Yaeger Kaplan, *Reproductions of Banality: Fascism, Literature, and French Intellectual Life* (Minneapolis: University of Minnesota Press, 1986); and Cinzia Sartini Blum, *The Other Modernism: F. T. Marinetti's Futurist Fiction of Power* (Berkeley: University of California Press, 1996).

12

MICHAEL INGHAM

Pound and music

I am glad you have got your voice, or part of it back. I have the organ of a tree toad, fortunately, for if I had ever been able to sing "My Country tiz of Theeee," without going off the key four times in each bar, I shd. have warbled & done no bloomin' thing else – che peccato & wot a loss to litterchure. *(P/J, 65)*

This is Ezra Pound to his friend James Joyce, who was a singer with, by some accounts, the potential for a career as such. On the other hand, all accounts of Pound's voice are pretty well in accord with his own jocular assessment – raucous, nasal, a scratchy phonograph. Recordings bear this out. When we say someone has a beautiful voice we usually mean a speaking or singing organ of great resonance, power, suppleness, freedom, range, capable of an infinitude of nuance, a strangely affecting *Gestalt* through which we experience a thrill akin to the sensation of flight. But there is another kind of voice than the merely frequency producing one, another kind of singer than the paragon of high notes – certain poets, who, either naturally, or by acquisition, have the ability to compose words which prescribe the voice which should utter them, poets with an "ear," poets who never separate word from sounding tone and the percussive rhythm of consonants. The list of such poets is relatively short but Pound is high on the list. His desire to "warble and do no bloomin' thing else" was to some degree accomplished (he certainly did things else) and not to the loss, but to the inestimable gain of "litterchure," scratchy yapper notwithstanding. It is virtually impossible to understand his poetry without, to some degree, understanding his relationship to music, and why he thought music and poetry cannot drift too far apart without grave damage to both arts. "Poetry," he once declaimed, "is a composition of words set to music" *(LE,* 437). I believe that all of Pound's verse, even the prosy Adams and Malatesta cantos, as well as the Chinese history cantos in which the many Chinese names ring as gongs or tink as tuned stone slabs, are composed to a singer's imperative.

In *How to Read* and elsewhere, Pound defines this quality of "ear" without which there can be no poetry, and which in fact makes poetry different from prose, this musical quality more peculiar to the singer than to the composer. (The singer must grasp not only the purely musical proportions of his piece but the precise way vowels and consonants of language [phonemes] must be apportioned and arranged in hierarchies within the grosser, prescribed, purely musical notes of pitch and duration.) Pound felt that poets who wrote poems to be sung, the Troubadours for example, were keenly aware of this quality of hearing which produced such a synergy of *motz et son*, and that all aspiring poets should practice it. This he called melopoeia. Melopoeia is the physical part of the music we hear as verse is spoken. It should be complex, vital and specific, as all good music is, and not a smear or lull for the brain. Also vital to poetry is logopoeia, the progression of ideas, the rhythmical sequence (not necessarily linear) with which our intellect is made to move and dance. This is also a "musical" quality of poetry, and when it is integrated with melopoeia it makes the complete music of sound and sense. Phanopoeia is the mood created by imagery (*LE*, 25).

At the reading of the entire *Cantos viva voce* at Brunnenburg in the summer of 1980, it was agreed that an indispensable key to understanding the poem existed not so much in explicating or translating as in identifying the "voice" of each passage; shifts from one voice to another meant identifying the temperament and viewpoint of each voice, which in turn clarified the text. We spent considerable time making these identifications, and, insofar as we were successful, many so-called obscurities became clear. We said "voice" instead of "speaker" because we were not trying to find merely a persona, but also a condition of that persona which produced that particular utterance. One persona may have 1,000 voices. Neither by "voice" did we mean merely timbre or quality of sound, but rather the manner of articulation and stress, the quality of accentuation, pitch, tempo, intensity. In other words, interpreting *The Cantos* as a certain kind of singer would interpret a vocal score unlocked a myriad of mysteries. A certain kind of singer, as defined by Pound's rather voluminous criticism of singers in performance, from which we infer that his ideal does not display his/her voice merely as an organ of abnormal size, agility or beauty, making the voice the athletic focal point of what should be a musico-poetic event, even though audiences clamor for just such displays, and the "success" of a singer often depends on them. His ideal singer becomes the voice *for* the poet, not perhaps a voice which would even please the poet, who can rarely imagine a voice other than an idealized version of his own. The merging of poetry and music causes something much more than, and very different from, a mere combination of the two, another thing entirely. Pound, more than any other modernist, was aware of this "chemical" and synergistic process which occurs on occasion when the right mixture of poetry and music precipitates song.

Pound cultivated this awareness, transformed it into knowledge which informed his own verse. "Song clarifies writing as long as they stick together," he declared (*ABCR*, 158). This served and satisfied him up to a point. But neither investigating the music of the troubadours (even though the musicological knowledge available to him on this subject at the time was both wrong and misleading); nor falling under the spell of Dolmetsch's reconstructed whistles and keyboards, viols, lutes and the music they brought back to life – Campion, Lawes, Dowland, for example; not his voluminous concert reviewing; nor his many stimulating musical friendships; nor his theoretical intuitions and insights quite alleviated his musical itch. So, like other literati – Nietzsche, Rousseau, Burgess – he was driven to compose.

The heart of Pound's musical oeuvre consists of two operas, *Le Testament de François Villon* (1921), and *Cavalcanti* (1932). Interesting as they are in themselves, their very existence poses even more interesting questions, and perhaps answers a few. Why did he not set to music any of his own poetic texts? He marks a section of Canto LXXXII "libretto." In his translation of the *Women of Trachis*, he indicates instrumentation. He punctuates one of his recorded readings – at Harvard in 1939 – with interestingly anagogic timpani strokes. He expresses admiration for the *motz et son* boys (the troubadours) and some of the Elizabethans who composed music for their texts. And to a very large degree, Pound satisfied his compositional need in creating his own verse. He composed musical scores consisting entirely of words, complete somehow for his own ear. It must have been frustrating for him, the most virtuoistic translator of his time, to pronounce Villon untranslatable. He had to give Villon life, to make him new, to place the thief in his own personal canon as he had Divus, Homer, Li Po, Arnaut Daniel, the poet of the Seafarer, Propertius, and Confucius. He could not have translated Villon (or chose not to) either by creating a New English poetry, as he did for the Chinese poets of *Cathay*, by giving him a modern tongue as he did Propertius, or by transposing forms as he did (much later) in the Confucian Odes. So he put an idea into action (much more efficiently, it seems, than when he got it into his head to bruise and mangle hunks of marble in the name of sculpture) and with a little help from his friends notably Agnes Bedford, composed an opera. It seemed to settle the Villon problem for him.

The opera itself is a curiosity, oddly prophetic of the noisy neo-medievalism of Peter Maxwell Davies, but with a disdain for harmony, even a quasi-cacophonous one, so intense is the focus on melody alone. Murray Schafer, whose *Ezra Pound and Music* is the masterly and indispensable volume for anyone interested in the subject, describes a conversation with Pound in which they "spoke of Arab music, which interested him because of its rhythms and unharmonized melodies" (*EPM*, 465). This rings a bell. Whether or not Pound imitated or indeed had any specific knowledge of Arabic music, his opera is very reminiscent of it. A number of knowledgeable composers have spoken very highly of *Le Testament*, among them Virgil Thomson, George Antheil, of course, and some seventy years after its première, Ernst Krenek, who on hearing its last scene remarked on its "curious vitality." Thanks to the indefatigable composer/conductors Robert Hughes and Reinbert de Lieuw, we have not one, but two marvelous recorded interpretations of two different versions of the score.

Cavalcanti is Pound's other opera. If he used music to "translate" the otherwise untranslatable Villon, why then did he need to compose music for a poet he so thoroughly and tirelessly "brought over" into English? He wanted all of his Cavalcanti translations to appear in a dual-language version with the original texts on facing pages. Many of the poems exist in multiple versions, indicating perhaps a kind of untranslatability, or at least a sense of incompleteness.

The opera would remain lost had not Robert Hughes exercised his perspicacity and skill in collating the manuscript in Olga Rudge's possession (prepared for an aborted BBC broadcast in 1933) with materials housed in the Beinecke Rare Book and Manuscript Library to create a complete score and parts for the world premiere in San Francisco on March 28, 1983 (program notes for first performance by Robert Hughes). My own impression on hearing this one performance of the opera is that it is composed roughly in the same hyper-melodic, almost oriental style of *Le Testament*, except that it is rhythmically less driven and complex. Without published opera scores, however, all commentary is likely to remain impressionistic.

Pound certainly knew musical notation – to a degree, even the neumes of the troubadour manuscripts (*EPM*, 6, 7). He played the bassoon, though no one has ever accused him of playing it well. Yet even "highly trained" musicians discover, when they compose, how difficult it is to write down what the mind's ear hears, or to know what they write down will sound like in performance. We assume that George Antheil, Agnes Bedford, Olga Rudge, and perhaps others "helped" Pound to realize his scores. (Olga Rudge told me that his dictation was always very precise.) It would be very interesting to know the exact nature and extent of this help, not to denigrate (especially in an age when a Hollywood composer writes a tune, then sends it out to be "orchestrated") or question the validity of Pound's compositions, but to understand more completely the processes of his transforming poetry to song. Such knowledge might in turn help us to understand more fully why these two poets, Villon and Cavalcanti, compelled him to compose music.

In addition to the two operas, Pound composed some violin pieces for Olga Rudge, lively and rhythmically compelling, like Olga Rudge herself. Robert Hughes in his notes for the premiere of *Cavalcanti* says that Pound had planned a third opera using the poetry of Catullus as libretto.

Ned Rorem's introduction to the Da Capo Press reprint of Pound's *Antheil and the Treatise on Harmony* is a wise, witty, tolerant, critical yet admiring commentary on an odd book (even for Pound). Pound's assertion that any pitch or chord can be followed by any other pitch or chord provided that the interval between them is right has several resonances, however, which Rorem does not explore. Any of the free atonalists *c.* 1920 would have agreed with Pound's idea (one thinks of Franz Schreker). Certainly it is a notion in sympathy with the aesthetic of *vers libre*. It is also a justifiable reaction against the harmonic thickness of late romanticism (though Boulez has shown us in his illuminating recordings that we are perhaps wrong, that Wagner is really a "horizontal" or contrapuntal composer.) But his prescription for just organic proportion is more resonant with the Confucian idea that the central tone from which all others are measured, if ill chosen, will foment chaos in society, and, if correctly chosen, stimulate order and harmony.

Pound's idea is that the *only* element of music is rhythm and, therefore, measure – even pitch, which is a frequency related to other frequencies – even form, which is an elongated rhythm – must evolve from the "absolute rhythm" which governs all musical relationships. (A look at the first page of Charles Ives' *Universe Symphony* reveals a startling congruence with Pound's great bass, a cosmic understanding which is virtually the same.) This is dangerously close to Schenker's reductive analytical theory, which attempts always to find the germ from which any musical composition is derived by various prolongations and adumbrations, although there is a different germ for each composition and not an absolute one for all of music. That would have been an odd theory for the poet whose musical analogue is Charles Ives, whose *Cantos* is the embodiment of the tradition of American inclusivism along with Melville's *Moby Dick* ("but a draft of a draft"), Whitman's *Leaves of Grass*, Ives's *Universe Symphony*, Henry Brant's spatial oratorios. They defy systematical analysis because they subsume systems, eating and digesting them like so much fodder. These works include everything but the kitchen sink, and then add the kitchen sink. All of them defy both Schenkerian analysis and deconstruction. How do you deconstruct a landslide, especially one onto which anyone may toss a rock or two? But Pound's idea had organic possibility to it, which mocks the hermetic. Harmony can be as chaotic as Nature herself.

Pound saw in the young George Antheil the energy of the Futurists, the hardness of the Vorticists, the defiance of the Dadaists. Alas, in spite of his boosting, Antheil degenerated into a witty Hollywood party-goer schmoozing for film contracts. Virgil Thomson lamented that George Antheil, "the bad boy of music," grew up to be a good boy. Katherine Ruth Heyman, a more perspicacious evaluator of new music (champion of Ives and Scriabin) said, "don't make a mountain out of an Antheil." Pound was clearly wrong to have seen him as superior to Stravinsky.

Pound's criticism under the pseudonym of William Atheling, and later in Rapallo under his own name, is often spectacularly wrong (Of all of Liszt's faults, stupidity is not one, nor is his alleged lack of knowledge of "chords" [*ANT*, 44]). But he is passionate in his support of clarity and understanding in performance, the lack of pretense many musicians are guilty of, and of liveliness and imagination in choosing repertoire, always steering performers and listeners away from the hackneyed. Many of his observations have the deadly acuity of a lynx in mid-leap ("If he [Sullivan] had had anything better than Gilbert to set, he would presumably have ruined it" [*EPM*, 187]). One doesn't, however, read the criticism for information, but for the animated thrusts Pound makes in an attempt to drive performers from their entrenched attitudes, and to stimulate listeners' perception of values other than thundering and bellowing.

Pound's "warbling" (i.e., composing verse) was very nearly throttled about 1908 by his devotion to one of his many musical muses, in the form of Katherine Ruth Heyman. He came within a hair's breadth of dumping poetry to manage the career of this brilliant pianist so prominent in the propagation of the works of Scriabin in this country. Faubion Bowers, Scriabin's marvelous biographer, paints a charming portrait of her (*Paideuma*, Vol. 2, No. 1) which shows how Pound's enthrallment was quite inevitable.[1] As a ten-year-old child appearing at a first piano lesson with a local teacher, on offering to play Liszt's eleventh Rhapsody, she said, "Do you want me to play the notes, or play it as it is?" One simply has to fall in love with that spirit. This propensity to manage, to instigate, to serve the talents of his musical friends was, however, not extinguished entirely when he failed to follow a career as a musical impresario. It quite significantly surfaced again in the Rapallo years when he made himself responsible for his town's musical well-being by organizing a series of innovative, didactic concerts which provided the type of programming he had so emphatically urged as William Atheling in London.

Through Katherine Ruth Heyman, Pound met the pianist and some-time composer, Walter Morse Rummel. Rummel was an acquaintance of Debussy, who approved of his playing. This was unusual, because Debussy was a grouchy critic of pianists. Pound was ambivalent towards Debussy, critical for the most part of his texts, and apparently unaware of the revolutionary treatment of words in *Pelléas et Melisande*: finding the most apt musical environment for each word, and eschewing the repetitive thematic formulae of opera composers of the past – an attitude which one would think Pound, as an admirer of (*le mot juste*) Flaubert, and propag-ator of sculpted and dense *vers libre*, as preferable to Edwardian jingles, would have found sympathetic. The foggy, mushy Maeterlinck libretto must have made him blind to it. At any rate, any positive feelings Pound might have had about Debussy must have been due to Rummel. As a composer, Rummel tended towards the rather sloppy emotional style appropriate to the Parisian salon, and most of his settings for voice and piano, including a number of early Pound lyric poems, today sound quaint, unremarkable, dated, and a little embarrassing. There is one masterful exception – "The Return." This poem stands out among Pound's early lyrics as a harbinger of the hard modernist style which renounced Yeatsian romance and re-volutionized English verse for generations to come. Rummel captures its essence as no modernist's setting could, because he embodies the romanti-cism the poem rejects. There is a painful loss expressed in its prophecy as Rummel finds the right horrified, excited musical atmosphere with none of the usual attenuating softness and conventionality.

Rummel's collaboration with Pound in setting *Neuf Chansons de Troubadour* in a collection quaintly titled *Hesternae Rosae* (1913), is a curiosity, valuable mainly for Pound's virtuoso translations, all the more impressive for having to fit existing tunes. Several conditions dictated that this effort would botch their intended revival of the music of the trouba-dours. They labored under a misconception about how the rhythms of the songs were to be executed. Jean Beck and Pierre Aubrey, two musical scholars who reportedly nearly fought a duel over who was the first to uncover a theory which has subsequently been proven to be dead wrong, caused Pound and Rummel to set the poems to what they thought were modernizations of ecclesiastical medieval rhythmical modes. That the trouba-dour melodies were to be sung to these rhythmical modes was the discovery Aubrey and Beck both claimed. That there is no evidence for this theory has been convincingly demonstrated by Hendrick van der Werf. No one can definitively say exactly how to interpret the songs rhythmically, but the best guess seems to be very freely, in the manner of Gregorian Chant with the text alone determining the hierarchy of durations.[2]

However that may be, the Rummel settings of Pound's translations, imprisoned in a folksy triple meter, thump along lustily, crudely savaging in the manner of a peasant dance, these delicate and nuanced texts. That nineteenth century behemoth, the grand piano, also lends its hob-nailed, percussive kicks. However, the Pound translations, sung to the troubadour tunes in a freely articulated rhythm and unaccompanied, yield a music of refinement. For some reason Pound did not complete his translation of Arnaut Daniel's sestina *Lo ferm volers*. At least it was not published in *Hesternae Rosae*. (Half a sestina is like – what? – half a chess game? Peter Whigham, in homage to Pound, completed shortly before his death, Pound's unfinished translation using the end-word scheme prescribed by Pound's first half.) Pound also produced singing translations for the American tours of the charismatic *chanteuse*, Yvette Guilbert. And he produced a singing translation of Massenet's *Cinderella* (never used) at the request of Thomas Beecham.

Though his interest in the ancient troubadour music was stimulated by his investigations of its texts, it was Arnold Dolmetsch and his "reconstructed century" which turned him towards the pre-baroque music of England, and canonized for him Lawes, Jenkins, Campion, and others. This music and this poetry was proof that both arts benefit from intimate contact. And no doubt the furniture maker in Pound was attracted to the lovely reconstruction of old instruments. Dolmetsch spawned what has become a thriving industry. Pound treasured his Dolmetsch clavichord until his death. The pianist Agnes Bedford, who helped Pound with the compositional notation of his operas, also collaborated with him in yet another transcription of troubadour tunes for voice and piano for which he supplied the English words in much in the manner that he had for Rummel's *Hesternae Rosae*.

Gerhart Münch, who played the complete Bach *Well-Tempered Clavier* for Pound's Rapallo concert series, and who accompanied Olga Rudge in the Mozart violin sonatas, is also the Gerhart who comes forth out of Phlegathon (out of the war) with music in his luggage (LXXV/450). The musical notation which follows the few beginning words of Canto LXXV is a transcription for violin of one of the vocal parts of Clement Janequin's five-part madrigal *Chant des Oiseaux*, which exists in several versions. It was played at one of the Rapallo concerts in 1933; Münch may have been the accompanist.

The famous madrigal is a quasi-cacophonous, almost Ivesean, concatenation of bird-calls. It is, of course, impossible to gather any inkling of the full force of the madrigal from one part, but this is how Pound remembered it and immortalized it in *The Cantos* (had he heard Olga Rudge practising it? [see also *ABCR*, 54]). There would be a touching performance of this fragment as it appears in *The Cantos* by the child prodigy, the violinist Paul Zukofsky, for Pound as he chafed in the cage of St. Elizabeths. Paul was brought to St. Elizabeths by his father, Louis, Pound's loyal friend and supporter, who began his own great epic "*A*," with "A round of fiddles playing Bach." The two Zukofskys (whose struggle is poetically chronicled in the elder's novel, *Little*) provided a moment of beauty for the imprisoned Pound, much as the appearance of Munch with music at St. Ambrogio must have ameliorated the chaotic destruction of the raging war in 1942.

Pound said that his *Cantos* was constructed in the form of a fugue (*SL*, 294). Some commentators have evolved complex interpretations of the structure of *The Cantos* which rigidly adhere to a nineteenth-century theoretical definition of the form of the fugue. "Form" is the troubling word here. They may well be right, but their arguments are unconvincing. If, by "fugue," Pound meant that "themes" are presented simultaneously, are developed, recur and are interrupted by "episodes" of unrelated thematic material, while distinct "voices" adumbrate themselves by staggered entrances, then I agree that *The Cantos* is, indeed, fugal, if not a "fugue." Neither *The Cantos* nor the fugues of, say, Bach adhere to a prescribed form with a fixed key structure, schematic development or return. The fugue as taught in college theory courses or required for examinations may well do so. The *form* of the fugue is not, however, so prescribed and, therefore, not a form which can always be predicted. The procedure or the rules of counterpoint, may, on the other hand, be fairly strictly prescribed according to the period.

Nevertheless, the revolutionary poetic methods used by Pound in *The Cantos* can be described accurately as contrapuntal or even "fugal." It has been frequently pointed out, for example, that in Canto I there exists a "counterpoint" of at least five simultaneous voices:

1. the eleventh book of Homer's *Odyssey*;
2. its Latin translation by Andreas Divus;
3. Pound's English translation of Divus;
4. the metrical and rhythmical procedures of "The Seafarer";
5. the beginning of a modern epic.

Perhaps there are more. The beginning of Canto II – "Hang it all, Robert Browning" – might be said to be an "episode" interrupting a multi-voiced counterpoint with a "chord" of juxtaposed images, the "developed" theme returning briefly with "And poor old Homer . . . ," followed by the "countertheme" of Ovid's *Metamorphosis*. One must always be cautious with analogies, although understanding *The Cantos* as fugal is helpful at a certain level.

That *The Cantos* can be perceived in the same way as a piece of music is axiomatic. One should read *The Cantos* as one studies a score, and not always from the beginning. Musicians do not necessarily learn difficult pieces from the first bar. Sometimes they will pick out the thorniest sections and grapple with them first. Or sometimes they will ease themselves into the piece by first examining those passage they readily understand. Only gradually, and in no specific order, do they come to see the logic of how each fragment achieves its meaning by its micro-form and by its placement in the larger form, and eventually are able to unfold the piece in performance from the beginning.

Donald Davie, following Pound, advises to begin reading in *The Cantos* anywhere and to keep reading, not bothering too much with what we do not understand. Later on, and the more we do understand, the more that which we don't understand, and the more any structure which may be there, will become clear to us. Starting "from the left edge" and insisting that we understand every nuance – or even the literal meaning – of every word of the text will not get us very far in *The Cantos* (at least I cannot imagine a reader so intrepid). This is evidence that *The Cantos* reveals itself in non-sequential fragments which, taken together, can be seen to unfold in time as music does, though our memory imposes an order on our perception which is not linear. Davie's advice would be poor if applied to Dante's *Comedy* or the *Aeneid*, but it is prescient for *The Cantos*. Pound's advice to read *The Cantos* as a fugue is well-taken only if we do not try to force the poem into a pre-ordained form, but perceive its contrapuntal and non-linear simultanieties.

Robert Hughes suggests that Pound, independent of any knowledge of Anton Webern's music, used the technique of *Klangfarbenmelodie* (the pointillistic use of a different instrumental "color" or timbre on each successive note of a melody) in his *Testament*. This is no doubt true, though I have been unable to perceive it aurally. Though I see no similarity whatsoever between Pound's musical compositions and Webern's, I do very strongly perceive in fragments of *The Cantos*, especially the later ones, the very qualities of sound and of musical tension or atmosphere evoked by Webern's music, not only *Klangfarbenmelodie*, but sculpted silences (it is as though the sounds are formed only to make us more aware of the silences they frame); extreme compression of utterance (the force and weight of large forms rendered in the space of very few notes or words) – whole perceptions, as opposed to developed thoughts.

Webern's sketches show that he had fully developed ideas which he would begin to notate, then break off. He would repeat the procedure numerous times, writing exactly the same fragment, breaking off in exactly the same place, unable to go on, sometimes for years, until finally he would suddenly, inexplicably, finish the piece completely. One feels that some of Pound's last fragmentary lines are the result of a similar process of vision struggling not to be betrayed by utterance. Whether or not Pound's *tempus tacendi* was a physical or mental aphasia, or a choice, it was important in drawing our attention to the medium in which music (or poetry) exists, and its scarcity. Silence. Could it be that since modernism both poetry and music have languished because of the oppressive omnipresence of sound, of music which is not meant to be listened to? We would "let the wind speak" but it can't be heard over MTV and car radios whether they are playing Mozart or rock and roll. Silence has lost its voice. We can no longer hear it. We no longer welcome it. There is no music except as it exists between silences. Without silence there can be no music. Is this the message of Pound's silence?

The twin pillars of American culture in the twentieth century are Ezra Pound and Charles Ives. Each dominated by innovation, by the creation of forms which show the way for generations to come. And if they have been momentarily eclipsed by more reactionary mechanics, it is only a fad, a chic political statement, the ever-present worship of the simple, the ignorance that nature, and thus art, are more complex than we can ever know. Ives and Pound both demonstrated that to seal art off from the life which produces it might well create "perfect" works, but it is always "perfection" achieved at the cost of vitality.

Stravinsky said that Ives ate the whole cake of contemporary music before any of the rest of us had a chance to sit at the table. This is not merely praise of innovation, but a recognition of his unanalysable fecundity of imagination. Pound, too, can be said to have created an attitude towards poetry and indeed all of the arts which supplies energy which others can benefit from. Several people who had contact with Pound during his St. Elizabeths years have told me independently that they are still operating, some forty years later, on the energy they received in their brief encounters with him. Ives is without question the *only* American composer who might be termed "great."[3] No poet has left a body of work as indelible as Pound's. This greatness is also uniquely American, inclusive in the tradition of Whitman, resourceful as the pioneers, creating solidly built structures out of whatever is at hand, recognizing both "high" and "low" cultures, and creating without pretense.

Pound and Ives share a long list of common traits. Both expressed themselves in speech and in writing in a populist "cracker-barrel" style designed to repel any hint of pretentiousness when talking of artistic subjects. Both grappled with the economic malady of being artists in a society which rewards only those artists who fluently conform, Ives by becoming a millionaire insurance executive, extinguishing his own compositional impulse in the process, Pound by trying to educate the world to an economic system in which artists are seen to have a value measurable in monetary terms, losing at times some clarity of thought in the process. Both were deeply traumatized by the great war, and both were moved to try single-handedly to end the system which creates wars, Ives by proposing a constitutional amendment requiring a popular referendum before war could be declared, Pound by demanding an economic system which would eliminate the possibility of profit by war. Both were capable of being physically stimulated by an issue or idea to the point of complete exhaustion and exacerbated intolerance.

Both composer and poet juxtaposed the vernacular and "high art" as elements in a multilayered "collage," or counterpoint, or ideogrammic technique. Ives included extramusical autobiographical elements as a part of the "sound" of his music, such as "wrong" notes, faulty ensemble, simultaneous tunes. Pound composed musical sounds into his poetry which command tempo, articulation, emphasis, pitch and voicing. Each saw his art as something indispensable to culture, yet each entered into silence which seemed to deny the value of his own work and expresses a kind of regret. Both were prolific in innovations which revolutionized their crafts. Each lived to see his patriotism disintegrate into disillusionment.

Ives and Pound were intent on bringing music and poetry closer together. Ives believed he could express with musical sounds alone, a flower growing in a crack in a stone wall, thus creating poetry. Pound created poems which are like musical scores in form and sound, thus creating music. Both presented to the world almost hyper-masculine personae, but each was capable of the utmost in delicacy, sensuality and refinement. Both used quotations extensively as elements of composition, creating aggregates of historical and personal pasts resulting in personal canons which excluded the hackneyed. Ives hated Mozart, Pound, Milton. Both he and Pound wanted to bring in a "new sensibility." Ives wanted you to "stand up and use your ears like a man." Pound wanted to get rid of "slither."

Pound's rejection of Edwardian verse, and the Latinate verse of Milton, his turning for models to the ancient poems of the troubadours, to Cavalcanti and Villon, to Anglo-Saxon and Chinese has an analogue in music. The centuries of Western Art Music known as the period of "common practice" – roughly the late baroque to late romanticism, from Bach to Mahler (the practices which the great modernist composers – Schoenberg, Stravinsky, Bartok and Ives either extended past the breaking point, or subverted by innovation until all possibility of a musical *lingua franca* was shattered) is the period described by Ernst Krenek in his *Music Here and Now* as the period of "symmetrical scanning," an apt name for the verse of the period as well. This is the music (and by extension, verse) before and after the common practice period he refers to as "freely articulated." In the latter, the articulations of text and music interact only with each other, while in the former they must conform as well to a background hierarchy predetermined by a prescribed meter. The free articulation concept encouraged highly prescribed procedures and forms (the isorhythmic motet, the sestina, serialism), while symmetrical scanning is more sympathetic to ambiguous forms and procedures, and to textures which are readily recognizable (sonatas, symphonies, the iambic foot, rhyming couplets, opera).

One great struggle in the music of the twentieth century has been to determine an aesthetic value for varying degrees of order. The aleatoric music of John Cage and the "total serialism" of the 1950s sound somewhat alike. When ordered sound becomes so highly ordered that the order can no longer be perceived by the ear, it resembles chaos. Pound, along with modernist composers, was willing to risk being accused of creating chaos in his *Cantos* (and perhaps in his operas) in order to galvanize, to "probe a spot on the brain which has not yet been de-sensitized," to create a radiant vortex. Even though to the neophyte *The Cantos* at first glance is chaotic, there is order. It is the order of the voice – the voice of song, of conversation, of contemplation, of exclamation, of ritual, of business and politics. Just as Ives heard a new music in the multiplicity of voices at Sunday School hymn time, each class singing a different tune, tempo, key, words, all at the same time, Pound created in his *Cantos* a simultaneity of voices, each rising to prominence in fragments amidst a seeming chaos of other voices, but always pure in its own music and purpose, forming together a gigantic universal symphony as exhilarating as a mountain range.

NOTES

1 Faubion Bowers, "Memoir within Memoirs," *Paideuma*, 2 (1973), 53–66. Also see in the same volume, George Antheil, "Why A Poet Quit the Muses," 3–6 and three essays on Pound's opera, "Le Testament De Villon," 7–22.
2 See Alejandro Planchart, "Introduction," in J. B. Beck, *The Music of the Troubadours*, trans Timothy Wardell (Santa Barbara: Ross-Erickson Press, 1979).
3 The greatness of Ives has recently been elaborated in Jan Swafford, *Charles Ives: A Life with Music* (New York: Norton, 1996).

13

TIM REDMAN

Pound's politics and economics

Ezra Pound made his first political statement when he was only seven years old. Reacting to the news that Grover Cleveland had defeated Benjamin Harrison in the presidential election of 1892, he threw his child's rocking chair across the room. Such a combination of rage and reaction would typify his approach to politics over his lifetime. But at that age his opinions were not yet his own, and his violent act was undoubtedly motivated by family discussions he had overheard. In his autobiography, *Indiscretions* (1920), he speculated:

> that a child of six [sic] should lift up its miniature rockingchair and hurl it across the room in displeasure at the result of a national election can only have been due to something "in the air"; to some preoccupation of its elders, and *not* to its own personal and rational deductions regarding the chief magistracy of the Virgin Republic.
>
> In this case it may have been that I was genuinely oppressed by the fear that my father would lose his job and that we would all be deprived of sustenance.[1]

As Pound remembered it, Homer Pound's job in the assayer's department at the US Mint in Philadelphia was not covered by the 1883 Pendleton Civil Service Reform Act, which dealt only with offices with more than fifty employees. But there may have been other family matters bearing upon Pound's temperamental flare-up.

Under Harrison, Congress had passed the Sherman Silver Purchase Act as well as the Sherman Antitrust Act, actions dear to Western populists. And James G. Blaine, an old enemy of Pound's grandfather, Thaddeus Coleman Pound, after serving as Harrison's Secretary of State, fell out with the president, whose renomination he challenged. Without the support of Blaine and other key Republican leaders, Harrison lost to Grover Cleveland, the incumbent he had successfully challenged in 1888.

Cleveland's second term of office saw the panic of 1893, a severe economic depression, and the repeal of the Silver Act. To understand Pound's first political act, as well as his subsequent economic and political beliefs, we must go more profoundly into his family background and the history of the United States in the second half of the nineteenth century. When we do that, we see that Pound's core political philosophy, instead of being eccentric or irrational, largely conforms to a set of populist beliefs deeply rooted in American history.

Pound once boasted that he "could write the whole social history of the United States" from his family annals.[2] While such a claim might seem exaggerated, there is some truth to it. The figure of Pound's paternal grandfather looms large in the history of his adopted state of Wisconsin and even in national politics during the decades following the Civil War. Thaddeus Coleman Pound was born of Quaker stock in the town of Elk, Warren County, Pennsylvania on December 6, 1832. He first came to Wisconsin in 1848 and in the spring of 1856 he settled in Chippewa Falls. Thad Pound was prominent in the early history of the Republican Party. He took a leading part in early railroad building in northwestern Wisconsin and also pursued business interests in logging, bottled spring water, and retail sales, making and losing several fortunes. He was a member of the Wisconsin State Assembly, Lieutenant Governor, and he served three terms as a member of Congress from 1876 to 1882, refusing to accept nomination for a fourth term. Thaddeus Coleman Pound ("TCP" as Pound referred to him) was mentioned as a possible Secretary of the Interior in the cabinet of James Garfield, but Blaine, who became Garfield's Secretary of State, blocked his appointment. When Blaine ran for the presidency in 1884, Thad Pound bolted from the Republican Party and supported the successful Democratic candidate Grover Cleveland, taking Wisconsin with him. In 1888, believing that Cleveland had not made good his promise of Civil Service reform, Thad Pound supported General Harrison.

Although he faded from national view, "the Governor's" views on national political questions were solicited by the Wisconsin press throughout his lifetime. In 1896 he opposed William Jennings Bryan's free silver platform, blaming the economic difficulties of the time on the democratic administration of Grover Cleveland, and endorsing William McKinley. Thad Pound believed in the *de facto* bimetallic system of the time, with its approximately equal ratios of gold and silver, because of the necessity of gold to international trade and the need for a stable currency.[3] His pro-tariff views show that he was aligned with the Western, "Main Street" wing of the Republican Party, and opposed to the Eastern, "Wall Street" wing with their laissez-faire ideology which predominated during the period 1865–1900. The Western agrarian radicals, as represented by Wisconsin Senator Robert M. La Follette, in alliance with Eastern progressivists such as Theodore Roosevelt, came to the fore in the party after 1900.[4] Thus Thaddeus Pound was associated with a wing of the party that advocated vigorous government intervention in the national economy. In many respects, Pound would follow in his grandfather's footsteps.

Pound's mother's side of the family had even more reason to boast of its ancestry, and he received a vivid sense of his family's place in US history from his mother Isabel. His maternal grandmother, Mary Parker Weston, was the daughter of Mary Wadsworth, of the distinguished Wadsworth clan, the first member of which came over on the Lion in 1632. Pound heard tales of the Wadsworths from his mother, and read about them in Horace Andrew Wadsworth's *Two Hundred and Fifty Years of the* WADSWORTH FAMILY *in America* (1883). Pound's paternal aunt, Frances Wessells Weston ("Aunt Frank"), also took an interest in politics, and "was in the habit of invading Washington at regular intervals."[5] She traveled there at least every four years for the Inaugural Ball; she had danced with President Grant and after she hung up her dancing shoes continued to travel to the capital to shake hands with the newly elected president, even, Pound recalled, "Cleveland's, 'who drank.'"[6] Thus from both sides of the family, Pound inherited a sense of participation in United States' politics, a sense of connectedness to the power structure, of speaking to the nation's leaders on a first-name basis.

Pound's first published poem was a limerick on the defeat of William Jennings Bryan by William McKinley in 1896, showing a prescient interest in national politics for a boy his age:

> There was a young man from the West,
> He did what he could for what he thought best;
>> But election came round;
>> He found himself downed,
> And the papers will tell you the rest.
>
> Aged 11 years E. L. Pound, Wyncote[7]

Despite his grandfather's support of McKinley, the poem shows a certain sympathy for Bryan, and reinforces our sense of early populist leanings in Pound's politics. As Alec Marsh has observed: "More than is generally realized, family annals, especially Thaddeus Coleman Pound's 'Scrapbook,' were an important source for the poet."[8]

Despite these early influences, Pound was no populist in his early adult years, but an aesthete and an elitist, a believer in art for art's sake, a poet convinced of the superiority of his vocation and the triviality of any mundane matter. Pound's political education came about slowly, in London during the decade of the 'teens, through his association with the influential

English left-wing journal, *The New Age,* and its editor A. R. Orage. Pound wrote on literary topics for it, and later under pseudonyms, art and music criticism. But his association with the *New Age* circle, with its Fabians and Guild Socialists, had a gradual influence on Pound's thinking, introducing him to the British tradition of social thought exemplified by Carlyle, John Ruskin, and William Morris.[9]

Orage's integration of the arts and politics had as its leading theme the oft-quoted clause "economic power precedes political power." Thus Pound's gradual political education was at the same time an economic education, though devotion to art was still his paramount concern. The onset of World War I made the aesthete's posture more and more ridiculous. When Pound's close friend, the sculptor Henri Gaudier-Brzeska, was killed in action at Neuville St. Vast on June 5, 1915, Pound was shaken to his core and forced to reevaluate his thinking about the relation of the artist to society. That and Orage's persistent efforts, including introducing Pound in 1918 to the unorthodox economist Major C. H. Douglas, led to an important shift in Pound's thinking, announced in his review of Douglas's *Credit Power and Democracy* in *Contact,* 4 (Summer 1921): "The symbolist position, artistic aloofness from world affairs, is no good now."

Pound himself marked the change as occurring during the period of his first acquaintance with Douglas: "1918 began investigation of causes of war, to oppose same," he wrote in his brief autobiographical preface to the New Directions edition of his *Selected Poems* that appeared in 1949. Orage was an early champion of Douglas and serialized his first two books, *Economic Democracy* and *Credit Power and Democracy,* in the pages of *The New Age.* Orage even allowed his own "Notes of the Week" columns for February 6 and 13, 1919 to be written by Douglas, an unusual display of confidence. Douglas was essentially an underconsumptionist, who believed that an inadequate supply of money and an overproduction of goods, led to the periodic depressions that had plagued capitalist societies since the nineteenth century. Douglas's views do not surprise us greatly today, but to economists of his time, they were seen as fringe attacks on the two ironclad laws of orthodox economics: Say's Law of Markets and the law of supply and demand. Both essentially state that in the manufacture of a good or the delivery of a service enough money is put into circulation through costs and wages to enable people to purchase the goods and services produced, or that supply creates its own demand. In Canto XXII, Pound wrote about a meeting he witnessed between the eminent and at the time still orthodox economist John Maynard Keynes and Major C. H. Douglas:

And C.H. said to the renowned Mr. Bukos:
"What is the cause of the H.C.L.?" and Mr. Bukos,
The economist consulted of nations, said:
                              "Lack of labour."
And there were two millions of men out of work.
And C.H. shut up, he said
He would save his breath to cool his own porridge,
But I didn't, and I went on plaguing Mr. Bukos
Who said finally: "I am an orthodox
"Economist." [. . .]
And Mr. H.B. wrote in to the office:
I would like to accept C.H.'s book
But it would make my own seem so out of date.
                    Heaven will protect
The lay reader. The whole fortune of
Mac Narpen and Company is founded
Upon Palgrave's Golden Treasury.   (XXII/101–02)

Here Pound exposes how Keynes (Bukos) is so caught up in the orthodox
economics of his time that he must give a completely illogical answer to
Douglas's question about the "H[igh]. C[ost]. [of] L[iving]." This damage
is similar to John A. Hobson's [Mr. H.B.] refusal to accept Douglas's
views, an action that recalls to Pound his own early attempt in proposing
a new anthology of English poetry "to replace that doddard Palgrave,"
Francis Turner Palgrave (1824–1897), editor of the Victorian best-seller
*Golden Treasury of the Best Songs and Lyrical Poems in the English Lan-
guage*. Pound proposed to do a new anthology to reflect the new sensibility
in English poetry, but he made the proposal to Palgrave's publisher and
was told "don't you know that the whole fortune of Mac Narpen &
Company is founded on Palgrave's *Golden Treasury*?" So his project was
turned down. The point is obviously how entrenched interests prevent the
circulation of new ideas, but another point to be noted is how much
Pound identified Douglas's struggle to reform economics with his own
struggle to reform poetry.

The problem that Douglas attempted to remedy was that increases in
productivity and the need for profit would lead to the eventual inability of
a capitalist system to clear its markets; this inability led to dumping and
layoffs, resulting in trade wars and depressions. To counter this problem,
additional money had to be introduced into the system, and Douglas proposed to do this through the payment of an annual Social Credit dividend
to all citizens. Douglas called attention to how easily the government could
accomplish this, explained by Pound in Canto XXXVIII:

> "I have of course never said that the cash is constant ["]
> (Douglas) and in fact the population (Britain 1914)
> was left with 800 millions of "*deposits*"
> after all the cash had been drawn, and
> these deposits were satisfied by the
> > printing of treasury notes.   (XXXVIII/190)

Faced with the problem of financing the First World War, Great Britain did not hesitate to print treasury notes. In the extreme national emergency of a war, the state took it upon itself to create credit. The problem that Douglas, Orage and Pound were addressing was that at that time war was the only enterprise for which a government would go into debt. Under normal conditions, there was no agreed upon method for the state to expand the amount of money in circulation to match and encourage economic growth, resulting in periodic depressions. The prevailing notion that money needed to be backed by gold locked the industrial nations into fierce competition for foreign markets and a boom and bust cycle for which war seemed the only solution. And arms merchants were always there to profit from the only state-subsidized activity, an activity that they therefore encouraged by selling arms to all possible belligerents. Again, in Canto XXXVIII:

> Said Herr Krupp (1842): guns are a merchandise
> I approach them from the industrial end,
> I approach them from the technical side,
> 1847 orders from Paris and Egypt. . . .
> > orders from the Crimea [. . .]
> > > At Sadowa
> > Austria had some Krupp cannon;
> > Prussia had some Krupp cannon.   (XXXVIII/191)

For Pound the causes of war were to be found in the economic system, and economic reform was the only way to prevent a future world war.

Pound and his wife Dorothy moved to Paris in 1921, maintaining their principal residence there but traveling extensively in Italy. In 1925 they moved to Italy, leasing a seafront apartment in the fashionable resort town of Rapallo, east of Genova. Ezra and Dorothy had long been attracted to Italy, and the politics of Benito Mussolini's new fascist government had little if anything to do with their move. Pound's political interests during the 'twenties were directly related to three issues affecting artists and his own freedom of movement: "the passport nuisance," the inadequate copyright laws of the United States (particularly the failure of the USA to sign the Bern Convention), and article 211 of the US Penal Code which, in Pound's words, confused "smutty postcards, condoms, and Catullus."[10] The latter two laws were a particular nuisance to Joyce's *Ulysses* as Samuel Roth had published an unauthorized version of that book in 1926 *and* it was banned in the United States. And Pound's interest in economics as an historical force certainly had an impact on his newly reworked edition of *The Cantos* as it appeared in the 'twenties, incorporating a number of economic themes. But his major turn towards politics, economics, and Italian fascism was yet to come.

Three events drove Pound back to serious study of economics in the early 1930s. By 1932 it was clear to everyone that the economic downturn that had begun with the Wall Street Crash of 1929 was not a temporary phenomenon, but that a worldwide depression of unprecedented scope and severity had begun. The Great Depression caused severe hardship in the United States, Franklin Delano Roosevelt defeated Herbert Hoover in 1932, and people were looking for new solutions. There was widespread distrust of bankers, economists, and politicians. As Joseph S. Davis has remarked, "the stage was set for the rise of charismatic political leaders [and] bold or even rash experimentation."[11]

Douglas's Social Credit doctrines had diagnosed the principal problem causing the economic collapse (inadequate monetization), and his movement gained new followers and attention. Pound's efforts on behalf of Douglas thus received favorable attention. The clearest evidence of Pound's turn from the more limited social concerns affecting artists of the 'twenties to the larger economic (and, for Pound, following Orage, therefore political) concerns of the 1930s comes in Pound's letter to Senator Cutting of March 20, 1931, in which Pound completely ignores Cutting's efforts on behalf of a revised copyright bill and focuses his attention instead on Senator Smith Brookhart's populist speech opposing the nomination of Eugene Meyer to the Federal Reserve Board.[12]

The second event that influenced Pound's new course in the early 1930s was the return of A. R. Orage. Orage had quit *The New Age* and left England in the autumn of 1922 to study with Gurdjieff. He returned to England in 1932 and founded the *New English Weekly*, and he and Pound resumed their old relationship. With a sympathetic editor willing to publish his economic and political journalism, Pound was to contribute more than two hundred items to the *New English Weekly* during the 'thirties.

The third event that was to have a decisive impact on Pound's political thinking was his meeting with Mussolini on January 30, 1933. Pound's companion, Olga Rudge, had given a private concert for *il Duce* on February 19, 1927, and was greatly impressed with the charismatic Italian leader. Pound was overwhelmed by Mussolini's charm and intelligence, and his subsequent references to the dictator are marked by an uncritical acclaim that resembles hero worship. News of Pound's interview was published on the front page of the Rapallo newspaper, bolstering his status in the town. The immediate effect was galvanizing: Pound started two books, *The ABC of Economics* and *Jefferson and/or Mussolini*, in February 1933.

Jefferson and/or Mussolini was not published until April of 1935; Pound claimed that forty publishers rejected it.[13] The book is an apologia for Italian fascism, but its principal focus is not on the fascist system but on Benito Mussolini. This focus reflected not only Pound's vast admiration for the man, but also the fascist regime's carefully cultivated myth of *mussolinismo*, the benevolent leader who was always right. Corollary to that belief was Pound's idea that fascism was a viable system of government only for Italy, that it was not for export. Similarly, Pound praises Lenin in *Jefferson and/or Mussolini*, but he did not believe that communism would work outside of Russia. The Anglo-American tradition of the rule of law is hastily discarded by Pound in his need to believe in his hero's omniscience. Great Britain and France are mentioned occasionally in the book, invariably in a critical manner. Pound in 1933 was ambivalent about Franklin Delano Roosevelt. Later he would be highly critical of Roosevelt, never understanding that the public works programs of the New Deal were identical in nature to Mussolini's public works programs that he praised. Jefferson, when treated at all, is made over into an American Duce; his prominent position in the title of the book was probably meant by Pound to startle American readers into favorable consideration of Italian fascism. Not that such consideration was needed at the time he wrote the book. As John P. Diggins has convincingly shown, the view of Mussolini that was held by most Americans was favorable at the time the book was written.[14] International public opinion shifted drastically, however, after the outbreak of Italy's war with Abyssinia in October 1935, shortly after the book was published.

Pound's political philosophy, was "very much influenced by his reading of Jefferson and Adams" and "is very close to an eighteenth-century ideal and praxis. Political movements, in this view, come into being through the understanding, will, and direction of individual[s]" who together orchestrate change.[15] Success is determined by the virtue of the individuals involved. Failure results from a defective *directio voluntatis*, not the will to power, but the direction of the will, a phrase that "brings us ultimately to Confucius and Dante."[16] No matter what the legal system of government, the ideal government should be one "composed of sincere men willing the national good."[17] Although such a rationalist view of politics has its appeal, it fails in that it locates all evil as a result of individual depravity or faulty volition, and cannot account for the all-too-common situation of bad results coming from good intentions. Furthermore, Pound's system needs villains, and it would eventually involve him "in search of the imaginary international malefactors who deliberately caused social collapse for personal profit."[18]

The next two major influences on Pound's developing ideas about economics and politics were his discovery of the writings of Silvio Gesell, a disciple of Proudhon, and his correspondence and friendship with Odon Por, both beginning in 1934. Gesell's principal work, *The Natural Economic Order*, first appeared in 1906, with a fifth section being added in 1911. By 1929 it was in its seventh edition. Gesell was an early advocate of what came to be known as the quantity theory of money, the view that is accepted today. Money, following this view, is not based on a valorized commodity such as gold, but is merely issued by the state according to the needs and the productive capacity of the nation. Pound first became aware of a Gesellite scheme when he heard of a monetary experiment in Woergl, a small town in Austria near Salzburg. To counteract the Depression, the mayor issued village scrip according to Gesell's recommendation: stamp scrip, where one needed to affix a stamp equal to 1 percent of the note's value each month to maintain that value. People were thus encouraged to spend freely, and Woergl prospered, paying the salaries of 1,500 workers for public works using the scrip. When the Austrian National Bank found out about the scheme it was brought to an end.

Pound was attracted to Gesell's stamp scrip because it was an easy, comprehensible, practical mechanism with which to remedy the economic problem diagnosed by Douglas. But despite Pound's efforts to convince him, Douglas resisted any incorporation of Gesellite ideas into his Social Credit movement. Pound's reading of Gesell represented a major step forward in his development as an economic thinker. Pound, who had also read a great deal of Karl Marx's *Kapital* and admired Marx's passion for social justice, adopted Gesell's critique that Marx never understood the nature of money. Like Proudhon, Gesell was sympathetic to the plight of labor, but believed that the best way to social reform was through monetary reform. "Proudhon (and Gesell) opened the way whereby the state could be expected, in times of crisis, to accelerate the productive capacity of the nation through the creation of capital at an expanded rate."[19] In 1935, John Maynard Keynes acknowledged Gesell's importance, calling him "an unduly neglected prophet . . . whose work contains flashes of deep insight."[20] Gesell, like Pound, might be considered a proto-monetarist.

The Hungarian Odon Por first wrote to Pound in April 1934, introducing himself as "an old New Age-Orage man . . . trying to propagate Social

Credit here."[21] Though Pound and he would not meet until the 1930s, Por had lived in London in 1912, serving as special correspondent for *Avanti* and contributing to *The New Age*. He defined himself in a letter of March 28, 1935: "Syndicalist. Guild Socialist. NOT fascist. Free lance." Por was a prolific writer and a frequent contributor to fascist journals. His correspondence with Pound was a rich one, and Pound relied upon Por's assessment that Mussolini's fascist regime was on its way towards adopting Social Credit policies. Por also helped Pound make contacts with journalists and fascist officials in Rome, and later encouraged him to offer his services to Rome Radio.

The final important influence on Pound's political and economic thought was his deepening understanding of Chinese and the writings of Confucius. Pound had first become interested in Chinese poetry through his work as the literary executor of Ernest Fenollosa in the early 1910s, and he continued to work as a student and translator of Chinese for fifty years. During the period of the late 1930s and particularly during the Second World War, Pound became convinced that the philosophy of Confucius, along with economic reform, offered the best hope for an enduring and just social order, and he worked to translate Confucius into Italian and publish his work in Italy.

Although he would continue to write and make radio speeches during the Second World War, probably the most complete synthesis of Pound's political and economic thought can be found in his *Guide to Kulchur*, written in 1937. The scope of the book is astonishing as Pound ranges over 2,500 years of human history, asserting that its two causes are "economic and moral" and that "at whichever end we begin we will, if clear headed and thorough, work out to the other."[22] Denouncing rapacity as the primary force in the West, Pound calls for a return to a Confucian concern for the entire social order. But by the time of its publication (1938) the West was heading for another global war.

Pound's antisemitism, which had been sporadically in evidence since the publication of "Patria Mia" in 1912, grew in virulence along with that of the Italian regime. With the passage of the racial laws in 1938, the onset of the Second World War in 1939, and the foundation of the Salo Republic, Pound's antisemitic outbursts grew in viciousness and frequency until the end of the war, when public awareness of the Holocaust forced a realization of the horrific consequences of hateful speech. This antisemitism makes it painful to consider at any length Pound's wartime radio speeches and journalism.

Pound did write further economic and political tracts of merit: an important series of articles for the prestigious journal *Meridiano di Roma* (a later selection of which would appear in the book *Orientamenti*, 1944); a bilingual edition (Chinese and Italian) of Confucius's *Ta S'eu* or *Studio Integrale* with Alberto Luchini (1942), and an Italian translation of Confucius's *Unwobbling Pivot* (*L'asse che non vacilla*, 1945); an Italian translation with modifications of *Jefferson and/or Mussolini* (1944); and three economic pamphlets, *L'America, Roosevelt e le cause della guerra presente* (America, Roosevelt, and the Causes of the Current War, 1944), *Oro e Lavoro* (Gold and Work, 1944), and *Introduzione alla natura economica degli S.U.A.* (Introduction to the Economic Nature of the United States of America, 1944). *L'America, Roosevelt e le cause della guerra presente* was printed March 23, 1944. Roosevelt and the Second World War are hardly mentioned. The booklet gives Pound's version of US economic history with an emphasis on the nineteenth century. It views the war as part of "a millenial war between usurers ... and whoever does an honest day's work with his hands or with his brains." Pound stresses his principal point, that "only the state has the right to issue credit and that this right was usurped by private citizens, 'usurers.'"[23] The "worldwide *usocracy* or the congregation of high finance" provokes a continual series of wars. *Oro e Lavoro* was sent to be printed in March 1944. It treats many of Pound's familiar concerns: that the usocracy foments war to drive nations into debt and then profits from that debt through currency manipulation. In late May 1944 Pound wrote another pamphlet, his *Introduzione alla natura economica degli S.U.A.*, largely a rehash of some of the chief points of his previous work. By this time his attention had almost completely shifted to Confucius.

Pound also made later discoveries, of the work of Brooks Adams around the beginning of the war, and of Alexander del Mar, during the period he spent in St. Elizabeths. But although some of his later writings contain interesting elaborations of Pound's economic and political thought, by the time of *Guide to Kulchur* his basic ideas are in place. Although he would later apologize for his antisemitism, he never recanted his support for Mussolini and the fascist regime. Indeed, his *Pisan Cantos*, along with being perhaps the most astonishing work of poetry of this century, can be read as a defiant *apologia* for the good that he saw in Italian fascism.

During his confinement (1946–1958) in St. Elizabeths Hospital in Washington DC, where he was placed after having been found unfit to stand trial on the charge of treason, Pound was largely reticent about political and economic issues, pleading ignorance of current affairs. Through his circle of regular visitors at the hospital, he came into contact with the white supremacist John Kaspar, and the resulting public embarrassment probably delayed his release for a year. Upon his return to Italy in 1958, he was photographed giving a fascist salute when his ship docked at Naples on its way to Genova, but he again refrained from any public comment about politics to the press. When the British fascist leader Sir Oswald Mosley visited Rome in 1961, Pound attended a meeting in his honor and was applauded sitting on stage, but again he declined to make any comment. During the last ten years of his life (1962–1972), Pound was in a severe depression. He rarely spoke, was filled with remorse and regret for his work, and suffered a variety of physical ills.

What are we to make of Pound's political and economic views? Are they mistaken, as his loyalty to Mussolini's fascist regime would suggest to most readers? Do they represent an abandonment of his American heritage? And what relevance to his poetry did his long study of economics have?

For Pound, an epic was a poem containing history, and no one could understand history without understanding economics. In this sense, Pound resembles Marx. Pound's understanding of economics and his *Cantos* are inextricably intertwined: no reader can hope to understand one without understanding the other. And despite Pound's often eccentric formulation of his views, his principal point, concerning the nature of money and credit, is one that is accepted today.

Pound's support of Italian fascism remains problematic. As Giano Accame points out:

> In the strict sense Ezra Pound was never a fascist . . . he didn't like uniforms; he wasn't a militarist; on the contrary, he was a pacifist . . . he scorned the Nietzschean will to power; he hated violence; in all his life he never raised a hand against anyone; he contradicted the climate of heroic exaltation, presenting war as the product of usurers; he did not encourage imperial dreams for the Third Rome; he loved America (he considered himself a true American patriot) even if he questioned the Establishment; he didn't see fascism as a model for export to Anglo-Saxon countries; and his spirit was as much elite as libertarian, intolerant of bureaucracies, universities, censorship . . . like Giovanni Gentile . . . he mistook fascism for a free system.[24]

Yet he was a supporter of Mussolini, and he was indicted for treason for his radio broadcasts from Rome during the Second World War, though the indictment was later dropped.

Accame denounces the kind of facile understanding of Pound that has remained in circulation for decades, leading a recent biographer to conjure up this fantastic scene:

> the neo-Fascist Movimento Sociale Italiano. . . . held a May Day parade, wearing jack-boots and black armbands, displaying the swastika, shouting antisemitic slogans, and goose-stepping. Among those photographed at the head of the parade was Ezra.[25]

Accame writes: "Pure legend. Even the most documented biographies have the credulity of their prejudices."[26] Of course, no such photograph exists.

Victor C. Ferkiss has argued that a coherent set of political beliefs among people such as Huey Long, Reverend Charles E. Coughlin, Gerald K. Smith, and Pound could be characterized as an American fascism.[27] According to Ferkiss, these beliefs had their roots in American populism:

> Both despaired of achieving a just society under the joint banners of liberalism and capitalism. The attacks on finance capitalism, the hatred of social democracy and socialism, the belief that representative democracy is a mask for rule by a predatory economic plutocracy, and that a strong executive is essential for the creation and preservation of a middle-class society composed of small independent landowners, suspicion of freedom of the press and civil liberties generally as the shields and instrumentalities of the plutocracy, ultra-nationalism, antisemitism (both latent and active), and, finally, a peculiar interpretation of history which sees in events a working-out of a dialectic which opposes the financier and the producer – these populist beliefs and attitudes form the core of Pound's philosophy.

This summary is a particularly apt attempt to show the roots of Pound's political and economic beliefs in American populism.[28] It is of further interest due to the violence of Pound's reaction to it. Pound's commentary on Ferkiss's article can be seen at the Lilly Library at Indiana University. Some of these notes are of interest:

> Ferkiss lies ... in his first line, from the cultivated ignorance of a N[ew]. Deal propagandist, or brain conditioned hireling.
> E.P. was a critic of fascism, and opponent of the historic blackout the roosveltian falsification of news, and the illegal encroachment of power by the executive. . . .
> Pound's political principles are those of John Adams and the U.S. Constitution. Mr. Ferkiss may lie from ignorance but he lies ...
> Mr. Ferkiss has probably NOT read E.P. trans/ of Confucius which define the basis of his philosophy. Freedom of the press precisely what is NOT functioning. . . .
> Living in Europe from 1908 onward, E.P. knew nothing of anything which Ferkiss calls american fascism. . . .
> E.P. has NEVER suggested that any ism is the only.[29]

Ferkiss continued with another article in which he further refined his arguments. Populism, for Ferkiss, was a generic term denoting

> not merely the People's party, or Populism properly so-called, but such closely allied movements as the Greenback party, the Bryan free silver crusades, La Follette [Wisconsin] Progressivism, and similar manifestations

of primarily agrarian revolt against domination by Eastern financial and industrial interests . . .

The class struggle throughout America history has traditionally been waged not by laborers against employers, but by debtors against creditors . . . A struggle began for a government which would regulate credit . . . This struggle reached its climax in Bryan's campaign of 1896.[30]

Ferkiss continues, quoting William Jennings Bryan:

"When we have restored the money of the Constitution all other necessary reforms will be possible". . . .

This, then, was the most important plank in the Populist economic platform – the restoration to the people of their "sovereign power" to control money; private control is held to be a violation of the Constitution and a usurpation of a governmental function.[31]

To some degree, certainly, Ferkiss is reading the history of American populist thought through the lens of Pound. Yet his analysis is surprisingly accurate. Although it does not completely explain the extraordinary range of Pound's economic and political writing, populist concerns do coincide with a great number of Pound's principal points, and give us the best overall explanation of his positions. Additional evidence is provided by Pound's family background, which Ferkiss did not know, both Thaddeus Coleman Pound's various crusades and positions, and the tension that existed between Pound's Western father Homer, whom he favored, and his Eastern mother Isabel. Thus to a surprising degree those early heated discussions over the Pound family table formed the unconscious background and emotional motivation for much of his subsequent writing on social issues. American populism forms a necessary though not a sufficient background for Pound's political and economic views.

NOTES

1 Ezra Pound, "Indiscretions or, Une Revue de Deux Mondes," in *Pavannes and Divagations* (New York: New Directions, 1974), p. 32.
2 "Indiscretions," p. 6.
3 Newspaper letter of Thaddeus Coleman Pound dated October 31, 1896, and in the TCP scrapbook at Brunnenburg.
4 Eric Foner and John A. Garraty (eds.), *The Reader's Companion to American History* (New York: Houghton Mifflin, 1991), p. 932.
5 *Indiscretions*, p. 18.
6 *Ibid.*, p. 9.
7 *Jenkintown Times-Chronicle*, November 7, 1896. Reprinted in Humphrey Carpenter, *A Serious Character: The Life of Ezra Pound* (Boston: Houghton Mifflin, 1988), p. 36n.
8 Alec Marsh, "Thaddeus Coleman Pound's 'Newspaper Scrapbook' as a Source for *The Cantos*," *Paideuma*, 24, 2 & 3 (Fall & Winter 1995), 163.

9 For an illuminating discussion of that influence, see Mary Ellis Gibson, *Epic Reinvented: Ezra Pound and the Victorians* (Ithaca, NY: Cornell University Press, 1995).

10 Letter to Senator Bronson Cutting, November 8, 1930. In E. P. Walkiewicz and Hugh Witemeyer (eds.), *Ezra Pound and Senator Bronson Cutting: A Political Correspondence 1930–1935* (Albuquerque, NM: University of New Mexico Press, 1995), p. 38.

11 Joseph S. Davis, *The World Between the Wars, 1919–1939: An Economist's View* (Baltimore, Md.: Johns Hopkins University Press, 1975), p. 296.

12 Walkiewicz and Witemeyer (eds.), *Ezra Pound and Senator Bronson Cutting*, p. 54. I have discussed that speech and Pound's reaction to it in great detail in my essay "An Epic is a Hypertext Containing Poetry: *Eleven New Cantos (31–41)* by Ezra Pound," in Lawrence Rainey (ed.), *A Poem Containing History* (Ann Arbor, MI: University of Michigan Press, 1997), pp. 117–149.

13 I have dealt extensively with this book in my *Ezra Pound and Italian Fascism* (New York: Cambridge University Press, 1991), chapter 4, "The Turn to Fascism," from which the following is summarized.

14 John P. Diggins, *Mussolini and Fascism: The View from America* (Princeton, NJ: Princeton University Press, 1972), especially chapter 4, "Mussolini as American Hero."

15 Redman, *Ezra Pound and Italian Fascism*, p. 112.

16 Pound, *Jefferson and/or Mussolini*, p. 16.

17 *Ibid.*, p. 95.

18 Redman, *Pound and Fascism*, p. 117.

19 *Ibid.*, p. 132. I have considered the importance of Gesell in depth in chapter 5, "The Discovery of Gesell."

20 Keynes, *The General Theory* (New York: Harcourt, Brace, Jovanovich, 1964), p. 353.

21 The Por letters are at Yale's Beinecke Library.

22 Pound, *Guide to Kulchur*, p. 31.

23 Redman, *Pound and Fascism*, pp. 245–247. Information about this period is taken from chapter 8, "The Republic of Salo' and Left-Wing Fascism."

24 Giano Accame, *Ezra Pound Economista* (Rome: Edizioni Settimo Sigillo, 1995), pp. 50–52.

25 Carpenter, *Life*, p. 874.

26 Accame, *Ezra Pound Economista*, p. 192.

27 Victor C. Ferkiss, "Ezra Pound and American Fascism," in *The Journal of Politics*, 17, 2 (1955), 173–197. This and a later article arose out of his PhD dissertation for the Department of Political Science at the University of Chicago, "The Political and Economic Philosophy of American Fascism," June 1954.

28 For an alternative view of this subject, see Jean-Michel Rabaté, "Pound populiste?" in the *Revue Francaise d'Etudes Américaines*, 12, 31 (February 1987), 41–52.

29 Lilly Library, Pound mss. II. Correspondence, Pound, Ezra.

30 Victor C. Ferkiss, "Populist Influences on American Fascism," in the *Western Political Quarterly*, June 1957, p. 352.

31 Ferkiss, "Populist Influences."

14

HELEN M. DENNIS

Pound, women and gender

Hugh Kenner's *The Pound Era* characterizes Ezra Pound as the driving force, the dynamo, the vortex which propelled, revitalized, energized the era of high modernism which began sometime around the beginning of the twentieth century and which survived World War II before becoming part of literary history. There are many different and differing accounts of modernism, and Peter Nicholls's *Modernisms* (1995) makes this clear in its very title, but one could argue that high literary modernism of the sort Pound promulgated and claimed to invent, neglected or misunderstood the significance of gender, and indeed relied on doing so. If this is the case, one could also argue that Pound's texts articulate a strenuous and at times exaggerated masculinity, and concomitantly, enunciate a range of profoundly traditional versions of the feminine.[1] This may seem odd, given that women feature so prominently in Pound's personal and professional life and as subjects in his writing. This essay investigates Pound's relationship with some of the significant women in his life and analyzes those moments in his poetry which inscribe the archetypal feminine while recalling individual women.

Of first consideration is the cultural value or status of the feminine in the context of early modernism. This differs from the question of the political position or social status of women at that time. Although the questions are related, the answers may be contradictory. The interrelation between the sexual and textual politics of high literary modernism and the phenomena of the New Woman is undoubtedly complicated since the two movements occupy the same historical period and on occasion share the same tea-rooms, drawing rooms and editorial offices, but they seem to exist in mutually unrecognized or unappreciated discourses. Pound's modernist texts replace notions of art as mimesis, substituting a discourse of critical inquiry which suggests radical valuations and significations of the materials of culture and tradition. His aesthetic implicitly assumes that the art object does not reflect society but, rather, constructs meaning and value for a particular society, rewriting the historical record to reshape the past according to artistic judgment.

At the very moment when *The New Freewoman* was putting the case for woman's suffrage, and when new women were attempting to break the mould of Victorian gender formations, masculine modernists were still working with a traditional aesthetic of the feminine. Nicholls argues that the "Men of 1914" saw the work of immediate precursors, such as the Decadents, as degenerate, as embodying the feminine and as associating the production of art with a feminine value system; and that they, therefore, felt and demonstrated an artistic necessity in their own work to re-establish a set of masculine values which would inform their modern(ist) production. However, this rejection of the degenerate identification with the feminine does not mean that the feminine has no function in their work. Despite the appearance of avant-gardisme in Pound's work, the function of the feminine in his poetics and his aesthetics draws on deeply traditional and conservative models of the archetypal feminine and of the feminine ideal. While Pound worked with some of the most culturally radical women of the Modernist era, his poetry encodes and enunciates conservative configurations of the feminine. There are evident contradictions between his work as promulgator, collaborator and colleague to literary women such as H.D., Gertrude Stein, Marianne Moore, and his sense of the ideal feminine. There is, too, a sense of an insoluble enigma when one contemplates the details of his personal life: the marriage to the painter, Dorothy Shakespear; the life-long alliance with the musician Olga Rudge; the other affairs which leave elusive traces in the poetry.

At the start of his career Pound traveled to Europe and in January 1909, newly arrived in London, he met Olivia Shakespear at the American, Mrs. Fowler's salon for young musicians and poets. She invited him to call for tea along with the Australian poet Frederic Manning at the end of that same month. Through Olivia Shakespear and through her daughter, Dorothy, Pound was not only introduced to Gaudier-Brzeska and Wyndham Lewis, but he also gained access to the London literary circles and to the artistic elite of pre-war London. Mrs. Fowler and Olivia Shakespear were only the first of many women who would, one way or another, become patrons, facilitating Pound's career as poet and man of letters. Others include Dora Marsden and Harriet Shaw Weaver, ediors of *The New Freewoman: An Individualist Review*, later to become *The Egoist*, which H.D. edited for a while during the First War; Harriet Monroe, editor of *Poetry: Chicago*; Alice Corbin Henderson, *Poetry's* sub-editor; Margaret Anderson and Jane Heap, editors of *The Little Review*; Caresse Crosby, whose Black Sun Press published Pound's *Imaginary Letters* in October 1930; Ethel Moorhead, joint editor of *This Quarter*. There were also a number of women artists: sometimes the relationship began as teacher/pupil, as with Iris Barry, but adopting the role of mentor arguably stimulated Pound in his own formulations and poetic output. Other women artists who facilitated and enriched his oeuvre, as well as benefited from the exchange themselves, include May Sinclair, Amy Lowell, Mary Barnard, and Marianne Moore. There were also a number of musicians with whom Pound collaborated, including Agnes Bedford and his life-long companion Olga Rudge.

Women facilitated his literary career in many ways, not all of them yet fully documented. One must mention Mrs. Mary Fenollosa, whose decision to entrust her late husband's papers to Pound resulted in *The Chinese Written Character as a Medium for Poetry* and his translations from the Noh; Sylvia Beach, whose bookshop, Shakespeare & Company, was a center of modernism in Paris in the 1920s; acquaintances who facilitated introductions both of Pound to other artists and of his works to potential editors, such as Bridget Patmore, Djuna Barnes and Caresse Crosby. And then there were the women who inspired his poetry: novelists, artists, poets and musicians, all muses and conjecturally more: these include Mary Moore of Trenton, H.D., Frances Gregg, Dorothy Shakespear, Margaret Cravens, Bride Scratton (Thiy), Olga Rudge, Marcella Spann, Sheri Martinelli. Older women, who mentored Pound, include Katherine Ruth Heyman, as well as Olivia Shakespear and Florence Farr. One should also pay tribute to his daughter, Mary de Rachewiltz, dedicated to the accurate transmission of *The Cantos* (her bilingual Italian translation has been acclaimed for its accuracy) and author of a memoir of her father which sympathetically captures the spirit of his work.

The impression is that Pound's relations with women at the start of his poetic career were multifarious if not ambiguous. Yet gender formations and sexuality seem to have complicated his perception of women and contributed to their poetic representations which associate them with an imaginary neo-Platonic landscape or with their role as divine intermediary or mantra. His sources for this conception were Provençal poetry, Renaissance love poets and Rossetti. Yet he sometimes perceived their "new Woman" modernity as intrusive and therefore dealt with it in a somewhat jokey fashion. The strong-minded women Pound collaborated with were struggling to establish their own autonomous identity, while Pound at times was still trying to ensnare them in amorous subject positions. Pound's "Tempora," written in 1913–14, wittily illustrates the confusions arising in a time of rapid transition in the definition of gender roles. Pound's effect on women may not always have been advantageous to their survival and happiness, but his tendency, and the tendency of the women themselves, seems to have been to assume that it was their responsibility to find the strategies to cope with this ambivalent eroticism and, if possible, use the experience to their advantage.[2]

But Margaret Cravens, a young American pianist living in Paris, was unable to withstand the tensions. She was instrumental in supporting Pound at the start of his career when her financial patronage made a crucial and enabling difference, which the details of their friendship, first published in 1988, confirm.[3] Describing Pound's artistic and financial position in London in 1909–10, the editors, Omar Pound and Robert Spoo, write: "[Pound] was still poor [. . .] Then he met Margaret Cravens who, on the basis of one or two day's acquaintance, offered him such a large sum of money that he was able to put everything out of mind except finishing *The Spirit of Romance* and getting on to new projects" (*EP/MC*, 6). The arrangement was kept secret. Pound did not disclose his source of income to his parents nor to Dorothy's parents. We can only conjecture whether he told Dorothy or not; there is no published evidence to confirm that he did.

There seems to have been considerable ambiguity about Pound's relations with a number of women at this time, if not throughout his life; and although the cause of Margaret Craven's suicide in 1912 is usually adduced to be Walter Rummel's marriage, we cannot rule out the possibility that her despair was increased by Pound's unofficial engagement to Dorothy. After all, H.D. had followed him to Europe in 1911, possibly still assuming that the relationship was "on" in some sense or other. Mary Moore of Trenton, to whom *Personae* (1909) was dedicated, also followed him to Europe, and Dorothy, who did not get a volume dedicated to her until 1911, and then along with her mother, found herself having to entertain Pound's previous women:

> My dear
> What am I to do about Miss Mary Moore? I dont know her address – nor any reason why I am to ask her to tea. Will you tell her the New Century Club on Tuesday at 4. ocl? (*EP/DS*, 92)

Dorothy hardly ever complained; doubtless the so-called "aloofness" was her preservation, but one could read veiled criticism of Pound's sexual mores in her letter of May 8, 1912:

> In answer to yours. No – of course, I can't manage Paris – as you say – a "strange female" and then I'm *here!* [. . .] You see if we were officially engaged it might do – But as Father "won't recognize" our engagement –
> You might thank "Margaret" very much though for proposing to invite me – it's extraordinarily good of her anyway. And don't talk to too many of your best friends about me. I have had to suppress M. Moore.

> I am glad the Hamadryad is not lost. Is "Richard" preferred to W.R. at
> present? (*EP/DS*, 96)

While still in the States, Pound had both conducted an intense, passionate friendship with Hilda Doolittle ("the Hamadryad") and also flirted with Mary Moore; the friendship with Margaret Cravens was ambiguous enough for the editors of their letters to suggest the possibility that "Margaret asked Ezra to marry her and received a negative response of some sort" (*EP/MC*, 113).

Despite the discretion of Dorothy's discourse, a careful reading of her letters to Pound reveals moments of anger and frustration, not only with the length of their unofficial engagement, but also with her having to abide by the constraints of social conventions, whereas Pound was able to continue to range freely, both socially and geographically. One cannot help but feel sympathy for her, and for her generation of women: they were expected to maintain Victorian moral values themselves, and at the same time be subjected to an explosion in sexual behaviour. The tensions for these women, who had been schooled in the manners dictated by late nineteenth-century etiquette, must have resulted in confused and painful identities. They had internalized injunctions on female decorum, compliance and submission; their formation included an emotional dependency on the provident male, and they were still expected to act as functions of the male psyche, as the Other to his desires, developments and self-definitions. Dorothy Shakespear survived the experience with dignity.

But is it surprising that Margaret Cravens, alone in a Paris flat, giving possibly two-thirds of her income to a charismatic young poet and fellow American – only to be told of his unofficial engagement to the daughter of a London novelist famous for her brief, passionate liaison with Yeats, only to be told that Walter Rummel, the object of her concealed, romantic attachment for some considerable time had become suddenly engaged to her former piano teacher Thérèse Chaigneau – calmly took her life after playing the tune that Pound and Rummel had written for her? What seems surprising is that so few modernist women in similar circumstances did not take their own lives but largely survived and in many cases contributed to the production and transformation of art in multiple ways.[4]

Evidently Margaret Cravens aspired to be such a transformative patron, but it is unclear what she expected in return. What Pound gave her, along with his gratitude, was the role of divine messenger or angel:

My Dear Miss Cravens:
[. . .]

You have given me so much – I dont mean the apparent gift – but restorations of faith. Your "largesse" in all that a forgotten word should mean! – and then the apparent gift comes, as a sort of sign from beyond that my work is accepted. It couldn't have come unless there was some real reason, behind us all, for the work to go on unfettered.

As for myself – and what it means to be free to attend to nothing but vowels and quantities, and the rest of the human part of the least known Technique of any of the arts; I sha'n't try to say what it means. I haven't quite found out yet. I suppose it means that I shall see the earth, the external apparent earth as a place in which I have some sort of a place provided – shall see material things other than hostile – am I writing nonsense voluminously?

(EP/MC, 12)

Did Margaret Cravens give too much and demand too little in exchange? Or was Pound incapable of returning such love? Certainly she seems to have boosted Pound's ego along with his bank balance; and although we may read as rhetoric the transcendental sense of her gift coming "as a sort of sign from beyond that my work is accepted," yet time and again we find that the woman's role for the poet is that of angelic messenger from the divine beyond, confirming for the male artist the preordained validity of his individual enterprise. Characteristically, the woman functions as an intermediary with the "beyond," which it will be the poet's life's work to translate into song, while at the same time her function is to provide the material conditions which will make his artistic production possible, by relieving his anxieties about his immediate contingent circumstances.

Pound's poetic response to Margaret's death expresses itself as an extraordinary transformation; extraordinary to me as reader, perhaps not extraordinary in the way the poet was envisioning phenomena at this stage of his career:

His Vision of a Certain Lady Post Mortem

A brown, fat babe sitting in the lotus,
And you were glad and laughing
    With a laughter not of this world.
It is good to splash in the water
And laughter is the end of all things.   (EP/MC, 124)

The poem is an irreverent lambaste of Margaret Cravens's belief in "[a]ll the beauty of eternity" (EP/MC, 116). Pound's jokiness about "such damp white-petaled beatitude" reads as a way of covering up any sense of guilt he might have experienced (EP/MC, 124). She recurs in The Pisan Cantos, in a remarkably similar image, which again associates the aestheticized, dead woman with religious iconography:

And Margherita's voice was clear as the notes of a clavichord
tending her rabbit hutch,
                        O Margaret of the seven griefs
who has entered the lotus   (LXXVII/491)

Margaret is still envisioned thirty years later as having entered the
lotus upon the occasion of her suicide. The significant transformation is
the way in which the poet's memory has associated this pianist, Margaret,
with the Tyrolean girl whom Mary de Rachewiltz grew up with. One
could describe this figure as a complex image cluster, combining simile and
metonymy. It is as much the contiguity of the women's names as the
unspoken musical association which connects Tyrolean ragazza with rabbit, Margherita with an American in pre-war Paris piano student, Margaret.
And, of course, this unit of a larger poem could be extracted from its
context and be read as an Imagist poem not untypical of the genre which
H.D. and Pound were formulating, composing and promoting around the
time of Margaret's death. In both instances the women are associated with
a musical clarity and a purification of daily life.

Hugh Kenner, in a reminiscence of Dorothy Pound, published after her
death, states, "I do not know who the girl was that Ezra Pound married"
and goes on to ask, "What did a young woman from an 'advanced' house-
hold [. . .] expect of life in those early years of the century?[5] The letters
between Dorothy and Ezra which cover the four years of their courtship
suggest that Dorothy was both dignified and discrete, and that she was
the intellectual and emotional equal of Pound. However, whereas H.D. had
to recover herself from their engagement in order to become an author,
Dorothy, as a visual artist, did not seem to suffer the same conflict between heterosexual desire and artistic autonomy. Evidently her preference
was for the more traditional role of wife, whereas H.D. would have preferred artistic collaboration and mutual inspiration. Pound appears to have
also been discrete in his inclusion of Dorothy in poetic texts. Her presence
is not an overt one, and even when she is celebrated or alluded to the poet
covers the traces. "Doria" (first published in *The Poetry Review* in February
1912) appears to be a poem to Dorothy which captures something of the
mood of their 1911 letters:

Δώρια
[*Doria*]

Be in me as the eternal moods
        of the bleak wind, and not
As transient things are –
        gaiety of flowers.

> Have me in the strong loneliness
>   of sunless cliffs
> And of grey waters.
>   Let the gods speak softly of us
> In days hereafter,
>   The shadowy flowers of Orcus
> Remember Thee.   (CEP/193)

Of interest is the way in which Dorothy, and the gifts she brings to the future marriage, is associated with a type of mythological landscape and the type of transcendental aspirations it evokes. In "Doria," if Doria is an approximation of Dorothy's name as well as the Greek word for gift, the poet addresses "Doria"/Dorothy, rather than speaks through her persona. A mutual act of giving is implied: "Be in me [...]" and "Have me [...]"; there is a reciprocity of gesture in the difference between the first and second imperative. This mutual giving and taking of the permanent (eternal moods) leads to the allusion or invocation to the "gods": the coming together of male and female will invoke the gods' speech – not silence. This sentiment is thus a reworking of the line from Propertius, which Pound renders as "My genius is no more than a girl" in "Homage to Sextus Propertius." The final two half-lines seem to contradict the rest of the poem, however:

>   The shadowy flowers of Orcus
> Remember thee.   (P, 1990, 213)

Orcus is the infernal regions, the underworld; eventually the shadows of transient things will be all that remember Doria (Dorothy), and the rest is presumably *hubris*, or the hopelessly absurd expression of human existential desire for strong permanence, for identification with the perdurable elements in nature and culture. Dorothy's role as wife, confirmed by the symbolic giving of the bride during the wedding ceremony, will be to be the "rock" but, finally, she is but another avatar of the Kore. However elusive and enigmatic this poem is, the impression the images conveys is of emotional sincerity in contrast to the uneasy, dismissive, parodic tone of his obituary poem for Margaret.

The evidence of their letters indicates that the extended period of courtship and unofficial understanding between the two, against the wishes of Dorothy's parents, instigated a process of refinement of desire, which one might describe as sublimation rather than a pandering to what Pound calls in *The Spirit of Romance* the "philoprogentive." Such a process would be analogous to Pound's interpretation of medieval Provençal *trobar clus* (hermetic or closed composition) which he viewed as evidence of a cult of erotic mysticism (*SR*, 95). Certainly there is a very strong drive to rechannel energies into artistic considerations prompted by the seemingly endless separations and deferrals. One consequence of this seems to be a strongly felt sense of place, and a displacement of emotional intensity or desire onto literary descriptions and visual representations of place.

A lifetime later, Hugh Kenner recalls March 22, 1965:

> Where was Ezra now? In Venice? Why no; nearby, as a matter of fact: up in Sant' Ambrogio, in the little house just below the church with Olga. She imparted this information as one imparts the location of a planet.
>
> She retired early, a black form ascending to a tiny room. In a dozen encounters since 1948, I never saw her in anything but black. (Kenner, 486)

Is this the metaphorical black of the Mediterranean widow? It certainly allows an imaginative identification with Kore/Persephone in her infernal manifestation. (Both Landor and Swinburne influenced Pound and his contemporaries, including H.D., in their interpretation of the myth of Persephone.)

Hugh Kenner concludes his "D. P. Remembered" with a comparison to Homer's Helen; and behind this comparison lies the assumption that the wife and mistress are functions of the poetic oeuvre:

> Ezra Pound's story is inextricable from hers [. . .] would Gaudier, or would Lewis, have to come to count for so much in Ezra's mind had Dorothy not lived through her eyes, and had her mother Olivia not purchased Lewises and Gaudiers? His alliance with Miss Rudge was with a musician, as though to redress some balance of the senses: an ear world. For years he loved both women. (Kenner, 493)

Ironically, Dorothy's presence is largely unacknowledged in the early poems and in *The Cantos*, however, as the "Dorian" invocation indicates, it was no less important for being so diffusely pervasive. More concretely we can say she influenced his concentration on the visual arts, on the work of Lewis and Brzeska during the First World War, and was as influential on his insistence on the direct observation of the thing, as H.D.'s modern Hellenics were instrumental in helping him out of *fin-de-siècle* imitations of the past masters, and into the vanguard of twentieth-century Imagism and literary modernism.

Culture formulates gender, and in its formation sexual difference affects individual identity to the extent that it enables or sometimes disables the achievement of a recognizable, acceptable, viable and relatively stable sense of self. Pound's 1912 poem, "Doria," expresses the notion of woman as gift or object of exchange within a patriarchal kinship system; and of course Dorothy, as the one who was given from father to son-in-law, was transformed into the legal wife; as such she was a mythical and later (after 1958) an actual guardian of Pound. Thus, while the individual woman may retain a political and legal identity, in the cultural exchange the female body is transformed into spiritual or aesthetic value.

The evidence of H.D.'s *roman-à-clef*, *Her*, is that she found Pound's proclivity to imaginatively transform her person into a mythological creature, which better suited his aesthetic stance, both seductive and profoundly disabling. H.D.'s solution was to enter and inhabit the identity that links woman with a mythopoetic version of natural phenomenon. H.D. remained the Dryad, or Hamadryad of Pound's perception, and hence, through a type of ludic imagination, achieved a *modus vivendi*. If gender were not an issue, H.D. and E.P. could have been poets speaking "each to each." As it was, gender informed their literary relationship throughout their lives. During the first years of their friendship, Pound wrote many poems to Hilda, some of which he gathered in a small, hand-bound, vellum-covered book called "Hilda's Book." He often addressed her as "Ysolt," or characterized her as a tree nymph, which is to say, rather than address her as an equal, he cast her in romantic versions of the archetypal feminine. The poem "A Girl" (*Ripostes* 1912) exemplifies the nature of that relationship as Pound perceived and expressed it:

A Girl

The tree has entered my hands,
The sap has ascended my arms,
The tree has grown in my breast –
Downward,
The branches grow out of me, like arms.

Tree you are
Moss you are,
You are violets with wind above them.
A child – *so* high – you are,
And all this is folly to the world.   (*CEP*, 186)

Pound included a version of "The Tree" in "Hilda's Book," and in *A Lume Spento* (1908) but I prefer "A Girl," which treats the same material and experience more successfully, relying on persona which could be usefully compared with H.D.'s "Oread."[6] Its premise is the identification of the girl with the tree, as in the Ovidian myth of Daphne and Apollo. In H.D.'s "Oread" the speaker throughout is the mountain nymph of the title. In Pound's "The Girl," there is a shift in the speaking subject. In the first stanza it is the girl in the process of metamorphosis into the tree, in the second stanza "she" is addressed directly by the romantic poet. The lyric bears an uncanny resemblance to Wordsworth's Lucy poems, the female child's human identity is obliterated and her participation in natural process is then celebrated rather than mourned. Moreover, the death of the female in human form and consummation into the natural cycle facilitates the poetic identity of the male speaker. Her transformation into tree, moss, violets with wind above them, erases the boundaries of her selfhood, but provides a privileged, poetic position of divine madness for the author. Note also the violation of the girl, the entry effected by the tree which totally smudges out the female body. Are the *viol*ets a linguistic pun which unconsciously acknowledge a cultural rape?

"Tempora" (1914), also about H.D., is aware of the irony of mythologizing the present, and allows H.D.'s modern, contemporary voice to intrude into the male poet's artificial perceptions of her. Two worlds, that of modernist mythopoeia and that of modern times and economic exigencies, intersect here. H.D.'s imagist poetry can be characterized as often presenting non-specific landscapes which could draw on her reading in classical Greek literature, or could draw on the refined memories of childhood holidays on the New England coast. The speaker is often a presence, immanent in the landscape, voicing an emotional reaction or interaction with elements of the landscape but, nevertheless, elusive and lacking a bodily definition. The association of the feminine with landscape occurs throughout nineteenth-century literature both in the British and the American canon; and H.D.'s textual strategy is to enter this cultural locus which has been defined as the feminine position but to speak from it. With a sleight of hand Pound seems to misunderstand creatively her tactics, and in Canto II writes what can be taken as a critique of the limitations of Imagism, starting as it does with a cruel parody of Richard Aldington's Imagist poem "Choricos." Is this Pound's definitive version of the "crystalline" H.D.?

> If you will lean over the rock,
> the coral face under wave-tinge,
> Rose-paleness under water-shift,
> Ileuthyeria, fair Dafne of sea-bords,
> The swimmer's arms turned to branches,
> Who will say in what year,
> fleeing what band of tritons,
> The smooth brows, seen, and half seen,
> now ivory stillness. (II/9)

What is his compulsion to write this fellow Imagist poet back into the myth of Daphne, back into the role of inspiring muse, a version of the tree nymph who features in one of the Ovidian myths of the origin of poetry?

In 1926 Pound published his translation of Remy de Gourmont's *Natural Philosophy of Love* and seems to have been drawn into its ethos of eroticism masquerading as post-Darwinian investigation of the relation between the human and other animal species. In her somewhat whimsical statement of personal and womanist aesthetics, *Notes on Thought and Vision*, H.D. seems to make a more healthy assessment of this aspect of Gourmont's work:

> There is plenty of pornographic literature that is interesting and amusing.
> If you cannot be entertained and instructed by Bocaccio, Rabelais, Montaigne, Sterne, Middleton, de Gourmont and de Régnier there is something wrong with you physically.[7]

Pound, added a "Translator's Postscript" where he picks up a suggestion made at the end of the chapter entitled "Love Organs," where Gourmont speculates that: "[t]here might be, perhaps, a certain correlation between complete and profound copulation and the development of the brain."[8] Pound develops this speculation in a pseudo-scientific discourse, that develops Gourmont's sense of correlation into a thesis of causal and, indeed, physiological connection between copulation and ideation: "Not only is this suggestion [...] both possible and probable, but it is more than likely that the brain itself, is, in origin and development, only a sort of great clot of genital fluid held in suspense or reserve [...]" (*NPL*, 169).

What follows is an apparently serious exposition of his belief that artistic genius is intimately connected with biological masculinity, whereas woman's role as conservator of culture is connected with her reproductive functions. The language of this postscript is revealing, for it combines the rhetoric of scientific objectivity with a strong reliance on the persuasive power of mythological discourse; moreover, he draws authority for his argument from his own subjective experience of heterosexual passion:

> There are traces of it in the symbolism of phallic religions, man really the phallus or spermatozoid charging, head-on, the female chaos; integration of the male in the male organ. Even oneself has felt it, driving any new idea into the great passive vulva of London, a sensation analogous to the male feeling in copulation.
>
> Without any digression on feminism, taking merely the division Gourmont has given (Aristotelian, if you like), one offers woman as the accumulation of hereditary aptitudes, better than man in the "useful gestures," the perfections; but to man, given what we have of history, the "inventions," the new gestures, the extravagance, the wild shots, the impractical, merely because in him occurs the new up-jut, the new bathing of their cerebral tissues in the residuum, in *la mousse* of the life sap. (*NPL*, 170–71)

Such blatant misogyny is followed by further stages in the pseudo-scientific argument which eventually brings Pound to the subject of a possible connection between the ascetic who "has tried to withhold all his sperm" in the attempt to "super-think" and other ways of seeking mystic experience throught he deferral of heterosexual gratification (*NPL*, 180). The final paragraph of the postscript presents a characteristic cluster of Poundian associations which include "priestess in the temple of Venus, stray priestesses in the streets," a reference to the line by Propertius "*Ingenium nobis ipsa puella fecit*," Dantescan metaphysics, Gourmont's *Le Latin Mystique* and Fenollosa's *The Chinese Written Character* (*NPL*, 180). Pound's theory seems to want to tease out a connection between the physiology of hetero-sexual desire, the image-making faculty and the visionary experience of the mystic or initiate. It is a theory which confers glamour on women and elevates them to the status of mantra or divine muse, but which sits un-easily with a full consideration of the political rights of individual women to autonomy and equality.

Gourmont's work also contains this ambivalence towards women. On the one hand, he talks of woman as culturally inferior to man: "L'homme créait; la femme apprenait par coeur." But on the other: "Toute la femme parle; elle est le langage même."[9] This elegant aphorism underlies his analysis of Dante's Beatrice and the ideal feminine, as well as his study of medieval love poetry.[10] Such ideas are familiar to students of Western culture. Woman is seen as biologically inferior to man, something of a biological mess at times; but the ideal image of her is essential to the psychology, or should that be the physiology of his superior creativity which bears the mark of "genius" rather than of mere cultural conserva-tion? The provenance of these ideas is obviously not restricted to Gourmont; indeed, it is virtually endemic in the culture. For Pound, his reading in the literature and art of the Pre-Raphaelites and the writings of Pater, together with his early studies of medieval Romance literature, gave him a thorough immersion in this conventional but compelling nexus of assumptions about gender at the formative stage of his intellectual and artistic career.

In 1926, the year of the Gourmont translation, Pound wrote to William Carlos Williams describing the ambience in post-war London. The First World War had decimated the young male population leaving "a greater proportion of females above that of males (which) makes it THE land for the male with phallus erectus. London THE cunt of the world."[11] Pound is talking here of a change in gender balance and, implicitly, a strain on marital fidelity. It is significant that while he uses the Latin, *phallus erectus*, for the male member, he refers to the female genitalia as "cunt." Again, Pound is not talking biology so much as culturally positioning himself within the dominant order which is phallogocentric. This concept of London forms the basis of a masculine theory of genius which he propounds in his translator's postscript, traces of which find their way into Canto XXIX, in some ways problematic for Poundian critics. The unstable tone of the canto prompts the question to what extent it reflects the poet's own moods, and to what extent it seeks to represent scientifically male attitudes towards the female, attitudes with which the poet does not necessarily agree? Is this a critique of male perceptions of the female, of masculinity as it is formed in our culture, both historically and in the contemporary moment; or is it a disguised "confessional" poem?

Wendy Flory in *Ezra Pound and "The Cantos"* argues that Canto XXIX is informed by personal preoccupations. The arena in question in the canto is the Roman arena at Verona, and Pound is there with "Thiy," or Bride Scratton, a married woman Pound much admired, as we later learn in Canto LXXVIII. The problem is how does the reader interpret the significance of the personal material? The allusion to Scratton is almost completely buried in this canto but are we to read the historical material as metonymically "about" her? Or should we, instead, accept her obliterated trace as the poet's personal mnemonic, which he did not entirely erase in the text? Is the canto an unselfconscious if guarded expression of adulterous love, or is it a conscious reflection on the diverse, dialogic nature of cultural manifestations of heterosexuality? Or, is it, in fact both? The canto also presents semantic difficulties. How are we to understand

> Wein, Weib TAN AOIDAN
> Chiefest of these the second, the female
> Is an element, the female
> Is a chaos
> An octopus
> A biological process
> > and we seek to fulfill . . .
> TAN AOIDAN, our desire, drift . . .
> > Ailas e que'm fau miey huelh
> > Quar no vezon so qu'ieu vuelh.
> > > (XXIX/144)

Flory suggests that the enunciation of this point of view is uncharacteristic because "Pound gives in to a Lewisian rhetoric and . . . demeans the female as 'a chaos.'"[12] But one cannot excuse the passage on the ground of excessive "Lewisitis." Pound expresses this view of women in other passages. In his "Translator's Postscript" to Gourmont's *The Natural Philosophy of Love*, he puts forward the same proposition, and there, too, the gesture of evenhandedness lapses almost immediately into crude biological essentialism (*NPL*, 170–71). It is important to recall that Gourmont is not only the direct instigator of this spurious, scientific argument for biological difference directly affecting intellectual capacity, but also one source of Pound's interest in Renaissance mysticism and a source for a post-Romantic interpretation of Dante's Beatrice which emphasizes the centrality of *l'ideal feminin*.[13] The medieval Provençal passage from Sordello, whom Dante placed in *Il Purgatorio*, captures the ethos of Courtly Love, with its emphasis, even reliance, on absence. The male poet needs to be distanced from the female beloved in order to transform and refine erotic desire into poetic utterance. Given Pound's consistency in associating sexual desire, eroticism and mysticism, one must accept authorial validation of the text, despite its confusions and contradictions. His preoccupation with Renaissance definitions of Love continues with *The Cantos*, most notably in Cantos XXXVI and XC.

Canto XXXVI suggests a dialogue between woman and man. But the lady's question is only the occasion of the canto; love is referred to as a function of natural reason, memory, intellect, and feeling. In other words it/he is a function of introspection rather than relationship, although paradoxically this highly stylized, philosophical canto denies actual introspection and depersonalizes the process. Love is another signifier, composed by the masculine tradition of philosophical poetry:

> Yet shall ye see of him That he is most often
> With folk who deserve him
> And his strange quality sets sights to move
> Willing man look into that forméd trace in his mind
> And with such uneasiness as rouseth the flame.
> Unskilled can not form his image,
> He himself moveth not, drawing all to his stillness,
> Neither turneth about to seek his delight
> Nor yet to seek out proving
> Be it so great or so small.   (XXXVI/178)

In her memoir of Pound, written on the occasion of his release from St. Elizabeths, H.D. recalls Pound's "kisses" and their effect/affect:

I was hiding myself and Ezra, standing before my father, caught "in the very act" you might say. For no "act" afterwards, though biologically fulfilled, had had the significance of the first demi-vierge embraces. The significance of "first love" can not be overestimated. . . . It filled my fantasies and dreams, my prose and poetry for ten years. But in the end, intellectual and physical perfection, the laurel wreath of the acclaimed achievement must be tempered, balanced, re-lived, re-focused or even sustained by the unpredictable, the inchoate, challenged by a myth, a legend – the poet (Vidal, shall we say), changed to Wolf or Panther, hunted down and captured.[14]

> There is a stir of dust from old leaves
> Will you trade roses for acorns . . .   (LXXIX/511)

These are lines from the lynx lyric in Canto LXXIX/507–12 which is about transformation, as well as about the choice to sublimate. It recreates a Bacchic ritual of transformation and distillation in which the mystery of the vine/wine and the mystery of woman in her archetypal manifestations are woven into lyrical evocation of the Dionysiac dance. Yet for all its realization of the icons, it ends with a Latin phrase:

> aram
> nemus
> vult
>   [The grove needs an altar]   (LXXIX/512)

The lyric still signifies desire and lack of completion. In reading *The Pisan Cantos* what is important is not the philosophical program, which can be read many different ways, nor knowledge of the exact provenance of the particulars of Pound's razor sharp recollections and perceptions, but the emotional transformations, the intellectual visions, the musical celebration; the transformation or metamorphosis of so many different influences, many of which are now annotated, into poetic utterance. In the end, it is the utterance which is important; in it women, metamorphosed natural land-scape, and a neo-Platonic locus in the mind and memory, combine in a gendered evocation of Love in its/his many aspects. In "D. P. Remembered," Kenner tells us that Dorothy thought of the lynx lyric as her chorus (491). It evidently caused a stirring of memories for Hilda, too. Who is to say whether Olga Rudge's presence is also immanent? And Bride Scratton? And Mary Moore of Trenton? And others?

Canto XC draws on the Latin Patrology for its epigram, on "How the Holy Spirit is the Love of the Father and the Son," but the occasion of the canto is also Pound's encountering the young American artist, Sheri Martinelli, while in St. Elizabeths. Noel Stock writes: "Miss Martinelli is said to appear in *Rock Drill* and to have inspired Canto XC, which is perhaps the most lyrical of the later cantos" (439). Carpenter concurs (801–4, 829–30). The repeated phrase, "*m'elevasti,*" in Canto XC/626 comes from Dante's *Paradiso*. And although the occasion of the canto might have been Miss Martinelli, Pound transforms her, like his other women, into poetic utterance which aspires to transcend the merely personal. Here, the poetry enunciates arrival at completion, "Grove hath its altar," which may have more to do with the process of the long poem, than with the accidental qualities of this particular encounter.

In this work, Pound associates women with an idealized landscape and the "permanent," divine world, especially when this is a transformed vision of Greek and other ancient iconography as translated by Italian Renaissance artists. Originating in the tradition of Provençal poetry, Pound adapts this technique to modernist concerns and private situations. Pound's Homeric *nostos* is gendered feminine, which in the male psyche tends to be associated with the image of the woman as (m)other. In the poetry of Pound, woman represents the permanent and the divine, but man's access to this is fragmentary. Pound, despite all the masks and voices he assumes, or symptomatically through them, is unable to sustain a stable sense of a unified wholeness. His relation to the symbolic order is also arguably unstable. As late as Canto LXXIV he enunciates the position of complete loss of personality, writing "I am noman, my name is noman" (446), in a passage which considers the power of language, the concept of *verbum paraclete*, and which then recalls the prefect at Gardone evoking the quintessential woman:

> 'La Donna' said Nicoletti
>   'la donna,
>   la donna!'   (LXXIV/447)

Desire for verbal perfection, the importance of male camaraderie, especially when thinking and writing about women, the desire not only to enunciate cultural artefacts in language but to eventually find and name beatitude through contemplation of the archetypal female, while evading definition of the masculine self beyond that conferred by the names of eponymous heroes; all these characteristics are enduring aspects of Pound's work, and all of them are gendered. The emotional transformations associated with Romance visions and evocations and which associate landscape (often meridional) with the feminine either human, divine, or semi-divine nymph, or mythic female, can be described as gendered feminine. The moral and ethical transformations tend to be gendered masculine. The world of Confucian candour and integrity is masculine; the work of establishing just laws is masculine. The female is a presence, immanent in the landscape(s), the male is the secretary of nature converting her wisdom into wise statutes.

Yet that is too neat a formulation, as H.D.'s comment aptly illustrates: "[b]ut in the end, intellectual and physical perfection, the laurel wreath of the acclaimed achievement must be tempered, balanced, re-lived, re-focused or even sustained by the unpredictable, the inchoate" (*END*, 26)

This is the underlying principle of *The Cantos'* production. The Confucian principle of balance and the contradictory need to recognize and allow "errors" coexist; depictions of the manifold manifestations of the Great Goddess and representations of the female as a Circean chaos also coexist. Modernist women did not necessarily eschew identification with the Great Goddess in her various aspects. Invocations and representations of her formed part of a modernist discourse, articulated by women authors as well as men, exploring alternatives to patriarchal monotheism. A generous reading of Pound's recurrent enunciations of the archetypal feminine in association with subdued or erased allusions to individual women could indeed be interpreted not as a patriarchal plot to mythologize, and thus silence the modern woman, but as an attempt to write the female back into the symbolic order. Similarly, his references to the female as a biological process, could be interpreted not as dismissive misogyny, but rather as a sane response to the excesses of Victorian discourses about women's bodies as either angelic or pathologically hysterical, but never normal.

If we take into account the historical era within which Pound was writing, his representations of the Great Goddess could be interpreted not as a patriarchal plot to fix woman as a conventional muse, even though many of his versions of Venus/Aphrodite draw on profoundly traditional, classical sources, but rather as part of a shared, modernist project to radically revise religious and symbolic expression. Aphrodite is invoked in Canto I, as worthy of worship, *venerandum*, and recurrently addressed throughout *The Cantos*, sometimes as Venus, sometimes as Cythera, sometimes as Kupris. I have argued elsewhere that in Canto LXXXI Pound traces the process whereby the transient, personal memories of the eyes of three women he has loved are transformed into the vision of Charis/Venus/Kore.[15] The women of Pound's generation would have been flattered to be associated with the Great Goddess of the Mystery Religions.

One of Pound's late translations, *The Women of Trachis* (1954), bears eloquent testimony to the preoccupations of a lifetime. Herakles' tragedy is the culmination of a situation not unlike Pound's own, in which the wife and mistress have to "figure out how [. . .] to manage this cohabitation" (*WT*, 25). The play enacts in a highly stylized fashion the consequences of marital infidelity, the pain and suffering that are the inescapable manifestations of desire. Running through it is a resignation or acceptance that Kupris or erotic love controls human action and destiny:

> KUPRIS bears trophies away.
> Kronos' Son, Dis and Poseidon,
> There is no one
>   shaker unshaken.

> Into dust go they all.
> Neath Her they must
>
> > > give way   (*WT*, 23)

She appears as "*dea ex machina*" and the stage instructions state, that the "apparition is fairly sudden, the fade out slightly slower: the audience is almost in doubt that she has appeared" (*WT*, 37). The key phrase in the play is Herakles' line, "SPLENDOUR, IT ALL COHERES" (*WT*, 50): – an insight which Pound appropriates in Canto CXVI, with wise humility, acknowledging that "it coheres all right / even if my notes do not cohere" (817).

For many years that was the final published canto, but recent editions have added late fragments. The New Directions, thirteenth printing (1995), ends:

> That her acts
> > Olga's acts
> > > of beauty
> > be remembered.
>
> Her name was Courage
> & is written Olga
>
> These lines are for the
> > ultimate CANTO
>
> whatever I may write
> > in the interim   (824)

In his final years Pound spent most of his time with Olga Rudge rather than his wife Dorothy. Humphrey Carpenter, his most recent biographer, reports that Dorothy Pound told Noel Stock: "Ezra needs a lot of looking after, and Olga's stronger than I am." Richard Stern observed "Miss Rudge was clearly the sea in which he floated" (Carpenter 877, 885). She, the younger woman, and the bedrock of his later years, outlasted both Dorothy and Ezra Pound to die in March 1996.

Did Pound think of Dorothy when he translated Daysair's lines, "My husband, her man, the new girl's man" (*WT*, 37)? And if so, should we criticize the multiplicity of his affections or praise him for the imaginative sympathy he displays here and for his lifelong effort to replace the patriarchal godhead with the divine presence of the barely perceptible *dea ex machina*? Pound's poetry fuses the archetypal feminine, which derives from his own psyche as well as from his voluminous reading, with transformed depictions of women who, for want of a better term, he "loved." While Canto XXXVI proffers one definition of love which "cometh of that perfection / Which is so postulate not by the reason / But 'tis felt" (178), Canto XC offers an opposite view. One can only conclude that however flawed, confused and complex Pound's love for women was, the traces which their presence leaves in *The Cantos* is fundamental to the overall coherence of its complicated design.

NOTES

1 See Peter Nicholls, *Modernisms: A Literary Guide* (Basingstoke: Macmillan, 1995), p. 194.

2 In this respect, Menie Muriel Dowie's *Gallia* (1895), which caused quite a stir when it was first published, is an illuminating novelistic investigation of the double standards in sexual mores at the turn of the century, how it affected women and what strategies they adopted to cope. See Menie Muriel Dowie, *Gallia*, ed. Helen Smith (London: J. M. Dent, 1995).

3 See Omar Pound and Robert Spoo (eds.), *Ezra Pound and Margaret Cravens: A Tragic Friendship* (Durham: Duke University Press, 1988). Hereafter *EP/MC*.

4 See Pound and Spoo, "Introduction," in *Ezra Pound and Margaret Cravens*, pp. 1–7; Humphrey Carpenter, *A Serious Character: The Life of Ezra Pound* (London: Faber & Faber, 1988), pp. 180–181.

5 Hugh Kenner, "D. P. Remembered," *PAI*, 2 (1973), pp. 492–3.

6 H.D., *Collected Poems 1912–1944*, ed. Louis L. Martz (New York: New Directions, 1983), p. 55.

7 H.D., "Notes on Thought and Vision," in Bonnie Kime Scott (ed.), *The Gender of Modernism* (Bloomington, IN: Indiana University Press, 1990), p. 99.

8 Remy de Gourmont, *The Natural Philosophy of Love*, tr. Ezra Pound (London: The Casanova Society, 1926), p. 55. Hereafter *NPL*.

9 Remy de Gourmont, *Le Chemin de Velours: Nouvelles Dissociations d'Idees*, 6th edn (Paris: Mercure de France, 1928), pp. 190, 195.

10 Remy de Gourmont, "La Beatrice de Dante: Et l'Ideal Feminin en Italie à la Fin du XIIIe Siecle," *Revue du Monde Latin* (1885), pp. 174–190, 286–296, 442–451.

11 Pound, in Carpenter, *Life*, p. 331.

12 Wendy Stallard Flory, *Ezra Pound and "The Cantos"* (New Haven: Yale University Press, 1980), p. 115. Also see Noel Stock, *The Life of Ezra Pound* (London: Routledge & Kegan Paul, 1970), pp. 83, 243–244, 254, 284, 441–442.

13 See Gourmont, "La Beatrice de Dante," *La Revue du Monde Latin*, pp. 174–190, 286–296, as well as Gourmont, *Le Latin Mystique* (Paris: Mercure de France, 1930).

14 H.D., *End to Torment: A Memoir of Ezra Pound* (Manchester: Carcanet, 1980), pp. 18–19.

15 Helen M. Dennis, *A New Approach to the Poetry of Ezra Pound* (Lewiston: Edwin Mellen Press, 1996), pp. 434–447.

15

WENDY STALLARD FLORY

Pound and antisemitism

When people speak of Pound's antisemitism, they are thinking primarily of the antisemitic tirades included in the speeches that he broadcast over Rome Radio between 1941 and 1943. Although, after the bombing of Pearl Harbor and America's entry into World War II, Pound stopped his broadcasts for two months, he resumed them on January 29, 1942. Since the United States was now at war with Italy, Pound's radio attacks on Franklin Delano Roosevelt and praise of Benito Mussolini seemed, to the United States government, to be the acts of a traitor and, on July 26, 1943, Pound was indicted for treason in Washington. On May 3, 1945, he was taken into custody by the American forces in Rapallo and was interned, from May 24 to November 16, at the US Army "Disciplinary Training Center" north of Pisa, a prison and rehabilitation camp for US military offenders. From there he was flown to Washington where the court found him "of unsound mind" and so unable to stand trial for treason. On December 21 he was incarcerated in St. Elizabeths Hospital, a federal psychiatric institution, where he would remain for twelve and a half years until, on April 18, 1958, the indictment against him was dismissed. Although the legal issue raised by the Rome Radio broadcasts was the charge of treason, in the over fifty years since Pound's indictment the antisemitism of the broadcasts has been the primary focus of the widespread outrage and outcry against him.

The issue of Pound's antisemitism can only now begin to be discussed in a reflective and analytical way. The understandable reason for this is the Holocaust context of his actions. That Pound should have been broadcasting accusations of Jewish conspiracies against the cultural and economic health of Europe and the USA at the time of the *Shoah* is explanation enough for the general denunciation of him as a rabid antisemite and the widespread suspicion that any analytical approach to the antisemitism of the broadcasts is likely to be apologist. The natural response to the revelations of Hitler's death camps was an anger all the more intense for being grounded in horror and fear. Pound, because of the highly public nature of his antisemitic broadcasts, provided a ready target for this anger and it continues to determine reactions to him today.

The strength of the initial anger is seen in those early responses to Pound that made no distinction between the nature of his guilt and that of those directly responsible for the mass murder of Jews. Contributors to the *New Masses* article of December 25, 1945, "Should Ezra Pound be Shot?", for example, advocated a death sentence without hesitation. Lion Feuchtwanger asserted that Pound could be imprisoned or hanged "with the clearest conscience" and to Albert Maltz, the statement, "I remember the corpses of Buchenwald, Dachau, Maidanek," was sufficient justification for calling for Pound's hanging. Arthur Miller judged Pound as even more malign than the Nazi High Command: "In his wildest moments of human vilification Hitler never approached our Ezra... he knew all America's weaknesses and he played them as expertly as Goebbels ever did." Norman Rosten argued that Pound "should be shot" as "a fascist hireling [who] contributed to the murder of the innocent." He rejected the "eccentricity" defense as no more legitimate in Pound's case than in the case of Hitler, Goebbels or Ribbentrop.

The issue of Pound's antisemitism has a very immediate bearing upon how he is perceived and evaluated as a poet. It determines not just *how* his poetry is read but, in many cases, *whether* it is read. In *The American Ezra Pound* (*AEP*), an analytic biography of the poet, I found it necessary to make the issue of Pound's antisemitism and the related issues of his insanity and his economic theories central concerns. I will refer directly to this study for two reasons. First, the statements made below about Pound's antisemitic and psychotic wartime state of mind constitute only a brief summary of conclusions based upon evidence presented in the book in detail. Secondly, I want to emphasize that, in presenting the following description and explanation of Pound's antisemitism, I am not summarizing a position that is "generally received." Such a position does not yet exist as this highly controversial issue has only recently begun to be investigated analytically and angry condemnation is still the prevalent reaction. The nature of the responses to Pound's antisemitism and the reasons for them constitute a context that needs to be addressed as a crucial dimension of Pound's case.

The over-forty-year delay before Pound's antisemitism could be discussed analytically is directly related to the delay in analytical investigation of the *Shoah* itself. Not until the late 1970s would historians and archivists in the United States be widely and concertedly engaged in discovering and preserving as many details as possible of all aspects of the Nazi genocide.

Survivors had had to wait for many year; to find people ready to listen to and record their testimony. The *Shoah* had been a subject too painful to discuss, not only because of the enormity of the mass torture and murder and of the guilt of those most directly responsible. Painful issues of a less direct yet serious kind of accountability went unaddressed for many years. The complicity of bystanders, the extent of collaboration within Nazi-occupied countries and the indifference in Britain and the United States to the Jews' fate showed that great numbers of people were sufficiently antisemitic either to acquiesce silently in the persecution of Jews or feel no commitment to acts of rescue. Neither American leaders nor the great majority of the American public had shown any willingness to help save the Jews of Europe – either militarily, by bombing the rail lines to the death camps, or, politically, by granting asylum to Jews. David Wyman has shown in *Paper Walls* (1968) and *The Abandonment of the Jews* (1984), how, during the war, strong antisemitic and anti-immigrant sentiment led to measures that succeeded in turning away the vast majority of Jewish refugees – including, on one occasion, 20,000 children under the age of fourteen. Allan Ryan's *Quiet Neighbors* (1984) tells how the Displaced Persons Act of 1948 was specifically designed by Congress to exclude as many Jewish concentration camp survivors as possible and to give preferential status to groups known to include many Nazi war criminals.

Widespread reluctance to confront the extent of American antisemitism at the time of the Holocaust has very directly determined attitudes toward Pound. At a time when any kinds of antisemitism short of documentable war-crimes were being generally disregarded, the blatant antisemitism of Pound's radio tirades stood out with particular obtrusiveness. He was quickly assigned the role of "National Monster" and continues to be thought of as such by many people, even today. The strength of the resistance to any subsequent examination of the facts of his case bespeaks a genuine concern that antisemitic guilt not be mitigated or brushed aside, yet it is possible to detect an unconscious motive here also. Pound-as-antisemite served as a convenient place-holder for all those whose antisemitism was not being confronted. In the context of a pervasive, institutionalized American antisemitism that no one wanted to acknowledge, the denouncing of Pound as the "real antisemite" became an effortless alternative to any serious analysis of the problem of antisemitism in America – and in oneself. The vilification of Pound was obviously a completely inadequate response to wartime antisemitism in the United States, yet, for many years, it was the *only* response of most American intellectuals.

This "National Monster" caricature, that has persisted with such tenacity since 1945, has strongly influenced readers' responses to Pound's poetry and critics' estimations of the significance of his achievement and the value of his writing. Critics adopt one of two, clear-cut, opposing views of Pound's character and moral guilt according to whether they decide that he was or was not in a psychotic mental state when he made the broadcasts. A commonly held conspiracy theory claims that, with the connivance of the superintendent of St. Elizabeths, Pound faked insanity to avoid possible execution. In fact, his medical records, letters, and the testimony of many visitors to St. Elizabeths show clear evidence of psychosis, as this is now defined. The hesitance of some of Pound's psychiatrists to label his psychosis definitively, reflects the incompleteness of the very narrow definition of that time that assumed that psychosis would be sustained rather than episodic and would seriously impair normal functioning (*AEP*, 156–73).

Beginning in 1935, Pound's mental condition deteriorated precipitously. From then on, characteristics of his behavior and his writings exactly fit the diagnostic criteria for paranoid psychosis – relabeled in 1987 "Delusional Disorder" – both of the "Grandiose Type" (involving "the conviction of having some great [but unrecognized] insight") and the "Persecutory Type" (the belief of "being conspired against . . . [and] obstructed in the pursuit of long-term goals") (*DSM-IV*, 296–301). The form that both of these took was determined by the context of his long-standing campaigning for world-wide economic reform. His "great insight" was his conviction of the ability of Social Credit policies to save the West from economic depressions and from a second world war. He tried to convey this insight to Roosevelt, to members of the US government, and to Mussolini and even believed that he could have convinced Stalin of it (*AEP*, 141–42).

Even before 1935, aspects of Pound's behavior, such as the frenetic letter-writing and grandiose objectives of his economic campaign, showed clear manic tendencies and, after 1935, these became so pronounced as to constitute a manic mood disorder that co-existed with his Delusional Disorder. His mood was, in fact, "abnormally and persistently . . . expansive [and] irritable" and a manic "flight of ideas" announced itself in a "nearly continuous flow of accelerated speech, with abrupt changes from one topic to another." His broadcasts were typical of manic speech in being "pressured, loud, rapid, and difficult to interpret"; "characterized by joking, punning, and . . . irrelevancies"; "theatrical, with dramatic mannerisms"; and "marked by complaints, hostile comments, [and] angry tirades" (*DSM-IV*, 328–32).

Pound's symptoms of Persecutory Delusion were also determined by his economic focus and here a complete body of ancient, hate-driven, paranoid theory lay ready-to-hand in the whole farrago of antisemitic stereotypes. In the radio broadcasts he speaks of a Jewish master-plan for world domination – "The Jews have ruin'd every country they have got hold of. The Jews have worked out a system, a very neat system, for the ruin of the rest of mankind, one nation after another" (*EPS*, 256); of nations dominated by secret conclaves of irresistibly powerful and malign Jewish international bankers; of Communism as set up by Jews, for Jewish ends – "The Talmud is the one and only begetter of the Bolshevik system" (*EPS*, 117); of Jewish control of the press; of the strategy whereby Jewish financiers start wars to make money from armament sales and then to take over the crippled economies of the combatants.

The texts of 120 of these broadcasts can conveniently be consulted in *"Ezra Pound Speaking"*. The overwhelming impression that they create is of the repulsiveness of their antisemitism. They also, as Thurman Arnold (who represented Pound in the case for dismissal of the indictment) wrote to the ACLU, "show insanity on their face" (*AEP*, 185). Pound's psychotic mind-set reveals itself most dramatically when a speech is read in its entirety, but it can also be seen in some individual passages such as his references to "the Jewish proposal to make Roosevelt world emperor and to locate the New Jerusalem on the Isthmus of Panama, with NO checks and controls imposed on it, by even the angry Saxons" (*EPS*, 258) to the "hook up between Masonry, its central control, Jewry, Anglo-Israel, and the British Intelligence Service" (*EPS*, 114) and to how "Abe Lincoln became target for assassination when he got round to resisting the desire of FOREIGN Jew bankers to control the currency of the USA" (*EPS*, 281).

To believe that Pound was "of sound mind" at the time of the broadcasts is necessarily to pronounce him guilty of deliberate, malicious, and callous antisemitism. The gravity of this accusation requires that the facts of the case be determined with careful accuracy. This involves a close examination of evidence of his state of mind in the 1930s and 40s to establish whether, why, and how it deteriorated. The conclusions arrived at in *The American Ezra Pound* are as follows. In his youth, Pound inevitably internalized some of the antisemitic attitudes that were pervasive at this time of mass immigration from central Europe and were widely institutionalized in discriminatory practices in university education, hiring, housing and at clubs, hotels and resorts. His parents, however, were less antisemitic and anti-immigrant than most, as is shown by their work with Italian immigrants and their willingness to rent their home, in 1902 and 1903, to the president of the Jewish Hospital Association.

The record of Pound's writings and behavior in his youth provides no evidence of particular antisemitic animus. In London, he was exposed to the supercilious and spiteful variety of antisemitism that was *de rigueur* for members of the upper and upper-middle classes such as Pound's wife, Dorothy Shakespear and Wyndham Lewis. Even here, antisemitic instances in his writings are very rare and include qualifications that betray his uneasiness. In his last *Little Review* "Imaginary Letter," he perversely includes his partly-remembered translation of an offensively antisemitic poem by Baudelaire, yet dismisses as too "facile" both the poem and his translation which he claims to have finished in fifteen minutes and then thrown away (*PD*, 74–75). Pound's 1912 serialized version of *Patria Mia* includes one antisemitic sentence: "The Jew alone can retain his detestable qualities, despite climatic conditions." Pound qualifies this also, first with, "That is, perhaps, an overstatement," then, in 1913, by omitting the statement altogether. Pound's position on immigration, in *Patria Mia*, is that its influence on American culture is primarily positive and energizing (*AEP*, 136–137).

The death of Pound's friend, the young French sculptor Henri Gaudier-Brzeska, in the trenches turned Pound's distress at the First World War into outrage. He renounced the "bohemian aesthete" persona of his Vorticist period and committed himself to study the causes of war. This change of direction is clearly announced in *Hugh Selwyn Mauberley* (1920), the first of his poems to include a reference to "usury." Through A. R. Orage of *The New Age*, Pound was introduced to Major C. H. Douglas's theory of Social Credit and quickly became convinced that this new economic program would remove one of the major causes of war by minimizing both reliance on debt-financing, and hence "loan-capital," and competition for overseas markets. Mussolini's economic reforms of the 1920s convinced Pound that the Duce was the only European leader committed to a sound, "anti-war" economic policy and, in 1924, Pound moved to Italy.

Unlike the USA, Britain or France, Italy was virtually without overt antisemitism in any form. It was not only the least antisemitic of all the countries in Europe, but until 1938 Mussolini himself, in his public pronouncements, was actively philosemitic. Mussolini's turn toward empire-building and his alliance with Hitler were followed by his racial laws of 1938. While these seriously limited the freedom of Jews in Italy, Mussolini adamantly opposed the murder of Jews and none was deported from Italy as long as he was in power. Jews were also safe in the Italian-occupied areas of Croatia, France and Greece which became havens or escape routes for Jewish refugees from German- or Bulgarian-occupied zones. The commonly made allegation that Pound's antisemitism accounts for his enthusiasm for Mussolini has no basis in fact.

Nothing that Pound wrote or is reported to have said before 1935 is comparable in tone and content to the antisemitic rantings of the broadcasts and the journalism of that period. The nature of his post-1935 antisemitism is determined by the marked deterioration of his state of mind after Mussolini's invasion of Abyssinia in October 1935. This decline into psychosis can readily be documented by considering his writings of this period chronologically (*AEP*, 102–30). Pound had taken seriously Mussolini's original commitment to revitalize Italy through internal economic reforms and to avoid war. Mussolini's reversal of his non-belligerent policy with his invasion of Abyssinia presented Pound with a crisis. Here was irrefutable evidence that the leader whom Pound saw as Europe's last hope for preserving peace was a warmonger. To acknowledge this evidence would be to abandon all hope and instead, Pound took the first fatal step in the process of lying to himself. Encouraged by the widespread enthusiasm within Italy for the Duce's colonialist ambitions and accepting the government's propaganda about Abyssianian atrocities against Italians, he began to rationalize away what he should have confronted.

Even this initial act of rationalization involved serious self-delusion, but to rationalize away what was to follow – Italian intervention in the Spanish Civil War, the racial laws, the invasion of Albania, the Pact of Steel, Mussolini's declaration of war against England and France, the attack on Greece, and finally the declaration of war against the United States – entailed an evasion of reality so extreme and so sustained as to be genuinely psychotic. By the time of the radio broadcasts, Pound's consistently reiterated position on the mission of the Allies and of the Axis exactly inverted the wartime roles of Hitler and Churchill, making Churchill the aggressor and Hitler a benevolent economic reformer. From the reasonable position that wars can have economic causes, Pound moved to the position that there are no causes of war except for economic ones. Hitler was not involved in a war of conquest, but, like Mussolini, committed to setting up a "usury-proof" economic system. Churchill and Roosevelt, acting as fronts for the international conspiracy of primarily Jewish usurers and arms dealers, were making war on the Axis powers to prevent this. Hitler invaded Russia to crush Communism with its pernicious economic system.

As Pound's fixation upon his economic conspiracy-theory entirely determined the content of his post-1935 antisemitism, so his growing psychosis and the "rapid shifts to anger" of its manic component determined its tone. An analysis of individual broadcasts quickly shows that the part and the whole create quite different impressions. Excerpted from a broadcast, its antisemitic passages convey a direct, unqualified, aggressive anger, the ugliness of which is indisputable. Yet the overall effect of such broadcasts is of frenetic disorganization and confusion. They function according to a reliable self-sabotaging dynamic that derails any attempt to move beyond antisemitic allegations to recommendations for antisemitic action. If Pound broaches the topic of action, he immediately qualifies his comments or changes the subject altogether. His strongest recommendations are to "look into," read about, and study the "real" causes of this and other wars and to "diagnose" FDR and the other "warmongers." The conflict between his strong drive to rationalize and his equally strong anxieties about his self-delusion generated such mental confusion that finally the only victim of the effects of his broadcasts was Pound himself (*AEP*, 140–55).

Throughout Pound's years in St. Elizabeths, political or economic topics invariably precipitated a psychotic response. Yet on any other topics, such as literary matters, Pound was able to be logical and reasonable and often to show an energetic enthusiasm. A change of topic would cause an instantaneous switch into or out of a psychotic mood in a way that has been noted by many people, from his daughter, describing how her father was at the time of the radio broadcasts, to his visitors during the St. Elizabeths years. Although clinical definitions of psychosis, of that time, assumed a sustained state, according to the current definition, "A common characteristic of people with Delusional Disorder is the apparent normality of their behavior and appearance when their delusional ideas are not being discussed or acted upon" (*DSM-IV*, 297).

Since literature was, for Pound, a "safe subject," although there are frequent antisemitic outbursts in the radio speeches, there are very few indeed in *The Cantos*. This fact has been obscured by the generally held but unexamined assumption that *The Cantos* contain many antisemitic passages. On December 14, 1988, for example, a *New York Times* reviewer of a Pound biography stated that "even the highly acclaimed Pisan Cantos . . . are riddled with antisemitic remarks." In fact, in this eleven-canto sequence of over 3,800 lines, there are three antisemitic passages, totalling thirteen lines. Although these are thirteen lines too many, they hardly "riddle" this section of the poem.

> Pétain defended Verdun while Blum
>   was defending a bidet   (LXXX/514)

> Meyer Anselm [Rothschild], a rrromance, yes, yes, certainly
> but more fool you if you fall for it two centuries later
>   . . .
>   from their seats the blond bastards, and cast 'em.
>   the yidd is a stimulant, and the goyim are cattle
>   in gt/ proportion and go to saleable slaughter
>   with the maximum of docility.   (LXXIV/459)

and the goyim are undoubtedly in great numbers cattle
whereas a jew will receive information
he will gather up information
faute de . . . something more solid
but not in all cases   (463)

Not surprisingly, all three are spill-overs from the radio speeches, for example: "[the USA and Britain are] bloody well hog tied by Rothschild. More is the pity. Goyim or cattle, milked, skinned alive, hog tied, sent out to the slaughter [in war] or drowned like blind mice in the steerage, to keep up the usual swindles. Usury at 60% being the quietest" (*EPS*, 339).

In the first thirty cantos Pound expresses no antisemitic sentiments. Canto XX describes the helpfulness and commonsense of the Jew, Yusuf, who showed Pound around Gibraltar and took him to a synagogue. The antisemitism reported here, is that of Mustafa, a muslim, who, when Pound says "Yusuf's a damn good feller," agrees but with the proviso, " 'But after all a chew / ees a chew' " (105). Pound recalls this synagogue visit when, in the *Pisan Cantos*, he credits the *Torah* with opposing usury and mandating economic justice:

> So that in the synagogue in Gibraltar
> the sense of humour seemed to prevail
> during the preliminary parts of the whatever
> but they respected at least the scrolls of the law
> from it, by it, redemption
> @ $8.50, @ $8.67 buy the field with good money
> no unrighteousness in meteyard or in measure (of prices)
>
> and there is no need for the Xtns to pretend that
> they wrote Leviticus   (LXXVI/474)

The Cantos written before 1935 are free from the ranting, paranoid antisemitism of the radio speeches. When arms dealers who are Jews are denounced, for example, they are not identified as Jews. Significantly, neither the ranting, condemnatory "Hell Cantos" (XIV and XV), nor the jeremiac "Usura Canto" (XLV) contain any antisemitic references. In *Eleven New Cantos: XXXI–XLI*, also published before 1935, we find two antisemitic instances. Canto XLI recounts with obvious approval an anecdote "told by the mezzo-yit ['half-Jew']" about Mussolini outsmarting profiteering businessmen (202). Canto XXXV includes derogatory comments and anecdotes, mainly about people Pound had met, intended to illustrate "the intramural, the almost intravaginal warmth of / hebrew affections, in the family, and nearly everything else" (172–173).

In *The Fifth Decad of Cantos, XLII–LI* of 1937, we find two instances of outright antisemitism and one potentially antisemitic reference to an observation by one of the Rothschilds (XLVI/233). Also, in Canto XLIV Pound, paraphrasing his Italian source, records that in 1799 a mob entered the Jewish quarter in Siena "to sack and burn hebrews" (225). The outright antisemitism occurs in Canto XLVIII ("Bismarck/ blamed american civil war on the jews;/ particularly on the Rothschild" [240–241]) and in Canto L ("Wellington was a jew's pimp" [248]).

With Canto LII, the angry, obsessive antisemitism of the economic and political writings uncontrollably spills over into the poetry.

> **Stinkschuld's** [Rothschild's] sin drawing vengeance, poor
> yitts paying for **Stinkschuld**
> paying for a few big jews' vendetta on goyim
> . . . .
> Remarked Ben [Franklin]: better keep out the jews
> or yr/ grand children will curse you
> jews, real jews, chazims, and *neschek* [usury]
> also super-neschek or the international racket
> **specialité of the Stinkschuld**
> **bomb-proof under their house in Paris**
> **where they cd/ store aht voiks**
> **fat slug with three body-guards**
> **soiling our sea front with a pot bellied yacht in the offing,**
> governments full of their gun-swine, bankbuzzards, poppinjays.
>
> (257–258)

The marked passages, censored by Pound's editors and replaced at his insistence with black bars, were restored in the tenth printing of 1986. The 1941 "Addendum" for Canto C, is a "sermon" against usury in the manner of Canto XLV, but, unlike the "Usura Canto," contains some antisemitic commentary. Here Pound uses the Hebrew for "usury" in "*neschek* whose name is known, the defiler,/ beyond race and against race" and writes "S[assoon] doing evil in place of the R[othschild]" (818–19).

Pound's unconscious impulse to save his poem from the contamination of the antisemitic ranting of Canto LII resulted in an act of radical "self-censorship." On this canto's second page he abruptly cut off this train of thought and, throughout the remaining twenty-nine cantos of this section, kept his focus steadily upon what were, for him, safe subjects. He recounted the actions of the rulers of China, appraising these according to a Confucian standard and celebrated the fortitude, good sense and political integrity of John Adams.

Although Pound's paranoid and antisemitic fixation upon his theory of an international economic conspiracy persisted unchanged during the St. Elizabeths years, he was able, with very few exceptions, to keep anti-semitic observations out of the Cantos. His villains are labelled "the usurer" (LXXXVII/589), "gold-bugs" (LXXXVII/592) and "Hoggers of harvest" (LXXXVIII/601) rather than "Jews" or "kikes." In the post-1945 cantos we find only one directly antisemitic comment, in the following outburst:

> Democracies electing their sewage
> till there is no clear thought about holiness
> a dung flow from 1913
> and, in this, their kikery functioned, Marx, Freud
>   and the American beaneries
> Filth under filth,
>   Maritain, Hutchins,
> or as Benda remarked: "La trahison"   (XCI/633–34)

In addition, there are six obliquely-worded antisemitic passages. An allusion to Hitler, "Evita, beer-halls ... / ... / not arrogant from habit, / but furious from perception" (XC/626) is reiterated as "Adolf furious from perception" (CIV/761). Pound twice mentions Sir Barry Domvile whose autobiography *From Cabin Boy to Admiral* includes antisemitic observa-tions – "And men even in our time (survivals) / as Domvile" (LXXXIX/619) and " 'The libraries' (Ingrid) 'have no Domvile.' Jan 1955 / as was natural" (CII/749). "Der Jud will Geld [The Jew wants money]" (LXXXIX/620) a comment made to Pound by a Tyrolean "considered the family's low in intelligence" is quoted by Pound, implicitly with approval (620). A sixth instance – " "800 years after En Bertrans / 'en gatje', had the four towers, / 'Dalleyrand Berigorrr!' " (CV/769) – intimates disapproval that a castle of the troubadour, Bertrans de Born, should now be owned by a Jew.

Given the long hiatus before the appearance of analytical studies of the Holocaust itself, it is not surprising that even more time had to elapse before Pound's antisemitism was approached analytically. In the interim, critics either followed Hugh Kenner in focusing on aesthetic issues and leaving the antisemitism unaddressed or else denounced Pound categoric-ally. The outcry against Pound's antisemitism was dramatically amplified when, on February 20, 1949, *The Pisan Cantos* was awarded the first annual Bollingen Prize for poetry. The main documents of the resulting controversy are collected in *A Casebook on Ezra Pound*. Any critic who held back from outright denunciation was expected to have and be willing to state an alternative position. Initially, such positions frequently reflected New Criticism's aestheticist tendency to separate text and writer. The

Bollingen jury anticipated objections to their decision by stating: "To permit other considerations than that of poetic achievement to sway the decision would destroy the significance of the award and would in principle deny the validity of that objective perception of value on which civilized society must rest" (O'Connor & Stone, *Casebook*, 45).

The New Critical tenor of defenses of Pound led his attackers to impute to him the positions taken by his defenders. Consequently, many later critics have condemned Pound for a New Critical aestheticism completely at odds with his decisive, post-World War I rejection of "art-for-art's-sake" in favor of economic reformism. While Marxist critics assume that Pound's enthusiasm for Mussolini strongly supports their position that modernism is, *sui generis*, "fascistic" and indifferent to the working classes, any attention to Pound's economics will show the opposite. For good reason the *Pisan Cantos* open with a reckoning of the personal cost of the failure of economic reform – "The enormous tragedy of the dream in the peasant's bent / shoulders" (LXXIV/445).

"The Case Against Pound" was an all-too-convenient stalking horse for critics bent on professional vendettas. A highly publicized instance of this strategy – and one that shows how long the "modernism is fascism" position has been current – was Robert Hillyer's "Treason's Strange Fruit," published in the *Saturday Review of Literature* of June 11, 1949. John Berryman's letter of protest, published with eighty-four signatures in *The Nation* for December 17, formally arraigned Hillyer's editor:

> Under the pretense of attacking the award of the Bollingen Prize to Ezra Pound, you sanctioned and guided a prepared attack on modern poetry and criticism, impugning not only the literary reputations but the personal characters of some of its foremost writers . . . Through the technique of the smear and of "guilt by association" you linked the names of T. S. Eliot, Ezra Pound, Paul Mellon, and Carl Jung, and adumbrated a Fascist conspiracy . . . [also implicating] not only certain of the Fellows in American Letters of the Library of Congress, but also a larger group of unnamed writers.

In Ray West's less formal version: "H. sees a conspiracy of poets, critics, psychoanalysts, publishers, and god-knows-what-all under the banner of obscurity in poetry, religio-mythology, and the New Criticism" (*Casebook*, 71–72). Although the strategy of focusing on Pound's poetry and setting aside the issue of his antisemitism was often attacked as apologist, it has proved in retrospect to have been the most productive recourse for two reasons. It established *The Cantos* as an important subject of literary study, making the poem far more accessible by providing source information and demonstrating ways of approaching this highly complex work. Further, even *had* a carefully analytical account of the nature, causes and culpability of Pound's antisemitism been possible, it would not have found a readership willing to give it a hearing.

By December 1959 Pound had fallen into a profound, at times suicidal, depression. A move to Rome in January 1960 temporarily revived his spirits, but by that summer he was again incapacitated by feelings of worthlessness, insisting that his life's work was a failure. By the next summer he chose silence, breaking this very infrequently and then mainly to insist again upon his errors and that *The Cantos* was a "botch." Though these facts are not in dispute, their significance is. Those who believe that he was sane all along, attribute his final self-accusations not to contrition, but to senile dementia. To see psychosis in his paranoid obsessiveness from 1935 on, is to see a movement beyond the antisemitic component of his psychosis after his release. During the St. Elizabeths years, his postponement of self-confrontation was an understandable and even necessary self-protective strategy. Freed from imprisonment among the insane, he began to address his long-repressed feelings of guilt and shame. Donald Hall describes in detail how, in March 1960, Pound's bursts of enthusiasm would be cut short by unannounced plunges into despair and physical collapse. Hall tells how, after having spontaneously repeated an inoffensive story about Bernard Berenson commenting on his own Jewishness, Pound's face collapsed into a mask of abject misery, shame and guilt (Hall, 167). In October 1967, when Allen Ginsberg visited him in Venice, Pound broke his silence to insist that his writing was "stupidity and ignorance all the way through" and that his "worst mistake" was his "stupid, suburban prejudice of antisemitism [which] all along . . . spoiled everything." His parting comment was, "I should have been able to do better" (Ginsberg, 13–15).

By 1980, some critics began to move beyond the options of denunciation or avoidance and to look at some of the evidence in the case. Initially, their hypotheses about Pound's motivations were either minimal, as in "Ezra Pound's Antisemitism" by Ben Kimpel and T. C. Eaves, or shaped to fit a pre-existing interpretive theory, such as Daniel Pearlman's psychoanalytic speculation that Pound's antisemitic anger may have originated with his childhood resentment of his father's lack of financial success. In *The Roots of Treason: Ezra Pound and the Secret of St. Elizabeths*, the psychiatrist E. Fuller Torrey, working with Pound's medical records, but only with secondary materials on his writings, relied on allegation rather than proof to urge his thesis that Pound at St. Elizabeths was not "of unsound mind." As damning to Pound as this contention is, Torrey seemed almost as interested in blackening the professional reputation of the then-superintendent of St. Elizabeths as in discrediting Pound. Torrey's book received much attention, partly because it was so calculatingly sensationalist

– it billed itself as an "exposé" of "the collaboration of psychiatrists and poets in maintaining the charade of Pound's insanity" – and partly because it said what so many wanted to hear. The *a priori* reasoning, definitional arbitrariness, and sweeping generalization of most poststructuralist commentaries on Pound's antisemitism make them inadvertently sensationalist.

In the 1970s and 1980s, when historians were undertaking searching analyses of Holocaust-related antisemitism, the influence on literary study in the United States of French anti-humanist poststructuralism – in particular, of the writings of Roland Barthes, Jacques Lacan, and Jacques Derrida – deferred, yet again, any careful examination of the evidence in Pound's case. In principle, deconstructive and Lacanian theorizing, by embracing radical indeterminacy, problematizing causality, and disallowing the concept of a definable – and hence accountable – self, had declared obsolete the only grounds upon which a morally responsible determination of the nature and extent of antisemitic (or fascist) guilt could be made (*AEP*, "Afterword," 221–28). Yet this was seen as no impediment to a proliferation of emphatic poststructuralist condemnations of Pound. Now, to the habitual accusations of political (antisemitic) fascism was added the charge of "aesthetic fascism." Any non-poststructuralist perspective was labeled "totalizing," meaning, in Pound's case, totalitarian. Read poststructurally, his whole body of work could easily be described as aesthetically "fascist." The extension of this charge to T. S. Eliot and his work was seen as sufficient grounds for alleging that American modernism itself was fascist. To be able to give a diminished account of the most influential high modernist poets and their writings was strategically very useful at a time when critical theory, having announced the "death of the author," was urging its own claim to the privileged status hitherto reserved for works of poetry, fiction, and drama.

In *The Genealogy of Demons: Anti-Semitism, Fascism, and the Myths of Ezra Pound*, Robert Casillo relied on Lacanian, Freudian, Girardian, Derridean, and Marxist paradigms to argue that "Point by point Pound's ideas and values figure unmistakeably within that wide current of proto-fascist and fascist thought which culminates at Auschwitz and Buchenwald." Casillo contended that Pound's "prose ... [and] abstract, discursive language," and the "ideas ... symbols, images, and metaphors" of his poetry are all thoroughly "fascist," and also that "the role of Anti-Semitism and fascism within the verbal economy and structure of *The Cantos*, show[s] above all else that the fascist ideology is indispensable to the poem's linguistic strategies and formal development" (154). Insisting that Pound's thinking after 1935 was essentially characteristic of Pound from the beginning, Casillo frequently quoted passages from the pre-1935 writings, gave a reading of their antisemitic "underlying meaning," and then offered, in support, post-1935 statements that he left undated in the text (Flory, "Review").

Alan Durant and Paul Smith claimed that Pound's enthusiasm for fascism (and concommitant antisemitism) were the inevitable consequence of a "visceral" authoritarianism attributable to his essentialist notions of language and identity. Durant's argument, derived from Lacan, is that "a continuity is established between an order of discourse dependent on the fetishized phallus, the assurance of ego this installs, and the declarations of allegiance to Italian Fascism in the 1930s and early 1940s" (124). Andrew Parker's Derridean strategy allowed him, in "Ezra Pound and the 'Economy' of Anti-Semitism," to "read into" virtually any textual or biographical data the totalizing and essentialist tendencies he expected to find. A highly generalized and symbolized terminology ensured that this could easily be done. Taking as a key "methodological *a priori* 'the formal similarity between linguistic and economic symbolization and production,'" Parker based his argument that Pound's poetics "'impel toward his Fascism and anti-Semitism'" upon "rhetorical connections between Pound's economics and his anti-Semitism" (104). Other *a priori* were Pound's "fear of writing" (119) and the assumption that Pound's "animus against Judaism [is] an animus against (his own) writing as such" (104). Parker's radically generalized definition of "Jewishness" allowed him to see Pound's "hostility towards Judaism as . . . an oblique confirmation of his own irreducible 'Jewishness'" (119).

Sweeping poststructuralist denunciations of modernism as fascism and of Pound as always inherently a "rabid antisemite" fulfil a need unrelated to any serious determination of guilt or innocence. As in 1945, such tactics provide an easy alternative to and a distraction from the far more painful task of analyzing the realities and implications of the full range of wartime antisemitism – in this case, among intellectuals in Germany and in countries under German occupation. Deconstruction's dematerializing of an accountable self forestalled confrontation of the humiliating record of French accomodations to Nazi occupation – in particular the almost universal failure of the French to resist or even to protest the deportations of Jews to the gas chambers. It also, for as along as possible, deflected inquiry into the record and implications of the enthusiastic Nazism of Martin Heidegger – an active collaborator and the intellectual hero of French poststructuralist thought.

By the late 1980s, the very tactics consistently used against Pound from 1945 on of dismissing the value of the work on the grounds of objectionable episodes from the life, began to be deployed against two of the authorities most revered by the very critics who had so enthusiastically and summarily indicted Pound. First came the revelations that Paul de Man, who established Derridean deconstruction in the United States, had, in his youth, contributed articles to fascist periodicals. Then followed the graver accusations against Heidegger whose works have been indispensable to the project of deconstruction. In his exculpation of de Man, Derrida, in the spirit of his own philosophical theorizing, resisted any suggestion of his friend's moral accountability.

The shockwaves of *"L'affaire Heidegger"* may prove sufficiently powerful, finally to blast away the impediments to an evenhanded and inclusive analysis of the antisemitism of intellectuals in the context of the Holocaust. Certainly, Heidegger's moral dereliction is far graver than Pound's. Thomas Sheehan, among many others, has examined the philospher's conviction of the "inner truth and greatness" of Nazism (88) and noted his insistence that "his engagement with Nazism came from the very essence of his philosophy" (92). Where Pound's antisemitic rantings brought harm to no one but himself (and his family), Heidegger lent the prestige of his reputation and academic position to the validation of Hitler's regime and energetically implemented the antisemitic "cleansing laws" against colleagues and students at Freiburg University (86–7). Unlike Pound (but exactly like de Man), he gave no indication of mental instability, nor expressed any subsequent self-criticism or remorse. We can now see Heidegger's calm as far more dangerous than Pound's ranting.

Holocaust research has dramatically exposed the strategy of focusing only on the exceptional, "rabid" antisemite for the comfortable evasion that it is. From the 1961 testimony of Adolf Eichmann (*AEP*, 133–34) to Christopher Browning's findings in *Ordinary Men* (1992) and the data (waiving the overall thesis) in Daniel Goldhagen's 1996 *Hitler's Willing Executioners: Ordinary Germans and the Holocaust*, the evidence is overwhelming that the truly lethal antisemitism – of those who conceived, implemented, facilitated, and countenanced the massmurder of Jews – was, with very few exceptions, not aberrantly "rabid" but matter-of-course. The many Germans who, like Heidegger, made the "Final Solution" possible by publically supporting or failing to protest antisemitic persecution, could proceed undisturbed by serious misgivings because they had voluntarily delegated to the regime the responsibility for moral choice. Pound, to his credit, never did this. The profound anxiety and mental conflict everywhere apparent in his broadcasts strikingly demonstrates the continuing influence over him of his moral sense.

We can now see how lethal that silent antisemitism was that, through collaboration or complicity, cumulatively made possible the perpetration of ultimate harm. We can also see how, as the result of a continuing angry refusal to examine the facts of his case, Pound as "designated fascist intellectual" has served since 1945 as stand-in for all those individuals of the silent majority in Germany, in occupied France and Belgium, in Britain and the United States who, by quietly aiding or standing quietly by, made the Holocaust possible.

WORKS CITED

Browning, Christopher. *Ordinary Men: Reserve Police Battalion 101 and the Final Solution in Poland*. New York: HarperCollins, 1992.

Casillo, Robert. *The Genealogy of Demons: Anti-Semitism, Fascism, and the Myths of Ezra Pound*. Evanston, IL: Northwestern University Press, 1988.

Durant, Alan. *Ezra Pound: Identity in Crisis*. Brighton: Harvester, 1981.

Flory, Wendy Stallard. *The American Ezra Pound*. New Haven: Yale University Press, 1989.

"Review: *The Genealogy of Demons. . . .* By Robert Casillo." *Modern Language Quarterly*, 50, 1 (1989), 82–88.

Ginsberg, Allen. "Encounters with Ezra Pound," in *City Lights Anthology*, ed. Lawrence Ferlinghetti. San Francisco, 1974.

Goldhagen, Daniel Jonah. *Hitler's Willing Executioners: Ordinary Germans and the Holcaust*. New York: Alfred A. Knopf, 1996.

Hall, Donald. *Remembering Poets*. New York: Harper & Row, 1978.

Kimpel, Ben, and Eaves, T. C. "Ezra Pound's Anti-Semitism." *South Atlantic Quarterly*, (Winter, 1982), 56–59.

O'Connor, William Van & Stone, Edward. *A Casebook on Ezra Pound*. New York: Thomas Y. Crowell, 1959.

Parker, Andrew. "Ezra Pound and the 'Economy' of Anti-Semitism." *Boundary/ 2*, 11 (Fall/Winter, 1983), 103–128.

Pearlman, Daniel. "Ezra Pound: America's Wandering Jew." *Paideuma*, 9 (Winter, 1980), 461–480.

Ryan, Allan. *Quiet Neighbors: Prosecuting Nazi War Criminals in America*. New York: Harcourt Brace Jovanovich, 1984.

Sheehan, Thomas. "Reading a Life: Heidegger and Hard Times." *The Cambridge Companion to Heidegger*, ed. Charles Guignon. Cambridge: Cambridge University Press, 1993.

Smith, Paul. *Pound Revised*. London: Croom Helm, 1983.

Torrey, E. Fuller. *The Roots of Treason: Ezra Pound and the Secret of St. Elizabeths*. New York: McGraw-Hill, 1984.

Wyman, David S. *The Abandonment of the Jews: America and the Holocaust, 1941–1945*. New York: Random House, 1984.

Paper Walls: America and the Refugee Crisis, 1938–1941. New York: Random House, [1968], 1985.

FURTHER READING

Biography

Ackroyd, Peter. *Ezra Pound and His World*. New York: Scribner's, 1980.

Carpenter, Humphrey. *A Serious Character: The Life of Ezra Pound*. London: Faber and Faber, 1988.

Cornell, Julian. *The Trial of Ezra Pound*. New York: John Day, 1966.

Davenport, Guy. "Ezra Pound 1885–1972," *Arion*, NS 1 (1973), 188–196.

de Rachewiltz, Mary. *Discretions*. Boston: Little Brown, 1971.

Diagnostic and Statistical Manual of Mental Disorders. Washington: American Psychiatric Association, 1952 [DSM, I–IV].

Doolittle, Hilda. *End to Torment: A Memoir of Ezra Pound*. New York: New Directions, 1979.

Hall, Donald. "Ezra Pound: An Interview," *Paris Review*, 28 (1962), 22–51.

Heymann, C. David. *Ezra Pound: The Last Rower*. New York: Viking, 1976.

Homberger, Eric. ed. *Ezra Pound: The Critical Heritage*. London: Routledge and Kegan Paul, 1972.

Hutchins, Patricia. *Ezra Pound's Kensington*. London: Faber & Faber, 1965.

Mullins, Eustace. *This Difficult Individual, Ezra Pound*. New York: Fleet, 1961.

Norman, Charles. *The Case of Ezra Pound*. Rev. ed. London: Macdonald, 1969.

Olson, Charles. *Charles Olson and Ezra Pound: An Encounter at St. Elizabeths*. Ed. Catherine Seelye. New York: Grossman, 1975.

Stock, Noel. *Life of Ezra Pound*. 2nd. ed. San Francisco: North Point Press, 1982.

Torrey, E. Fuller. *The Roots of Treason: Ezra Pound and the Secret of St. Elizabeths*. New York: McGraw-Hill, 1984.

Tytell, John. *Ezra Pound: The Solitary Volcano*. New York: Doubleday, 1987.

Wilhelm, J. J. *The American Roots of Ezra Pound*. New York: Garland, 1985.

Ezra Pound in London and Paris 1908–1925. University Park: Penn State University Press, 1990.

Ezra Pound, The Tragic Years 1925–1972. University Park: Penn State University Press, 1994.

Letters

DK/Some Letters of Ezra Pound. Ed. Louis Dudek. Montreal: DC Books, 1974. The years 1949–1967.

Pound/Ford: The Story of A Literary Friendship. Ed. Brita Lindberg-Seyersted. New York: New Directions, 1982.

Ezra and Dorothy Pound: Letters in Captivity, 1945–1946. Ed. Omar Pound and Robert Spoo. New York: Oxford University Press, 1998.

Ezra Pound and Dorothy Shakespear: Their Letters 1909–1914. Ed. Omar Pound and A. Walton Litz. New York: New Directions, 1984.

Ezra Pound and Japan: Letters and Essays. Ed. Sanehide Hodama. Redding Ridge, CT: Black Swan, 1987.

Ezra Pound and James Laughlin, Selected Letters. Ed. David M. Gordon. New York: W. W. Norton, 1994.

Ezra Pound and Margaret Cravens, A Tragic Friendship 1910–1912. Ed. Omar Pound and Robert Spoo. Durham: Duke University Press, 1988.

Ezra Pound and Senator Bronson Cutting, A Political Correspondence, 1930–1935. Ed. E. P. Walkiewicz and Hugh Witemeyer. Albuquerque: University of New Mexico Press, 1995.

Ezra Pound to Alice Corbin Henderson. Ed. Ira B. Nadel. Austin: University of Texas Press, 1993.

Letters to Ibbotson, 1935–1952. Ed. V. I. Mondolfo and M. Hurley. Orono, MA: National Poetry Foundation, 1979.

Pound/Cummings, The Correspondence of Ezra Pound and E. E. Cummings. Ed. Barry Ahearn. Ann Arbor: University of Michigan Press, 1997.

Pound/Joyce, The Letters of Ezra Pound and James Joyce. Ed. Forrest Read. New York: New Directions, 1967; rpt. 1970.

Pound/Lewis: The Letters of Ezra Pound and Wyndham Lewis. Ed. Timothy Materer. New York: New Directions: 1985.

Pound/The Little Review, The Letters of Ezra Pound to Margaret Anderson: The Little Review Correspondence. Ed. Thomas L. Scott, Melvin J. Friedman with the assistance of Jackson R. Bryer. New York: New Directions, 1988.

Pound, Thayer, Watson and The Dial, A Story in Letters. Ed. Walter Sutton. Gainesville: University Press of Florida, 1994.

Pound/Williams, Selected Letters. Ed. Hugh Witemeyer. New York: New Directions, 1996.

Pound/Zukofsky, Selected Letters. Ed. Barry Ahearn. New York: New Directions, 1987.

Selected Letters of Ezra Pound, 1907–1941. Ed. D. D. Paige. New York: New Directions, 1971.

Selected Letters of Ezra Pound to John Quinn, 1915–1924. Ed. Timothy Materer. Durham: Duke University Press, 1991.

Criticism and bibliography

A Casebook on Ezra Pound. Ed. William Van O'Connor and Edward Stone. New York: Thomas Y. Crowell, 1959.

Alexander, Michael. *The Poetic Achievement of Ezra Pound.* Berkeley: University of California Press, 1979.

Anderson, David. *Pound's Cavalcanti, Edition of the Translation, Notes and Essays.* Princeton: Princeton University Press, 1983.

Bacigalupo, Massimo. *The Forméd Trace: The Later Poetry of Ezra Pound.* New York: Columbia University Press, 1980.

Beach, Christopher. *ABC of Influence: Ezra Pound and the Remaking of American Poetic Tradition.* Berkeley: University of California Press, 1992.

Bell, Ian F. *Critic as Scientist: The Modernist Poetics of Ezra Pound.* New York: Methuen, 1981.

Ezra Pound: Tactics for Reading. Totowa, NJ: Barnes and Noble, 1982.

Bernstein, Michael André. *The Tale of the Tribe: Ezra Pound and the Modern Verse Epic.* Princeton: Princeton University Press, 1980.

Bischoff, Volker. *Ezra Pound Criticism 1905–1985, A Chronological Listing of Publications in English.* Marburg: Universitatsbibliothek Marburg, 1991.

Bornstein, George. *The Postromantic Consciousness of Ezra Pound.* Victoria, BC: University of Victoria, English Literary Studies, 1977.

ed. *Ezra Pound Among the Poets.* Chicago: University of Chicago Press, 1985.

Bush, Ronald. *The Genesis of Ezra Pound's Cantos.* Princeton: Princeton University Press, 1976; rpt. 1989.

Case Against The Saturday Review of Literature. Chicago: Poetry, 1949. On *The Pisan Cantos* and the Bollingen Prize.

Casillo, Robert. *The Geneaology of Demons: Anti-Semitism, Fascism, and the Myths of Ezra Pound.* Evanston: Northwestern University Press, 1988.

Cookson, William. *A Guide to the Cantos of Ezra Pound.* London: Croom Helm, 1985.

ed. *Ezra Pound: Selected Prose, 1909–1965.* New York: New Directions, 1973.

Dasenbrock, Reed Way. *The Literary Vorticism of Ezra Pound and Wyndham Lewis.* Baltimore: Johns Hopkins University Press, 1985.

de Rachewiltz, Mary. "Ezra Pound's Library: What Remains," *Ezra Pound and Europe.* Ed. Richard Taylor and Claus Melchior. Amsterdam: Rodopi, 1993, pp. 1–18.

Eastman, Barbara. *Ezra Pound's "Cantos": The Story of the Text.* Orono, MA: National Poetry Foundation, 1979.

Espey, John. *Ezra Pound's "Mauberley".* Berkeley: University of California Press, 1955.

"Ezra Pound," *Sixteen Modern American Authors II: A Survey of Research and Criticism Since 1972.* Ed. J. R. Bryer. Durham: Duke University Press, 1990.

Flory, Wendy Stallard. *The American Ezra Pound.* New Haven: Yale University Press, 1989.

Ezra Pound and "The Cantos": A Record of Struggle. New Haven: Yale University Press, 1980.

Froula, Christine. *A Guide to Ezra Pound's "Selected Poems".* New York: New Directions, 1983.

To Write Paradise: Style and Error in Pound's Cantos. New Haven: Yale University Press, 1984.

Gallup, Donald. *Ezra Pound: A Bibliography.* Charlottesville: University Press of Virginia, 1983.

Gibson, Mary Ellis. *Epic Reinvented, Pound and the Victorians.* Ithaca: Cornell University Press, 1995.

Hesse, Eva. ed. *New Approaches to Ezra Pound.* Berkeley: University of California Press, 1969.

Kenner, Hugh. *The Poetry of Ezra Pound*. New York: New Directions, 1951.
The Pound Era. Berkeley: University of California Press, 1971.
Laughlin, James. *Pound as Wuz*. St. Paul, MN: Graywolf, 1987.
Longenbach, James. *Stone Cottage: Pound, Yeats and Modernism*. Oxford: Oxford University Press, 1988.
McDonald, Gail. *Learning to be Modern: Pound, Eliot and the American University*. Oxford: Oxford University Press, 1993.
McDougal, Stuart Y. *Ezra Pound and the Troubadour Tradition*. Princeton: Princeton University Press, 1972.
McGann, Jerome J. "The Cantos of Ezra Pound, The Truth in Contradiction," *Towards a Literature of Knowledge*. Chicago: University of Chicago Press, 1989, pp. 96–128.
"Ezra Pound in the Sixth Chamber," *The Textual Condition*. Princeton: Princeton University Press, 1991, pp. 101–176.
Makin, Peter. *Provence and Pound*. Berkeley: University of California Press, 1978.
Mondolfo, Vittoria. "An Annotated Bibliography of Criticism of Ezra Pound, 1918–24," *PAI*, 5 (1976), 303–325.
Morrison, Paul. *The Poetics of Fascism, Ezra Pound, T. S. Eliot, Paul de Man*. New York: Oxford, 1996.
North, Michael. *The Political Aesthetic of Yeats, Eliot and Pound*. New York: Cambridge University Press, 1991.
Paideuma. A Journal Devoted to Ezra Pound Scholarship. 1972–
Pearlman, Daniel. *The Barb of Time: On the Unity of Ezra Pound's Cantos*. Oxford: Oxford University Press, 1969.
Perloff, Marjorie. *The Dance of the Intellect: Studies in the Poetry of the Pound Tradition*. Cambridge: Cambridge University Press, 1985.
The Poetics of Indeterminacy. Princeton: Princeton University Press, 1981.
Pound, Ezra. *A Walking Tour in Southern France, Ezra Pound Among the Troubadors*. Ed. Richard Sieburth. New York: New Directions, 1992.
Ezra Pound and Music. Ed. R. Murray Schafer. New York: New Directions, 1977.
Ezra Pound and The Visual Arts. Ed. Harriet Zinnes. New York: New Directions, 1980.
Ezra Pound's Poetry and Prose Contributions to Periodicals. 11 vols. Ed. Lea Baechler, A. Walton Litz and James Longenbach. New York: Garland, 1991.
"Ezra Pound Speaking": Radio Speeches of World War II. ed. Leonard W. Doob. Westport, CT: Greenwood, 1978.
I Cantos. Ed. with Italian trans. Mary de Rachewiltz. Milan: Mondadori, 1985. Bilingual edition.
Impact, Essays On Ignorance and the Decline of American Civilzation. Ed. Noel Stock. Chicago: Henry Regnery, 1960.
Machine Art and Other Writings, The Lost Thought of the Italian Years. Ed. Maria Luisa Ardizzone. Durham: Duke University Press, 1996.
Pound's Artist, Ezra Pound and The Visual Arts in London, Paris and Italy. Intr: Richard Humphreys. London: Tate Gallery, 1985.
Rabaté, Jean-Michel. *Language, Sexuality and Ideology in Ezra Pound's Cantos*. Albany: State University of New York Press, 1986.
Rainey, Lawrence. *Ezra Pound and the Monument of Culture, Text, History and the Malatesta Cantos*. Chicago: University of Chicago Press, 1991.

ed. *A Poem Containing History: Textual Studies in The Cantos.* Ann Arbor: University of Michigan Press, 1997.

Redman, Timothy. "Pound's Library: A Preliminary Catalogue," *PAI*, 15 (1986), 213–237.

Ezra Pound and Italian Fascism. New York: Cambridge University Press, 1991.

Ricks, Beatrice. *Ezra Pound: A Bibliography of Secondary Works.* Metuchen, NJ: Scarecrow Press, 1986.

Sherry, Vincent. *Ezra Pound, Wyndham Lewis, and Radical Modernism.* New York: Oxford University Press, 1993.

Sieburth, Richard, *Instigations: Ezra Pound and Remy de Gourmont.* Cambridge: Harvard University Press, 1978.

Singh, G. *Ezra Pound as Critic.* New York: St. Martin's Press, 1994.

Smith, Marcel and William A. Ulmer, eds. *Ezra Pound, The Legacy of Kulchur.* Tuscaloosa: University of Alabahma Press, 1988.

Stoicheff, Peter. *The Hall of Mirrors, Drafts & Fragments and the End of Ezra Pound's Cantos.* Ann Arbor, MI: University of Michigan Press, 1995.

Sullivan, J. P., ed. *Ezra Pound, A Critical Anthology.* Harmondsworth: Penguin, 1970.

Surette, Leon. *A Light from Eleusis: A Study of Ezra Pound's Cantos.* Oxford: Oxford University Press, 1979.

Tate Gallery. *Pound's Artists, Ezra Pound and the Visual Arts in London, Paris and Italy.* London: Tate Gallery, 1985.

Taylor, Richard and Claus Melcheor, eds. *Ezra Pound and Europe.* Amsterdam: Rodopi, 1993.

Terrell, Carroll F. *A Companion to the Cantos of Ezra Pound.* 2 vols. Berkeley: University of California Press, 1980, 1984.

Tiffany, Daniel. *Radio Corpse, Imagism and The Cryptaesthetic of Ezra Pound.* Cambridge: Harvard University press, 1995.

Wilson, Peter, *A Preface to Ezra Pound.* London: Longman, 1997.

Witemeyer, Hugh. *The Poetry of Ezra Pound: Forms and Renewal, 1908–1920.* Berkeley: University of California Press, 1969.

INDEX

Scheiwiller, Vanni 176, 177
Schelling, Felix 35
Schoenberg, Arnold 247
Schwartz, Delmore 9
science 195
Scratton, Bride 20, 266, 277, 279
Scriabin, Aleksandr 241
Scriptor Ignotus 43
Second World War 31, 111, 112, 213, 215,
  244, 258, 259, 260, 264, 284, 287
Seldes, Gilbert 35
Seneca 201
sestina 82
Seurat, Georges 228
Shakespear (Pound), Dorothy 11, 20, 24,
  69, 110, 113, 116, 117, 125, 126,
  129, 130, 131, 135, 136, 137, 138,
  174, 254, 265, 266, 267, 268, 270,
  271, 279, 282, 289
Shakespear, Olivia 24, 45, 265, 266
Shakespeare & Company 39, 266
Shakespeare, William 192, 201, 203, 216,
  219
  King Lear 219
Shoah 284, 285, 286
Shoptaw, John 151, 152, 159, 160
Shu Ching (Book of History) 218
Siena 7, 15, 92, 93, 95, 104, 106, 200, 293
Sinclair, May 266
Sirmione 39, 69
Smart Set 12
Smith, P. H. 94
Snyder, Gary 146
Social Credit 10, 19, 53, 54, 55, 253, 255,
  257–8, 287, 289
song 192, 238, 248
Sophocles (Sophokles) 118, 214, 215, 217,
  221
Sordello 31, 52, 62, 114, 191, 278
Spanish 70, 204
Spanish Civil War 290
Spann, Marcella 125, 126, 129, 130, 266
Spoo, Robert 267, 283
St. Elizabeths Hospital 11, 13, 15, 20, 31,
  36, 110, 117, 118, 128, 137, 139,
  140, 143, 146, 182, 213, 244, 246,
  259, 278, 279, 284, 287, 291, 294,
  296
Stalin, Joseph 201, 287
Stein, Gertrude 24, 40, 41, 151, 152, 158,
  201, 265
  Autobiography of Alice B. Toklas 24, 41,
  201

Stendhal 195, 199
Stock, Noel 222, 279, 282, 283
Stoicheff, Peter 14, 132, 133, 138, 182,
  186
Stone Cottage 2, 12, 26, 27, 45, 65, 195
Stony Brook 185
Stravinsky, Igor 241, 246, 247
Sullivan, Arthur 241
Sumac 185
Surrealism 150, 151, 152, 158, 159
Swinburne, Algernon 56, 197, 272
symbolism 26, 28, 123, 124

Tagore, Rabindranath 26, 29, 31
Talmud 288
Tate, Allen 118
Taylor, Frederick Winslow 104
Taylor, Richard 13, 16, 17, 138, 187
Tempio 72, 74, 84, 85, 113, 135
Tennyson, Alfred Lord 211
Terrell, Carroll F. 14, 136, 137
textual criticism 161–4, 203
Thayer, Scofield 35
This Quarter 266
Thomson, Virgil 239, 241
Thompson, E. P. 102, 104, 105, 108
Three Mountains Press 39
Threshold 183
Tinham, George Holden 9
Titian 230, 231
tone 189, 193, 209, 236, 240
Torah 292
Torcello 126
Torrey, E. Fuller 296, 300
  Roots of Treason 296, 300
Tovey, Donald 82, 91
translation 17, 18, 43, 118, 181, 197, 200,
  201, 202, 204–23, 238, 239, 242,
  243, 289
treason 11, 20, 259
troubadour 45, 62, 67, 72, 74, 75, 82, 88,
  192, 205, 213, 217, 220, 222, 238,
  239, 242, 243, 248
Troubadours 57, 188, 189, 199, 237
Tuscany 15, 63, 92

Upward, Allan 28
usury 7, 10, 15, 53, 55, 78, 92, 93, 94, 95,
  99, 104, 108, 118 259, 260, 289,
  290, 292, 293, 294

van Gogh, Vincent 226
Van Buren, Martin 10